"The Prime Minister does a good job of taking you back to the country, and the time, that gave birth to the national game."

—*The Globe and Mail*

"[A] readable and entertaining historical exposition of the early organizational days of Canada's most beloved sport. . . . [Harper is] an unreconstructed sentimentalist about hockey. He romances the game, focusing on its sepia-toned infancy."

—*Toronto Star*

"Harper has a deep curiosity about all aspects of Canadian history and a love of hockey—making a natural fit for his book."

—*Postmedia.com*

"An illustration of hockey's special place in the Canadian heart and mind. . . . Harper has written a finely detailed history of the struggle between professionalism and amateurism in early 20th-century Ontario hockey. . . . It includes insightful examinations of class and religion and the roles they played in a country that still saw itself as a pillar of the British Empire, all viewed through the prism of hockey at the dawn of the pro era."

—*The New York Times*

"It's a rare achievement for a world leader to write a book while in office. It's a rarer achievement still when the book isn't a personal memoir, but rather concentrates on a radically different topic. Stephen Harper, Canada's 22nd prime minister, has done just that. . . . Mr. Harper's book . . . is a well-written and tightly researched history of Canada's national pastime in the early 20th century."

—*The Washington Times*

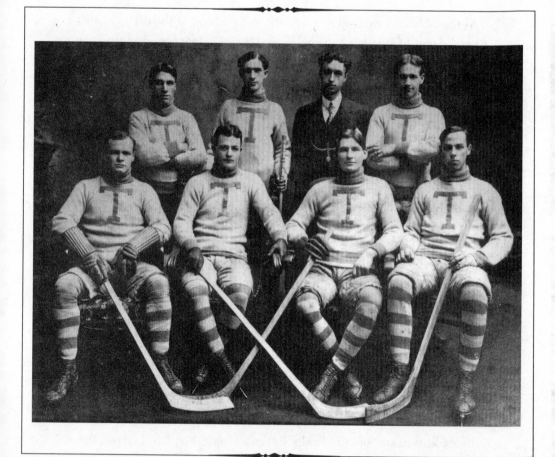

Toronto Professional Hockey Team, 1907

A GREAT GAME

THE FORGOTTEN LEAFS
AND THE
RISE OF PROFESSIONAL HOCKEY

Stephen J. Harper

Published by Simon & Schuster Canada

NEW YORK   LONDON   TORONTO   SYDNEY   NEW DELHI

Simon & Schuster Canada
A Division of Simon & Schuster, Inc.
166 King Street East, Suite 300
Toronto, Ontario M5A 1J3

This Simon & Schuster Canada edition October 2014

SIMON & SCHUSTER CANADA and colophon are
registered trademarks of Simon & Schuster, Inc.

For information about special discounts for bulk purchases,
please contact Simon & Schuster Special Sales at 1-800-268-3216
or CustomerService@simonandschuster.ca.

Cover photograph courtesy of the Hockey Hall of Fame;
spine: Bibliothèque et Archives nationales du Québec
Cover design by PGB

Manufactured in Canada

1   3   5   7   9   10   8   6   4   2

ISBN 978-1-4767-1653-4
ISBN 978-1-4767-1654-1 (pbk)
ISBN 978-1-4767-1655-8 (ebook)

MIX
Paper from
responsible sources
FSC® C016245

To Canada's military families, past and present.

*We have a great game, a great country,
and a great empire—if you gentlemen are as great
as the possibilities of the O.H.A, if we Canadians
are as great as the possibilities of Canada,
and if we Britons are as great as the glory of our
Empire—the flag of amateurism in your hands will be
as safe from harm as the Union Jack was
in the hands of your fathers and mine!*

—JOHN ROSS ROBERTSON, PRESIDENT,
ONTARIO HOCKEY ASSOCIATION, 1905

Contents

FACING OFF

March 14, 1908: Saturday night at the Montreal Arena at the corner of St. Catherine Street and Wood Avenue. Also known as Westmount Arena, the ten-year-old hockey rink with the natural ice and the novel rounded corners is the largest in the country. Along with many hundreds who will stand, 4,500 fans will cram into the rows of hard wooden seats they can soften and warm with rugs available for rent.

Outdoors, it has been a mild, springlike day at the tail end of a soft winter in which the St. Lawrence River has remained open longer than it has for thirty years. Indoors, a battle for the Stanley Cup is about to begin.

The visitors from Toronto step onto the ice amid the polite applause of the spectators. The local papers have reported that this upstart team is a decent aggregation, but no one expects them to beat the home side. Their Montreal Wanderers have successfully dominated hockey's top tier for the better part of three seasons.

One of the Ontario challengers is well known to—and highly regarded by—the Montreal fans. He is a grizzled veteran pro lining up in the key position of rover. He is flanked, however, by two even better forwards.

At centre stands a young French Canadian who will someday be regarded as one of the greatest competitors of all time. And at left wing is the best player the city of Toronto has yet produced, with both great triumph and tragedy ahead of him. In a moment, the game will start and this handsome young star's speed and skill will stun the overconfident Montrealers.

The Wanderers are about to have the fight of their lives.

But if the visiting team has been underestimated by Montreal observers, the hockey establishment back home in Toronto holds it in utter contempt. They may resent Montreal, but they detest this club, their *own* club, even more. Toronto's leading newspaper has dismissed its Cup aspirations as the delusions of "false alarm hockey statesmen"[1] hoping to collect some fast bucks from the gate receipts.

In fact, from its beginnings the club has been the object of disdain and ridicule by the hockey powers in its hometown. Upon its formation in the fall of 1906, the same journal had wishfully mused that "professional hockey in Toronto promises to flourish till the frost comes. Then like other flowers it will fade away and die."[2] When the team lost its first game—an exhibition affair—by a score of 7–0, a rival paper said ticket buyers had only proved there truly was "a sucker born every minute."[3]

Things got no better the following season, when the team joined a full-fledged pro league. "All the world is laughing," declared the powerful *Toronto Telegram*, "at a so-called professional hockey league that can only get players that real professional leagues don't want. It's not a professional league at all. It's a disqualified amateurs' league."[4]

In fact, the whole league experiment seemed jinxed. For the first game, a team from Berlin (later to be renamed Kitchener) had come to town by train, but the Saturday papers were not even thinking about hockey. They were consumed with the sudden passing of Ned Hanlan at the age of fifty-two. The "Boy in Blue" had been Canada's first-ever world champion—a rowing prize he captured before 100,000 spectators on the River Thames—and he had been the city's most beloved athlete for years. "The death of Edward Hanlan removed the most famous oarsman that ever lived," proclaimed the *Globe*. "Nor is it likely that any other who comes after him will occupy so large a share of public attention."[5]

Things were even worse inside the rink, where a big winter thaw had taken its toll. The Monday papers were far more interested in the playing conditions than the play. The *News* labelled it "Hockey on Bare Floor" and observed that "by the time play ceased there was not ten yards of solid ice in the rink."[6] The *World* was no less kind, summing up the match with "The Flying Dutchmen of Berlin proved better mud horses than the Torontos."[7] The team had again lost its season opener by a shut-out, this time 3–0. It seemed some local scribes even held them responsible for the weather.

Yet the progress of the organization has proven remarkably steady and swift. Indeed, by the time of its arrival in Montreal less than three months later, it has been able to ice the best hockey team ever to wear a Toronto uniform. Less than a year and a half into its existence, the club has genuine hopes of capturing the Cup, much to the delight of its fans— but only of its fans.

The truth is that in Toronto the hockey bosses are hoping the team will lose the game. They would rather "their" team and Lord Stanley's mug did not even exist. We know this because they say so—often and loudly.

Who were these Stanley Cup contenders and what happened to them? History has told us they were the original "Toronto Maple Leafs." In fact, they were never, ever, called by this name.[8] They were simply the "Torontos," sometimes (at times sarcastically) the "Toronto Professionals." So determined—and successful—would be their naysayers in obliterating their existence that even their name would be long forgotten.

Their opponents are some of the most powerful people in Toronto. They are in the midst of leading one side in the national "Athletic War." It is an extraordinary chapter in Canada's social history—a sort of witch hunt against professional sports so intense and so divisive that the country may not enter the coming summer's Olympics in London, England.

Today, none of this makes any sense, not in a time when *Forbes* magazine has certified that Toronto boasts the most valuable professional hockey franchise in the world.[9]

A century ago, however, Toronto was a very different place.

A GREAT GAME

CHAPTER ONE

THE OLD ORDER IN HOCKEY'S SECOND CITY

From Good Beginnings to the Osgoodes

———•◦•———

It's grand to be an Englishman in 1910
King Edward's on the throne
It's the age of men[1]

— "THE LIFE I LEAD," FROM *Mary Poppins*

It was the dawn of a new century. The sun, it was said, never set on the British Empire, and Toronto was a burgeoning bit of the Empire's vast Canadian dominion. Toronto liked to be called the "Queen City," which was certainly preferable to the pejorative "Hogtown." The moniker reflected perfectly the self-image and aspiration of its—exclusively WASP and male—civic leaders. As the song from the Disney musical *Mary Poppins* would so perfectly put it, it was considered a "grand" time to be alive if you were part of the English realm.

There was great optimism in the air. Prime Minister Sir Wilfrid Laurier perhaps best expressed it in 1904, in an address to the Canadian Club in Ottawa: "I think that we can claim that it is Canada that shall fill the twentieth century."[2] Such was the growing confidence across the land.

What links the Toronto of the early 1900s to that of the early 2000s is the experience of change and growth. Though a primitive time by today's standards, technological progress had been sufficiently bold and rapid that it was unmistakable. Further, such advancement—and the positive social development it would make possible—was keenly anticipated.

Throughout the world, but especially in Canada, the most meaningful developments had occurred in transportation. The steam-engine locomotive had replaced the horse and cart (or winter sleigh) for intercity travel, reducing travel times exponentially. The age of the horse had not been displaced locally, but wealthy citizens could purchase the new motor vehicles, while the many rode bicycles or travelled by electric streetcar for a five-cent piece of silver.

The railways had their communications parallel in the telegraph, by which news could be rapidly transmitted throughout the world's urban network. A growing array of daily newspapers could then disseminate it within hours rather than days, and to a much wider array of citizens. Toronto had six daily papers: the *Globe*, *Mail and Empire* and *World* in the morning, and the *News*, *Star* and *Telegram* in the evening.[3] Citizens of reasonable means now also had their own telegraph parallel, the telephone.

They were good times to be raising a family in the Ontario capital. It was said a woman could be outfitted for twenty-five dollars, a man could get three squares ("breakfast, dinner, tea") for fifteen cents and a family could buy a home for $1,200. However, with a full-time labourer earning twenty-five cents per hour at best—ten hours a day, six days a week—life for many was not easy. Trade union troubles were growing. Nonetheless, compared to the past, the times were prosperous and generally becoming more so.[4]

The growing wealth was sparked by the rapid expansion of industry and manufacturing. It was accompanied by the noticeable spread of urbanization and the rising values of city land, along with an increase in the time for and the type of leisure activities. These ranged from high culture to, as one newspaper advertisement read, "Stage always filled with lovely women."[5] However, all activity—except church services—shut down on Sundays.

Recreational activities and sports entertainment were experiencing explosive growth. In 1908 alone, the city's strict authorities charged 1,200 boys and girls for playing their games on public streets. When not playing, the lads and lasses would follow the exploits of their hockey heroes in the winter and their lacrosse, baseball and football counterparts in the summer. Without television or even radio, newspapers gave detailed sports coverage at every level of competition. Big games would often be reprinted literally play by play.

It was the age of heavyweight champ Jack Johnson and his Canadian adversary, Tommy Burns. Ty Cobb ruled baseball. In track and field, no one was bigger than the country's own Tom Longboat. Few were the days between scuttlebutt—good or bad—about the Onondaga long-distance runner from the Six Nations reserve near Brantford, Ontario.

Sports took minds off the many challenges and problems those in the growing city faced. Despite the prevailing Protestant moral ethos, alcohol use and abuse were rampant. Major occasions would be marked by energetic celebrations into the night, followed by brawling till the early morning. At the same time, there was an obsessive concern about personal health. Every newspaper of the time was overloaded with potential remedies for infirmities of all varieties.[6]

While basic services were improving, unreliable water quality, infestations of rats and the pollution caused by the widespread use of coal were commonplace. This was especially true for the poor. Toronto was not known for its poverty, but slums, squalor and desperate privation were certainly to be found if one looked. Divorce was exceedingly rare, but spousal abandonment was not.

Nothing like the government payments and social services of our age existed. Active benevolent work was undertaken by extended families, neighbourhood interests and, especially, religious institutions. These were particularly important in Toronto's central "foreign district"—the poor areas that already contained 7,000 Italians and 22,000 "Hebrews" according to the census of 1911.[7]

Crime was also regularly reported, although one does not get the sense it was top of mind. This changed with the spread of the automobile. In the years leading up to the Great War that began in 1914, the escalating numbers of pedestrian injuries involving cars became a major issue. It was yet another sign of the changing times. Only a few years earlier, Edouard Cyrille "Newsy" Lalonde, the famous Cornwall athlete (and future Toronto Professional), had been robbed by bandits while driving his horse and buggy on an Ontario country road.

All told, the problems of the era were notably lower in profile than the bold new ventures, emerging corporate empires and ambitious civic projects that were taking shape. The business district was growing rapidly, moving up Yonge Street beyond its traditional northern limit at College. Two-thirds of the roads of "Muddy York" were now paved, and electric lighting was soon to appear above them. The affluent had already established summer homes in Muskoka.

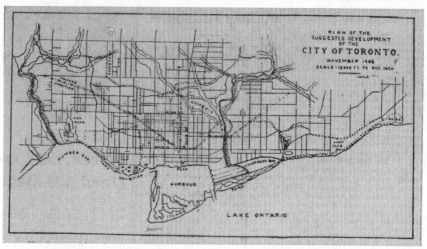

Toronto in the early twentieth century covered only a fraction of its present-day territory.

More than anything, Toronto was growing. From 1901 to 1911, Canada expanded from five million–plus inhabitants to just over seven million. The city, absorbing its growing suburbs, climbed from some 200,000 souls to around 375,000. By way of comparison, Toronto's closest provincial rivals, Ottawa and Hamilton, would barely cross the 80,000 mark by the end of the decade. There was already no doubt as to where the power lay in the new country's largest province.

A "new" country it was. The Confederation that brought together the colonies of Canada West (Ontario), Canada East (Quebec), Nova Scotia and New Brunswick in 1867 had since added Manitoba, British Columbia, Prince Edward Island and the immense lands that would later make up the Prairie provinces and northern territories. The Dominion now stretched *a mari usque ad mare*, from coast to coast (to coast), and was the world's second-largest country, next only to sprawling Russia. And yet, still commonly heard was the terminology of pre-Confederation days: the "West" meaning Ontario, the "East" being Quebec. The Atlantic realms and the provinces and territories of the vast Northwest—increasingly stocked by people neither British nor French—seemed still somewhat beyond the everyday "national" consciousness of central Canadians.

Canada then had only two cities of national significance, Montreal and Toronto. Of these, Montreal was clearly both the larger and more dominant in numbers and influence. It had grown earlier and its economy was more diverse. Although Toronto was beginning to make gains, it still trailed the Quebec metropolis by a good hundred thousand.

Montreal was not, however, merely bigger and more powerful than Toronto. It was a decidedly different place. Whereas Toronto was dominated by its "British" character, Montreal was defined by its cultural diversity. "Us, them and the Irish" was the city's reality, a reality marked not so much by hostility as by "much indifference and ignorance."[8]

Montreal had its class distinctions, but these were much less ethnically based than modern mythology suggests. It is true that the business elite was largely Anglophone, living in brownstone mansions on Dorchester Boulevard and Sherbrooke Street. However, there was also a new class emerging between the rich on the Mountain and the poverty-stricken closer to the river, a middle stratum "composed of both French Canadians and Anglo-Canadians."[9]

The other difference in Montreal was its palpably more flexible character. Whether this was a consequence of the accommodations of cultural difference is hard to say, but Quebec's urban centre seemed a less rigid place than its Ontario counterpart. Ironically, this made it more in line with the contemporary mores of the Mother Country. There, the fashionable, adventurous and sometimes scandalous Edward VII, who had ascended to the throne in January 1901 upon the death of Queen Victoria, was defining a new age.

In Toronto, however, to be British still meant to stand for the stern and solid moralism of Edward's late mother. She had ruled for nearly sixty-four years, from 1837 on, and her rigid personality and values had wielded as much influence in the world as had her army and navy. Toronto did not call itself the Queen City for nothing. Victorian morals continued to reign supreme and had begun to morph into a phenomenon called the "social purity" movement.

Queen Street in the Queen City, 1901.

This movement believed that a systematic, "scientific" approach to moral education could expunge social problems and vices. Ontario was a beachhead for the Women's Christian Temperance Union, which had started up in Ohio in the 1850s. Drinking men were advised by doctors

to switch their drink of choice, as there would be "few ___
pure milk." Many Ontario schools had their young m___
day to say, "Jesus Christ and Canada expect me to be an___
nounced was the trend in English Canada that youngst___
warned to avoid "the leprosy of vice."[10] This puritanical culture ___
have a profound influence in the area of sport.

The cultural differences between the two cities served only to underscore Toronto's restlessness with its second-place status. Reading the
journals and debates of the period, one is soon struck by the city's sense of
its inevitable and rightful rise to power in the new Dominion. The idea
that Montreal had a birthright to Canadian leadership—so obvious to
that city's older establishment—was not accepted in the Queen City. A
British Canada, Toronto believed, needed the unequivocal British leadership that only it could provide.

———

Toronto's status as the second city of hockey is embedded in this period
of history—the period during which the modern sport first developed.
Kingston, Halifax (or, more precisely, Windsor, Nova Scotia) and many
other Canadian sites have staked claims as the birthplace of hockey. In
fact, stick-and-ball games on ice can be traced back centuries to different
parts of northern Europe. Field hockey's ancestors are even older. Aboriginal Canadians probably had similar rudimentary pastimes. There is
little doubt, however, that ice hockey as an organized endeavour traces its
evolution from Montreal, then the only centre truly capable of defining a
new national sport.

Montreal was the location of ice hockey's first formal game (1875), its
first published rules (1877), its first official club (1877), its first major tournament (1883), its first intercity league (1886) and its first national champion (1893).[11] That occurred when the reigning governor general, Lord
Frederick Stanley of Preston, presented his famous Cup, and a five-team
league—three of which were from Montreal—settled on its winner.[12] For
much of this time, hockey as an organized sport had been marginal and
largely unknown in Toronto.

Hockey's slower emergence in the Ontario capital was not an accident history. While there are early accounts of boys playing shinny on Toronto's frozen harbour and ponds, the city had natural disadvantages. Its winters are significantly milder than Montreal's and given to much more frequent thaws. This was a serious impediment to the development of the sport before the arrival of artificial ice.

Yet Toronto, as an important city in its own right, had a vibrant sporting life. The local papers of the era are replete with articles on winter activities of all kinds. There was skating, snowshoeing, tobogganing, ice yachting, boxing, fencing, pedestrianism (walking races), indoor baseball, billiards, shooting, checkers, card games, dog shows and, most important of all, curling. Yet, until well into the 1880s, little mention is made of hockey in the local newspapers of the day. One then finds only the odd brief report of some contest before a large gathering in Montreal.

As the decade of the 1880s progressed, however, hockey was beginning to firmly entrench itself beyond Montreal. It first settled into Montreal's hinterland in Quebec and eastern Ontario. Each place hockey arrived, interest would quickly escalate. Canada needed a sport that would speak to its winter soul the way lacrosse had captured its summer heart. It was only a matter of time before hockey would find its way to Toronto.

The introduction of the modern game to the Queen City is credited to Tom Paton, goalkeeper of the Montreal Wheelers. The house team of the Montreal Amateur Athletic Association (MAAA) was soon to become elite hockey's first dynasty. On a trip to the city in the winter of 1887, Paton found Torontonians oblivious to the rage sweeping the East. He decided to order a bunch of sticks and pucks from Montreal, and then organized practices among associates in Toronto. It being the end of the season, these efforts seemed to come to naught as the spring thaw arrived—but the seed had been planted.

The following winter, some of these athletic gentlemen would proceed to organize a hockey team out of the Caledonian Curling Club. About the same time, others started one at the Granite Curling Club. And, on February 16, 1888, the Granites hosted and beat the Caledonians 4–1 in Toronto's first official hockey match.

For the two clubs, at least, this was a watershed. The Granites had taken the first step in a storied journey through hockey history. The Caledonians vanished from the scene early, leaving but one important mark. Their rink on Mutual Street would become the city's premier hockey venue for many years to come.

Most students of the Toronto Maple Leafs, or of National Hockey League history in general, know that the team's first home was the Arena Gardens, a.k.a. the Mutual Street Arena. Less well remembered is that Mutual Street was itself the site of an even earlier rink. In fact, it was twice the site of natural-ice facilities before the arrival of the artificial variety.

The first mention of a rink on the west side of Mutual between Shuter and Cruickshank (later Dundas Street) can be traced to 1874. On that date the land belonged to John Willoughby Crawford, the lieutenant governor of Ontario, and would soon pass to his widow, Helen. The following year, the outdoor facility was formally christened by the Caledonians.

On December 10, 1885, a permanent indoor structure replaced the open ice sheet. One week later, to the music of the Royal Grenadiers band, patrons attended a "grand fancy dress carnival" to officially inaugurate the state-of-the-art "New Caledonian Rink."[13] The club would continue to open its ice to the paying public six days a week for curling and skating. The "Mutual Street Rink," as it quickly became known, had clearly not been intended for hockey; nevertheless, in the years that followed it established itself as the city's leading site for sport and trade exhibitions of all kinds.

Despite its official birth in the winter of 1888, Toronto hockey would remain an infant orphan for a couple more years. Little subsequent activity appears to have occurred during either that or the following season. Teams seem to have been loosely formed and games organized just as informally. The country's top league, the Montreal-based Amateur Hockey Association of Canada (AHAC), tried to contact clubs in the Toronto area in the fall of 1888, but heard nothing back. The Queen City just did not seem all that interested.

The seminal moment for Toronto hockey would not come until the 1889–90 season, and the visit of Ottawa's Rideau Rebels.

There may never have been a less appropriately nicknamed team than the Rebels. Officially the Vice-Regal and Parliamentary Hockey Club, it consisted of members and officials from both houses of Parliament as well as representatives of Rideau Hall. Among its players were some of Lord Stanley's children; future Cup trustee Philip Dansken Ross; and James George Aylwin Creighton, the man behind Montreal's first organized hockey match back in 1875.

Ottawa Rebels (1888–89). Based at Rideau Hall, this club was one of the most influential in the early development of Canada's national winter sport. Standing: C. Wingfield, A. Stanley, L. Power, H. Ward, J. Lemoine. Seated: E. Stanley, J. Creighton, A. MacMahon, J. Barron, H. Hawkes.

The Rebels initially belonged to no league, sought no championships and played only exhibition matches. Sporting plain crimson sweaters with white accessories, the club existed to promote the new game across the young country. Through it the members, including Stanley sons Edward, Victor and Arthur,[14] demonstrated both a deep commitment to the sport of hockey and a wider sense of nation-building.

The prospective visit of the Rebels seems to have spurred hockey activity and organization in Toronto that season. Genuine excitement built as the famous team approached the city in the governor general's private rail car. For the very first time, real hockey passion was sweeping Ontario's capital.

"The visit of the Parliamentary and Viceregal hockey team of Ottawa to Toronto has been looked forward to with great interest for some time," reported the *Daily Mail*. "Hockey is one of the most popular winter games in Ottawa, Montreal, Quebec, and other eastern cities, while in Toronto the game has not been extensively played."[15] It declared that the game "is somewhat like lacrosse, but far quicker, and the excitement is at fever heat all the time."[16]

The sport, at this time, was but a distant relative of the game Canadians would come to worship. It was played on natural ice by seven a side, rather than today's six. Teams carried no more than two spares. The participants wore skates that involved a leather boot and rudimentary blades: the Starr Manufacturing Company of Dartmouth, Nova Scotia, a major skate manufacturer, sold "Silver King" hockey blades—early tubes—for $10 a pair. It also carried sticks carved from a single piece of wood.

The skaters wore no special protective equipment apart from short, simple shin pads (with no knee protection) and padded "gauntlet" gloves that could be purchased at Eaton's for $1.75 a pair. Goalies wore cricket pads and were not allowed to drop down to stop or smother the puck. There was no forward passing. Players could carry the puck—in the earliest years, a round wooden disc, by the mid-1890s made of vulcanized rubber—up the ice and past checkers only by using a series of lateral passes. More often, they would simply backhand the puck high down the ice and then pursue it. There was no such thing as a slap shot.

The Vice-Regals had arranged two games with local sports clubs, and big crowds were expected for both. The visitors received a huge ovation as they stepped onto Toronto ice that afternoon of February 8, 1890. The presence of Arthur Stanley added considerable enthusiasm to the proceedings.

The Rebels were coming off a 4–3 victory over the Lindsay club the previous evening. Alas, their schedule was a tad intense for a group of middle-aged men. Despite quickly taking a lead of 5–0, they barely held on to beat the Granites 5–4. "The excitement towards the close was intense," reported the *Mail*, "as the home team were having the best of the play and were making strenuous efforts to equalize, which, however, they failed to do." [17]

That night, playing their third game in twenty-four hours, the Ottawa club lost 4–1 to the Toronto St. Georges at the Victoria rink. The two teams played "before a very large and fashionable attendance, who took great interest in the game, applauding the good play of the visitors and local men alike." Ice conditions were superb, and though the Rebels were clearly exhausted from so much hockey, the play was described as "excellent." The newspaper account was long and detailed, describing the play lavishly for those who had not attended. Young Stanley made "a clever shot for goal" that was stopped by St. Georges' point F. W. Jackson. Rush after rush is described: tides turned, shots were taken, all while "the applause was deafening, the fair sex heartily joining in." [18]

The games had been exciting—full of skating, passing, scoring, checking and even a bit of fighting. The club attended a couple of banquets before heading back to Ottawa the following evening, but they left behind a city transformed. Winter would never again be the same in Toronto. Soon the Granites and the St. Georges, along with the Victorias and the New Forts (from the local infantry school), were organizing a tournament for a loosely defined Toronto championship. Out-of-town dates were also being arranged. And teams of all kinds—institutional, commercial, church, school, ethnic, women's—would begin to appear.

Toronto was following the same pattern of development in its early hockey scene as had occurred elsewhere, particularly in Montreal and Ottawa, where the game was already well entrenched. This was the opposite of how an established sport grows. Today, it is the hockey league or association that is first established. The league creates franchises and schedules, and only later do its teams enter into competitions with outside entities. In the early days, however, clubs were organized first, and independently, with no overriding agency governing the structure of teams or players.

Typically, the first hockey clubs were established by existing institutions. In Toronto and elsewhere, the leading organizations were the athletic clubs. Teams were also started by the athletic branches of colleges and government organizations (particularly such institutions as police and fire departments and the military). Commercial entities as well were an important source of hockey clubs. In Toronto, the chartered banks produced some of the earliest and highest-quality teams.

Once hockey clubs came into existence, they would seek to arrange games. These "challenges" would grow to multi-team affairs and lead to the creation of tournaments. The final organizational step would be the creation of a league with an annual schedule.

By the end of the 1889–90 season, the preconditions for the founding of a hockey league had been met. This was not just true in Toronto; thanks in part to the work of the Rideau Rebels, it was also the case throughout much of southern Ontario.

Thus, on November 27, 1890, the "Hockey Association of Ontario" was established at Toronto's Queen's Hotel. Here again, the influence of the Rebels club was critical. Among the sixteen mainly middle-aged gentlemen who attended the founding meeting were the Honourable Arthur Stanley and Lindsay's John Augustus Barron, MP, the Rideau captain and chair of the meeting.[19] The governor general, Lord Stanley, had agreed to be honorary patron.

The Ontario Hockey Association, or OHA, as it quickly came to be known, set out to establish much-needed order among the province's emerging hockey scene. This order, however, would reflect the exclusively British, bourgeois character of these Ontario organizers, and from the outset it had a distinctly puritanical and authoritarian streak. The first item of business, not surprisingly, dealt with the issue of rough play. Barron, speaking as chair, noted that the Vice-Regals had found Toronto hockey—then largely unconnected to the rest of the shinny world— tending to the violent side.

Others had made similar observations. The impression given is of something like lacrosse on ice. Toronto the Good was troubled, as the *Mail* stiffly observed in its report of the Rebels–Granites contest: "It is greatly to be regretted that in a game between amateur teams some players should so forget themselves before such a number of spectators, a good proportion of whom on the occasion referred to being ladies, as to indulge in fisticuffs."[20] The OHA was not out just to establish a schedule. It would make sure that Ontario hockey was "clean" hockey.

Under the guidance of the OHA, hockey boomed throughout the province. The OHA ran senior, intermediate and junior series touching virtually every corner of the province. By its 1898 annual meeting, it had expanded from thirteen clubs to forty-two, accounting for fifty-four teams, and was growing rapidly. Only a decade after its first game, it could be said that "Toronto has more hockey clubs than it has any other kinds of athletic organizations." [21]

Besides numerous clubs in all three provincial divisions, Toronto possessed an array of hockey associations that fed into the OHA system. These included the Toronto Church Boys Brigade Hockey League, the Toronto Junior Hockey League and the Toronto Lacrosse Hockey League, founded by lacrosse clubs to give themselves a winter activity. At the top of the totem pole was the Toronto Bank Hockey League, a high-calibre senior circuit with an on-again, off-again relationship to the OHA.

In the Ontario Association itself there had been six Toronto clubs among the thirteen founding members. The first to emerge from the pack was Osgoode Hall. In 1893–94, the famous law school became the city's first senior provincial champion. However, the achievement was marred by controversy. Indeed, the first Osgoode title would highlight the first of the two recurring themes that underlay virtually every OHA controversy: an alleged Toronto bias.

The groundwork for the trouble was laid at the OHA annual meeting in December 1893. Toronto delegates won virtually every position on the executive, leading the Hamilton *Times* to label it the "Toronto Hoggy Association"[22]—a shot at the Queen City's derogatory nickname of Hogtown. The proverbial stuff hit the fan, however, when the executive ordered that the OHA senior final be played at the Mutual Street rink on February 28.

For the Ottawa Hockey Club, this was the final outrage. Now the reigning Ontario champions for three seasons, it believed it had earned the right to host the final. Going to Toronto would not only mean additional travel expense, but a higher risk that the ice would be poor at season's end. Before their semifinal against Queen's University, the Ottawas pulled out of the competition. Even in Kingston, public opinion was on their side.

Osgoode Hall Law School produced Toronto's first provincial senior champion. Yet, despite winning the OHA title twice, the Osgoodes never did get a shot at the Stanley Cup.

The Ottawa–OHA spat got ugly. After Osgoode defeated Queen's on slushy ice to win the championship, the Ottawas refused to return the OHA's Cosby Cup. They claimed that, as three-time winners, they were taking permanent possession of the trophy—a common sports tradition of the era. Only after Major A. Morgan Cosby himself refuted that interpretation—and the Ottawa club received lawyer's letters—did the former champs relent.

The motives of the OHA in this dispute remain unclear. Perhaps Toronto interests did not want a far superior and far-off club. Perhaps they were tired of scheduling around Ottawa's dual membership in the OHA and AHAC. In any case, Ottawa was gone from the Ontario league forever. Henceforth they would play exclusively in the Quebec association.

Of course, by 1894 the OHA championship was no longer the highest prize to which an Ontario team could aspire. The "Dominion Hockey Challenge Cup from Stanley of Preston," almost immediately known as the Stanley Cup, now embodied national supremacy, as far as Canadian hockey fans were concerned. And the Toronto Osgoodes wanted their shot. This time, however, a scheduling controversy would work against the provincial capital.

The Cup trustees, P. D. Ross and Sheriff John Sweetland, both of Ottawa, had decided that the league holding the trophy would first settle its own title and then accept challenges. Unfortunately, the AHAC regular season that year resulted in a four-way tie, which led to protracted negotiations between the clubs, followed by a lengthy period of playoffs. Accommodating the OHA was the least of the AHAC's concerns.

The defending champion Montreal Wheelers were eventually victorious. But by the time they clinched, on March 22, the chances of playable ice for a Cup final, even in Montreal, were remote. Osgoode Hall, now out of practice, let its challenge to the MAAA quietly pass.

The Toronto Osgoodes remained a serious OHA contender for the next several years. After the departure of the Ottawa Hockey Club, however, the next OHA dynasty fell to Queen's University. The Kingston club won the senior title in four of the next five years. The one exception was 1897–98, when the "Legalites" again beat Queen's to take the title. For whatever reason, Osgoode made no attempt to challenge for the Dominion championship and quietly vanished from the Stanley Cup scene.

———

The year of the Toronto Osgoodes' second senior title coincided with a big battle over the second of the OHA's recurring themes of controversy: the definition of an "amateur." When the founders of the OHA spoke of "clean" hockey, they meant far more than an absence of rough play; they also had in mind a moral philosophy of athletics. That philosophy was "amateurism"—and the term then meant much more than not paying athletes.

Amateurism embraced the belief that sport for its own sake, not for money, was the root of all virtue in athletics. Indeed, professionalism in athletics was believed to be the source of all vice. Without money, sport was regarded as a noble calling in which the young man nurtured heroic qualities—endurance, courage, self-sacrifice for the team—all to attain the glory of the championship. Once paid, the athlete was labelled socially disreputable, morally deviant and, as we shall see, even disloyal to the nation. The belief was simply that, once professionalized, athletics were no longer "sport" at all, but simply the worst kind of illicit moneygrubbing.

Today, such a stark dichotomy may strike the reader as almost unbelievable. It is, however, exactly how hard-line amateur advocates saw the world. Indeed, a significant element of society was determined to destroy the career—on *and* off the ice—of any young athlete who accepted money to play sports.

Hockey.
The Week in Hockey.
Something of "Jack" Carpmichael.

The life of a professional athlete, the penalized and ostracized variety is hard. Not only is debarred from the active sport, but his amateur brethren fiendishly delight in enforcing the restriction imposed upon his class. Last week J. P. Carpmichael, the now notorious professional, of Guelph National fame, an employe of Messrs. W. R. Johnson and Company, and a member of the hockey club, was subjected to a hardship incident to his unfortunate plight. Lining up against the Messrs. H. S. Howland and Company's champion Commercial League team, Carpmichael was at once objected to. Captain Wright setting up the fact of Carpmichael's suspension from the O. H. A. Carpmichael did not play. The same player was also refused a lucrative position not long since by a supposedly bright up-to-date business man. "Were you not concerned in a discreditable affair with the hockey people?" was the tradesman's leading question. Explanation would not suffice. The prospective employer could not be dissuaded from an altogether false impression. So the "professional" lost what might have been a splendid position. Such is the status of the "professional" as seen through not a few, but surprising as it appears, the eyes of a great many people, generally credited with the endowment of fair intelligence. Talking of "Jack" Carpmi-

This article highlights the social discrimination to which the professional athlete was subjected a century ago. Such attitudes were already becoming controversial.

J. P. CARPMICHAEL.

An account of the plight of young John P. "Jack" Carmichael, which appeared in the *Toronto News* on February 2, 1901 (with his name misspelled), illustrates perfectly the disgrace in which some held paid athletes. Carmichael's previous hockey friends refused to be on the same ice surface with the "now notorious professional" and a prospective employer denied him "a lucrative position." His crime? He is reputed to have accepted a small fee for playing a game "gentlemen" played only for sport and fun.

In the eyes of the amateur sporting authorities of the day, to be professional warranted a lifetime ban. One would be barred not just from the sport in question, but from any sanctioned athletic activity and all associated social circles. And a professional was not merely someone who accepted pay for play; it included anyone who ever played with or against a professional. So serious was the charge of professionalism that, contrary to British legal traditions, the accused was required to prove his innocence.

The reality is that the argument over professionalism in sport was one of the great moral debates of the era throughout the Anglo-American world. The paying of athletes in those days has been compared with the use of performance-enhancing drugs today. The key difference is that the latter is almost universally condemned—at least where such drugs are intentionally employed. Conversely, the question of professionalism a century ago created deep social divisions.

Why amateur advocates believed these things so passionately— indeed, fanatically—is now rather hard to explain. Suffice it to say that "respectable" sports in Great Britain had long been the preserve of "gentlemen" who neither needed nor sought remuneration. There were clear class distinctions when it came to sporting activities. "Gentlemen" were, of course, amateurs. "Professionals" were, for all intents and purposes, "undesirables."[23]

Amateurism had its roots in the noncommercial society of the aristocracy. The nobility had established elite recreations as an offshoot of military training. In an evolving United Kingdom, the ascendant bourgeoisie gradually assumed aspects of this athletic culture. It also developed the exclusive sports clubs, with a proscription on pay gradually replacing explicit class criteria.[24]

Amateurism also dovetailed with the dominant Christian thinking of the period. The idea that "play" could be "work" seemed nonsensical to the values of both industrious Protestantism and otherworldly Catholicism. Play was for boys; work was for men. Athletics could not be seen as an occupation. Rather, its social utility was viewed as restricted to the development of the young.[25]

The most robust manifestation of such ideas in the Victorian era was the concept of "muscular Christianity." While the idea could be traced back to the apostle Paul, it was the contemporary writings of such authors as Thomas Hughes in England and Ralph Connor in Canada that re-energized the thinking. Hughes's *Tom Brown's School Days*, published in 1857, was hugely popular for decades.

The simple story portrayed the friendship between two youngsters, Tom and Arthur, and their development as God-fearing, decent young men who were as diligent with their nightly prayers as they were as fair-playing, determined teammates on the cricket pitch or rugby field. As true "gentlemen," the notion of playing any game for rewards other than health, fitness and friendship would have appalled them.

Hockey on Ottawa's Rideau Canal, Christmas 1901.

It was believed that such athletic activity, by instilling the values of toughness and teamwork in young men, would engender a dedication to wider civic responsibilities. As in aristocratic times, this would include both the fitness and the willingness to participate in military service. Robert Baden-Powell's scouting movement famously began as an exercise in such training, building up the manhood of young boys through the teaching of noncombat skills that could be applied to battlefield situations. Lord Baden-Powell had been influenced by the writings of Canadian author and naturalist Ernest Thompson Seton, himself a firm believer in muscular Christianity.

Amateurism in Canada had experienced some unique frontier twists. Although the country never had an aristocratic "leisure class," its first amateur codes did contain the old-world restrictions against labourers. To these it added barriers based on race and ethnicity. Often cited is the 1873 rule of the Montreal Pedestrian Club, one of the country's earliest definitions of an amateur: "One who has never competed in any open competition or for public money, or for admission money, or with professionals for a prize, public money or admission money, nor has ever, at any period of his life taught or assisted in the pursuit of athletic exercises as a means of livelihood, or is a labourer or an Indian."[26]

As in Britain, Canadian amateurism by the end of the nineteenth century had come to be defined by the absence of pay rather than the absence of social standing. What remained incontrovertible, however, was that amateurism by its nature was rooted in an agenda of social exclusion. The "amateur" was never himself defined; he was only what he was "not." The amateur was not the "professional"—that is, not one who possessed professional characteristics or engaged in professional behaviours. Exclusion was thus the essence of all amateur definitions.

In its defence—although such rationalizations are difficult—this aversion to professionalism also had a basis in historical experience. "Professional" sports had their origin in the culture of the working-class tavern and the travelling show, realities that had likewise been brought from the Mother Country. Sports as business had thus long been associated with things like bare-knuckle fisticuffs, cockfighting and "hippodroming." The last were barnstorming tours of the countryside exhibiting "supposedly authentic athletic contests engaged in solely as a means of making money and drawing a large gate."[27] Usually such "contests" involved horses, but also team sports and fighters, and are considered to be the precursor to professional wrestling.

This early "pro" athletic culture was not pretty. Promoters and their clients did often engage in cheating, rigging, intimidation, violence, hooliganism, gambling and even less savoury activities. Most shockingly, they did not hesitate to desecrate the Sabbath, an affront that was particularly unacceptable to those who lived in and believed in "Toronto the Good." To the social establishment—the bourgeois leaders who were establishing the various forms of modern, organized, "scientific" sport—all such behaviour was ultimately attributable to the very nature of "professionalism" itself.

Of course, amateur definitions were in practice self-fulfilling. Those denied "respectable" sponsorship and status in all sports as "professionals" were relegated to disreputable activity and standing. Further, it was argued even at the time, the prohibition on pay was just a thin veneer covering deeper issues of class and racism. Athletes who most required pay were those who tended to come from underprivileged or ethnic backgrounds.

Yet one should not underestimate the degree to which amateurism had consciously evolved from a social system to a moral one. By the time the OHA arrived, it was personal character, not personal characteristics, that had become the focus. Amateurism's avowed goal was now to evangelize its values to all. Indeed, as long as one did not accept money, OHA hockey was widely accessible to the population. But being paid to play the sport was viewed as little more than a form of prostitution.

In reality, when the OHA was founded, professionalism in serious athletics was exceedingly rare in the young Dominion. International champion rower Edward "Ned" Hanlan—by far the most famous Canadian of his era—would be the notable exception. It was virtually unknown in team sports outside of the American importation of baseball. Hockey in 1890, though on the cusp of its explosive growth, could certainly not have then supported a pro athlete.

This did not stop the league from defending the faith with zeal. As hockey's following grew and its competitions intensified, the OHA became ever more vigilant against any taint of professionalism. One manifestation was an ever-stricter residency rule, designed to weed out suspicious player movements. Then, at its annual meeting of 1897, the association unanimously adopted the notorious "reverse onus" rule—in a stark reversal of the principles of British justice, anyone accused of professionalism was presumed guilty.

The rule would soon be tested. As the 1897–98 season began, there were rampant rumours of professionalism around the hockey clubs of southwestern Ontario. The Berlin (now Kitchener) Hockey Club was favoured to repeat as the league's intermediate champion. After a big win over rival Waterloo, city mayor and club manager Oscar Rumpel presented the boys with $10 gold coins in the dressing room.

There would have been no problem if the gifts had been, say, gold watches or gold rings. With these souvenirs in the form of currency, however, the OHA stepped in and accused the club of engaging in remuneration. The team was thus expelled for professionalism—even though the coins had been returned.

The OHA was not finished there. Waterloo was thrown out next. Accusations had surfaced that star forward Joseph "Grindy" Forrester had once competed in a bicycle race for cash prizes. While no one suggested Forrester had taken any money, he was judged unable to convincingly "prove" his innocence.

Most of the Berlin and Waterloo players were eventually reinstated by the OHA, but by then the season was over. It was to be the beginning of a history of strained relations between the provincial association and the leading cities of the region. The controversy would also give rise to two of the most interesting builders in hockey's long history.

One of these was John Liddell MacDonald Gibson. "Jack" Gibson was the star defenceman of the Berlin team. Exiled by the OHA, he would wander outside its jurisdiction and eventually, in the United States rather than Canada, become widely known as the "father of professional hockey."

The other man is perhaps the most powerful, charitable, tyrannical and enigmatic figure in the history of the sport. Drawn by the OHA's demonstrated commitment to amateurism, he would take its crusade to a level that would divide not only the hockey world, but the country itself.

His name was John Ross Robertson.

CHAPTER TWO

THE RISE OF "THE PAPER TYRANT"

All Is Well Under the Wellingtons

———•◦•———

The Ontario Hockey Association is a patriotic organization, not in name exactly, but in nature most assuredly. A force we stand for is fair play in sport, and sport is one of the elements in the work of building up the character of a young nation. . . . We have tried to live up to the ideals which are part of our birthright as Canadian sons of the greatest of countries, and as British citizens of the grandest of empires.[1]

—JOHN ROSS ROBERTSON

More than a half century after his passing, his biography was published under the title *The Paper Tyrant*—words that would suggest his power and influence, yet only hint at the breadth of John Ross Robertson's reach.[2] His was a life of great adventure—at one point he was even imprisoned by Louis Riel during the Red River Rebellion. Robertson found enormous financial success as a Toronto newspaper publisher, became a philanthropist of the first order and, not least of all, was for many years the aspiring hockey professional's worst enemy.

Robertson's reputation as a puritanical tyrant has had great lasting power. In a 2012 episode of the popular Canadian television series *Murdoch Mysteries* the long-ago head of the Ontario Hockey Association is portrayed as a central figure in an episode entitled "Murdoch Night in Canada" that involved the fictionalized death of a star Toronto hockey player. "This game is being taken over by rogues and capitalists, Mr. Murdoch," Robertson, played by actor Guy Bannerman, complains at one point. "I'm doing all within my power to stop it."[3] The hockey murder and dialogue might have been made up, but John Ross Robertson was very, very real.

Robertson was the founder of the *Toronto Telegram*, which by the end of the nineteenth century was the country's most powerful newspaper. He was also an ardent British imperialist who distrusted the involvement of the United Kingdom in Canada's affairs; an antiracist, antislavery advocate who regularly employed racial slurs and railed against French Canadians and the Catholic Church; a staunch Tory who consistently opposed the Conservative Party; a strict disciplinarian who indulged his children to their ruin; a figure popular and respected, yet authoritarian and controversial. John Ross Robertson was nothing if not complex.

The dichotomies of his life seem endless. He ran for Parliament demanding sweeping change, won spectacularly and then chose not to pursue his political career. He established the *Telegram* as a leading publication, yet sowed the seeds for its eventual demise after his own passing. He had a high opinion of his own social standing, but would later turn down both a British knighthood and a Canadian Senate seat.

Robertson had a large head, expanded by fleshy jowls and a beard worn in variations of the style made popular by U.S. president Abraham Lincoln. This, along with deep-set eyes under forbidding brows and an overbearing, powerful personality, may have made him seem larger than life. Contemporaries described him as standing six feet, tall for the age, yet his own grandson, John Gilbee Robertson, described him as "short and pudgy." And while Toronto charities, particularly the Children's Hospital, heaped praise upon Robertson for his generosity and for such touching contributions as his willingness to dress up as Santa Claus, the grandson had a decidedly different impression: "I did not like the son of a bitch."[4]

Yet there was one thing on which Robertson was not complicated: he was opposed to professionalism in all sports, but particularly in the one he loved the most: hockey. As he succinctly put it: "There can never be the shadow of a justification for professionalism in hockey."[5] He would live every breathing moment of his six-year tenure as president of the Ontario Hockey Association as if his very existence depended on that principle. He was "the embodiment of the OHA's iron fist."[6]

There can be little doubt that John Ross Robertson's devotion to amateurism was bred at Upper Canada College, the country's leading private school. There, as a sixteen-year-old in 1857, he founded Canada's first student newspaper, the *College Times*, leading to a confrontation with the institution's authorities. He had nevertheless fully absorbed their doctrine. As he proclaimed at his first address to the OHA in 1898: "Sport should be pursued for its own sake; for when professionalism begins true sport ends."[7]

After his school experience with the *College Times*—and also with a satirical magazine he called *The Grumbler*—Robertson became a journalist, first working for the *Globe*, then trying to found his own newspaper, the *Daily Telegraph*, which failed. He was twenty-eight years old when he found himself sent to the Northwest Territories to cover the Riel uprising. His reports were more graphic than the staid, impersonal accounts that were traditional in the *Globe*. It was this style he later brought to the *Telegram*, which he founded in 1876 and which soon became a pre-eminent journal in the city and the country. The *Telegram* was staunchly Orange—this zealous devotion to all causes Protestant perhaps having something to do with Riel's treatment of the young reporter. At his death he was said to have marched in fifty-three Twelfth of July Orange parades.[8]

A man of prodigious energy, he was politician, publisher, philanthropist and hockey head all at the same time—and still it did not use up all his available time. His restlessness could be seen in his fingernails, which his second wife, Jessie, insisted he stop biting. Robertson's "crusty benevolence"[9] was by no means limited to hockey, where he was exceedingly generous with both his time and his money. He was Toronto's most renowned early historian and archivist, leaving his collection to the city's library system. Most significantly, his dedication to helping the young almost single-handedly created the Hospital for Sick Children, an organization to which he bequeathed a considerable endowment.

In 1890 he became grand master of the Grand Masonic Lodge of

Canada West and, in a single year, travelled 10,000 miles in order to pay visits to some 130 lodges. "Wincing most of the way," biographer Ron Poulton wrote. "His lumbago was particularly bad the day he hired a boy on skates to haul him in a sleigh across Rice Lake to visit some lodge brothers in Keene."[10]

Although Robertson had his detractors at the time, admirers were much more numerous. In 1896, with Toronto in an uproar over a series of unpopular concessions to the Catholic Church and the French language, he succumbed to public pressure to run for Parliament in East Toronto. Robertson aligned himself loosely with the small but radical McCarthyite League, made up of followers of D'Alton McCarthy, a one-time Conservative cabinet minister who had broken with the party over French-language issues and reform of protective tariffs. Presenting himself as an "Independent Conservative," the Orangeman was swept to office—very rare for a third-party candidate in that era. He would later become one of very few Canadians to turn down both a knighthood and a senatorship.

His leadership skills were also much admired by the Toronto hockey community. Robertson had already been involved in the sport for some time when he attended the OHA's annual meeting in 1898. Robertson's son, J. S. Robertson, better known as "Cully," was a great sports fan and already on the OHA executive. Apparently impressed by its controversial defence of amateur principles the previous season, J.R. presented the association with a stunning new championship trophy, the John Ross Robertson Cup, and delivered "delightfully smart"[11] remarks that brought the house down. History then records that at the next meeting, in 1899, he was by acclamation "persuaded to accept the position of President."[12]

Robertson's well-known opinions were happily embraced by his fellow members of the executive. As he succinctly put it at one annual meeting: "Hockey as a recreation is all right, but hockey as a business is all wrong."[13]

———

The new president, however, did bring a new dimension to amateur advocacy: Canadian nationalism. Put simply, according to Robertson's followers, to advance professionalism was to undermine the country itself. To be clear, this perspective was based on a national identity then firmly defined within a much different context from today. To his contemporary OHA audiences, their president's message would have been clear: Canada, as an outpost of the traditions of the British Empire, had to stand on guard against the encroachment of the values of the American Republic.

The idea that there was a patriotic cause here was not as far-fetched as it may seem now. The bourgeois establishments of Canada and the United States saw the world quite differently. Much of this country's contemporary elite—particularly old-line Tories like Robertson—were the conscious heirs to a long evolution of British practices and traditions that, they believed, had created the greatest and most enlightened power in history: the British Empire. They saw U.S. society as inherently chaotic and their American counterparts as the offspring of rootless—and potentially dangerous—revolutionaries.

Robertson and his colleagues felt more imminently threatened by the United States than do the anti-Americans of today. Indeed, our concerns at their worst would be minor compared to the sovereignty worries of those years. Although Canadian–American relations had improved considerably over the decades, the two countries were not then bound in alliance. Robertson's cohorts had witnessed frequent periods of grave tension between the two countries. They might have known men who had lived and fought during the War of 1812; they certainly knew those who had lived through the American Civil War. "Muscular Christianity" was to them no mere theoretical concept. Developing young Canadian boys into tough men who could defend British North America against the possibility of U.S. invasion was a national imperative. In fact, Lord Stanley's patronage of hockey was motivated, in significant part, by precisely this line of thought.[14]

The OHA leaders could also look across the Great Lakes—at states like Pennsylvania and later Michigan—and see the corruption of their country's beloved national winter sport by professionalism. There, hockey players had been more or less openly paid for some time—with hardly the slightest sense of outrage or offended public mores. This was not the under-the-table pay, or "shamateurism," that was creeping into Canada's senior leagues. It was the unbridled commercial excess of American culture, complete with all the violence and plebeian evils they believed it inflicted on athletics.

It mattered not that precisely the same amateur-versus-professional debates were being played out both in the United States and the United Kingdom. Indeed, in much of the United States—where the clean-playing amateur star Hobey Baker was the game's role model—the professional corruption of hockey was viewed as a Canadian phenomenon.[15] Nevertheless, according to Canada's amateur purists, this was a fight for Canada's national game and national soul.

Powerful institutions, especially those rooted in Anglo-Canadian culture, promoted strands of this thinking. One example could be found in the British schools, of which Robertson's alma mater, Upper Canada College, was the quintessential Canadian example. There were also the military and paramilitary organizations, such as police and fire departments, as well as the homegrown North-West Mounted Police.

Not surprisingly, the ultimate fortress of this philosophy became the Ontario Hockey Association under Robertson's leadership. In effect, Robertson took the moral and social theories of amateurism and wedded them to a political ideology. At the 1903 annual meeting, he provided perhaps as clear and concise a contemporary articulation of this ideology as one will find:

> The Ontario Hockey Association is a patriotic organization, not in name exactly, but in nature most assuredly. A force we stand for is fair play in sport, and sport is one of the elements in the work of building up the character of a young nation . . . We have tried to live up to the ideals which are part of our birthright as Canadian sons of the greatest of countries, and as British citizens of the grandest of empires.[16]

———

The fanaticism of Robertson's convictions has obscured his contribution to the sport. He had, in fact, been enthralled by hockey since he cobbled together a shinny team, the Simcoes, from among his boyhood friends.

As OHA president, he virtually doubled the size of an already large organization, making it the richest and by far the biggest sports body in the country. Under his guidance, the association pioneered and promoted numerous rule changes that grasped the subtlety of the game: the delayed penalty, the goal net, the intermediary role of the captain, flexible interpretations of the offside pass, dropping the puck for a faceoff instead of laying it between the two centres' stick blades. Other sporting entities envied and emulated the OHA's publications and its organizational methods.

John Ross Robertson. Love him or hate him, there was no figure in early Toronto hockey more powerful or more compelling.

However, Robertson's contributions came with a price: his breathtaking proclivity to control. This power was built not only through long hours of dedicated service, but also by constitutional manipulation and self-promotion bordering on self-mythologizing. He was hailed as the "father of pure amateur hockey in Ontario"[17] and, quite erroneously, as the "father of the association."[18] Any person who had helped build up the OHA over the nine years before his presidency either became a follower or was simply swept away. Even his donation of the eponymous championship trophy had the side benefit of brushing aside the Cosby Cup, which had been named after the organization's real first president, Toronto investment manager Major A. Morgan Cosby.

The new president sought total, unconditional victory over his opponents, wherever they might be. For example, by 1902 professionalism was widely known to be practised in the Western Pennsylvania Hockey League. Thus, Robertson told the annual meeting that "every guilty player should be given to understand that the axe of the O.H.A. will fall upon his neck just as surely for an offence committed in Pittsburg [sic] as for an offence committed in Toronto."[19] He gloated openly about his power to ruin such athletes in lacrosse and football just as easily as he could in hockey.

In the name of amateur principles, Robertson would almost immediately begin tightening his personal hold over the OHA. At the annual meeting of 1900, a constitutional amendment allowed him to directly name two of the executive's ten other members, ostensibly to ensure better regional representation. The next year, all but the immediate past president were dropped from the governing body.

However, Robertson did have a vision. His speeches on amateur hockey were eloquent, powerful mixtures of morality, inclusiveness and unbridled nationalism. Take this passage from his address to the annual meeting of 1902: "You are with few exceptions, young Canadians. I am not exactly in the junior class, but, thank God, I also am a Canadian, and I am as young as any of you in my love for this country and this country's winter game." [20]

Those who doubted him—and an increasing number did as the years passed—simply could not compete with his command, conviction and charisma. Four decades after his death, his younger colleague and confidant, former *Star* sports editor W. A. Hewitt, still marvelled that "Mr. Robertson was a big man in every way." [21]

Helping Robertson consolidate his power was newspaper ally Francis Nelson, the sports editor of the *Toronto Globe*. Nelson had joined the OHA executive with his *Tely* colleague in 1899. Two years later he would be named first vice-president. Nelson was also deeply involved with lacrosse, serving as first vice-president of the Canadian Lacrosse Association, and was, like Robertson, an unyielding opponent of professionalism in athletics. Alongside Robertson, he would find far more success in fighting it in the new winter sport than the much older and more established summer game. The *Telegram* and the *Globe*, then the two most powerful newspapers in the province, soon to be joined by Hewitt's *Star*, would increasingly act as bully pulpits for Robertson's iron control of Ontario hockey.

———

Robertson's ascendency to the presidency of the OHA would coincide with the rise of a provincial championship team that embodied the principles he stood for. This was the Wellington Hockey Club, which would be Toronto's first genuine hockey dynasty. And it would, of course, be purely amateur.

As was common in athletic clubs of the era, the Wellingtons were active in many facets of the Toronto sports scene—soccer, rugby, baseball and more. Also typically, its members were multi-sport athletes, and so the player roster varied little from sport to sport. The founding meeting of its hockey team took place in the fall of 1891.

The progress of the Wellingtons was steady. The young team, led by captain Charles "Chummy" Hill, appears to have first played challenges before moving into the Toronto Junior league. In 1895–96 the club also put an entry in the junior division of the OHA. That season they took the Cox Cup, representing the

Francis "Frank" Nelson. Sports editor of the *Globe* and first vice-president, under John Ross Robertson, of the Ontario Hockey Association.

city's junior championship. The next year they took the provincial junior crown.

By the fall of 1898 the Toronto Wellingtons felt ready to compete in the top division of the Ontario Hockey Association, and their incredible run began the following season. In the winter of 1899–1900, they stormed back from a loss at home to upset the defending champions from Queen's University 6–4 in a two-game, total-goals final. They again took the J. Ross Robertson Cup in 1900–01.

The "Iron Dukes," as the rising team was nicknamed,[22] were known both for skill and toughness and were then captained by George McKay. As an eighteen-year-old McKay had scored the only goal for Queen's University in its 1895 Stanley Cup game against the Montreal AAA. Queen's losses that year and in 1899 had been the only Stanley Cup contests involving OHA teams to date. Nonetheless, the Wellingtons' aggressive young secretary-treasurer, Alexander Miln, issued a challenge for the national title in December 1901.

This was the era in which the Stanley Cup trustees, not the leagues themselves, decided which teams would be allowed to play for the championship of the Dominion. In this case, the Wellingtons' challenge was promptly accepted by the trustees and a best-of-three series was slated for mid-January.[23]

The Wellingtons would face the famed Victoria Hockey Club of Winnipeg, consistently one of Canada's top teams. The Vics had been champions of the top-tier Manitoba Hockey Association nine consecutive times. In 1896 they had become the first non-Montreal team to hold the Cup, though only briefly. Since 1899 they had been in a series of toughly fought annual challenges, finally wrestling the Stanley Cup from the Montreal Shamrocks at the Montreal Arena in January 1901.

The OHA challenger was viewed with considerable skepticism in the established hockey circles of Quebec and Manitoba. Ontario had never won the national championship—or even been close. The Wellingtons lacked recognized national hockey stars to match Winnipeg's Dan Bain or Tony Gingras. Some doubted whether a Toronto club could skate on the same ice as a Stanley Cup champion.

The Toronto papers shot back in defence of the OHA. They noted that the Victorias were the champions of a mere two-team Winnipeg league. Manitoba's exclusion of the Thistles, a promising club from Rat Portage (later Kenora), was increasingly controversial.

The Toronto Wellingtons' trip to Winnipeg in early 1902 is often noted as the city's first Stanley Cup voyage. It also constituted a quintessential display of the traditions and values of amateurism. Every facet of the adventure highlighted the concept of the amateur sportsman and his commitment to gallantry, toughness and fair play.

The Iron Dukes were seen off at Union Station by a big crowd led by John Ross Robertson himself. To get to the Manitoba capital, they faced a railway journey of two days. They boarded with boisterous wishes of good luck, the OHA president chorusing a hearty cheer for the men.

The party of team officials and nine players (seven starters plus two spares) were met at the other end by hundreds of wildly cheering Winnipeggers. Players and officials from the Victorias and other local sporting organizations then led the Wellingtons in carriages to their hotel. Their procession followed a route decorated brightly with the colours of the

The Queen's Hotel, Toronto.
In 1890, this landmark stood on the site of the Royal York.
Even then, it was a prestigious address.

HOCKEY! HOCKEY!

WANDERERS OF MONTREAL,
CHAMPIONS OF CANADA,
VS. PORTAGE LAKES
UNITED STATES CHAMPIONS,

FOR WORLD'S CHAMPIONSHIP.

MONDAY AND TUESDAY,

MARCH 21 AND 22
at AMPHIDROME.

These will be the Greatest Hockey Games that were ever seen in America

Just think of it! A chance to see Canada's Champion Hockey Team go against Portage Lakes, United States Champions. You are not likely to have another chance to see such a game.

SPECIAL RATES AND TRAINS
FROM ALL PARTS OF THE STATE.
See Railroad Advertisements for Rates and Leaving Time.

SEATS ON SALE
At Barry's Drug Store, Houghton; Nichols' Drug Store, Hancock; Sodergren & Sodergren's Drug Store, Calumet.

Prices--First three rows on side $2.00.   Balance of sides $1.50.   General Admission $1.00
Wire all Orders to Manager Amphidrome.

The victory of Doc Gibson's Portage Lakers over the Montreal Wanderers in 1904 showed that open professionalism would be the future of championship hockey.

The Schenley Park Casino (c.1895), the predecessor of Pittsburgh's Duquesne Gardens, was North America's first artificial-ice arena.

Main Street looking North, Winnipeg, Man.

Winnipeg's Main Street in 1907, five years after the Toronto Wellingtons' Stanley Cup excursion to the city.

Winter sports were quite varied in Toronto. As in most of Canada, hockey became the pre-eminent one by the 1890s.

SKATING ON TORONTO BAY.

The Aberdeen
Pavilion, site of the
Ottawa–Marlboros
Stanley Cup
confrontation of 1904.

This depiction of a ladies' hockey team is from about 1910. Starting with the governor general's daughter, Isobel Stanley, female players were a feature of the game.

The Amphidrome in Houghton, Michigan, was the home of Doc Gibson's Portage Lakers, the first avowedly professional team.

This postcard illustrates an 1890s match between the Montreal (AAA) Winged Wheelers and Victorias at the latter's rink, now considered the birthplace of hockey as an organized sport.

Toronto Osgoodes jersey (1897–98).

Toronto Wellingtons jersey (1901–02).

Montreal Wheelers jersey (1901–02).

Toronto Marlboros jersey (1903–04).

clubs. The train being late on the night before the first game, the Vics graciously gave their practice hours over to the visitors that evening.

Although the Manitoba hockey world harboured strong doubts about the calibre of the Ontario champions, interest in the series was raging. The Cup was on display in the window of Dingwall's jewellery store with large pictures of the two teams. Over 5,000 spectators squeezed into the Winnipeg Auditorium, with hundreds more left outside when the doors finally closed. The fans loudly waved pennants and streamers of their team's colours as the marching band of the 90th Regiment provided pregame entertainment.

Newspapers in both cities noted with pride that the Manitoba crowd gave the Wellingtons almost as big a welcome as the hometown champions and periodically cheered good play by the visitors. Even the referee was warmly applauded by the spectators. Still, gentlemanly wagers went between 2½ and 3 to 1 against the Iron Dukes throughout the week.

Interest was high back in Toronto as well. On both evenings, January 21 and 23, hockey fans spent hours at the offices of the newspapers, following the reports of the games sent by telegraph. The operators would loudly read out the Morse code "play-by-play" while fans cheered or groaned at the very latest news from Winnipeg. Robertson had made things a bit easier for the general public by arranging the results to be broadcast by way of a giant whistle at the Toronto railway powerhouse. Between 11:00 and 11:30 p.m. two soundings would mean the Wellingtons had won whereas three would mean the Victorias had kept the championship.[24]

It would have been a fine game for Toronto fans to witness, if only there had been radio or television in 1902. The Winnipeg Auditorium, with a surface that measured 205 feet by 90 and had been hardened by frigid temperatures, provided a fast, exciting and toughly fought series. The Victorias beat the challengers two games in the best-of-three, both by a close margin of 5–3. While still a loss in their quest for the Stanley Cup, the Iron Dukes had won a measure of respect for the OHA game.

The second game of the series saw an interesting innovation. Both clubs unfortunately sported the same dark red colour, which posed somewhat of a problem. Before the televising of games in 1950s black and white, clubs usually maintained only one set of jerseys, and each member of a league was expected to have a unique colour scheme. Thus, dilemmas like this could arise when teams from different leagues met. In this case it was agreed that the Wellingtons would use the jersey of the Victorias' crosstown competitor, the Winnipegs, for the first game, while the Vics would do the same for the second. However, for game two the Vics appeared in a new, white club jersey—a very early foreshadowing of the protocol of the TV age.

This Toronto–Winnipeg Stanley Cup series also became legendary for a number of incidents involving the puck. In one instance, a backhand lift became lodged in the rafters, forcing the players to throw their sticks up to dislodge it. In another case, the Wellingtons scored with half a puck when the disc split during play. Although the referee allowed the marker, future rulings forbade the granting of a goal for anything other than the full rubber entering the net. Finally, a fan refused to throw back a disc that had gone into the crowd, as had been the practice up to that point. Thus the tradition of the souvenir puck was born.

That said, in the amateur era only a small part of the action took place with the puck or on the ice. The terms "visitors" and "home" were not mere labels on a score sheet. The Victorias were expected not only to provide the competition inside the rink, but to host the Wellingtons away from it as well. Mrs. J. C. Armytage, spouse of the club president, offered the Iron Dukes a bouquet of pink and white carnations at the conclusion of game one. The "Bisons" promptly followed up by hosting the Iron Dukes at a local theatre.

After game two, the victors banqueted their guests at the Queen's Hotel—the same hotel that had been kind enough to supply the Wellingtons with food and refreshments in their dressing rooms. Senior officials of the two clubs rose in turn to toast the hard but gentlemanly play of their opponents throughout the series. The Wellingtons' Miln was particularly diplomatic: "The Victorias are all good sports and play good hockey. Our boys are not at all sore over their defeat, but are proud to think that they gave the champions of the world such a hard rustle for their win."[25]

The next morning, the Victorias gave the Wellingtons one final breakfast banquet before passing them over to other city dignitaries. The rival Winnipeg Hockey Club provided a luncheon for the men at the Commercial Club. They were then taken by Mrs. E. L. Drewry, the Victorias' "Lady Patron," who hosted a reception for 200 in honour of the Iron Dukes, who received "three hearty cheers"[26] upon arrival. Unfortunately, a trip to Silver Heights to view the buffalo had to be cancelled due to the freezing weather. The evening concluded pleasantly, nevertheless, in the officers' mess of the Canadian Mounted Rifles.

This is Lord Stanley's trophy as it looked after 1903. It's a safe bet the early champs found it a lot easier to hoist over their heads.

Although there was no third game, hospitality extended into Saturday the 25th. At noon, the Wellingtons were the guests of honour for a luncheon at the Cavalry Barracks put on by Major Gardiner. The final reception was hosted by a Mrs. R. F. Manning, the purpose of which was to have the fellows entertain some local young ladies. In charmingly chivalrous wordage, it was noted that "their success in this particular was even more marked than against the Victorias."[27]

Needless to say, the Wellingtons could expect no less attention from their hometown. A crowd, smaller than expected due to "Arctic weather" and a seven-hour train delay, greeted the Wellingtons at Union Station. With Mayor Oliver Howland in tow, President Robertson, who had transmitted laudatory telegrams to the boys throughout, led the delegation in "three cheers and a tiger for the plucky Wellingtons!"[28] He and his executive then promptly took the crew for dinner.

The Toronto Wellingtons, also known as the Iron Dukes, were the city's first genuine hockey dynasty. This picture shows the club as it neared the end of its four-year reign. Standing: A. Ardagh, M. Irish, W. Lamont, W. Loudon, W. Smart, C. Pringle. Sitting: J. Worts, I. Ardagh, G. Chadwick, C. Hill, F. McLaren. Reclining: A. Miln.

A grand public reception awaited the team as the players arrived at Shea's Theatre later that evening. They were escorted to boxes decorated in the team's red and white for the purpose of viewing the show. However, time and again cheers broke out for the hometown heroes, all interest in the performance being utterly forgotten. It mattered not in the least that the Wellingtons had lost. The club, as one local paper observed, "by their gallant and sportsmanlike conduct, both on and off the ice, attained to a degree of popularity far greater than was ever before."[29]

The Wellingtons returned the accolades. They prominently published thanks to their supporters along with a detailed list of the patrons who had underwritten the eleven-day trip to Winnipeg. It was noted that the whole affair, after a $1,000 share of the gate, had almost broken even.

However, none of the generous hospitality or kind words directed towards the Torontonians by the Winnipeggers should suggest that this had been a tame affair. The national championship was on the line in what was regarded as a tough, manly sport. By the end of the two matches the Iron Dukes, to use the phraseology of the day, were "badly used up."

The Victorias had sensed the relatively poor conditioning of the Wellingtons early in the Toronto season[30] and had taken the body to them with a vengeance. One Toronto player had a dislocated shoulder. Another sported damage around the eye. Yet another hobbled on a crippled leg. One was so sick with injuries he had to leave Shea's early (and was later diagnosed with a mild case of scarlet fever). The Vics were not pristine either, one member having a badly damaged rib cage.

It should be noted that the beginnings of a less genteel era were also on display in Winnipeg. At halftime of game two, a large black Newfoundland dog suddenly appeared on the ice surface, pursued by a frantic owner. More serious was the crush when the auditorium gates had opened for the series, a stampede and critical injuries being only narrowly averted. And pure hooliganism occurred when youths who had been shut out climbed high in the building and smashed some upper windows to gain free admission. The times, indeed, were changing, although few then realized how quickly those changes would come.

Following the Stanley Cup challenge, the Wellingtons went on to win the Ontario senior series again in 1901–02 and an unprecedented fourth consecutive title the following year. They were known to be actively planning another run at the Cup when, at their annual banquet on November 30, 1903, the club abruptly announced it was disbanding. Too many veterans, it seems, would be unavailable—and irreplaceable—for the coming season.

The Vics were the first non-Montreal team to win the Stanley Cup.
They were a formidable opponent for anyone.

Chummy Hill, with the Wellingtons since their inception, was just
one player reported to have broken down upon the news of their demise.

In fact, Toronto's OHA establishment—including team patron John Ross Robertson—was stunned by the unexpected end of the venerable club. The OHA had laboured mightily to create the perfect order in hockey in the province and the Iron Dukes represented the epitome of its ideals.

In truth, the series between the Toronto Wellingtons and Winnipeg Victorias was the last gasp of the gentleman amateur in Stanley Cup play. Before the end of 1901–02, the Vics would lose the championship to the Montreal AAA. That team would, at the end of the next season, defect en masse to the newly formed Montreal Wanderers—a decidedly entrepreneurial act that certainly hinted at professionalism. The Cup itself would be taken by the Ottawa Silver Seven. They were a gang not merely suspected of accepting pay, but employing dirty play as part of a deliberate strategy of winning at all cost.

In other words, the demise of the Wellingtons would prove to be a relatively minor blow to hockey's old order. Much bigger challenges were about to confront the amateur world that John Ross Robertson had sought to entrench.

CHAPTER THREE

THE ENEMY IN THE OPEN

The Ascent of the Marlboros

———⋅•⋅———

We have met the enemy and he is us.

—POGO (COMIC-STRIP CHARACTER
CREATED BY WALT KELLY)[1]

The great irony of the efforts John Ross Robertson and his cohort undertook to preserve the amateur order is the degree to which those efforts would serve to undermine it. More than once, in their search for an enemy, the Ontario Hockey Association brain trust would create one. Their first such target was Jack Gibson. It all began with that $10 coin Gibson received from the mayor of Berlin (later Kitchener), Ontario, in 1898—a coin he never asked for and in fact had offered to return.

Gibson was a local boy and an accomplished athlete who excelled in virtually every sport he took up: lacrosse, baseball, rowing, swimming, cycling, soccer, curling, cricket, tennis and skating. He played his first organized hockey when he was sent to Pickering College, a private school in what was then a rural setting just east of Toronto. At fifteen, he was captain of the school team. At seventeen, he was a member of the Berlin intermediate team that was soon to be disgraced by the OHA's heavy-handed actions. Even though the players' suspensions were to be lifted at

Doc Gibson. When the Ontario Hockey Association exiled John Liddell MacDonald Gibson, it turned out to be one in a series of grand miscalculations by John Ross Robertson's organization. The wandering Gibson would become "the father of professional hockey."

the end of the season, the experience had a profound effect on the handsome young hockey star.[2]

Gibson moved from his Ontario hometown to Detroit, where he played some non-OHA hockey and studied dentistry. He then settled in the copper-mining town of Houghton, on Michigan's Upper Peninsula, where he set up a dental practice. There, in 1900, "Doc" Gibson would establish the Portage Lake Hockey Club, giving it Berlin's green and white colours. With the 200-pound Gibson as its star, and bolstered by other Canadians from Gibson's Detroit college team, Portage Lake soon emerged as a force. At one point, Houghton ran off fourteen straight victories, defeating all comers in the States and some reputable Canadian challengers as well.

Then, in the fall of 1903, Gibson made a momentous decision. He resolved to make his Houghton Portage Lakers hockey's first avowedly professional club. Setting out to build the strongest possible team in an area with few homegrown recruits, he determined that he would openly remunerate the players by dividing any gate receipts among them.

For the OHA zealots, the enemy had finally come into the open. However, this adversary was no longer some callow youngster suspected—rightly or wrongly—of breaking the finer interpretations of ancient dogma. Gibson's action was to rapidly transform paid hockey from a hidden and isolated exception to a systemic development across clubs and leagues. The kid with the $10 coin who had been driven into OHA exile was about to become the "father of professional hockey."

The first effects of Gibson's move were felt in other parts of Michigan and neighbouring northern Ontario, specifically in Sault Ste. Marie. The birth of a pro team in the Canadian "Soo" was perhaps inevitable. The city had built a large arena, incurring much debt in the process. There being no serious OHA competition in the area, the city's newly formed Algonquin Hockey Club turned to the only nearby rival: a competitor of Gibson's in Sault Ste. Marie, Michigan, that the OHA clearly considered professional. The Canadian-side Algonquins said they would rather remain amateur, but according to the rules of the day, they were branded as professional as soon as they skated out against the team from across the St. Marys River.

Semi-professionalism had already taken hold in another U.S. state, hundreds of miles south of Gibson's Michigan realm. In 1896, the Western Pennsylvania Hockey League had been founded in Pittsburgh.[3] After a false start (the local arena burned down that December), the WPHL was relaunched in 1899, making its home in an enormous, modern arena called the Duquesne Gardens. In addition to its status as a former streetcar barn, what set the Gardens apart from other rinks was its still-novel artificial-ice plant. The league needed paying fans to cover its costs. However, just as had happened in Michigan, hockey in the Pittsburgh area saw its status as a spectator sport quickly outgrow its local talent pool, creating a market for paid players. As early as 1901–02, the Pittsburgh league had been drawing quality Canadian players with promises of modest dollars and side jobs. And in 1903, the WPHL champion Pittsburgh Bankers met, and were narrowly defeated by, the Portage Lakers for the first-ever "United States Hockey Championship." John Ross Robertson's *Telegram* had run an exposé on the organization's professionalism, leading—not surprisingly—to an OHA ban against any Ontario boy who might play there.

These commercial pressures south of the border were already having repercussions in Canada. For example, the new Stanley Cup champions, the Ottawa Hockey Club, had seen their clandestine payroll creep from a nominal $100 to about $250 in the preceding years. Battles over anything with financial implications—league membership, scheduling dates, Cup challenges—were thus growing ever more serious in eastern hockey. The combination of the overt demands of hockey's popularity with the covert ones of its sham amateurism could not be contained by the sport's existing structures for much longer.

On December 1, 1903, came the announcement of a rival to Canada's elite eastern hockey league. Since its founding in 1886, the Amateur Hockey Association of Canada—which became the Canadian Amateur Hockey League in 1898—had been the country's leading organization. Yet, during a period of rapidly expanding interest in the sport, it consisted of just five clubs: Montreal's Wheelers (a.k.a. the AAA), Victorias and Shamrocks, plus the Quebec Bulldogs and Ottawa Silver Seven.[4] That exclusivity had been the key to maintaining the calibre of play and the league's dominance. But it had also engendered increasing controversy and resentment that contributed to the rise of the new Federal Amateur Hockey League.

The Federal League—loosely, a successor to an Ottawa-based league called the Central Canada Hockey Association—would consist of organizations long shut out of the older circuit: Cornwall, the Capital club of Ottawa and the Francophone Nationals of Montreal.

However, it was the flagship English Montreal team that really raised eyebrows: the suitably named Wanderers.[5] Not backed by any established athletic club, the Wanderers became a contender overnight with the defection of virtually the entire roster of the Montreal Wheelers. The "Little Men of Iron," who had lost the Stanley Cup the previous spring, claimed to have been badly treated by Wheelers management. They were joined by a couple of disgruntled Victorias. The Montreal amateur authorities were blissfully unconcerned about local star players apparently receiving better offers to leave their clubs and suit up with the Wanderers.

The establishment CAHL initially scoffed at the upstart circuit, only to have its position gravely weakened when the champion Ottawa Silver Seven abruptly quit the older league during the 1903–04 season. In taking the Stanley Cup with them, as well as toying with membership in the FAHL, they had measurably altered the balance of power in eastern hockey. The Silver Seven were soon to establish an on-ice rivalry and business camaraderie with the Wanderers that would dominate hockey for almost a decade.

In short, the two best teams in Canadian hockey, the Silver Seven and the Wanderers, were now professional in all but name.

With embryonic professional hockey taking hold on its eastern and northern fringes, the OHA held its fourteenth annual meeting at Toronto on December 5, 1903. Notwithstanding the changing landscape around it, the organization was strong and united under the iron-clad control of John Ross Robertson. Its more open nature (compared to the CAHL) had brought the association wealth and growth, facts for which it never ceased congratulating itself.

Ottawa Silver Seven (1904–05). The defection of this Stanley Cup champion, a tough and sometimes dirty team, to the new Federal Amateur Hockey League showed that the hockey world's order was changing rapidly.

President Robertson did have some concerns. He scolded the growing trend of "offside interference" (essentially, forward blocking). He also bemoaned slackness in the wearing of uniforms, which he declared part of the "harmony, propriety and attractiveness of the game."[6] However, secure in his office, his fire was largely turned outward—and upward.

Robertson launched into a lengthy denunciation of the nation's governing sports body, the Canadian Amateur Athletic Union. He decried not only the CAAU's Montreal-centric nature, but also its lax enforcement of amateur principles. He noted, for example, that amateurism had hit "a low ebb"[7] at all levels of baseball. Tired of waiting for the CAAU

W. J. Bellingham. Billy "Turkey" Bellingham appears to be the first man to attempt to organize a professional Toronto Hockey Club, in the fall of 1903.

to deal with the situation, he instead called for the blanket banning of *all* baseball players from Ontario hockey.

On one level, Robertson's suspicion of baseball was understandable. Less than two months earlier, the first modern World Series had been played between the Boston Americans of the American League and the National League's Pittsburgh Pirates. It had been a sensation. Ropes were required to hold back overflow crowds at Pittsburgh's Exposition Park and Boston's Huntington Avenue Baseball Grounds. Boston won the best-of-nine series in eight games, but not before more than 100,000 fans had paid for tickets and shelled out even more in wagers.[8]

Baseball was the first incontrovertibly professional team sport. Robertson no doubt saw this as a U.S. phenomenon, but in fact, professionalism was appearing in all the games that were native to either side of the North American border. And, of course, it did not follow from the rampant commercialism of the World Series that every baseball player at every level in Ontario was being secretly paid.

Robertson clearly viewed any professionalism, in any sport, anywhere, as a challenge for the OHA. Although this view was clearly extreme, there was evidence that the murky semi-professionalism of the Montreal hockey world could impact affairs in amateur Toronto.

For the past month, W. J. "Turkey" Bellingham, one of the Wheeler defectors, had been in town. His main purpose seems to have been to put together a team of nonlocal players—to be called, rather oddly, the Toronto Hockey Club.[9] The Federal League was reputed to be looking to place such a franchise in its circuit. In any case, the scheme fizzled and Bellingham returned to Montreal.

The upshot, however, was that Robertson, not content to limit OHA jurisdiction to its own rink, called for consideration of a new national governing body for Canadian sports—one that would be stricter and more representative of the country as a whole. The meeting passed a unanimous motion giving him a mandate to pursue the project. This was a sign not only of his power in the OHA, but also of his growing influence on the Canadian sports scene. To leave no doubt, at the OHA annual banquet there were only two toasts on the menu—one to the King and the other to Robertson.

———

President John Ross Robertson would soon be joined by another influential media ally. The late 1903 meeting concluded with the election of W. A. Hewitt as secretary of the OHA. An all-round sportsman as well as sports editor of the *Toronto Star*, Hewitt would use his newspaper address for association business. President Robertson of the *Toronto Telegram* and First Vice-President Francis Nelson of the *Toronto Globe* were again elected by acclamation. There would not be much doubt as to how these papers would come down on future OHA controversies.

William Abraham Hewitt was involved in sports of all kinds at all levels. Billy was also the third newspaperman to become a fixture on the OHA executive. Men like Hewitt saw no contradiction in running the OHA while also reporting on it—or even keeping some association matters secret.

"Billy" Hewitt was the perfect aide-de-camp for the commandeering Robertson. Short, young and mild-mannered, he assumed the position of secretary on what he believed was a temporary basis. Hewitt came from a family of journalists, yet he never learned to use a typewriter. At a time when there was no separation between sports journalism and sports promotion, Billy not only was secretary of the very hockey body his paper would be reporting on, but he later served as manager of the Argonaut football team. He acted as steward at the Woodbine horse-racing track and was manager of Canada's Olympic gold medal–winning hockey team three separate times. He not only reported on the very first Olympic

hockey match—Sweden versus Belgium at the 1920 Antwerp Games—
he refereed it as well.[10]

Hewitt began his career as sports editor at the *Montreal Herald*, where
he worked for Joseph E. Atkinson. When Atkinson left Montreal to take
over the *Toronto Star*, Hewitt joined him. He was already a longtime
friend of the *Globe*'s Nelson, the two of them being early promoters of
hockey's goal net. Though the idea was ridiculed by players and other
sportswriters, the OHA was quick to approve the idea of nets and they
soon became standard equipment.[11]

"Joe" Atkinson had become convinced that sports coverage would
attract more subscribers to his paper, so he convinced Billy Hewitt to
return to Toronto with him. "In my own department I had some ideas
on sports writing that were considered unique," Hewitt later wrote in his
memoirs. "One was the story had to be accurate, and another that it had
to be brief."[12] He said nothing about conflict of interest.

The new OHA secretary would soon find himself in the midst of
a series of controversies over the rising trend of professionalism. It all
started when Robertson, apparently convinced that all in the organization were safe from such outside influence, went on an extended business
trip to Egypt and Europe. Shortly thereafter an association director, A. B.
Cox of London, moved for the reinstatement of one Harry Peel.

The Peel case was a nuanced affair. The London boy had been
thrown out of the OHA more than two years earlier when his team was
declared professional. There was, however, no evidence Peel himself had
known or done anything wrong. Unable to play in the association, he had
then gone briefly to Pittsburgh, where he had been paid the weekly rate.
He soon regretted the decision to accept money for playing hockey and
came back to Ontario for the amateur game. Cox made his case based
on strong character references, including one from one of the province's
leading clerics.

When Peel's reinstatement was narrowly accepted, all hell broke
loose. The first consequence was the resignation of an outraged Francis
Nelson from the executive. The reinstatement was a break from the strict
OHA policy of lifetime banishment for professionalism. A storm of denunciation came from the Toronto papers and their network of agents in
the hinterland.

The executive refused to accept the Nelson resignation. Yet Cox was unrepentant, stressing the concept of rehabilitation: "We are dealing with boys playing games, and not with criminals."[13] Besides, he warned, accumulating exiles would only lead to a whole network of potentially professional players and teams in the province.

The presence or absence of various executive members had an ongoing effect on this and other OHA disputes—most notably a simmering issue concerning Aeneas "Reddy" McMillan. McMillan was the star of the Belleville Red & Whites, a team steamrolling towards the intermediate championship. When Reddy was accused of a fast run around the association's residency rule, the case soon came before the executive, in which Belleville's member of Parliament, Gus Porter, was a member.

Porter and Nelson's on-again, off-again resignations, along with new and conflicting information, led to farcical consequences. The executive suspended McMillan, let him play again, suspended him a second time and then threw out the whole club for refusing to go along. The fact that the suspension resolution was moved by the executive member from Peterborough, whose team then became the district champion, did not help matters.

It was the second bitter blow to Belleville's championship aspirations. The year before, the OHA executive had intervened to overturn the club's apparent victory over the Toronto Marlboros in the playoffs. It had suddenly ruled forward Jack Marks ineligible because he had once played pro baseball—a fact the OHA had known but had never had problems with before.

It is interesting to note that, in both cases, new secretary Hewitt had strongly supported the resolutions, which strengthened the title hopes of the Marlboros. This would tie into growing rumours of Hewitt's favouritism towards that club, which his sports department often lauded. In the meantime, with Belleville now doubly enraged, Porter decided to take his case to court. In a lawsuit that dragged on for months, he eventually persuaded a local judge to block Peterborough from playing for the OHA championship.

Perhaps the most serious case, from a long-term perspective, originated with the earlier defection of Sault Ste. Marie. The complication of a pro team in Ontario became immensely worse when Toronto's Varsity squad was invited to play in the Soo. The players accepted the invitation, took the trip north and faced off against both its Canadian and American professional teams.

Although the university itself was furious about the northern hockey excursion, it did not see things in quite the same light as the OHA. The fact was that the colleges recognized professionalism as playing for real money, not merely playing in an exhibition, as the Varsity team had against the two Soos. The CAAU likewise refused to apply full sanctions. Thus the OHA was left to expel the University of Toronto—effectively ending the OHA's governance of intercollegiate hockey in Ontario.

———

With amateurism reversals outside Ontario and professionalism crises inside the province, 1903–04 was a difficult season for Toronto's hockey establishment. It had begun with the death of the beloved Wellingtons. Yet there were to be some highlights that suggested all was far from lost. Chief among these new was the emergence of a new troop of amateur heroes: the Toronto Marlboros.

Like its Wellington counterpart, the Marlborough Athletic Club had long been active in Toronto team sports. It set up its hockey branch in 1899, initially joining the Toronto Lacrosse Hockey League. The club took the league's junior honours in 1900–01 and added the senior title the following year. The shorter spelling of the official team name took hold in those early seasons and the "Marlboros" were soon a household name in Toronto.

Recognized early as a skilled if light septet, the Marlboros formally applied for admission to the OHA intermediate and junior divisions in the fall of 1902. The manager of the team was Fred Waghorne, later to gain renown as the first referee credited with dropping the puck for face-offs. That first year, the "Little Dukes"[14] were finalists in the intermediate series while winning the junior circuit outright. They were ready to aim higher.

The new Marlboro seniors would join an OHA loop that included ten other teams, one being the Toronto St. Georges, a well-established rival that had been quick to pick up most of the available Wellingtons. On paper, it seemed the St. Georges would reign supreme, but the Marlboros would prove far stronger than had been anticipated for a rookie senior outfit.

The new Queen City aggregation began the year in impressive fashion, hosting the powerful Montreal Wanderers for two games. The Marlboros tied one match against this squad of former Stanley Cup champs and lost the other by a single goal. They then went undefeated in the OHA season—a feat the Wellingtons had never accomplished. In the home-and-home total-goals final against the Perth Crescents, the Dukes won by an incredible margin of 28–9.

A big reason for the season's success was the addition of a tall, dark-haired young man from Rat Portage, Tom Phillips. The sheer speed and skill of the Marlboro rover caught everyone's eye immediately. The *News* summarized local opinion nicely: "Phillips is without doubt the best hockey player that has ever been seen on Toronto ice, and is a whole team in himself." [15]

This should not really have been a surprise. Phillips had long been a top prospect in the Manitoba Association. He had also spent the previous season in Montreal, where, with the Wheelers, he had starred in their defence of the Stanley Cup against the Winnipeg Victorias. As well, he had been rumoured as a candidate for Bellingham's abandoned Toronto pro club. Interestingly, none of this rapid shifting around seems to have bothered the Toronto-centric OHA brass.

The official reason for Phillips's appearance with the Marlboros was the same one that had taken him to Montreal—a change in his college studies. That was good enough for the normally suspicious amateur barons of the Queen City. Toronto now believed it had a real shot at the Stanley Cup, something that few wished to see more than the *Star*'s own Billy Hewitt. The gentlemen sportsmen of the OHA badly wanted a crack at the Ottawas, the team that had angrily defected from their ranks a decade before. It was widely believed the Silver Seven had taken the Cup more by brute force than through lightning skill. Secretary Hewitt personally filed the challenge before the playoffs had even concluded. Toronto was not going to wait till the next winter and repeat the problems with early-season conditioning that it believed had sunk the Wellingtons.

Toronto Marlboros (1903–04). The pride of the OHA would prove no match for the Ottawa Silver Seven. Standing: G. Vivian, J. C. Earls, E. Marriott, J. Earls, R. Burns, F. Waghorne, W. Smith. Sitting: F. McLaren, A. Wright, P. Charlton, T. Phillips, E. Giroux, L. Earls. Reclining: E. Winchester, H. Birmingham.

The Stanley Cup trustees accepted the challenge and the series was scheduled to be a best-of-three in the Dominion capital. The visitors arrived in Ottawa a day early, with about a hundred supporters from Toronto in tow, and skated through a light practice. Local Ottawa hockey scouts were generally impressed, especially after another peek at Phillips. He looked big, fast and dangerous. Nevertheless, informed odds still had the champion Silver Seven as two-to-one favourites.

The Marlboros arrived with a couple of spares from their own system. They hadn't acted on rumours they would pick up a couple of heavier players from other elite OHA clubs. The Ontario Association felt that such a move, while strictly permitted, would not be appropriate for a club of sporting gentlemen. According to Phillips, the confidence was warranted: "Don't you believe all you hear. There are just as good hockey players in Toronto as in the east, and I think that the Stanley Cup is about due to come here."[16]

It looked that way for the first half of game one at the Aberdeen Pavilion on February 23, 1904, with the Marlboros outscoring the Ottawas 3–1. Then the roof fell in. The Silver Seven came back with five unanswered goals in the second segment to win 6–3. Future Hall of Famer "One-Eyed" Frank McGee[17] had netted three of them before the 2,000 Ottawa fans. What caused the turnaround would become a source of furious accusations between the two cities.

Everyone seems to agree that the Marlboros outplayed the Silver Seven in the first frame. After that, the complexion of the game—and the coverage of the series—changed dramatically. According to the Toronto papers, Ottawa had turned it all around by resorting to nothing short of thuggery. Francis Nelson's *Globe*, for example, claimed the capital septet "endeavor [*sic*] to incapacitate their opponents, rather than to excel them in skill and speed." The paper sniffed that "so long as the game was hockey the Marlboros were the leaders" and that the famed Silver Seven were not up to the skill level of "an O.H.A. intermediate team."[18]

Hewitt's *Star* offered the ready excuse that the Marlboros "were unaccustomed to the style of game that permits downright brutality, cross checking in the face and neck, tripping, hacking, slashing over the head and boarding an opponent with intent to do bodily harm."[19] Both Toronto journals were defensive and protective, listing a litany of injuries to the various Dukes while proudly noting their club's general disinclination to retaliate.

Ottawa observers told a far different story. The *Citizen* felt the Silver Seven had simply played poorly in the first half, but had got back on track in the second. It found the game rough on both sides and singled out Marlboro star Phillips for dirty play. The local newspaper also tried to claim there were no ill feelings at the end of the first match.[20]

There is more agreement on what occurred in game two on February 25. It was a thoroughly gentlemanly affair—and the Marlboros got creamed. McGee had five tallies in the 11–2 thrashing. The Ottawa papers emphasized the superior skill of the Silver Seven in every department. However, Toronto's take was again at odds. Queen City reporters suggested instead that their team was banged up, dispirited, even intimidated. Most agreed that only goalkeeper Eddie Giroux and Phillips seemed to have their hearts in it. Ottawa opinion was blunter, though, calling Phillips "much too fast a man for the company in which he is traveling." As for the rest of the Marlboro skaters, they "looked like a bunch of old women chasing a hen."[21]

The *Citizen* poured on the disdain: "The squealers from Squealville-on-the-Don raised an awful howl against the alleged brutality of the holders of Lord Stanley's silverware." The paper even ripped the Toronto newspapers for claiming the outcome would have been different had the teams stuck to hockey: "But they got their answer good and hard last night."[22]

There is strong reason to believe that neither side was telling the whole truth. For instance, a careful reading of the *Citizen*'s game-one report makes clear that Marlboro players were hurt by hits on several different occasions. And dirty play by Ottawa in Cup games had been witnessed on more than one occasion.

However, if the Ottawas were really so vicious, would at least elite opinion in the capital not have expressed some dismay? There seems to be no evidence it did. Indeed, it is hard to believe that His Excellency Governor General Lord Minto would have agreed to drop the ceremonial puck for the series if the champions were the butchers the Toronto press made them out to be.

In reality, in spite of all the documented bangs and bruises of the Marlboro players, all but one played in the second game two nights later. Lal Earls replaced Edgar Winchester at left wing, but he did so to give the team more weight, not because of injury. It was also conceded that the most serious mishap by far—right winger Frank McLaren breaking his ribs in game two—was accidental.

There are other holes in the tale told by the client papers of the OHA's Toronto headquarters. Why, if Ottawa's play was so flagrantly illicit, did no one blame the referee for not calling it? The independent *Toronto News* hinted at a rather different version of events. Its initial postgame report conceded rough play, especially by Ottawa, but also acknowledged the champs' superior skill.[23]

At the series' conclusion, the *News* also printed a telling, if anonymous, letter. It blamed the Marlboro debacle on the Ontario Hockey Association for not permitting tougher hockey.[24] Another outside organ, the *Belleville Intelligencer*, took the argument further. It accused the

OHA of "making hockey a sort of cross between croquet and ping-pong, instructing their referees to rule men off for what is considered perfectly fair in other associations." [25] The charge was repeated by the era's greatest player, William Hodgson "Hod" Stuart. The rough-and-tumble Ottawa native, who had turned professional with the Pittsburgh Bankers a year earlier, claimed that in the OHA, "I could not lift my stick off the ice." [26]

SLUGGED AND BODIED INTO SUBMISSION

Marlboros Beaten by Ottawa, But Not at Hockey—Flail the O. H. A. Champions Over the Head and Cripple Arms and Legs.

Special to The Toronto Star.

Ottawa, Ont., Feb. 24.—Ottawa defeated the Marlboros of Toronto at the Aberdeen Pavilion last night in the first of the Stanley Cup games by 6 goals to 3. The half-time score was 3 to 1 in favor of the visitors. The first half was played under Quebec rules and the second half under the Ontario rules, so that both teams did their best work while playing under the regulations of their opponents. Taken all round it was a poor exhibition of hockey, but an excellent exemplification of the rough-house sport that travels under the name in this section of the country.

KILL THE MAN.

The Marlboros encountered a far different proposition to any they had met in their O. H. A. experience. They were unaccustomed to the style of game that permits downright brutality, cross checking in the face and neck, tripping, hacking, slashing over the head, and boarding an opponent with intent to do bodily injury. All went unpunished

kick the puck, and permitted a continuance of the rough play, it being evidently the only style of hockey with which he was acquainted.

THE CASUALTY LIST.

In the first half Moore, Smith, and Phillips were penalized two minutes each, while McGee rested for three minutes in the second half. There were delays in the first half owing to injuries to Charlton, who was rendered unconscious by Smith's cross check against the boards, McLaren, who was practically out of the play in the same way by Pulford, and to Wright, who got a flying skate in the thigh and a stick in the nose. In the second half Phillips retired for a while from a crack in the mouth. Later in the game Moore nearly broke McLaren's back with a cross cheeck over the fence, and McGee cracked Geroux several times on the top of the head with his stick, when attacks were being made on the Marlboro goal.

Summary:

—First Half.—

1—Marlboros	....	Birmingham	... 1.4?
2—Marlboros	....	Birmingham	... 2.0?
3—Ottawa	......	F. McGee	.... 1.47
4—Marlboros		Birmingham	19.5?

OTTAWAS WIN FIRST STANLEY CUP MATCH

The Marlboros Had Decidedly the Better of the First Half Which Was Poorly Contested, Ending Three to One in Their Favor.

In the Second Half the Champions Redeemed Themselves and Shut the Challengers Out—Other Sporting News.

The Tale of Two Cities. Someone reading the rival press accounts would have found it hard to believe that the reporters had watched the same game.

There can be no doubt that the OHA was using its iron grip to consciously develop a less physical brand of hockey in the province. At the end of the 1904–05 season, First Vice-President Nelson bragged to a reception in Berlin that the OHA had not had a single serious injury.[27] This was quite a record, given the nature of the sport and the hundreds of games that constituted an OHA campaign. Nor was it coincidence that only Phillips seemed not to be slowed by Ottawa's hitting. Though born in Toronto, he had grown up and learned his hockey at Rat Portage, under the control of the Manitoba Hockey Association.

In truth, the OHA had been linking a Marlboro defeat to "eastern" rough play before the series had even begun. Robertson's *Telegram* had proclaimed that "to beat Ottawa on Ottawa ice under an eastern referee is a big undertaking."[28] Faulting the referee was contrary to OHA culture, but throughout the series there were suggestions that non-OHA officials simply did not understand the fine points of OHA rules.

It is clear, however, that not everyone agreed with this direction in Ontario hockey. Teddy Marriott, the Marlboros' manager at the time of the series and a notable Toronto proponent of tough hockey, was not making any excuses. Contradicting his OHA superiors, he stated simply that "we were beaten by a better team."[29]

There would be one other intriguing take on the series—that of W. A. Hewitt. In his autobiography, published some fifty-four years later, the OHA secretary suggested the Ottawas had salted the ice during the halftime of game one to slow down the speedier Marlboros.[30] The problem is that there is no contemporary reference to any such theory, even in Hewitt's own *Toronto Star*. So it seems that, a half century later, Billy Hewitt was still making excuses for the home team.[31]

———

There is no doubt that the OHA brass was genuinely upset by the roughhouse eastern hockey that had taken down the Marlboros. Nonetheless, they must have been much more worried about the state of their own association. The uneven handling of the Peel and McMillan cases had greatly aggravated already controversial situations. With Robertson overseas and absent for much of the season, there were increasing questions about the way the OHA was being run.

Few were prepared for how the returning OHA president would respond. Robertson not only backed the expulsion of both Peel and McMillan, he went further—much further. Shortly before the 1904 annual meeting, he announced the expulsion of all senior lacrosse players from Ontario hockey—on his personal authority. Such a ruling would have a huge impact on the OHA game, as a great many of its top performers were lacrosse stars in summer.

While it was true that the CAAU had already labelled the Canadian Lacrosse Association a professional organization, the president was acting on dubious constitutional authority. It seemed more as if he was railing, Lear-like, at the professional world closing in around him.

There may, however, have been some method in Robertson's apparent madness. The mass lacrosse expulsion galvanized opposition to his autocratic rule, but it also polarized debate about his control around an issue of principle. Threatening to resign, he quickly brought the executive behind the McMillan suspension, his lacrosse edict and the reversal of the Peel reinstatement.

These decisions also had immediate consequences that strengthened Robertson's hand. By backing the McMillan expulsion he secured the continued participation of ally Francis Nelson and rid the executive of Gus Porter for good. Likewise, the lacrosse decision purged the body of opposition member Duff Adams, who was associated with Brantford's lacrosse club. A general message had also been delivered to those thinking of attending the upcoming OHA convention: associate with lacrosse or hockey, but not both.

No doubt this dynamic was undercutting the campaign of Hamilton's William Wyndham, who had decided to challenge for the presidency. Yet Robertson's re-election bid did not restrict itself to executive manoeuvres. Prior to the convention, a slander campaign against Wyndham was launched by OHA-friendly papers across Ontario. The essence of the undertaking was, of course, to accuse the opponent of planning to scrap the OHA's principles in favour of professionalism.

As a matter of fact, William Wyndham was not campaigning for professionalism—or even semi-professionalism—but against Robertson's increasingly despotic leadership style. The challenger proposed, for example, to end secret proceedings at meetings of the OHA executive. This was a sharp rebuke to a body that included three high-ranking Toronto journalists. Nevertheless, the president had successfully framed the issue: it was about the Peel decision and amateur principles.

BARRED THE DOORS TO PROFESSIONALS

O.H.A. Convention Decides There Shall Not be a Recurrence of the Peel Case—President J. Ross Robertson Re-Elected by a Large Vote.

The business of the annual O. H. A. convention, held in the Temple Building on Saturday, was concluded about 6.40 p.m., and was probably the longest and liveliest in the history of the Association.

The delegates, representing altogether 75 teams, emphatically endorsed "the government" by the re-election of President J. Ross Robertson and the passage of a resolution reaffirming the final decision of the 1903-4 Executive Committee in the Harry Peel case, by which the London player was returned to the professional class. The convention stood by the motto "Once a professional always a professional," and declared for amateurism in its purest form.

through without opposition. Bank, mercantile, church, or any other league players may now play for the O. H. A. teams of their towns, if they are good enough and are otherwise qualified.

It was agreed that clubs and players refusing to accept and obey the rulings of the executive should thereby forfeit their membership in the association.

The time of the annual meeting was brought forward a couple of weeks, and in future it will be held on the second Saturday in November.

The proposal to abolish proxies at the convention was withdrawn, and it was agreed that teams holding membership in both the O. H. A. and some other league must accept the schedule arranged at the O. H. A. district meeting.

The proposition to fix a minimum rent

After the 1904 annual meeting of the OHA, no view of professionalism other than John Ross Robertson's would be permitted.

The annual meeting of December 3, 1904, was stormy. Robertson began with a thundering defence of amateurism and the actions of the executive. In an unprecedented move, one executive member then took the floor to deliver a pointed rebuttal. Next, Nelson moved that the meeting back the reversal of the Peel reinstatement and his credentials to do so were challenged.

A heated debate raged for two hours but ended decisively. The removal of Peel was carried by a vote of 43–26. The annual meeting had asserted the principle "once a professional, always a professional" and forbade any future executive from reopening the question. Robertson defeated Wyndham by a wider margin, 49–22.

This meeting marked a turning point in the history of the Ontario

Hockey Association. The forces of rigid amateurism, championed by President John Ross Robertson, had carried the day. They would not, however, be content with just their clear victory at the convention. Having gained the upper hand, Robertson and his supporters set out to drive all remaining dissent and debate from the organization.

The agenda of enforced conformity to the president's views became evident shortly after the annual meeting. The OHA newspapers continued their assault on those who had opposed Robertson. Press allies Nelson and Hewitt had been re-elected to the executive by acclamation. This, according to the president, was as it should be. After all, he had concluded, the "growing evil of canvassing for votes"[32] was responsible for all the turmoil in the association.

Henceforth, Robertson instructed OHA clubs, delegates should come to the annual meeting unpledged and there should be no campaigning. As he put it: "Office should seek the man and not the man the office." Likewise, all aspirants must have "the highest interests of amateurism at heart."[33]

In other words, even as Doc Gibson's bold embrace of open professionalism was changing top-level hockey in every other jurisdiction, amateurism had been declared absolute and eternal in Ontario. In its defence, and with the enemy all around him, John Ross Robertson was determined to rule—absolutely and forever.

CHAPTER FOUR

THE ROAD TO WAR

The Defection of the Marlboros

———•◆•———

You know that Abe Lincoln said that the Union could not exist half slave and half free. I believe that the O.H.A. cannot honorably be half amateur and half professional.[1]

—JOHN ROSS ROBERTSON

With the Ontario Hockey Association's amateurism permanently entrenched in its rules, John Ross Robertson's executive launched the 1904–05 season with a renewed determination to stamp out professionalism. As a first line of defence, virtually no exceptions were permitted to the rule against change of residence after October 1. One so refused was a young Fred Taylor. This would prove to be an epic blunder by Robertson's organization, creating yet another powerful opponent of the amateur order it sought to uphold.

In his 1977 biography, Frederick Wellington Taylor described the infamous moment that changed his hockey career forever. Preparing to leave the junior ranks in the fall of 1904, Taylor received a call from the OHA's powerful secretary, W. A. Hewitt.[2] Hewitt once again asked Taylor to join the Toronto Marlboros. When he refused, the angry executive "told me straight out, 'All right, if you won't play for the Marlboros, you won't play anywhere!'. . . I never forgave Billy Hewitt for that."[3]

The story has been widely referenced—and widely believed—ever since. It fits to a tee the modern-day image of the arbitrary, controlling nature of the amateur fanatics who ran the OHA of the early 1900s.[4] It must be pointed out, however, that prominent hockey author Eric Zweig has recently questioned the veracity of the tale.

According to Zweig, the then ninety-three-year-old Taylor—a two-time winner of the Stanley Cup and early member of the Hockey Hall of Fame—had a notoriously unreliable memory. The last living player of his era, the legend often confused the facts of his career with the myths that had grown up around it. Zweig points to a number of instances where Taylor's stories cannot be squared with contemporary newspaper reports. Even as a young man, Taylor had given conflicting accounts of his actual date of birth.[5]

Zweig goes on to raise some specific questions about the story. First, Hewitt had no formal connection to the Marlboro club, so why would he be recruiting for the Dukes? Second, is it not odd that, of some half-dozen clubs reported to be after Taylor in 1904, the Marlboros were not one of them?

These are good questions, but it is far from obvious that they exonerate the OHA secretary. For one thing, Hewitt's lack of official connection to the Marlies does not mean he had no interest in their welfare. He was one of Toronto's most important hockey organizers. As a league executive, he was also bitterly disappointed in the OHA's failure to win the Stanley Cup the previous spring. The more pertinent question is: How emotionally vested was Hewitt in the Marlboros' goal of becoming the association's first Cup champion?

As Zweig admits, Hewitt would have known that the defending Ontario champs had some gaps in the lineup that needed addressing if they were to challenge again for the national trophy. True, it would have been highly unethical for the league secretary to do some recruiting on his own, all the while keeping the matter out of the newspapers (including his own *Toronto Star*). Of course, that doesn't mean it did not happen. Hewitt was widely rumoured at the time to be willing to bend the rules to help the Marlboros. Furthermore, collusion between the OHA and key Toronto newspapers not only transpired, it was, in fact, notorious.

What is not disputed is that the OHA forbade Taylor to move from his Listowel juniors to the intermediate squad in Thessalon. It is clear that other clubs were much closer to the boy's home. It is even clearer that the OHA had an interest in stopping players from shopping themselves around—a habit that smacked of professionalism. Whatever the real reason, the OHA apparently could not accommodate Taylor, and the twenty-year-old star sat out the entire 1904–05 season.

Hewitt passed away many years before Taylor and apparently never said anything on the matter. In his biography, published nearly twenty years before Taylor's, Hewitt glossed over the prodigy's departure from the OHA. He remembered only that Fred had played in the junior final of 1904 and that "soon after, the young 'Cyclone' was pursued by profes-

Fred "Cyclone" Taylor. Was his story legend or myth?

sional clubs."[6] There are, of course, issues around memory and myth in Hewitt's book as well, his story about Ottawa salting the ice in the Marlboros' Stanley Cup challenge being the perfect illustration.

Regardless of what might have happened between Hewitt and Taylor, the result was far-reaching. Effectively banned by the OHA, the youthful prospect headed for Portage la Prairie of the quasi-pro Manitoba league the following season. There, he made the contacts that quickly led him down to the burgeoning pro hockey scene in the United States.

South of the border, Taylor would join the world rapidly building up around another OHA exile, Doc Gibson. Indeed, the season that Taylor left the OHA, 1904–1905, would be the one in which Gibson and a growing cast of hockey managers and players brought the International Hockey League into being. It united under one umbrella the clubs in Pittsburgh, Michigan's "copper country" and Sault Ste. Marie on both sides of the border. It was hockey's first unabashedly professional intercity league.

The Western Pennsylvania Hockey League had paid salaries before, but usually at a modest, fixed rate of $10 to $20 per week, supplemented by an outside "position." In contrast, the IHL recruited and negotiated with players individually—that is, with true professional athletes. Some salaries were said to be over four figures for the short season, comparing well to sports like baseball and lacrosse. Beginning with the Portage Lakers, who had beaten the Federal league champion Montreal Wanderers in a "World Series" in March 1904, the IHL was assembling some of the best teams in hockey.

It was here that Taylor and others like him would hone the skills and images that define the career pro athlete. At this, no one was better than young Fred. As adept at promotion off the ice as he was at performance on it, he was rapidly evolving into the man that Governor General Earl Grey would famously dub the "Cyclone," a name that stuck so firmly that few people remember his Christian one.

And so, an OHA ban gave birth to "Cyclone Taylor," the professional game's first colourful superstar, and he would prove to be a key to the building of the widespread fan base the sport required.

Back in the Canadian hockey world—at least outside Ontario—the pace of change was accelerating. The eastern hockey war was getting more intense and more complex. The Federal Amateur Hockey League grew stronger. The champion Wanderers had fought a tough but inconclusive Stanley Cup series against Ottawa in the spring of 1904. Now the Silver Seven were joining the wandering "Redbands" in the new circuit.

The Canadian Amateur Hockey League answered by enticing the Nationals to switch associations and by adding a new club from Westmount. The Federal League retaliated by substituting a rival Francophone club, the Montagnards, and placing a team in Brockville, Ontario. Eastern hockey had gone from five elite teams to eleven in just two years.

Competition to the CAHL was also coming from more distant corners. The Manitoba league was the base of a growing powerhouse, the Rat Portage Thistles, who had startled the hockey establishment in the 1905 playoffs by dispensing entirely with "lifting" in favour of greater "combination." In effect, instead of clearing the puck from their end by backhanding it high and pursuing it, the Thistles rushed from the defence and transitioned to offence through passing and puck control. They came within a hair of taking the Stanley Cup.

Dawson City Nuggets (1904–05). The Klondike team got slaughtered, but left no doubt that the Stanley Cup was now a truly national championship.

Cup competition was becoming truly national. As early as 1900, for instance, the first Maritime team, the Halifax Crescents, had played for the trophy. However, 1904–05 would feature the most memorable—and most disastrous—attempt ever at Lord Stanley's mug. Entrepreneur and adventurer Joe Boyle spent $10,000 and took three weeks to move the Dawson City Nuggets 4,000 miles from Yukon, only to lose to Ottawa by scores of 9–2 and 23–2. Frank McGee's fourteen-goal performance in the second Cup match will never be equalled.

The expanding range of Stanley Cup contenders, the cost of challenges and the increasing movement of players confirmed a growing certainty that financial inducements were involved. This was doubtlessly true in both Quebec and Manitoba. Yet the Montreal-based Canadian Amateur Athletic Union, tightly tied to the eastern leagues and their financial interests, had none of the OHA's zeal for investigation. Besides, those leagues weren't just in the midst of their own player war, they were now also fighting the commercial pull of the new International circuit.

Whereas the Toronto-centric hockey realm was ideologically opposed to this professionalism, the Montreal-dominated region was pragmatic-ally adapting. Robertson's OHA dismissed every departure of a young star to the United States with "good riddance." Indeed, it had proactively exiled any athlete who also played lacrosse—and in the summer that was a fair number. Conversely, the eastern and other "amateur" leagues wanted those players to come back from the States. They bid accordingly. Thus, there was a growing transit of players between the International and the Canadian senior leagues—except for the hidebound OHA.

The Ontario Hockey Association was becoming increasingly vocal about the CAAU's growing tendency to "whitewash" such obvious viola-tions of amateur standing. In the case of lacrosse, the national governing body was in essence allowing the sport to professionalize. As Robertson had told the annual meeting:

> The Canadian Amateur Athletic Union, *whose headquarters are at Montreal* . . . has so far retrograded from its natural and essential pos-ition that it has offered to declare as amateurs all the professionals in the country if they will only join some organization that will affiliate with the C.A.A.U.[7] (emphasis added)

Nevertheless, the OHA was still prepared to permit games between its clubs and those of the supposedly amateur, but less pristine, Canadian leagues.

The OHA had to, if it wanted to win the Stanley Cup.

———

And there is no doubt that the Ontario Hockey Association, which rated itself the nation's best hockey organization, still wanted to win the Cup that had become so emblematic of the championship of the Dominion. As the 1904–05 season got under way, the OHA's greatest hope again rested with the Toronto Marlboros. As the year progressed, there were more questions about how far the association—Secretary Hewitt, in particular—was prepared to go to help them get it.

The Marlboros began the season with some big holes to fill. Tom Phillips had returned to Rat Portage and taken goaltender Eddie Giroux with him. Stalwart defender Doc Wright had retired. And veteran Frank McLaren was lost in the OHA's lacrosse decision.

There were, however, some new bright lights in the Dukes' lineup. Chuck Tyner was an all-round athlete and quality goalkeeper. McMaster University student Rolly Young was known as a talented stickhandler and tough defenceman (or sometimes rover). And at right wing was a new offensive star, Bruce Ridpath.

"Riddy," as the fans knew him, would quickly become the Queen City's most popular athlete. He had come up through the Westerns, an OHA junior team associated with Toronto's Parkdale Canoe Club. Indeed, Ridpath was such an accomplished canoeist that he would give mass exhibitions of canoe and paddling stunts—from headstands using the portaging thwart to "jumping" the canoe fast through the water by riding the gunwales. So in demand was the "aquatic wonder"[8] that Bruce would perform throughout North America and Europe in the off-season. Though small, Riddy was exceptionally fit, fast and surprisingly ready to mix it up. The fans loved him.

The Marlboros had another stellar season. They breezed through all the way to a first-game victory in the Ontario final against Smiths Falls at the Mutual Street Rink. They had scored eight goals on a future goal-tending legend, Percy LeSueur, while allowing only three.

Then trouble hit.

On the return trip to the eastern Ontario town, the game turned very rough. Due to injuries, the teams were down to five a side at the half, with the champs losing 6–4. The smaller Marlboros, claiming that all but two players were unable to continue, refused to take the ice for the second half.

Standard practice at this point would have been to declare the game a forfeit. Instead, referee Rose called the match off and referred the matter to the OHA executive. Smiths Falls went crazy. A red-faced Hewitt was sent packing by the local club without any gate receipts.

Newspaper accounts of what transpired vary wildly. In Smiths Falls (and a few other places), they brushed it off as a hard-hitting game with some accidental injuries. The Toronto papers (and their network of allies) labelled it a bloodbath.

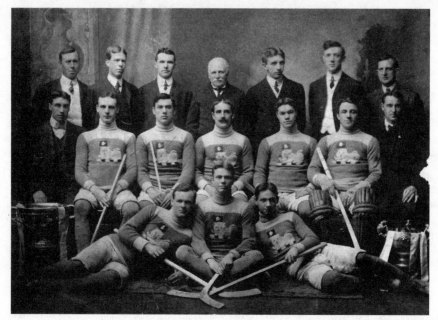

Toronto Marlboros (1904–05). This OHA senior champion would provide the nucleus of the future Toronto Professionals. Standing: T. Harmon, A. H. Birmingham, R. Burns, J. Earls, F. St. Leger, T. Welch, E. Marriott. Sitting: W. Slean, H. Armstrong, B. Andrews, P. Charlton, E. Winchester, C. Tyner, W. Smith. Reclining: R. Young, H. Birmingham, B. Ridpath.

The game likely was quite dirty, but there was a story behind it. Referee Rose had called twelve penalties against Smiths Falls, versus just two against Toronto. The home team was clearly seeking revenge for rough play by the Marlboros at Mutual. There, a "hard body check"[9] by Rolly Young, severe enough to warrant a major penalty, had put one of the Smiths Falls players out of the game.

The OHA executive—once it got its money out of Smiths Falls— decided on a rather unusual resolution to the whole mess. First, it declared both games null and void. Then it ordered a sudden-death final to be played March 7 on neutral ground in Peterborough.

Hundreds came in by train from both places to see the showdown, paying as much as five dollars a ticket. A near riot ensued when the travelling Marlie fans initially could not get into the building. In the end, Toronto beat Smiths Falls by a convincing 9–3 score, Bruce Ridpath leading the Marlboros with four tallies. Knowing that any spark could set off fireworks, Referee Fraser had called literally everything from the outset.

The officiating in the final game was certainly strict, but was it fair? The Marlboros, not known to be much in the tough going, were bound to benefit. Smiths Falls claimed that Hewitt, there representing the OHA, was actually giving instructions to the referee from the sidelines. To some, it all just confirmed the long-alleged Hogtown bias of the OHA.

This version of events, combined with the legendary Taylor saga and the earlier Belleville rulings, paints a not-so-pretty picture of the OHA secretary and his apparent conflicts of interest. If it is to be believed, Hewitt's machinations consistently catered to the Marlboros' Stanley Cup aspirations. And there was much bitterness. Although Toronto proclaimed itself satisfied the best team had won, Smiths Falls, disgusted with the wrong they believed had been inflicted on them, was finished with the OHA. It quit the association and joined the Federal Amateur Hockey League for the next season, completing the OHA's loss of senior hockey jurisdiction east of Kingston.

In truth, it did not really matter whether Hewitt was trying to engineer another Stanley Cup run for the Marlboros. The delay in deciding the OHA championship had effectively scuttled any immediate shot they might have had at the mug. The Dukes did manage to get in a couple of well-attended exhibitions at Mutual against Rat Portage on that team's way home from Ottawa. They also played a postseason series against Winnipeg's Rowing Club in the Manitoba capital. While competitive against both the Thistles and the Rowers, this was as close to the national playoffs as they would get in 1905.

It was apparent that the odds of the OHA winning the Stanley Cup would be even longer in 1905–06. The war between the CAHL and FAHL was largely resolved. Under pressure from the owners of the Montreal Arena, the best clubs of the two leagues combined. The new, stronger organization would be known as the Eastern Canada Amateur Hockey Association. The ECAHA included both the Ottawas and the Wanderers, two teams that met in an epic Cup showdown at the end of the season.

Competition to the west was also stronger. By "the west," one now meant not just Manitoba, but the professional parts of the United States as well. The International Hockey League had had its hiccups, yet it was still going strong. IHL scouts were scouring Canada for recruits, and the sincerely "amateur" OHA was easy pickings. At the end of the previous season, the league had sent its Michigan pros to play some exhibitions in Winnipeg. The missionary work of hockey was beginning to flow both ways.

As usual, the OHA began its campaign with delegates heading to Toronto in late 1905 for the annual powwow. They did so with the knowledge that John Ross Robertson would not be seeking re-election after an unprecedented six years as president. In his final address, his advocacy of strict amateur principles reached new extremes.

Professionalism might be rampant outside Ontario, said Robertson, but fidelity to amateurism in hockey was not merely about loyalty to the OHA; it was a question of patriotism itself:

> We have a great game, a great country and a great empire—if you gentlemen are as great as the possibilities of the O.H.A., if we Canadians are as great as the possibilities of Canada, and if we Britons are as great as the glory of our Empire—the flag of amateurism in your hands will be as safe from harm as the Union Jack was in the hands of your fathers and mine![10]

Robertson said he was departing with "a regret that is deep and sincere."[11] Yet if anyone thought he was actually leaving, they were terribly wrong. He was simply preparing to run the OHA without the bother of seeking election.

Shortly after the annual meeting, the OHA executive created a powerful new "subcommittee." Soon to be famously dubbed the "Three White Czars," it would consist of Robertson, Hewitt and a third, rotating member. According to Hewitt, the men rather enjoyed their nickname. "Occasionally we exiled members to hockey's Siberia," he later wrote, "but generally we weren't too severe."[12] To the subcommittee were delegated virtually all routine matters, including questions of player eligibility.

In short, through his control of this small group, Robertson was still effectively in command of the OHA. And Robertson was preparing the ground for his most controversial decision yet: to take Ontario out of

Stanley Cup competition. At the annual meeting, he had talked about the possibility of an OHA challenge, but not if the Cup defenders were "ineligible according to our rules."[13] Since the other Canadian senior leagues were clearly not eligible for amateur play in the eyes of the OHA, the die had been cast.

John Ross Robertson's *Telegram* office—a modest chamber for the OHA's great "Czar."

In reality, the trustees of the Stanley Cup had long since given up fighting professionalism. If the Cup was to be contested by the very best players, they had concluded, such resistance was hopeless. P. D. Ross, one of the Stanley Cup trustees as well as the editor of the *Ottawa Journal*, was increasingly outspoken on the matter:

To tell the plain truth, I feel rather bewildered about the conditions in our athletic sports. I can't help feeling sympathy for the men at the heads of our various senior lacrosse, football and hockey leagues.

They all would prefer simon pure amateur sport. And none of them
know how to get it. Neither do I.[14]

The matter came to a head in late January. Ross had written the country's three major leagues—the Eastern Canada, Manitoba and Ontario
associations—to propose that they set up a permanent committee to gov-
ern the national playoffs. The reply of the OHA executive, under the pen
of Hewitt, was not subtle:

The feeling was that the O.H.A. senior championship was sufficient
honor [sic] for any one club, and that it would not be wise to mix with
the other leagues named, where veiled professionalism is winked at.[15]

Outside the OHA elite, this edict was undoubtedly very divisive. While
the usual voices—including Ross's *Telegram*, Nelson's *Globe* and Hewitt's *Star*—chanted approval, the *News* vocalized the outrage of many
Toronto fans. It declared bluntly that Ontario wanted its champion "up
against the real thing." Its further contention that "the O.H.A. seems dis-
posed to mind everybody else's business rather than its own"[16] reflected
a widespread belief that financial incentives were as prevalent in Ontario
as anywhere else.

The OHA was not only aware of such suspicion; it was determined to
address it—with a vengeance. Soon, in a pre-emptive crackdown, dozens of players were being hauled before the subcommittee and ordered
to make amateur declarations. New president D. L. Darroch, evidently
under the sway of Robertson, declared that the association was prepared
to lose as many teams as necessary to retain its principles.

The OHA's hunt for transgressors led to more ugly public scraps. In
1905–06, the circus revolved around Bobby Rowe, the youthful star of a
serious senior-level contender that was emerging in Barrie. Rowe had
been excused after admitting to a couple of games with the Houghton
Portage Lakers in 1902–03, when he was still a teenager. However, a letter from "one of the most prominent men in the copper country . . . over
this gentleman's signature,"[17] which enclosed a picture of Rowe on the
team, persuaded the OHA to change its mind. So, on the eve of a playoff
game between Barrie and the Toronto Argonauts, the association decided
to suspend Rowe after all. Feelings ran so high that Darroch was pelted

with eggs when he attempted to walk down a Barrie street.

It got worse. Harry Jamieson, the OHA's executive member from Barrie, took the association to court. At trial division he won a clear victory. Chief Justice William Glenholme Falconbridge slammed the OHA for proceedings that he declared unwarranted and void, transacted without reasonable notice and lacking any valid legal evidence.

If the czars were embarrassed, they did not show it. Nelson's *Globe* dismissed the judge's injunction by simply declaring, "in the meantime the season is over."[18] Robertson's *Telegram* wrote that "the Rowe case is in the courts but it is quite settled in the O.H.A. councils."[19] The association would later get the decision overturned on appeal, but for an organization based on the maxim of gentlemanly fair play, the whole episode did not look terribly "principled."

Philip Dansken Ross. Former Ottawa star player P. D. Ross became an influential newspaperman and a Stanley Cup trustee. Originally a proponent of amateurism, he found his views evolving with the times.

Unfortunately, the public spectacles at the OHA's Toronto headquarters in 1905–06 were not compensated for by performances on local ice. An extended early-season thaw delayed the start of the campaign. It also kept the city's players dangerously out of condition. Very quickly, it became evident that area clubs were not going to have great seasons—especially the fan-favourite Marlboros.

The Marlboros had again lost some key men in the off-season. This time, however, no new crop of regulars stood ready to bridge the gaps. Despite the allegations in Barrie and elsewhere of a capital-city bias, no OHA rulings came to the club's rescue, either. The subcommittee's pre-emptive crackdown gave the Marlboros no breaks on amateur declarations or residency certificates. Jack Earls, son of club founder John Earls and brother of former captain Lal Earls, was denied permission to play after returning from a work stint in Buffalo. Conversely, mainstay defenceman Pete Charlton was permitted to defect to Berlin.

There were other player losses as well. Cover point Harold Armstrong joined Smiths Falls in the Federal league. Studies took Chuck Tyner and Rolly Young out for much of the season. Bruce Ridpath, along with veterans Herb Birmingham and Edgar Winchester, anchored a decent forward unit, but the rest of the lineup was a shifting mess. After two almost perfect years, the Marlboros started losing games consistently—and sometimes badly.

It was becoming inevitable that Toronto would hear calls for an alternative to the OHA. While the *Telegram* and its allies bragged that even OHA intermediates could win the Stanley Cup, no one was buying it. Toronto was out of the running for the national championship because of the provincial association's edict. To top it all off, the amateur season concluded sourly, with the Argonauts losing the city's provincial title to Berlin—the first non-Toronto champion in seven years.

Then, on March 7, a bombshell hit the newsstands. It was a story out of the boomtown Temiskaming League—a circuit known for wild betting backed by frantic player recruiting. Bobby Rowe had headed up there, to Haileybury, when it was clear his OHA career was over. Now it seemed irrefutable that Marlboros idol Bruce Ridpath and teammates Rolly Young and Harry Burgoyne had appeared as Rowe's opponents in a game at New Liskeard.

The Haileybury–New Liskeard game had occurred back on February 23. The Marlboro trio had initially escaped detection by playing under assumed names. When the gate receipts proved insufficient to pay these ringers, local proprietors passed the hat and came up with $265. It was sham amateurism at its worst. It was also very clear that the Marlboro stars were going professional.

Nevertheless, while the Marlboro case appeared to be open and shut, the OHA suddenly chose to proceed with unusual caution. The executive met and decided it would hear more from the men themselves before acting. In the meantime, Ridpath and company kept dressing for the Dukes. Was this because the club's president and secretary, both fine Toronto gentlemen, had assured the subcommittee the boys could be cleared? Was the OHA a bit gun-shy because of the ongoing Rowe litigation? Was it simply in denial of the possibility that its chosen successor to the thoroughbred Wellingtons could actually be a Trojan horse of professionalism?

The truth was that OHA leaders were considering the full implications of expelling the Marlboro stars. The *Telegram* warned that such a move would remove the final hurdle to the assembling of an "out-and-out professional organization"[20] in Toronto. Worse, the *Globe* opined, it might suggest "the Marlboros are not now, and never were, on the level as an amateur organization."[21]

The panic among the executive ranks of the OHA literally spills off the pages. And their concerns were fully justified. For one, out-and-out professionalism was inching ever closer to reality in the Queen City. Bellingham's abortive efforts to form a "Toronto Hockey Club" back in 1903–04 were being repeated by others. In 1904–05, the risk had been the number of lacrosse outcasts around the city, although, in the end, the most

Hockey

MARLBORO PLAYERS IN "PRO" HOCKEY

Participated in Famous Game at New Liskeard.

VAIR AND REGAN THERE TOO

Smith's Falls Scared Ottawa--Peterboro' Intermediate Champions-- Argos' Protest Turned Down.

Startling information is handed out by the Haileyburian in its report of the match between Haileybury and New Liskeard, on Feb. 23, at the latter town. Such well known players as Vair, of Barrie; and Ridpath, Burgoyne, and Young, of Marlboros, are reported to have participated in the game. Regan, of the Canadian Soo pro. team, also played. The O.H.A. will probably have some very pertinent questions to ask in regard to the whole affair. It is rumored that these players are not the only ones, but that one or two other hockey celebrities disported themselves on the ice under assumed names. The Haileyburian's account of the "doings" up north is appended.

The defection of key members from its flagship franchise proved to be a rare occasion on which the OHA would hesitate to deal with professionalism.

talented went to the International League. This season, though, there was now more than just a player pool on which to build in Toronto. The OHA had provided the raison d'être for professionalism: to compete for the Stanley Cup.

In fact, by February 1906, a Toronto professional hockey club was taking shape in the city. Eight senior players were known to be practising full-time. They included veteran hockey travellers Roy Brown (cover point), Bert Morrison (centre), Charlie Liffiton and Jack Marshall (wings), who were joined by locals Clarence Gorrie (goal), Hugh Lambe (point), Jack Carmichael (rover) and Frank McLaren (spare), the only man to play on both the Wellington and Marlboro teams that challenged for the Stanley Cup. It was a creditable lot.

Three different names were associated with these efforts to get a paid Queen City team together. One was local promoter W. A. Patterson, who was known to be trying to arrange games with International League teams. Another was Chaucer Elliott. A highly rated OHA referee who had gone to the IHL for the season, he had become a big advocate of the professional game in the Toronto press. In March, he managed to sign Walter Forrest of the Portage Lakers to the fledgling pros in the hopes they might get into the IHL the following season.

The most important of the trio was Alexander Miln, now manager of the Mutual Street Rink. Mutual was the home base of the pro club. Since none of its men played anywhere else in 1905–06, one can surmise that Miln was paying their retainer. He was also talking to the management of Pittsburgh's Duquesne Gardens about plans for artificial-ice rinks— and a corresponding league—for Toronto and the other large cities of northeastern North America.

Throughout February it was reported that games between the Toronto pros and IHL clubs were imminent. There were also notices of a coming match against a similar group of southwest Ontario pros being organized by Brown in Brantford. Nevertheless, the winter wound down without anything happening on the ice.

The OHA leaders may have thus felt that they could simply dodge the pro hockey bullet in Toronto. It seemed to make sense. If they delayed dealing with the Marlboro situation, the outfit at Mutual would scatter harmlessly to other regions of the hockey world. Soon, however, any thoughts that the OHA could easily work around the growth of professionalism were to be shattered.

On April 28, 1906, the country's largest sports club, the Montreal Amateur Athletic Association, voted to allow professionals to play with amateurs on its sports teams. The pressures on the MAAA had been most acute in lacrosse, where other major clubs were openly going professional. Indeed, the country's leading summer league, the National Amateur Lacrosse Union, would soon vote to remove the word "Amateur" from its name. It was evident that Canada's hockey capital, Montreal, would be a base for unapologetic professionalism the following winter.

The overwhelming attitude of the Montreal men was that they were simply accepting reality. One vocal opponent had warned that the city would be visited by floods, earthquakes and other signs of God's wrath as punishment.[22] But for the vast majority, the time had come to end the hypocrisy.

The prevailing view was very different in the Queen City. John Ross Robertson had been presented with the possibility of mixing pro-

An early all-round professional athlete, Edwin "Chaucer" Elliott was best known in hockey as a colourful and exceptional referee. He was one of three men associated with the effort to organize a Toronto pro club in 1905–06.

fessionals and amateurs in the same club, but he could abide it no more now than he could those $10 gold coins in Berlin years earlier. Indeed, at the 1904 annual meeting of the OHA, he had addressed this very subject. Quoting Lincoln on freedom and slavery, he declared that the organization "cannot honorably [sic] be half amateur and half professional."[23]

Honest Abe and his men had chosen to take their nation to war to defend their principles. Faced with insurrection in Montreal, Robertson and the amateur sport leaders of Toronto were prepared to do no less.

CHAPTER FIVE

THE REBELLION BEGINS

The Toronto Hockey Club Is Born

*Professional hockey in Toronto promises to flourish till the frost comes.
Then like other flowers it will fade away and die.*[1]

—*Toronto Telegram*

As 1906 unfolded, John Ross Robertson's world must have felt increasingly under siege. Professionalism in hockey was everywhere. Even in Toronto, the capital of the Ontario Hockey Association, some pro hockey players had been openly practising with the intention of forming a team. Worse still, the Toronto Marlboros were maintaining on their roster men who, there could be no reasonable doubt, had played for pay. In three short years, this club, which was meant to succeed the Wellingtons as the epitome of the OHA's amateur principles, had instead become a symbol of the changing times.

Even more ominously, the highest bodies in Canadian sports were on the verge of endorsing professionalism outright. The Montreal Amateur Athletic Association, long the country's most powerful such organization, had announced it would hire pro players for its (otherwise amateur) teams, including hockey's legendary Montreal Wheelers. It seemed only a matter of time before the country's national governing body, the Canadian Amateur Athletic Union, would follow suit.

The truth is that, for some years now, the gap between the principles and realities of amateur sport in Canada had been widening. The CAAU had been attempting to paper this over with an uneasy compromise: it would not go after professionalism in team games as long as the practice remained unofficial. This was also the approach taken by the trustees of the Stanley Cup. After all, when Lord Stanley had first announced his intentions of contributing a "challenge cup" in March 1892, it was stated that the trophy would go to "the champion hockey team in the Dominion." Nothing was said of the winners being "amateurs." Of course, no one then imagined the possibility of "professional" ice hockey. Outside of a handful of elite players, the sport was largely a pastime being enjoyed by, among many others, the governor general's own children.

To Robertson and his acolytes at the OHA, the CAAU's notion of compromise was simply an abandonment of principle. As the country's most powerful advocate of pure amateurism, the association could not tolerate such thinking, and, early in 1906, Robertson's group had taken the extraordinary step of officially dropping out of Stanley Cup competition. The OHA, from this point on, would have nothing to do with the increasingly famous and coveted mug. Robertson was also using the association to increasingly rally opinion in Toronto sports circles against the actions of the Montreal-based CAAU.

The amateur athletic leaders of Montreal and Toronto were now headed for an inevitable collision. True, they were all rapidly coming to the view that the hypocrisy of amateur athletics was no longer acceptable. It was an open secret that many of the best players were being paid under the table. However, they had two diametrically opposed ways of resolving the situation.

In Montreal, Canada's leading commercial and sports city, the opinion was that amateurism had to accommodate the inescapable professional pressures in team sports. In Toronto, the country's rival power centre, the position was that pure amateurism had to be enforced.

The 1906 annual meeting of the CAAU was set for October 27 in Montreal. Topping the agenda would be a proposal to amend the definition of amateurism to allow amateurs and professionals to mix in team sports. As the big date approached, opposing bands of sports leaders in Quebec and Ontario escalated the conflict. Each threatened to secede from the CAAU if its position was not upheld.

The Montreal men were confident of victory. This Anglophone elite had long been the source of the nation's top sports executives, and as such, they were convinced of the wisdom of their conclusions. To them, it was clear that professionalism at the senior level of popular team games like hockey was inevitable. After all, baseball and lacrosse—then still the country's most popular summer sport—had already turned pro. But there were soon signs that they had overreached.

FRANK GRIERSON NAMES MONTREAL "SUSPECTS"

C. A. A. U. Investigation Will Start Shortly at the Capital—Ottawa Man on the Committee

From Our Own Correspondent.

Ottawa, Nov. 14.—The C. A. A. U. Investigation will probably start in Ottawa in the course of the next few days, when all players on the "suspect" list will be called upon to appear and prove their amateur standing or else be professionalized by that body.

Ottawa Hockey Club—J. Ebbs.

The following list gives the hockey "suspects" in Montreal:

Victoria (Montreal)—O. Waugh, W. Bellingham, H. Grier, R. Bowie, C. Grier, R. Gilbert, B. Russell, N. Frye, G. Davidson, F. Church, R. Griffiths, R. Wagor.

Montreal. W. Brophy, G. Sargent, S.

The determination of hard-line Canadian Amateur Athletic Union leaders to pursue a witch hunt against their opponents would make Canada's Athletic War inevitable. It would not be pretty.

Despite the powerful MAAA's backing for commingling, there was strong resistance—even in Quebec. The CAAU's outgoing president, Captain P. Gorman, was known to strongly favour stricter amateurism and was, in fact, far closer to Robertson's thinking than to that of his fellow Montrealers. Gorman had come to believe that the leniency shown lacrosse was a mistake. The organizers of lacrosse's main rival, rugby football, were also resisting the idea of professionalism at the senior level.

The showdown turned into a rout. To the shock of the Montreal

TORONTO'S FIRST PRO. HOCKEY TEAM

The first professional hockey team in Toronto was organized at a meeting last night in the Mutual Street Rink. The new team is called the Toronto Hockey Club, and the Committee of Management consists of Rolly Young, Bruce Ridpath, Pete Charlton, and Hughie Lambe as secretary. The players are confident of a prosperous season and enthusiastic over the prospects. Games with the International League teams on their way to and from Pittsburg will be arranged ; also with teams of the Eastern League in Montreal and Ottawa, opening with a game here with the Wanderers on New Year's Day. The Wanderers at present hold the Stanley Cup.

The Michigan Soo team are due here on Jan. 16. There is plenty of material available, as in the city are Bergoine, Bert Morrison, Menzies, Gorrie, Frank McLaren and Jack Carmichael. Charlie Liffiton, who is at present out of the city, has written and expressed a desire to play in this combination.

Even in the relatively sympathetic *News*, the founding of the Toronto Professionals was only briefly noted.

establishment, and to the delight of John Ross Robertson's followers, mixing pros with amateurs was defeated by a majority of 39 to 13. Some delegates went further, openly suggesting that the MAAA should be thrown out of the Union altogether. And a Toronto purist, the aptly named William Stark, the city's deputy chief of police, was voted the new president of the CAAU.

But the victors were not content to stop there. Stark, egged on by another Ontario hard-liner, Frank Grierson of Ottawa's Civil Service Amateur Athletic Association, was soon announcing a special investigation of eastern team sports. It was claimed that, in an environment of rampant professionalism, eastern hockey players were making as much as $1,350 per season. Grierson began to publicly name dozens of suspects. These included some of the country's most prominent athletes, whom he labelled as "scum."[2]

Under Stark's leadership, the CAAU investigation would be handled by a new National Registration Committee. Akin to the OHA's Robertson-led subcommittee known as the "Three White Czars," this body would conduct ongoing accreditation of and investigations into amateur athletics countrywide. An OHA man, James G. Merrick of the Argonauts, was Toronto's point person on the new committee. It seemed, for the moment, that the Robertson forces had taken not only the day, but the country itself.

However, if the Union's new leadership thought the Montreal gentlemen would simply sit back and allow themselves to be tried, condemned and executed by the registration committee, they were badly mistaken. On February 1, 1907, after considerable groundwork by the 2,000-strong MAAA, the Amateur Athletic Federation of Canada was announced.

The AAFC would be the "realistic" alternative to the new fundamentalism of the CAAU.

With Canada now possessing two "national" athletic organizations, the first shots had been fired in what would quickly come to be known as the "Athletic War." Both the CAAU and AAFC claimed to be the true governing sports body of the country. To prove their respective claims, each began blacklisting the other's athletes, clubs, meets and associations. Across all sports—and across all of Canada—sides were being taken.

The country's national winter game would be a prime battleground.

Originally from Lakefield, Ontario, David Bruce Ridpath moved to Toronto as a teenager. "Riddy" was only twenty-two when he announced the founding of the Toronto Professionals.

———

It at first appeared that the pragmatists had the upper hand in hockey. The Montreal-centric leagues—the Eastern Canada Amateur Hockey Association and the residual Federal Amateur Hockey League—had aligned themselves with the AAFC. The decision of the ECAHA to withdraw from the CAAU, taken on November 10, 1906, was particularly important.

By making the Stanley Cup champion Montreal Wanderers officially open to professional players for the 1906–07 season,[3] the ECAHA effectively forced the hand of everyone in the hockey world. The Manitoba Hockey League split, with most of the teams going openly professional while the venerable Winnipeg Victorias and others left in protest. The Maritime Provinces Amateur Athletic Association forbade New Glasgow to pursue its Stanley Cup challenge against the Montreal Wanderers in December. It did anyway and was expelled, setting Atlantic hockey on a professional course.

The amateur purists, so triumphant at the October 27 meeting, were instantly and unequivocally on the retreat, especially in the hockey world. Even as far away as New York, it was observed that "there is a gen-

Roland Wilbur "Rolly" Young of Waterloo was talented and tough, if somewhat undisciplined. In the Torontos' first season, Rolly combined pre-medical studies at McMaster with playing for the club, moonlighting in other pro leagues, and coaching the OHA junior team at Upper Canada College.

eral rebellion in Canada against the Canadian Amateur Athletic Union."[4] The big exception was Ontario, where professionalism existed only on the northern and eastern fringes—the former embodied by the International, Manitoba and Temiskaming leagues, the latter by the ECAHA and FAHL. In Canada's biggest province stood the one force resolutely resisting the trend: the Toronto-headquartered, Robertson-led Ontario Hockey Association.

Indeed, the OHA had come foursquare behind the newly Simon-pure CAAU. At the annual meeting in November, the *Globe*'s Francis Nelson moved for formal affiliation with the Union. Like Robertson, he had not sought re-election at the annual meeting in 1905, but he was nevertheless aiming to become a permanent fixture on the executive. Membership in the CAAU would be his vehicle. Shortly thereafter, Nelson was named the OHA's representative on the Union's national board.

As the country's self-described bastion of amateurism, the OHA once again set out to keep hockey in Canada's largest province unsullied. It tightened its residency rule further, changing the deadline to August 1, and put curbs on its clubs playing exhibition games. As Nelson's *Globe* observed, professionalism in hockey was on the rise, and "in view of the strenuous fight that must be waged for amateur hockey, the O.H.A. must at once look to its fences and tighten up for the trouble."[5]

However, the OHA had a fundamental problem: it was now on the outside of competition for Canada's national hockey championship, the Stanley Cup. Thus, the association made a remarkable and self-serving discovery: not only had an OHA team never won the Stanley Cup, but the association was now proclaiming it had never really wanted to win the Cup anyway.

"The O.H.A. has never considered that its function was the development of champion teams," the *Globe* announced in rather arch tones, "... and it has not cared who won the Stanley Cup or any other of the cups that are a detriment to the games they were expected to promote. The O.H.A. looks with indifference on the battles for the Stanley Cup." [6]

The difficulty for the OHA was that many fans in Ontario—including, most pointedly, Toronto hockey fans—wanted a shot at the Cup. They saw what the Stanley Cup meant to followers in places like Montreal, Ottawa and Winnipeg. It symbolized hockey supremacy, no matter what Nelson's *Globe*, Robertson's *Telegram*, Hewitt's *Star* or the OHA might believe, and they wanted their local heroes to challenge for it. And it seems those local heroes,

Harry Burgoyne, the third of the original Marlboro defectors, would spend several years as a journeyman in the pro ranks.

the top Toronto players, increasingly felt the same way. By the end of the 1905–06 season, not only were eight well-known pros practising at the Mutual Street Rink, but three of the fan-favourite Marlboros, including star Bruce Ridpath, had been exposed as closet professionals.

There can be little doubt that the threat of professionalism encroaching on its home turf was the reason why the OHA, uncharacteristically, procrastinated in dealing with the Marlboros. Despite overwhelming evidence of their activities as paid ringers in the Temiskaming league, winter, spring and finally summer went by with no action from the normally draconian association. The OHA had to be aware that this threesome, led by the immensely popular Ridpath, if joined to the nascent pro squad at Mutual, could become a potent combination in favour of Toronto professional hockey.

The OHA had no choice in the matter, however, if it was to hold its treasured moral ground and lead the national fight against open professionalism. Thus, on November 14, 1906, more than eight months after learning of their infamous game at New Liskeard, the OHA finally ruled that Ridpath and teammates Rolly Young and Harry Burgoyne were professionals and threw them out of the association. In better days, when it had exiled the likes of Doc Gibson and Cyclone Taylor, the

Hugh Lambe, star defender of the Toronto Lacrosse Club, was always a fan favourite. Though a good stickhandler, his lack of speed made him a stay-at-home defenceman.

OHA probably could not have foreseen that it was laying the institutional foundations of pro hockey. This time, it had to know that it was creating the critical mass for a bona fide Toronto pro team.

That team was not long in coming. A mere eight days later, Bruce Ridpath announced the formation of the Toronto Hockey Club. "Riddy" would be the captain of the Torontos and head of their executive committee. The leading members would come from both the Marlboros and the aborted professional club of 1905–06.

Ridpath would be joined on the Torontos' committee by Young and Pete Charlton. Charlton, having migrated to Berlin after two previous years with the Marlboros, had won three consecutive OHA senior championships. His ongoing movements had long been the basis of rumours that he was a clandestine professional. The final committee member was Hugh Boydell Lambe of the Mutual pros, who would act as secretary-treasurer. Lambe, a former defenceman with the Toronto St. Georges, was one of the many senior OHA players expelled in the lacrosse decision of 1904.

The hockey club announced that a manager would be appointed later. Indeed, an unknown figure, a Mr. B. Spanner,[7] apparently did carry the title for a time. But the real boss had been there all along: Alexander Miln.

Ridpath may have been the captain of the Toronto Hockey Club in name, but it quickly became evident that the real skipper was the twenty-eight-year-old Miln. Aggressive and ambitious, the Scottish-born "Alex" had been around Toronto sports circles for years. He was a noted cyclist, horseman and sailor, belonging to both the Toronto Hunt Club and the Royal Canadian Yacht Club.

Miln was most noted, however, for his involvement in hockey. He had been associated with a number of organizations, but by far the most important was the legendary Toronto Wellingtons. While it appears he played briefly with the club, his key role had been as manager of the squad in its heyday and, later, as its secretary-treasurer. After the men's hockey team folded, he remained permanent secretary of the Wellington alumni and its ladies' organization.

A bookkeeper by profession, Miln became a full-time hockey executive in the fall of 1905. John J. Palmer of the Toronto Type Foundry had purchased the Mutual Street Rink from the Caledonian Curling Club for the princely sum of $25,000. Shortly thereafter, he named Miln its manager. The *Toronto News* noted that it was a popular choice: "Mr. Miln has been connected with hockey clubs for many years, and a better man for the position could not have been secured by the new owners of the rink."[8]

There is no doubt Alexander Miln was the driving force behind the Toronto Professionals. He is shown here holding the Robertson Cup in his days as secretary of the Wellingtons.

It appears that Miln's hockey ambitions from the outset were focused on the Stanley Cup, the very prize that Robertson's OHA so disparaged. It was Miln, after all, who had secured the Wellingtons' challenge against the Winnipeg Victorias in 1902, and he had acted as the team's spokesman in the Manitoba capital. A bitingly sarcastic letter in the Toronto papers the previous February had also betrayed a man not afraid to question the judgments of the association.

Although, like Robertson, a Conservative[9] in politics, Miln's independence on hockey matters became even clearer almost as soon as he took over at Mutual. He was publicly associated with the pro practice squad of 1905–06. He was also immediately engaged in extensive renovations of the old rink that betrayed bigger plans. Although the Caledonian building had been the preferred location of Toronto's top-rank shinny almost from the beginning, by the end of the nineteenth century it was also widely considered deficient for the national winter sport of a major Canadian city.

The first problem was the capacity of the building. On January 16, 1904, the facility managed to cram in 2,674 paying customers (and no

doubt a few others) to witness a showdown between the archrival Marlboros and St. Georges. This was a pittance compared with Montreal's
great Westmount Arena, which offered seating for 4,500 and standing
room for hundreds more. The new Winnipeg Arena, opened in 1905,
could take in 4,000. In Toronto's much smaller venue, important games
were often quick to sell out, leading to ticket scalping that could drive
prices up tenfold.

The second problem was the size of the ice surface. This was linked to
the first problem, because significant seating had been put in for hockey
spectators only after the fact. Known to be jerry-built, these stands significantly reduced the width of the original, squarish skating area. "To
settle all disputes," the *Toronto Star* measured Mutual's surface. It was a
mere 153 feet, 4 inches long and 73 feet, 5 inches wide.[10]

This put the playing area well below the standard established in
Montreal. The surface of its Victoria Skating Rink of 1875 had been
200 feet by 85 feet (the National Hockey League standard to this day).
The ice of the contemporary Montreal Arena was even slightly larger.
Mutual's small surface could help against a visiting team of strong skat-
ers, but it would handicap any Toronto team that aspired to take the
Stanley Cup on a full-size sheet.

The final problem was the amenities—or rather, the virtual lack of
them. There were also design flaws for a major spectator facility, like
windows low enough for young boys to crawl through for free admission.
Most of all, this was the pre-Zamboni era, when "natural" ice had to be
painstakingly created by work and weather. This sheet was constructed
on top of sand, which, combined with the era's poor lighting, made for
a murky-coloured surface that rendered the puck only semi-visible to
spectators.

No Canadian city of the time had an artificial skating rink; however,
Toronto's milder winters (compared to cities like Montreal and Winnipeg) were a more serious challenge. They made schedules much less
reliable. They also caused regular practices to begin comparatively later
in the season—sometimes as late as January—another disadvantage for a
Toronto team seeking a national championship.[11]

As early as the 1890s, Mutual's weaknesses were leading to stories
about a "new rink" for Toronto. Soon, these reports began to follow an
annual and predictable cycle. In the fall would come word of plans to

construct a new artificial-ice complex the following off-season, usually said to be located on the site of the New Caledonian Rink. The idea would inevitably be based on the contemporary gold standard, Pittsburgh's Duquesne Gardens.

The New Caledonian Rink—the home of the Toronto Professionals— was the second of three rinks that stood on the Mutual Street site. It was designed for curling, not hockey.

Duquesne, comprehensively converted to a sports arena in 1895, was a 6,500-seat amphitheatre of brick and iron. It succeeded the Schenley Park Casino, North America's first artificial-ice arena. Estimated to cost an enormous $300,000, Duquesne boasted a spacious promenade and palm garden, a soda fountain, heated stands and, of course, an artificial-ice system. Thus, hockey season in Pittsburgh commenced in November and lasted through the end of March, weather notwithstanding.

Everyone knew that if Toronto wanted a big-league champion, it had to get a big-league arena—and no one knew that better than Alex Miln. From his first day at the helm of Mutual, he had started remodelling the old building. There was a new entrance lobby, additional end seating, cosmetic and lighting improvements indoors, upgraded shower and locker areas, a large time clock and gongs for the goal judges. Teddy Marriott, the departing manager of the Marlboros, was put in charge of a new restaurant upstairs.

The only thing not done, observers noted, was the installation of an artificial-ice plant. Yet this was also clearly part of Miln's design. He was actively putting together plans to construct an advanced, 10,000-seat arena with amphitheatre seating. This was not the usual "new rink" story; Mutual's owners were buying additional land around the old facility in preparation for a larger building.

Reports from around North America indicated that similar schemes were being pursued in other major centres. Ever since the International Hockey League had been founded by Doc Gibson and his U.S. backers, proposals had circulated for a genuine "big league of hockey," rumoured to include the leading cities of eastern Canada and the northeast United States. Now it looked as if something was genuinely afoot. Only two days after the pro team's founding, Miln attended a meeting of the IHL in Chicago. There, he secured a franchise for Toronto for the 1907–08 season.

For the time being, however, the Pros would be an independent, "barnstorming" team, seeking exhibition matches against clubs from the pro leagues surrounding Ontario, splitting their gate share between the players. The IHL teams were an obvious target, given the Torontos' intention of joining the league next season. Those squads frequently came through Toronto on road trips between Pennsylvania, Michigan and family in Canada. Closer to home, it appeared the new Queen City club would have a sister organization and competitor in Barrie.

The OHA had expelled its Barrie club over the Bobby Rowe affair. Now, with Miln's younger brother Jack as secretary-treasurer, Barrie was establishing its own professional team. It would also include key forward Steve Vair, who had played with Rowe—as well as Marlboros Ridpath, Young and Burgoyne—at New Liskeard. The OHA tried a bit of public-relations face-saving by announcing that Barrie's all-star cover point, Howard Gee, would be doing the right thing by remaining an amateur and becoming a Marlboro. It backfired: Gee subsequently declared that he, too, was going pro—along with the entire Barrie team.

Having secured an organization, a manager, a rink, a league franchise, a local opponent and a plan for the season, the Torontos now needed only players to round out those locals who were already committed. It was apparent there would be no shortage of men looking for a place in the Torontos' lineup. Between OHA expulsions and the lure of the pro option, a growing number of quality city players were keen to be given a tryout. There were soon about two dozen men seeking spots.

But there was a rub: professional athletes were not club property like their amateur counterparts. Once a professional, an athlete could play anywhere there was a willing employer. In other words, the professional of the day was a perennial unrestricted free agent, free to sign with whatever team he wished to play for so long as he lacked a better offer. In the burgeoning world of pro hockey, competition from other potential employers was intense, especially for established performers.

Some veteran players from the 1905–06 gang were already pursuing offers elsewhere. Jack Marshall and Charlie Liffiton were heading to the ECAHA, with Roy Brown and Bert Morrison going to the IHL. Most troubling was the loss of Pete Charlton to the States. His $50 per week salary was far more than a barnstorming outfit could promise. A top star in the IHL could aim for at least $75.

These defections led the OHA-supporting papers to confidently predict that the professional team would not be viable. Billy Hewitt's *Star* sarcastically observed that the club—after the rink got two-thirds of the gate, the visitors received a fee and each player a share—"should simply coin money."[12] At Robertson's *Telegram*, the dismissal was complete.

"Professional hockey in Toronto promises to flourish till the frost comes," the paper predicted ominously. "Then like other flowers it will fade away and die."[13]

Before long, however, the Toronto Hockey Club had scheduled its first game. It was announced that, on December 28, 1906, the opponent would be Ontario's original pro rebels, the Canadian Soo team of the International league. They were led by Roy Brown at point and included Marty Walsh, an amateur star who had recently defected from Queen's University. The Mutual Street Rink also declared that out-of-town scores would be broadcast during the game.

The message was clear: this was the big leagues.

As the date approached, the Toronto Professionals—as the club was soon labelled—were coming together. The only players remaining from the 1905–06 experiment were Lambe at point, Jack Carmichael at centre and Frank McLaren at right wing. With Clarence Gorrie oddly deciding to return to amateur in the Toronto Aquatic Hockey League, Manager Miln secured former Marlboro prospect Mark Tooze to play goal. He rounded out the lineup by adding Young at cover, Ridpath at rover and Burgoyne at left wing.

Was this a group ready to take on an established professional club? With five men from the Marlboro organization, it was a credible senior-level team. However, although Carmichael had at one time been a top OHA performer, only Ridpath was a league all-star. And Lambe, with just a few games in Pittsburgh, was the sole member with any real pro credentials.

Observers also questioned whether the team had the conditioning for such an early contest. They had not looked ready in some early scrimmages. There was also an ominous sign in the 12–4 drubbing the Soo delivered to the Barrie Pros on Christmas Day. Worse, it was done with Ridpath and Tooze in the northern town's lineup.

Nevertheless, anticipation was high as the Torontos skated onto Mutual Street ice at 8:00 that Friday night. With paid athletes playing hockey for the first time ever in Toronto, everyone understood that new ground was being broken. Even the *Globe* predicted that "the contest should prove fast and exciting."[14]

A large crowd had turned out, excitedly waiting to see the new club.

It would have been a bit surprised by the lineup. Among those dressed was Gee at cover, lent to Toronto by Barrie for the occasion. Burgoyne had become the spare man, left to sit out that first game. The fans, however, were likely even more startled by the team's jerseys. Torontonians had been told the new club would be resplendent in white and purple. As their uniforms had not yet arrived, trainer William Slean—yet another Marlboro defector—gave them their old sweaters. Thus, the Professionals greeted the fans wearing the uniform of the Marlboros.

For Bruce Ridpath and company, it was a defiant farewell to John Ross Robertson and the OHA.

CHAPTER SIX

THE UPRISING SPREADS

Professional Hockey Appears Across Ontario

The O.H.A. have thrown Guelph out of their (amateur?) organization and have professionalized three of the players . . . But they have not broken the spirit of our warriors, nor can they prevent them from putting one of the fastest teams in Ontario on the ice.[1]

—Guelph Mercury

What would it be like to travel back to the Mutual Street Rink of 1906 and witness the Toronto Professionals taking on the Sault Ste. Marie Algonquins?

Anyone under the impression that the very first professional hockey game played in Toronto might bear much resemblance to a National Hockey League match played by Maple Leafs at the Air Canada Centre would be, at various times, disappointed, intrigued and amazed. The matches of the early pro era bear only a vague likeness to their modern offspring.

The first conspicuous difference would be on the ice surface itself. The familiar red and blue markings would be entirely absent. The only lines would be in black, connecting each set of goalposts. These existed primarily for the benefit of the goal judges, called "umpires," who stood on the ice directly behind the nets. With arena lighting very dim compared to today's requirements for television, fans in the rink could hardly be expected to see these inky smudges.

It is difficult to convey the vast difference between the shadowy atmosphere in the typical arena of a century ago and the brightly lit modern amphitheatres of today. To illustrate the difference, the Berlin Auditorium was lauded for its new lighting during the 1909–10 season. Two new "sun-lights" of 3,000 candlepower each had been installed, in addition to the ten existing "arc lamps" of 700 candlepower. Today, a flashlight alone can project as much as 75,000 candlepower.[2]

The next major discrepancy would be the seven men, lining up in a "T" formation for the opening faceoff. The centre, flanked by the left and right wings, would be familiar. They would be expected to stick to their positions. Behind the centre, however, would stand the *rover*, the position played by Bruce Ridpath on the new professional club. Usually the strongest skater on the team, the rover was the key transition man. He would often lead the attack as well as augment the defence.

The defensive alignment was particularly distinctive. Behind the rover would stand the *cover point* (or just *cover*), the more offensive-minded defenceman. Behind him was the stay-at-home *point*. While the two defencemen generally played both up and back, it was not unheard-of for them to be on either side of the ice. Indeed, it was considered bad form for them to be in an exactly straight line to the goal.

Of course, behind the point stood the perennial goalkeeper, guarding a target of six feet by four feet, filled out with the now-standard netting promoted just a few years earlier by Frank Nelson and Billy Hewitt. The goal dimensions are one of the very few constants of the game, virtually unaltered since its founding. Nor has the size of the puck—which by this time was made of rubber—changed. Likewise, the stick, while then wooden, has always had the familiar shape essential to the sport.

It would be some time before the dimensions of Montreal's Victoria Skating Rink—200 feet by 85—would become standard. In the 1890s, proportions as small as 112 feet by 58 were tolerated. By the 1900s, the minimums had been raised to 160 feet by 60. Few facilities had yet been built specifically for hockey; all but the newest buildings were converted curling clubs. The corners of their ice surfaces were, literally, ninety degrees.

At the big-league level, early hockey was always played indoors—notwithstanding the modern myth of the "heritage game," as the NHL has called its outdoor matches of recent years in Canada. Indeed, it was the decision of James Creighton to take shinny indoors, giving it a fixed number of players on a surface with fixed boundaries, that launched the modern sport.

The players themselves—like the population generally—were much smaller than nowadays. The best pros would typically be in the 145-to-165-pound range. Undersized players would tip the scales at much less. Claude Borland of the 1904 Stanley Cup challenger Winnipeg Rowing Club was reported to weigh only 97 pounds. A man of 180 or more (like 200-pound Doc Gibson) would be a veritable giant. Still, the essential skills—skating, stickhandling, passing, shooting, checking—have not changed, although using one's feet to control the puck was not permitted in hockey's first decades.

The early participants also wore very modest equipment, making them look much lighter than today's gladiators. Goalies relied on mere cricket pads to cover their shins. The protective gear of the others would be little more than thick padding to cover the more vulnerable parts of the body. Yet neither the players' heads nor the goalkeepers' faces were apparently considered vulnerable.

Nevertheless, such men were expected to play the whole game, even when hurt. Should an injury be serious enough, each side would generally drop a player (leading, occasionally, to "strategic" injuries). Substitution by agreement did sometimes occur, but it was comparatively rare. As a consequence, one would not see a bevy of alternate players staffing a large bench. There would be one, maybe two extras in uniform, plus a trainer and a small handful of club officials off to the side. The team's captain was usually the de facto coach of the squad.

It also follows that the pace of the game would not be nearly as fast as with the twenty-man NHL lineups of our era. As in a marathon street-hockey game, players would rotate positions to preserve their energy, forwards dropping back when exhausted. However, it should be noted that the top-level pros were much younger. It would be very rare indeed to find a man over thirty playing against twenty-somethings for a full sixty minutes. This hour was played in just two thirty-minute halves (stop-time at the elite level), with a brief ten-minute rest in between.

Advertisements for hockey matches were often seen in the newspapers. Sometimes, like this one for the first pro game, they took the form of promotional articles.

The more variable tempo—much like soccer matches to this day—also gave penalties less importance. The lack of analysis of power-play or shorthanded situations in game reports of the period is quite striking. An individual penalty was not seen as a significant disadvantage, although an accumulation definitely was—and there was no limit to the number who could be sent off. Penalties, though defined similarly to today, were also variable in length. A player was assigned one to four minutes (but usually two or three) for a routine offence, while serious fouls would receive five or ten minutes, or more.

As the game unfolded, the biggest difference a modern spectator would immediately grasp was the lack of forward passing. Hockey in that era was an "onside" game, meaning a player had to be on his own side of the puck to join the play. If not, the resultant "offside" would lead to an immediate faceoff wherever the infraction occurred. Then again, the Ontario Hockey Association—which, despite its extreme conservatism when it came to amateurism, was otherwise a remarkably innovative organization—had developed two important exceptions to the offside rule.

First, taking the puck off a save by one's goalie within three feet of the goal line did not constitute offside in Ontario hockey. In other provinces, such a situation would lead to dangerous faceoffs in front of the goal, or worse, an inability to clear rebounds. This 1905 innovation—first proposed by W. A. Hewitt—was rapidly adopted by other leagues, including the new professional circuits. Soon, an actual three-foot line was put across the ice surface (again in black)—the earliest forerunner of today's blue line.

Second, in the OHA a puck carrier could move the disc to a receiving teammate, provided he had drawn even with the teammate before the exchange. This was deemed to bring the pass receiver onside. This deviation was not widely accepted, leading to considerable confusion when Ontario clubs played against those from outside the jurisdiction. Among the early Ontario pros, a hybrid version was frequently employed, although no one seems to be able to describe precisely how it was supposed to work.

Although deliberately "loafing" offside in order to rest could earn a player a penalty, there is no doubt that offside rulings still led to more stoppages than we experience now. Conversely, there was also no such thing as icing a century ago. "Lifting" the puck down the ice to relieve the pressure was considered a legitimate, if somewhat archaic and boring, tactic. In the semi-darkness of many rinks, a high lift could disappear from sight, becoming stuck in the rafters or, quite plausibly, dropping unexpectedly into the net behind the opposing goalkeeper.

The goalie had a particularly tough job. He could not hold the puck with his hands and had to remain standing at all times. Falling or kneeling to block a shot constituted a penalty—which had to be served by the goalie himself. Unsurprisingly, then, games were generally high-scoring by today's standards. The goalkeepers' inability to bounce up and down also explains why many of the time were large, even fat, men. As in lacrosse, where the goal nets were narrower, they were often sought more for their size than their athleticism.

Many of these differences are interrelated. For example, the absence of substitution eliminated the need for the modern coach. Teams had managers, but nobody behind the bench. If anyone served a position akin to today's coaches, it would be the playing captain of the team. Likewise, the nonexistence of icing, fixed faceoff locations and offside zones are consistent with the lack of markings on the ice surface.

The approach to the game was quite unlike today's version of the sport. Offensive styles were limited. Emphasis was put on tight teamwork among the forwards, who ideally would exchange the puck back or laterally in a method more akin to rugby than modern-day hockey. The

John P. "Jack" Car-
michael had never
actually been hired to
play hockey. He was
first expelled from
the OHA in 1900
because his Guelph
club was caught
paying some other
men. Reinstated after
refusing to join
the moneyed ranks,
he was thrown out
again for playing
lacrosse.

player who could move up quickly and pass in this manner was considered the key man. Indeed, the playmaker (often the rover) was the star of the team. Much less importance was attributed to the goal scorer (often the centre).

Given a hockey culture that valued play-makers over goal scorers, it is ironic that assists were seldom noted. In truth, individual statistical records—even goal-scoring records—were rather paltry in this era. For example, historians have made much note of the fact that Toronto's Newsy Lalonde led the Ontario Professional Hockey League in scoring in 1907–08. However, these records were compiled decades later. There was never any "scoring race" mentioned in the newspapers that season.

Nevertheless, those watching the games would have little trouble conversing with twenty-first-century fans. Hockey jargon was already moving into recognizable territory. Earlier lingo of "games" and "bulls" was giving way to "goals" and "faces" (faceoffs). Both would quickly understand that "combination play" meant "passing" and that a "hockeyist" was really just a hockey player.

Even then, the principal official was the referee, but he usually carried a bell instead of a whistle. After all, in a frigid rink, a metal whistle might freeze to his lips. The referee would put offenders "on the fence" rather than in the penalty box. In some jurisdictions (but not the OHA or OPHL), the referee would be assisted by a "judge of play." He would focus on penalties while the referee looked after offsides. (Obviously, there could be no linesmen, since there were no lines.) At the side would be two timekeepers—one from each club—carefully watching each other as well as their timepieces.

Around the rink sat and stood the fans—people made of sterner stuff, watching in tougher conditions. Except for a stove in the dressing room, rinks were not heated. With buildings housing "natural" ice made meticulously from buckets and shovels, it could not be any other way. Huddling under blankets and unsupported by sound systems,[3] fans sang and cheered not just to encourage their team, but to keep warm enough to stay alive. Many would also smoke, defying management and often creating clouds so thick they obscured the action on the ice for those higher up in the stands.

Frank McLaren, one of seven hockey-playing brothers from Perth, had been kicked out of the OHA in its 1904 lacrosse decision. He had since sought to be part of a Toronto pro team.

Hockey, beyond any doubt, was already the nation's passion. A team's followers did not just come to their own rink draped in the colours of their club. They would often attend practices, especially the preseason tryouts. Mascot in tow (a child or a pet, rather than a team employee in a costume), they would also follow the boys when the squad went on the road. The vehicle to do this was the "special train," set up by enterprising railways.

Again, the societal changes that followed the explosion in rail transportation cannot be underestimated. Train travel was critical to the rise of professional sports teams and leagues all over the world.

The supporters' expenses did not end with the train or game tickets— as much as $3 total for a road trip within Ontario. A team's true follower would invariably feel the need to lay down wagers against opposing rooters. Somehow, whether "toasting their winnings" or "drowning their sorrows," the fans of a century ago managed, one way or another, to end up at the bar—much like their descendants.

Those headed to the bar after the game of December 28, 1906, would have been feeling a sense of anticlimax. Despite a vigorous contest, the Canadian Soo had walked away with a 7–0 shutout.

Yet the defeat was not as bad as the score would indicate. The score had been only 2–0 at the half, with the Torontos clearly in it. Conditioning had unquestionably been their undoing in the late going, when the Algonquins netted most of their goals. Although the ice surface was

Mark Harold Tooze was a goalkeeper on the Marlboros' intermediate-level roster when he was banned by the OHA in its 1904 lacrosse edict. He had been inactive for two seasons when the Professionals took him on.

not yet fully hardened, the play had been intense throughout—notably more physical than was typical in the OHA.

There was a fair range of reaction to that first professional game. The *Mail and Empire* thought the Professionals showed real promise and that with more practice and better conditioning, "it will take a speedy aggregation to put the kibosh on them."[4] Billy Hewitt's *Star* was the most persistently hostile to the new club, calling the game "of an inferior quality"[5] and the crowd a product of "a sucker born every minute."[6]

The OHA was sending a message: the war against pro hockey in Toronto had only just begun.

For now, though, things were clearly looking up for the paid men in the Queen City. Nearly 1,500 people had shelled out for admission on that opening night. The best seats went for seventy-five cents—a 50 percent increase in price from OHA senior games. Half that number had attended the OHA's first headline act of the year, a contest between the Marlboros and the defending intermediate champion from Peterborough. Despite the ongoing boosterism of OHA matches by the *Globe*, *Star* and *Telegram*—and frequent sarcasm towards the Torontos—interest in further professional matches was high.

Unfortunately, mild weather forced the cancellation of encounters with Barrie on January 1 and Calumet (Michigan) of the International league on January 7. The former was costly to the northern pro experiment. Faced with a severe shortage of playing time—and cash—Barrie's key men began to sign elsewhere. Rowe and Vair returned to the Temiskaming league, while Gee went first to the IHL and then to the Manitoba pro circuit.

It was not until January 17 that another IHL team was available to play the Torontos, this time from Sault Ste. Marie, Michigan. The

"American Soo"[7] brought with them early French Canadian stars Jack Laviolette and Didier Pitre, as well as Toronto defector Pete Charlton. In the meantime, to avoid the problems of his brother's outfit in Barrie, Alex Miln had been scouring the continent for additional men to bolster his club.

This would prove to be Miln's style as a manager. Throughout this season—and the ones to come—he constantly kept the lines of communication open, always ready to reel reinforcements into the roster. His first catch was Charlie Liffiton, lured back from Montreal. Once a big star with the Winged Wheelers of the Montreal AAA, Liffiton at twenty-eight was on the back end of his career. Nevertheless, in providing another winger and keeping Burgoyne as the spare man, he was widely seen as strengthening the lineup.

Whereas the jury was still out after the first game, the second was a smashing success. It was a furious back-and-forth battle, with the Wolverines[8] coming on in the second half as the Torontos faded. Then Carmichael banged in a Ridpath rebound with three minutes left to give the Pros their first victory, 8–7.

The Toronto newspapers' treatment of Howard Gee of Barrie exemplified the double standard they operated by. As an OHA player, he was the object of their lavish praise. Once he turned professional, they suddenly found him decidedly ordinary.

Media opinion was undivided on this one. The *News* called the game "easily the most spectacular, the most interesting, the most exciting seen here this year."[9] With Mutual still reverberating from 2,000 cheering spectators, even the *Globe* felt obliged to concede that "professional hockey has caught on in Toronto."[10]

Rolly Young was universally deemed the star of the game. His lone goal was the Torontos' first ever—a spectacular end-to-end rush that brought the house down. This was quite a turnaround from the previous outing, when Young had been widely singled out for particularly poor conditioning.

On the whole, the Torontos had played well. Liffiton proved

Once considered a great player, Charles Albert Liffiton had been in top-level hockey for a decade. He was a member of the Montreal AAA's "Little Men of Iron," who captured the Stanley Cup in 1902.

adequate but a bit of a disappointment, as was McLaren. The play of Carmichael, Lambe and Ridpath—who had half of Toronto's eight goals—was generally praised. The goaltender Tooze, of whom not much was expected, had also performed admirably. On the Soo side, the speed of Laviolette and Pitre had awed the crowd. There was simply nothing in the OHA to compare to such players.

Toronto had seen the real big-league article—and wanted more of it.

———

Soon came proof that Ontario's capital city was, indeed, finally part of hockey's top level. Almost immediately after the American Soo game, it was announced that the Manitoba champion Kenora[11] Thistles would play the Toronto Professionals at Mutual on January 25. Fans witnessing the Pros' first win had been updated by megaphone on the Thistles' first-game victory over the defending Stanley Cup champion Montreal Wanderers. Four days later, the Thistles took the Cup.

For many years, notable travellers from across Canada and the United States had come to play in Toronto. As early as February 1895, a future Stanley Cup aspirant from the West had performed on its way through town. In that case, it was the Winnipeg Victorias, featuring the famous Dan Bain.[12] In 1901, the Vics had even displayed the trophy in a Toronto store window on their way through town. However, never before had a Cup champion skated on Queen City ice.

Yet the Kenora team was no far-flung curiosity. Even then, Canadian hockey fans everywhere followed the top contenders religiously. The Thistles, with ex-Marlboro stars Tom Phillips and Eddie Giroux, were hometown favourites. Their lineup would include no fewer than five future Hall of Famers. The city's hockey fans went crazy.

Miln immediately postponed the OHA's scheduled games at the Mutual Street Rink. The old association, with its purely amateur teams, was plagued with dismal attendance anyway. In contrast, for the Kenora game, the rink management had to announce a limit of six tickets per buyer "to prevent speculation."[13] That was with top prices hiked to a shocking $1.

The Friday night game itself turned out to be an indifferent affair. The Thistles were cramped on the small Mutual Street ice.[14] They were also worn out and coming down after their epic victory in Montreal and a subsequent exhibition match in Ottawa. Observers thought Phillips seemed particularly off-colour, although he did score three goals. Instead, Si Griffis and Roxy Beaudro carried the offence in great style.

The Kenora Thistles came from the smallest place ever to win the Stanley Cup. They were the first such champions to play a game in Toronto. Standing: R. Phillips, J. McGillivray, J. Link, F. Hudson. Sitting: R. Beaudro, T. Hooper, T. Phillips, W. McGimsie, J. Hall. Reclining: S. Griffis, E. Giroux, A. Ross.

Ridpath and Young, the emerging core of the Torontos, led the home team. Just the same, everyone had contributed to the effort—even McLaren, who came on as the spare man. Nevertheless, the Professionals were simply not of the same calibre as the Thistles. The champs played just well enough to win—which they did by a score of 9–8.

But the more significant number was in the stands. Close to two and a half thousand people had crammed into the old barn to see the best team in the country. As the two squads skated onto the ice, the roar was deafening—and it continued through much of the contest.

Toronto had never had a hockey moment quite like it.

Toronto also had a newcomer on the ice that historic night against Kenora. He was a left winger named Joe Ouelette, borrowed for the occasion from another new pro club. A third such entity had just been formed in the heartland of the OHA.

Contrary to what John Ross Robertson's *Telegram* had predicted, the professional flower was blooming rather than fading with the cold weather. The rebellion against the OHA's amateur order was beginning to spread—in a very big way. Indeed, a ringleader had emerged. He was a maverick named Norman Edgar "Buck" Irving, formerly the secretary-treasurer of the OHA's Guelph Hockey Club and son of the owner of the Royal City Rink.

The Guelph trouble began not long before the Kenora game. The local club had assembled a good OHA senior team and was having a great season. From the outset, there was suspicion about how the team had come together, but after initial doubts had been raised, the OHA approved all residency certificates.

Then some solid evidence surfaced that the lineup had been "assembled" by management, likely with inducements. The Guelph club and a number of its officials and skaters, including Ouelette, were thrown out of the OHA. It was a bad enough situation, but the association made it worse by ruling even innocent Guelph players ineligible to perform anywhere else by virtue of the residency rule.

However, it was Buck Irving who would turn Guelph's fight with the OHA into a wider insurrection. After his club had been scuttled, the Royal City promoter published an open letter alleging widespread professionalism in the OHA. He named about two dozen of the association's top stars—all presumed to be pure amateurs and stamped as such by the OHA. Irving demanded an investigation as rigorous as the one imposed on his club.

GUELPH MAKES WHOLESALE CHARGES OF PROFESSIONALISM

Amateur Status of Berlin, Galt, Peterborough and Toronto Players is Questioned in a Statement Forwarded to the O.H.A.

From Our Own Correspondent.

Guelph, Jan. 28.—Mr. N. E. Irving this morning forwarded to Secretary Fitzgerald the statement regarding the amateur standing of the different senior teams of the O. H. A. He takes each team separately, and a synopsis follows :—

Berlin—Will McGinnis is charged with receiving $5 for every game that he played with Preston during 1903-04, and is also asked if he did not play with Port Dalhousie in the Niagara League the same season.

ing to press only part of it had been received, as follows :—
J. P. Fitzgerald,
    Secretary O. H. A., Toronto.
  Re Berlin :
  "Will McGinnis deny that he received $5 per game for every game that he played with the Preston team during the season of 1903 and 1904, the same year that the famous 'Texas' Gillard played with Preston, and 'Texas' was not playing for his health ? He at this time was a suspended player from the O. H. A. And can McGinnis swear that, during the same season, he did not also play with Port Dalhousie in

The infamous "Irving charges" were designed to turn the OHA's in-
quiries into players' amateur status into a fiasco.

Irving's charges had scant direct evidence but a certain ring of truth. Semi-professionalism in the senior ranks of the OHA was widely suspected. For example, among those accused were Chuck Tyner and Herb Birmingham. Along with Edgar Winchester, they were the only Marlboro starters from the 1904–05 OHA champions who had not gone professional—and the rumours had been rife.

President D. L. Darroch of the OHA immediately committed to a full investigation but, for the association, this could not be coming at a worse time. Secretary Hewitt, generally the workhorse for such matters, was out of commission with a life-threatening bout of pneumonia. John Ross Robertson's *Telegram* provided a temporary replacement in the person of reporter J. P. Fitzgerald, yet nothing seemed to control the swirl of accusation and innuendo in the media. Eventually, even Past President Robertson himself attended some of the hearings in an attempt to contain the story.

Despite the high-level intervention, the matter was never really resolved in a satisfactory manner. The OHA had planned a wide-ranging inquisition but was faced with revolt from the affected clubs and the risk of a collapse of the senior series. The association opted to generally back off, instead settling for affidavits by the players and public counterattacks on Irving. Buck and other OHA skeptics then had a field day, charging the organization with hypocrisy, double standards and "whitewashing."

By the time of the historic Torontos–Thistles contest, virtually all of Guelph's OHA players had gone to a new professional club. Thus, on January 30, the Toronto Professionals headed west for their first-ever away game against the Guelph Royals. With Liffiton unavailable and Ouelette playing for Guelph, McLaren was back as a starter and Burgoyne got into the lineup for the first time.

To the surprise of everyone, the Royals thumped the Torontos by the score of 9–4. Ouelette scored three for Guelph. Also noteworthy were two goals by right winger Walter Mercer, previously a Guelph junior.

For the Torontos, the play of Young was the most commented on. He had again rushed spectacularly, but was very weak in tending to his defensive chores. Burgoyne netted two for the visitors, suggesting he might have helped earlier lineups had he been played. The papers also noted that Carmichael, once a star performer with the OHA's Guelph Nationals, had lost little of his old speed.

Overall, the hockey provided solid entertainment for the home fans. There had been some disappointment that Irving had not delivered Reddy McMillan to the Guelph lineup as promised—a sign of things to come. Nevertheless, the *Guelph Mercury* denounced the OHA and proclaimed that "it was truly a great game . . . Guelph would support a team which can put up an exhibition like that of last night." [15]

Ontario's pro rebels had established another beachhead.

The Torontos' next match was back at Mutual just five days later against another International league team, the Pittsburgh Pirates. In the visitors' lineup was Ernie Liffiton, younger brother of Toronto's Charlie. The homesters had the elder sibling back on the ice and again borrowed Ouelette from Guelph. Burgoyne was once more shunted to the side, along with McLaren. In point of fact, Frank, scoreless in three and a half outings, had seen his last action of the season.

A full house saw the Professionals beat the Pirates by a convincing 9–5 margin. The reviews were generally positive, especially for the second half. As the *Mail and Empire* commented: "The game demonstrated the fact that professional hockey does not necessarily need to be played in a rough-house style, and there is no doubt that if the game is played cleanly that it will pay in Toronto. The play was very interesting to watch, abounding in splendid combination, good individual work, and checking."[16]

The Torontos had played particularly well. All skaters but Ouelette had scored at least one goal; Ridpath led the team with three. Liffiton, with two goals, was dubbed Toronto's first star, his mix-ups with his brother providing some colour for the evening. All in all, it was another good outing for pro hockey in the Queen City.

After the Pittsburgh visit, the team had no games scheduled for the immediate future. The various Toronto players used the break to head elsewhere to perform as ringers. In these early pro days, it was not uncommon for players, when available, to rent themselves out to a second team in another league.

Young left town in the company of the Pirates to spend some time in the IHL. His play in the Smoky City—at $40 per week—was the subject of rave reviews. He was brought back later for another week at the (then huge) sum of $200. As this illustrates, it was possible back then to be an unrestricted free agent several times a season.

Rolly also played some hockey that year in the wild Temiskaming league. That circuit, fuelled by mining money, hired players literally on a game-to-game basis. Virtually all the Torontos played some games up north that winter—at $15 a shot plus expenses. In one outing, Young, Ridpath, McLaren and Ouelette faced off for Cobalt against Latchford, which had dressed Burgoyne and Tooze.

LOCAL PROS. GO TO COBALT.

Mark Tooze, Oulette, Rowley Young, Burgoyne and a number of other local pro. hockeyists left for Cobalt last night, where they will play against a Latchford team at the opening of the new Cobalt rink.

In the early days of professionalism, hockey players were as much entrepreneurs as employees.

Indeed, the papers that season are full of reports and rumours of the Professionals' players seeking work elsewhere—Carmichael being the curious exception. Lambe also did not play for another club, although he was the subject of some interesting speculation. Both he and Young were cited as possible recruits for Kenora in their Stanley Cup rematch against the Wanderers at season's end. However, the Cup trustees, P. D. Ross and William Foran, were beginning to worry about the effect such movements were having on the mug's image. Their subsequent rulings against such hiring put an end to that story.[17]

In any case, the Toronto players would be needed again by their home club before the end of the month. They had yet another new opponent in southern Ontario. This time, it was the reigning OHA senior champion. Berlin's defection from the amateur ranks was a consequence of the "Irving charges" set against a long history of bad blood between the Dutchmen and the old association.

Ever since the infamous "gold coin" incident had cost Berlin the 1897–98 intermediate title, relations with the OHA had been troubled. In 1899, Berlin led a number of southwestern Ontario towns in forming the separate Western Ontario Athletic Association, of which it won the championship every year. Unable to get a Stanley Cup challenge accepted by the trustees, Berlin rejoined the OHA for the 1904–05 season. Its intermediate team was edged out for the title that year, but went senior and won it all the next season.

After Guelph was expelled from the OHA senior series, the western district increasingly looked like a race between the defending champs and the Toronto St. Georges. On February 16, the two teams were to meet for a big showdown at Mutual. But before the game began, St. Georges pointed out that Berlin's Jim McGinnis had never been cleared of Irving's charges.

At this point, the OHA would clearly have preferred to forget the whole Irving investigation. Unfortunately, when questioned by league officials, McGinnis gave suspicious and contradictory answers. The OHA was compelled to make him sit out. The Dutchmen, without a spare man, offered to play the St. Georges six on six. The Toronto team demanded the game be played seven on six or defaulted.

For over an hour and a half the management of the two clubs yelled at each other while a big Saturday-night crowd grew impatient for the game to start. Rather than risk a riot by his customers, Miln finally stepped in and persuaded the teams to play an exhibition. Meanwhile, the matter was referred to the OHA executive.

Buck Irving had already been hanging around Berlin, laying the groundwork for a new pro team. Thus, when the OHA took the St. Georges' side of the dispute and started expelling Berliners, things were ready to go. Two hundred people representing the management and leading patrons of the Dutchmen met immediately to pull their club out of the amateur association. The champions' entire lineup went with them.

In no time, the Toronto Professionals had set up home-and-home games with the Berlin Dutchmen. On February 26, they tied 7–all in

Joseph "Frenchy" Ouelette was renowned for his crouched skating style. The Guelph left winger was borrowed by the Torontos for a couple of their barnstorming matches of 1906–07.

Berlin, while the defending OHA champs won 8–3 at Mutual three nights later. The first game was particularly remarkable because 2,000 Berliners had waited two and a half hours for it to start after a wreck on the tracks had delayed the arrival of the Torontos' train. The crowd then stayed till midnight, not leaving until the game had ended.

Berlin's first professional game had featured great hockey. The Torontos, down 7–2 at one point, got their offence untracked and roared back in the second half. Bruce Ridpath, once again the star, scored his fourth goal of the night to tie the game with thirty seconds left.

The game in Toronto was not so great, but did supply an amusing tale. The home team was missing Liffiton, again away on business. When Miln's expected recruits did not show, the team was a man short. Doing some quick thinking, captain Ridpath recruited the referee into the lineup. He was Bert Brown, another former Marlboro.

The newly converted professional did not help much. Outclassed, the Torontos fell behind 7–0, and this time there was no comeback. Truth be told, the last twenty minutes were played in virtual darkness when the lighting failed. One observer called the game "almost as tame and slow, in fact, as the average O.H.A. games we have become accustomed to seeing this winter."[18]

That was not a statement John Ross Robertson or his followers could take any solace from.

———

Yet another defector from the Marlboro organization, Bert Brown was considered a good cover point. However, he appeared out of condition in his lone, last-minute appearance with the Professionals.

Through the ups and downs of their improvised first season, interest in the Toronto Professionals had remained keen. Part of the reason was the mediocre year transpiring in the OHA. One measure of that state of affairs was a disastrous OHA exhibition game played at Mutual on March 9.

On that date, a select squad assembled from Toronto's senior Argonauts, Marlboros and St. Georges went down to the University of Toronto by a humiliating score of 25–6. A desperate OHA had pressed an aging George McKay into service. He was reported not to have played since the demise of the Wellingtons—a fate, by the way, soon to be met by the remnants of the Marlboro team.

While the humiliating amateur blowout was taking place, Toronto's real hockey excitement revolved around the pending visit of the professional Montreal Wanderers. The Wanderers, despite having lost the Stanley Cup to Kenora earlier in the season, had taken the championship of the Eastern association for the third straight year. They would be headed west for a repeat showdown with the Thistles, again champions of the Manitoba league.

As Kenora and Montreal haggled over the terms of their encounter—including controversial questions of player eligibility—Wanderer manager Tom Hodge came through Toronto to meet with Alex Miln. It was said that Hodge wanted his team to play at Mutual in order to prepare for the real possibility the Cup games could be held on the small Kenora rink. It was also rumoured that Miln had paid up to $900 for the honour. Whatever the reason, a date was set for March 11.

"Big Ezra" Dumart was a rugged forward with a hard, accurate shot. His 160 pounds would make him a large man for this era.

In the star-studded Wanderer lineup that night was "Hod" Stuart, widely considered the greatest player of the day. Stuart, who also played football, had left Ottawa and performed in the Western Pennsylvania and International leagues before ending up with the Wanderers. Stuart was the Bobby Orr of his era. Big, fast and rough, he dominated the game not just through superior skill, but by quarterbacking the offence from his own end forward. Playing that night with a broken finger, Stuart led the Redbands to an easy 4–1 lead before retiring early.

From there on, the game got tight. Though much smaller than their Montreal opponents, the Torontos, led by the determined Ridpath, threw themselves at the Wanderers with a fury. Riddy brought the crowd to its feet by decking the lanky Lester Patrick with a hard check. The game was quick, tough and intense throughout.

While generally clean as well, the contest also featured a notable fight. Wanderer Ernie "Moose" Johnson had given Hughie Lambe what his defence partner, Rolly Young, considered a cheap shot. Young went after Johnson, and several others joined in. During the excitement, one overwrought fan hurled his seat onto the ice surface. He was arrested, but, when later ascertained to be a Toronto supporter, he was promptly released.

The Torontos recovered from their early-game jitters to become increasingly confident. With eight minutes left, the Professionals had pulled ahead 9–8. However, having let the game completely open up, they could not keep pace with the Wanderers' offence and eventually fell away by a count of 12–10. Charlie Liffiton, eager to show the Montrealers he still had it, was the best Toronto player, with five goals. But Ernie Russell, with an incredible nine for the Redbands, had sunk the local team.

There were differing opinions on what the game said about the Queen City club. Strengthened by Berlin forward Ezra Dumart, no one doubted that the Torontos had played well. Conversely, analysts pointed to Wanderer injuries, the soft ice, the small surface and an off night by Montreal goalie William Milton "Riley" Hern to suggest the visitors had perhaps done just enough to win. Subsequent events indicate that, in truth, the local pros were not that bad a team.

This midseason photo is the sole known picture of the first pro lineup. Goaltender Mark Tooze is the only regular who is absent.

By the time the Wanderers arrived in Toronto, the OHA stomping grounds, amateur hockey's last bastion, had become home to no fewer than five professional hockey clubs. The latest was out of Belleville, still smarting from the Reddy McMillan fiasco. Guelph and Berlin were clearly the strongest, so that is where the Montreal gang headed next on their road trip.

The other Ontario pro games bore a strong resemblance to the Toronto affair. In Guelph, the visitors from Montreal had to come from behind to beat the Royals 5–3. In Berlin, however, they could not pull off the same feat for a third time and were edged out 9–8 by the Dutchmen.

It all proved a good warmup for the Wanderers. They took the Stanley Cup back from the Thistles less than two weeks later.

These games had shown, in a nutshell, that the new Ontario professional teams could hold their own against the club that reigned as champions of the Dominion. The message they took from it was undeniable: they might themselves challenge for the Stanley Cup.

All things considered, the first professional hockey season in Toronto had been a fair success. The Professionals probably did not make money, and their record was only 2–5–1, but they had become the club of choice for a good chunk of local fans. As far as the city's dreams of a first Stanley Cup were concerned, the Torontos were also the only choice.

To make this go, however, Miln needed more than a handful of exhibition games at Mutual. Next year, his Toronto Professionals would have to be in a league, for which he already had a franchise. But, the best-laid plans notwithstanding, that league would not be the International Hockey League.

CHAPTER SEVEN

THE PROS ON THE MARCH

The Ontario Professional Hockey League Is Formed

———•◦•———

*All the hockey world is laughing at a so-called professional hockey league
that can only get players that real professional leagues don't want. It's not a
professional league at all. It's a disqualified amateurs' league.*[1]

—*Toronto Telegram*

As 1907 progressed, Alexander Miln was putting together the next phase
of his plan: a shot at the Stanley Cup for his Toronto Professionals. We
can only guess, however, as to what he was thinking about developments
in the sports world around him. There can be no question that he was
acutely aware of them. This was the era of the Athletic War, a vicious
power struggle between elites in Montreal and Toronto over control of
the country's amateur sports, not just hockey. Miln's team was operating
in the epicentre of amateur purism, Toronto, and in the backyard of its
most zealous advocate, John Ross Robertson's OHA.

It is hard to exaggerate the incongruities and absurdities that grew
out of Canada's Athletic War. Historically, the promoters of professional
sports had often been seen as suspect characters. But, by the fall of 1907,
it was the governors of amateur athletics who were increasingly viewed
as disreputable. Rival "national" sports bodies—the Toronto-based

Canadian Amateur Athletic Union and the Montreal-based Amateur Athletic Federation of Canada—were stuck in a quagmire of mutual disqualifications. So savage was the squabble that the very capacity of the Dominion for self-government—at least in sports—would soon be called into question.

There could be no doubt that the CAAU was gradually gaining the upper hand in the battle for sports supremacy. Already the larger and more established organization, it embarked on an aggressive campaign to organize Canadian athletics from coast to coast. Key to its efforts was the creation of a series of provincial wings that mirrored the federal nature of the country. Amid competing charges of hypocrisy, it seemed only fitting that the Union would be organized as a federation, while the Federation was a unitary body.

However, the CAAU, infused as it now was with John Ross Robertson's ideology, was also plagued with all the governance disputes that had racked the Ontario Hockey Association under his leadership. As in the OHA, lacrosse players were expelled from the Union en masse, with no exceptions. During the year, there were on-again, off-again ruptures with associations governing skating, canoeing, bowling and, most notably, rugby football. The last occurred after the CAAU thought it had scored a big coup in the country's rising summer game.

The new Interprovincial Rugby Football Union, also known as the "Big Four," had been formed under the auspices of the CAAU. It would consist of the Montreal (AAA) Winged Wheelers and Ottawa Rough Riders in the east and the Toronto Argonauts and Hamilton Tigers in the west. Almost immediately, however, the CAAU and IRFU descended into an ugly scrap. The issue was the amateur status of Montrealer Ernie Russell, who also happened to be a member of the (professional) Stanley Cup champion Wanderers. The IRFU and the Argonauts—home club of the chair of the CAAU's registration committee, J. G. Merrick— promptly left the organization.

As a consequence, though, the CAAU began to manage such disputes more pragmatically. Knowing that an affiliation with the Federation was lurking round the corner, the Union started to resolve rule conflicts by agreeing to forgive past transgressions in exchange for future adherence. This was a significant deviation from its own strict amateur code, but the CAAU was clearly prepared to do so if it would strengthen the organization. Such expediency would prove particularly troublesome in one high-profile case.

That would involve the sensational aboriginal runner Tom Longboat from the Six Nations reserve near Brantford, Ontario. The Onondaga runner had gained notoriety by winning area races while still a teenager. He was six weeks short of his twentieth birthday when he entered the Boston Marathon for the first (and only) time—and he went on to win in 2:24:24, shattering the previous record by a remarkable five minutes.

Longboat's win in Boston had been phenomenal. Running with a

Tom Longboat was now a national hero, but this champion long-distance runner was about to become the highest-profile pawn in the Athletic War.

bad cold, in rain and chilly weather, the youngster quickly won over the crowd that braved the elements. As the Boston *Globe* reported, "they saw in Tom Longboat the most marvellous runner who has ever sped along our roads. With a smile for everyone, he raced along and at the finish he looked anything but like a youth who had covered more miles in a couple of hours than the average man walks in a week."[2]

There was a problem, though. Through the eyes of those who wish to see nothing but amateur purity, the kid the Canadian newspapers were calling "the noble red man"[3] sure looked like a professional athlete. Accused of irregular training, he had no evident occupation other than running. His manager, the flamboyant promoter Tom Flanagan, claimed he controlled all the cash and paid Longboat only expenses.

Based on accumulating evidence—and perhaps some jealousy—Longboat ran afoul of American authorities. James E. Sullivan, the powerful boss of the Amateur Athletic Union of the United States, wanted him declared a professional. The CAAU's nationalistic defence of Longboat quickly became another factor in worsening relations with the American body. Finally, the AAU severed its link with the CAAU and affiliated with the AAFC instead. The already complex world of athletic sanction and censure now became doubly so for any Canadian contestant crossing the border.

There was, however, an even bigger complication on the horizon: the Olympics. The Summer Games of 1908 had originally been awarded to Rome, but would now be held in London. Relocation had been deemed necessary due to increased concern over volcanic eruptions.

Italy, it turned out, was not the only country where the Games were being threatened by explosion. Back in Canada, it was dawning on people that a team had to be named—but by whom, and including whom? All the country's top athletes had been banned by either the CAAU or the AAFC—or both. Technically, the responsibility for it all fell on the British Olympic Committee, which still had formal jurisdiction for the Dominion. Wanting nothing to do with this "colonial" problem, the British assigned the task to the governor general, Earl Grey, who in turn passed off the unholy mess to his secretary, Colonel John Hanbury-Williams, who then turned for help to prominent Ottawa publisher P. D. Ross. And Ross, of course, just happened to be a Stanley Cup trustee. As such, he had long been annoyed with the rigid CAAU and insisted that it had to work with the more flexible AAFC.

Throughout the winter, Hanbury-Williams struggled to put together an arrangement. Every time a deal seemed close, one side or the other would balk or face internal dissension. Petty and pompous public denunciations rang back and forth between the two groups of Edwardian gentlemen. The Union accused the AAFC's leaders of being "professionals." The Federation replied that the CAAU men were "shamateurs." During it all, Hanbury-Williams publicly articulated useful, if somewhat condescending, pearls of wisdom in an effort to encourage an agreement. In exasperation, he observed simply that "this is a big country, and we have to have big minds and big views to settle difficult points."[4]

However, while the great debate over amateurism dragged on, the hockey world had already moved on. As the 1907–08 season approached, professional hockey was no longer a curiosity—anywhere. It had become a reality in every part of the country. Nor were there any serious attempts to hide this professionalism from view. It was a proud and open world of competition.

The country's elite hockey organization, the Eastern Canada Amateur Hockey Association, still paid lip service to the formalities of amateurism. The league, home to the Stanley Cup champion Montreal Wanderers, would meticulously publish lists of its amateur and admitted pro players. But except for the also-ran Montreal Victorias, the league was essentially professional.

All around the ECAHA were competitor leagues that practised professionalism pure and simple. Also based in eastern Ontario and Quebec, the Federal league was still crawling along. Farther west and north, there was the ascendant Upper Ottawa Valley circuit. Even farther west and north, the Temiskaming league paid out money—in wages and wagers—by the wheelbarrow.

Pro leagues had also set up shop in the farther-flung sections of the Dominion. Manitoba, long a hockey power in its own right, had a credible association that stretched from Brandon to Kenora. The New Ontario Hockey League pulled together the other towns in the northwestern portion of the province. In the former territories of Alberta and Saskatchewan, the Interprovincial league had been established. Efforts were being made to do the same in the Maritimes.

All of this made the job of the Stanley Cup trustees increasingly complicated. Any pro league in the country could file a challenge for the trophy. Even the Canadian Soo team of the U.S.-headquartered International league was eligible if it could take the title. In December, the trustees mandated a semifinal for the first time, requiring the champions of the Federal league, the Ottawa Victorias, to take on the Upper Ottawa Valley's Renfrew Creamery Kings before they got a shot at the Wanderers.

The new world of professional hockey was a chaotic, booming business. Matches between the country's two leading clubs, the Wanderers and the Ottawa Silver Seven, were drawing as many as 7,000 spectators. Tickets in Montreal were reportedly scalped for as much as $15. Even a country town like Pembroke could pull in two and a half thousand for a big game.

As profitable as hockey could be, however, this new industry lacked any real structure. The only unifying element was the quest for the Stanley Cup, whose guardians had long maintained a hands-off policy on league governance. Periodic suggestions of a "national commission" between the various circuits did not lead to any serious discussions.

With no body to enforce agreements, "contract jumping" by players was widespread. Salaries escalated as teams openly raided each other for players, sometimes even within the same league. It was not uncommon for a quality performer to suit up with multiple teams in the same year, or to be employed in two different leagues at the same time. The phenomenon was reaching its logical extreme in Edmonton, where local management began buying star players from across the country as part of its plan to assemble a Cup contender.

Another downside of unregulated competition was the inability of pro leagues to enforce on-ice discipline. It should be noted that, contrary to what the amateur organizers claimed, violence in hockey was by no means a professional phenomenon. The papers of the day are full of on-ice assaults, all-out brawls and spectator bedlam in the unpaid ranks. However, when amateur leagues dealt with these, they could enforce their rulings throughout the amateur world.

When it came to violence in sports, Canadian hockey stood in intriguing contrast to American football in these early years. In the 1890s, the United States had moved to ban such dangerous plays as the flying wedge, a strategy taken from Napoleon that involved a "V" formation of players zeroing in on a single opponent. By 1905, the American press was so concerned with the rising death and injury tolls on the gridiron that universities across the country began banning the sport. It ultimately took the intervention of President Theodore Roosevelt to bring about the changes—such as the forward pass—that would deal with the issue.[5]

Hockey took no such actions at any level.[6] Professional hockey in particular lacked the system-wide rules necessary to control violence. For example, when "Bad" Joe Hall and Harry Smith of the Winnipeg Maple Leafs were suspended by the Manitoba league for particularly brutal play, they promptly received offers of employment in other parts of the country. The league then backed off. Smith was the same one who, along with his brother Alf and Baldy Spittal, had been involved in a vicious stick-swinging attack during an Ottawa–Wanderer contest the previous season.

The Ottawa–Wanderer incident had underscored the impotence of even the ECAHA. With the league unable to act, Montreal Arena management had to call in the police, who decided to arrest the three capital city players. Indeed, intervention by the authorities that season culminated in a murder charge against Charles Masson of the Ottawa Vics. He was apprehended after the Federal league's leading scorer, Owen "Bud" McCourt, died as a result of a multiplayer altercation at Cornwall.

Nonetheless, the year's tragedy with the most lasting consequence actually occurred during the off-season. Before the 1907–08 campaign began, it was reported that Hod Stuart, widely acknowledged as the game's greatest player, had perished in a diving accident. To raise funds for his widow and children, the

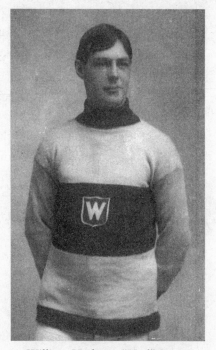

William Hodgson "Hod" Stuart was considered hockey's greatest player at the time of his premature death in 1907. His passing led to the staging of the first professional all-star game.

ECAHA assembled a team of its best players to take on the remaining Wanderers in an exhibition contest played on January 2, 1908, before 3,800 paying spectators in Montreal.

The professional all-star game had been born.

If John Ross Robertson seems less of a force in these times, there was more to it than the growth of professionalism in hockey. Now in his late sixties, he was beginning to consciously pattern himself after that other aging ruler, Edward VII. Like the king, Robertson increasingly spoke in favour of leisure and attempted to seek it himself.

"His concept of it was unique," biographer Ron Poulton wrote. "He was really a compulsive worker, but Edwardian enough to pose with ease as an absentee owner. The lid of an ever-ready steamer trunk was constantly being slammed; and word would filter through the lower echelons of the *Telegram* that he was prowling again through the hospitals, libraries and museums of Europe, or lolling the lobby of some favoured Southern hotel, adding to his collection of 'darkie' jokes."[7]

Robertson had so many other interests, it is a wonder he had any time at all for the game. He had other "causes" at which to aim his newspaper's slings and arrows, chief among them the suffragette movement. As a dedicated Edwardian, he believed absolutely in "the age of men," not the vote of women.

Robertson also became fascinated with the automobile and loved to show off his latest acquisition while being driven about Toronto by his chauffeur, Frank Yewman. He was involved in horse racing and in charity fundraising (mostly for the Children's Hospital) and he travelled extensively to add to his growing collection of artefacts. His eccentricities were both charming—like the five dollars' worth of change he carried in his pocket each day for the panhandlers he would encounter on his way to the office—and curious. He had an insatiable appetite for funerals, going to as many as five in one week. Yewman liked to claim his boss held "the all-Canadian record" for attending such memorials "and he always cried quicker than anyone else."[8]

The old man was increasingly leaving the job of daily editing the *Telegram* to his trusted second, John "Black Jack" Robinson. Likewise, he had formally passed the mundane matters of the OHA to its future presidents. He did, however, continue to be the power behind the throne. With his position of past president set to expire at the upcoming OHA annual meeting, it was arranged for Robertson to be declared a "life member" of the executive. Along with his perennial colleagues, Secretary Hewitt and CAAU representative Nelson, and their Three White Czars subcommittee, John Ross could wield his power whenever it suited him, just like at the *Tely*.

———

It is not clear whether Robertson felt the need. Professionalism might be rampant, but it was also now effectively outside his Ontario Hockey Association. In fact, he and his followers were taking considerable satisfaction from the on- and off-ice challenges facing the pro game. Similarly, where senior amateur hockey elsewhere might be in disarray, the OHA was still the leading league in Canada's largest province. In Toronto, Alex Miln's new artificial-ice arena at Mutual had not yet materialized, putting the International Hockey League franchise for his fledgling local pro club in doubt.

In truth, Toronto was the least of the IHL's concerns. Not only had its ambitious expansion plans failed to pan out, but early in November the outfit folded altogether. While the softening economy was blamed, the truth was that growing pro competition had been slowly undermining the league. In just three years, bidding for players from back home had driven up salaries by two-thirds. The growth of professionalism in Canada, initially fuelled by the IHL, would ultimately finish the IHL.

The American pro game did not disappear immediately. In Pittsburgh, the Western Pennsylvania Hockey League was re-established. The clubs of Sault Ste. Marie and Houghton, home of Doc Gibson, went amateur, but continued to barnstorm. Every preseason, reports on the imminent founding of a new U.S. pro league would circulate. Nonetheless, the IHL's day had passed.

This led outgoing OHA President D. L. Darroch to dismiss the pro threat in his final address, a speech that could have been written by Robertson himself. Darroch attributed the previous year's rebellion to mercenary rink managers—which would include both Miln and Guelph's Buck Irving. He blamed Irving especially, seeing his famous "charges" as an orchestrated plot to encourage professionalism. This reading was probably accurate, but his assertion that the Ontario pros had given up all hope was just wishful thinking.

While the Barrie and Belleville professional clubs had quietly fizzled, Toronto, Guelph and Berlin had completed the previous year on a high note. Games with the Montreal Wanderers and with each other had been well attended. Now a flood of exiled OHA talent was pouring back into Ontario from the defunct International league. With professional hockey already flourishing on the province's periphery, conditions were set for the first pro league in the OHA's heartland.

On November 12, 1907, the remaining Ontario professional clubs gathered in Berlin to form the Canadian Hockey League. Despite its official name, the organization was widely called the Ontario Professional

TORONTO CLUB IN PRO. LEAGUE

Berlin, Guelph, and Brantford the Other Towns Represented— Alex. Miln President.

Berlin, Nov. 13.—The Canadian Hockey League, composed of professional hockey clubs of Toronto, Guelph, Berlin, and Brantford, was organized here yesterday. Delegates were present from four towns, and were enthusiastic, with prospects for a successful season.

The circuit is compact, and traveling expenses will be small. Officers were elected as follows:

Hon. President, J. P. Downey, M.L.A. Guelph.

President, Alex. Milne, Toronto.

Vice-President, A. B. Burnley, Brantford.

Secretary, N. E. Irving, Guelph.

Treasurer—O. Vogelsang, Berlin.

Executive—J. C. Palmer, Toronto; J. A. Fitzgerald, Guelph; Roy Brown, Brantford, and Geo. Boehmer, Berlin.

An adjourned meeting of the Executive will be held Friday, Nov. 22, at which the constitution will be adopted and the schedule arranged for the season.

The league will play under O.H.A. rules. Provision has been made whereby teams will not outbid each other for players.

The barnstorming circuit of the previous season had become a full-fledged organization.

Hockey League almost immediately. Brantford was admitted as the circuit's fourth member.

Although the Telephone City was alone in not having an existing club, Brantford had been a rumoured centre of pro insurrection for some time. It had been hit hard by the OHA's expulsion of lacrosse players in 1904. In the winter of 1905–06, local exile Roy Brown had attempted to organize a team in the city while he was also part of Toronto's pro practice squad. A top defenceman, Brown had wanted to play in Ontario rather than the International league. He was immediately named the playing manager of the new team.

The OPHL was clearly feeling confident. Before it had played a single game, it announced that its champion would challenge for the Stanley Cup.

Alex Miln found himself wearing two hats as president of the new Ontario pro league and manager of its Toronto club.[9] After his IHL plans had fallen through, he had worked with Irving—now OPHL secretary—to put together the new provincial body. He had not pursued a rumoured possibility of getting Toronto into the big Eastern league; without a larger building to pay the freight, he wanted a more compact circuit with modest travel costs.

This does not mean Miln had given up on making Toronto's "new rink" a reality. His backers were buying the land all around the existing building. By the end of 1907 they had everything along Shuter Street from Mutual to Dalhousie Street. In truth, the venture seemed only a matter of time.

In the meantime, Miln's Ontario partners had carefully chosen each other from a number of applicants. They were trying to put together a stable and collegial outfit. They also sought to address some of the complaints against professionalism. Miln was particularly clear about getting rid of late-season ringers:

> The addition of a very strong residence rule . . . will not give the clubs a chance to import players at any stage of the season, as was done by Kenora last year in the Western League when they brought in nearly all the Ottawa team. We don't intend to have any farce of this kind.[10]

However, President Miln's number-one job was to keep the Ontario teams from raiding each other. This was essential, given the intense competition already coming from the other pro circuits. The OHA news organs—the *Telegram*, *Star* and *Globe*—needled the OPHL every time it lost a player to its competitors. As noted, Robertson's *Tely* was particularly savage:

> All the hockey world is laughing at a so-called professional hockey league that can only get players that real professional leagues don't want. It's not a professional league at all. It's a disqualified amateurs' league.[11]

Henry John "Con" Corbeau hailed from the Francophone community of Penetanguishene. Berlin signed him to be captain, but he was allowed to go to Toronto after the Dutchmen replaced their management.

Long rumoured to be headed from the Marlboros to the Professionals, Charles Rowland "Chuck" Tyner was a quality goalkeeper. This photograph comes from a set of postcards of the 1907–08 team, of which it appears only two still exist.

The unfortunate truth for the OHA was that, whatever the OPHL lost to other pro leagues, it made up for by raiding the old association. It had already taken all of Guelph and Berlin—probably the two best OHA teams before their defection. To these it added a few new amateur signings. It also grabbed many of the Ontarians returning from the States, although some would wait till after Christmas in order to first play for a few weeks on Pittsburgh's artificial ice.

On the whole, the Ontario teams looked decent. Roy Brown brought fellow International travellers like Billy "Lady" Taylor, Jack Marks, John Ward and Alfred "Cap" McDonald back to Brantford with him. Berlin had preserved a quality core of men who had been performing together for years. They had, of course, been OHA senior champions in 1905–06. Among the group, only Guelph was suspect. The Royals had had the best record of the barnstorming teams of 1906–07; however, while hyping his efforts to sign IHL star Fred Taylor, Irving had let much of his local talent slip away.

The Toronto Hockey Club was building on its lineup from that first year. While the team had come in for some criticism over its shifting personnel, there had been a stable core of familiar names. Mark Tooze (goal), Hugh Lambe (point), Rolly Young (usually cover), Bruce Ridpath (usually rover) and Jack Carmichael (centre) had played all eight games in 1906–07. With Frank McLaren apparently retired, Charlie Liffiton and Harry Burgoyne had settled in at the wings.

Preseason reports indicated all the veterans were available, but that

PROGRAM FOR CANADIAN CURLERS IN SCOTLAND

Rev. John Kerr Sends Details of Arrangements for the Reception of the Toronto—Western Ontario Men to Meet in Toronto To-morrow Afternoon.

CLARENCE DOHENY PLAYED ROVER

Former St. Michael's College Goalkeeper Starred for Cobourg at Peterboro.

CHAMPIONS BY A BIG SCORE

Stratford Midgets Defeated Mary's by 14 to 4—Woodstock and Bracebridge Winners.

When Engines Get Weary and Cars Take a Rest
A Story of a Broken Rail.

Accidents happen---when rails break---and men fail--- on roads not protected by automatic safety devices

List to the story of the broken rail. It is on one of the biggest railroads in America. The track inspector has just passed, and everything to him is O.K. A heavy train follows. The enormous strain breaks a weak rail, but the heavy train passes in safety, leaving a death trap behind. The Limited Express comes booming by. It strikes the broken rail.

With a bump—thump—and jolt it jumps from the ties and topples over. One thing only prevents the entire train from dropping over an 18-foot embankment—that—the framework of the Signal Bridge.

Three men killed, many injured, traffic tied up, rolling stock damaged because of the broken rail.

Accidents like this cannot happen with the Price System for Automatic Stopping and Controlling of Trains, for the broken rail would have actuated the device, and the train would have been stopped in safety.

We can prove this to your absolute satisfaction if you will call at our Exhibition Rooms, 12-14 Wellington St. East, top floor, Norwich Union Building, any day, between 9 a.m. and 6 p.m.

Universal Signal Co., Ltd.
12-14 Wellington St. East, Toronto.

SHRUBB SAW LONGBOAT BEAT DORANDO SATURDAY

Little Englishman Looking for Pointers for His New York Race With the Indian—Some Comment on the Coming Race.

ICE RACES POSTPONED UNTIL TO-MORROW

O.H.A. CHAMPIONS BEAT CLIFFSIDES

14th Regiment of Kingston Easily Defeated Inter-Provincial Team by 10 Goals to 5.

GEO. VAN HORNE CAPTAIN

Soldiers, at a Meeting Before the Game, Elect Their Leader for the Current Season.

AT THE PRO. HOCKEY GAME.

Fred Taylor of Ottawa didn't see why he should go off.

Chuck Tyner, in the net for the local pros., was O.K.

How the Ottawa bunch stopped the Toronto forwards.

Before action photos were feasible, it was common for newspapers like the *Toronto Star* to run sketches of matches in its game reports.

Ottawa's Dey's Arena (*above and below*) was a significant hockey landmark, but an unlikely one for Hobey Baker's final game as a member of the Princeton team.

WALKING ON WATER NO MIRACLE FOR CANADIAN

1—Ridpath standing on his hands on water shoes. 2—Sailing. 3—Walking, aiding legs with hands. 4—Walking upright. 5—Ridpath and his shoes, showing on the left the bottom of the shoe and the fins, and on the right the deck and cockpit of the shoe. 6— Ridpath carrying his canoe while walking in water.

Special to the Reporter.

Toronto, July 1.—When one walks on the water, moves along rapidly without meeting accident, and does it with an ease that would grace a pedestrian on a public street, he is doing something remarkable, although it is hardly a miracle.

Bruce Ridpath, canoe expert, walks upon the water. Ridpath is of an inventive turn of mind. After he had tired somewhat of the comparative ease in which he shot his canoe over the surface he set about the construction of a pair of "water shoes" that would enable him to travel, with "foot motion," over the deep.

The "water shoes" are constructed on the principle of snow shoes. Ridpath can walk on water at a five-mile an hour gait.

Bruce Ridpath displaying his canoeing prowess.

This postcard shows Pittsburgh's Duquesne Gardens – hockey's leading artificial-ice arena – in its heyday.

Toronto Professionals jersey (1906–07).

Montreal Wanderers jersey (1907–08).

Toronto Professionals jersey (1908–09).

Kenora Thistles jersey (1906–07).

Toronto Professionals jersey (1907–08).

Toronto St. Michael's College jersey (1910–11).

Toronto Tecumsehs jersey (1912–13).

Montreal Canadiens jersey (1912–13).

Toronto Blue Shirts jersey (1913–14).

Renfrew's Creamery Kings became known as the Millionaires, but their all-star lineup never did land the Stanley Cup.

E.D. LALONDE

BRUCE RIDPATH

K. MALLEN

DON SMITH

SKEIN RONAN

LESTER PATRICK OF RENFREW CLUB

FRANK PATRICK OF RENFREW CLUB

Early hockey trading cards such as these were included in packages of tobacco and cigarettes.

Whether it was played on the big city rinks or the frozen ponds of Sarnia Bay,
hockey quickly became a permanent part of Canadian life.

they would have to compete against a wider talent pool. Ridpath, who was in Europe on a canoe tour, was considered safe. So was Young, who succeeded him as captain. The rest would be tested in December tryouts against IHL returnees and a number of Varsity students wanting to turn pro. Only Bert Brown, the team's spare man at last season's end, was trying to get back into amateur athletics.

The consensus was that the Torontos would enter the year with a strengthened roster. Howard Gee returned from Manitoba to play cover once again. He would be joined on defence by point man Con Corbeau. Corbeau was a 185-pound International league veteran who had once captained Victoria Harbour, the OHA intermediate champion of 1904–05. Bert Morrison also returned to squeeze out Carmichael at centre. A former star at Upper Can-

As an emerging young star, Bertram Clifford Morrison had played for a select Toronto squad against the Stanley Cup challenger Winnipeg Victorias when they came through town in 1900. Much travelled since, Bert was one of the first career pro hockey players.

ada College, Morrison had been on American payrolls for years, although he had also been part of the stillborn Toronto pro team of 1905–06.

The real coup for the Professionals was getting the goalie they had wanted all along: Chuck Tyner of the disbanding Marlboros. Tyner was another in the long line of players who had been the subject of Irving's charges, been given a clean bill of health by the OHA and then gone pro anyway. The aspiring doctor would be joined by IHL forward Ken Mallen. Soon to play rover, Mallen was said to be Tyner's fellow student at the University of Toronto. Tooze was forced to look elsewhere, as were Liffiton and Burgoyne, while Lambe was retained as the spare man.

By the time this lineup had come together, Toronto was within a week of its home opener. In the lead-up to the big event, it was announced the club would be changing its colours for the upcoming campaign. Brantford wanted purple and white, so the locals decided to switch to garnet and grey. The inspiration for the choice was likely an OHA junior club, the Toronto Simcoes. The irony was that the Simcoes had been started up many years earlier by no less than John Ross Robertson himself.

The Simcoes of this day were managed by Edward Marriott. "Teddy" had taken over the club after leaving the Marlboros in 1905.[12] When Miln became the boss at Mutual, he recruited Marriott for increasingly important assignments, including as icemaker and boss of the building's restaurant. For all practical purposes, Teddy became the assistant manager of the Toronto Professionals.

The Professionals would wear the new colours on Saturday night, January 4, when Berlin would be their scheduled guests at the old Mutual Street Rink. The Dutchmen were an ensemble that had endured since the players were youngsters in the Western Ontario Athletic Association. They would face what was, at best, a two-piece outfit.

One part was the previous year's barnstorming team and its antecedent, the Toronto Marlboros. Ridpath and Young—moved to left and right wing respectively—had been together for three seasons. They had been joined by Lambe and (briefly) Gee the previous year. Tyner had played with them the two years before that. The other half was the former Calumet Miners of the International league. That was where Mallen had spent most of the past three winters. Corbeau had been there part of the past two. Morrison became their teammate in 1906–07.

Berlin almost did not come to town. During the preseason, a serious dispute had arisen with the other OPHL owners. Guelph's Irving had signed one Berlin star, Nelson "Uncle" Gross, while Brantford manager Brown and owner Fred Westbrook had poached another, Edward "Goldie" Cochrane. The Dutchmen threatened to quit the league if they were not returned. The rivals relented and Berlin stuck.

Even so, the Torontos' season opener seemed jinxed from the beginning. The morning newspapers were not even thinking hockey. They were instead consumed with the sudden passing of Ned Hanlan at age fifty-two. The "Boy in Blue" had been Canada's first-ever world champion—a rowing prize he captured before 100,000 spectators on the River Thames—and he had been the city's most beloved athlete for years. "The death of Edward Hanlan removed the most famous oarsman that ever lived," reported the *Globe*. "Nor is it likely that any other who comes after him will occupy so large a share of public attention." [13]

An early thaw in the winter of 1907–08 played havoc with the city's winter sports. It would leave the Mutual Street Rink with virtually no ice for the Torontos' home opener.

There was yet another serious distraction: the weather. Toronto was experiencing a sustained early-season thaw. As a contemporary cartoon illustrates (above), the ice was disappearing everywhere. Besides threatening game conditions, the situation left little opportunity for the home team to practice.

Nevertheless, 1,800 spectators streamed into the rink that night to see the match, again demonstrating Toronto's hunger for top-rank hockey. The crowd included a couple of hundred who had come down on a special train from Berlin.

Berlin won by a score of 3–0, but the game reports focused more on the appalling circumstances than on the actual play. The *News* labelled

Harvey Corbeau was considered a better skater than cousin Con. Although an OPHL all-star in 1907–08, he did not match his relative's eventual success in the pro game.

it "Hockey on Bare Floor" and observed that "by the time play ceased there was not ten yards of solid ice in the rink." [14] In such conditions, players hitting exposed boards were thrown headlong. The puck was often indistinguishable from the sugary slush mixing with the sand beneath.

The consensus was best summed up by the *World*: "The Flying Dutchmen of Berlin proved better mud horses than the Torontos." [15]

The Professionals, like the Marlboros before them, were a fast, skilled but light unit, especially up front. They had decent goaltending, but suspect defence. Predictions generally held that they could take the Dutchmen in a real contest on good ice, and these predictions were prescient, for Toronto's games against Berlin would be the pivotal matches of that first OPHL season.

The Toronto Professionals' second match of the season was out of town against Brantford, the team many considered the strongest in the league. Just the same, "Brown's Braves" [16] were also off to a rough start, having lost their first game to Guelph. The Pros did some shuffling. As Gee was down with a bad cold, Lambe came in at point and Corbeau moved up to cover.

The Torontos again lost. They fell 7–6 after Morrison, who had led the visitors' attack, broke a skate and had to sit out. By this time even Robertson's *Tely* raved about the encounter on Brantford ice, calling it "a tremendously fast game, with brilliant combination . . . played before a record crowd." [17] Readers must have wondered how the *Telegram*'s sports department managed to get such copy past the publisher.

For Brantford, Taylor and Marks had led the charge. A side story was the Braves' attempt to slip the ageless Pete Charlton into their lineup. He had come from Pittsburgh for the occasion. Alas, old Pete arrived with two right skates and could not lace up. Despite some inkling he had really come only to sign up players for the Western Pennsylvania league, a generous management paid him anyway.

Only three days after losing in Brantford, the Torontos would face their next road test at Guelph. This first of two matches against the Royal City septet was gaining a sense of urgency. While the twelve-game OPHL season was long by Ontario standards—an OHA team typically played four to eight—being in last place with a 0–2 record was still worrisome. The Royals were supposed to be the league's weak sisters. Victories against them were thus essential.

An expert speed and figure skater, William Kenneth Russell Mallen was a frequent target of opponents when in close quarters. Malicious reports following Kenny's departure from Toronto depicted him as unhappy about a lack of media attention.

The hometown had a couple of interesting characters in its lineup. Harvey Corbeau, at cover, was the cousin of Toronto's Con. Also dressed was none other than Buck Irving himself. The league's secretary, the rink owner's son and the team's manager was also Guelph's point man. However, Irving injured a knee early in what would prove to be his last game as a player.

For the Torontos, Lambe[18] got his second straight start, with Corbeau again moved to cover. This time, no explanation was given for Gee's absence on defence. One presumes he was quietly cut at some point. Hereafter, his name vanishes from all reports.

Toronto defeated Guelph 4–3 and was judged very lucky to have won. Despite leading 2–0 at the half and 3–1 early in the second, they were badly outplayed and the score was tied with less than two minutes remaining in the game. Tyner had been great in what the Guelph *Mercury* considered the best hockey game ever played there. It ruefully described the winning marker, a hat-trick goal by Toronto's centre:

> Finally, Bert Morrison lifted a shot from the side. Booth got in front of it, but the puck went through his skates and rolled tantalizingly and slowly, but very surely into the nets. It was all over but the shouting, and there wasn't much of that.[19]

With the bare victory, one particular gripe among Toronto hockey fans was reaching a crescendo: the decision to play Rolly Young at right wing while moving Mallen to rover—a peculiar arrangement from the outset. Young had played rover before, whereas Mallen had been sought specifically to fill the right-wing position. Although Rolly had worked hard in the first three games, his "serpentine" rushing style left him constantly out of position. At the same time, Mallen, while clearly having speed to burn, had sometimes seemed indifferent in his efforts.

This photograph of the 1907–08 Toronto Professionals was clearly taken early in the season. Standing (L to R): F. Carroll, B. Morrison, H. Lambe, C. Corbeau, B. Ridpath. Sitting (L to R): K. Mallen, R. Young, C. Tyner.

Whatever the reason for this odd placement, the situation was resolved when Mallen defected to the ECAHA's Montreal Wheelers shortly after the game at Guelph. Next came word that Morrison—to this point the team's best performer—was also going to Montreal, to play for the Shamrocks. His stint there was said to be a temporary, second-employer arrangement. If the management of the Toronto Professionals were not worried before, they surely were now.

Miln quickly brought in two new men. One was Walter Mercer, Guelph's former star right winger. Irving cried foul, but he had already lost Wally before the season began. Mercer had been with the Ottawa Vics for their Stanley Cup semifinal against Renfrew. Interestingly, Mercer had played against Con Corbeau, then a ringer with the Creamery Kings.

The other man was a young French Canadian far better known— and better rated—at the time as a lacrosse player. He was the star goalkeeper of the Cornwall Lacrosse Club, one of the country's best. Soon, however, the potential of "Newsy" Lalonde in the national winter sport would become evident for all to see.

Without Lalonde, the Toronto Professionals were a good team. With him, they would become a Stanley Cup contender.

CHAPTER EIGHT

A BRUSH WITH ETERNITY

The Torontos Reach for the Stanley Cup

———•—•—•———

For the quintessence of gall commend us to this aggregation of false alarm
hockey statesmen, who have wired a challenge for the Stanley Cup: to wit
and namely the Toronto professionals. There can be no doubt but that the
Wanderers upon receiving the wire last night laughed themselves to sleep.[1]

—*Toronto Telegram*

None of the notices in Toronto had prepared fans for the significance of this new arrival. Newsy Lalonde's weight and toughness would add real punch to the Torontos' forward line, something it had been missing ever since the departure of Tommy Phillips back in the Marlboro era. Also unknown was the fierceness of Newsy's competitive streak and temper—attributes that were to make him a perpetual source of controversy.

The idea of signing Lalonde had come from Jimmy Murphy, manager of the Toronto Lacrosse Club and a respected local hockey coach. Besides the lacrosse connection, both Lalonde and Murphy hailed from Cornwall, the most easterly city in Ontario. The manufacturing centre was a significant sports hub of the day. Newsy had come up through the town's OHA and Federal league teams before moving on to the Canadian Soo for the International league's final campaign. He had had a good season there. However, he had started 1907–08 in Portage la Prairie, where the reviews had been poor.

The new lineup would face a return match with Guelph at Mutual on Saturday, January 18, 1908. Despite sticky ice and a poorly rated opponent, well over 2,000 jammed in to get a look at their team's overhaul. They were not disappointed. The reconfigured Torontos completely dominated the Royals and coasted to a 7–2 victory.

It should be noted that Guelph felt disadvantaged from the outset. Goaltender Bert Booth had not been able to make his train connection on time. There being no such thing as a backup goalie then, the Royals recruited local boy Tooze, the discarded Torontos backstopper, for the occasion. The Toronto papers gave him decent reviews, but Guelph's was sarcastic:

> One does not desire to be unduly harsh, but really Mark would be perfectly safe in enlisting for active service. He could go through quite a few campaigns without stopping anything.[2]

In reality, there were many good signs for the Torontos in the win. Young finally played rover and got two goals. Ridpath, scoreless in three decent efforts, at last got one of his own. The new man Mercer, though small, was the fastest on the ice and notched one as well.

The revelation was Newsy Lalonde. The new centre was anything but fancy on skates and, only hours off a two-day train ride from the west, he was tired. But he was also husky and aggressive with a hard, accurate shot. Always dangerous, he netted three for his new club. Guelph's reporter observed simply, but accurately, that he would be "one of the stars of the league in no time."[3]

With the home-and-away wins against Guelph, the Torontos had averted disaster. At 2–2, their record now compared favourably with those of both Berlin and Brantford, who were tied with two wins and one loss apiece. However, the Toronto squad had not beaten either of those competitors. As they headed to Berlin for a match the following Friday, the question was: were they a middling team or a genuine contender?

The Professionals would play the Dutchmen with the same lineup that had beaten Guelph at Mutual. Morrison was still away in Montreal, where his play with the Shamrocks had been stellar, but he had suffered an arm injury. It was unclear at this point whether he was temporarily recovering or planning to stay down east permanently.

The Torontos were plagued with rumours of other defections as well. It was known that Montreal interests had been approaching Tyner and Young. The Pittsburgh league had also been after the goalie and Ridpath for at least three seasons. On the other hand, Miln had just nailed down Lalonde. His $600 for the balance of the season was at that moment a decent big-league salary.

The Lalonde signing represented a clear and final shift away from the team's previous "cooperative" basis. Since their barnstorming days, the players had maintained a gate-sharing arrangement. However, the trend in the expanding world of pro hockey was unmistakably to employer-employee relationships. This development was probably inevitable. Some of the other OPHL clubs were already joint-stock companies. In Toronto, though, the employer would be the rink. The players' committee elected in November consisted of Young, the captain; Morrison, the veteran; and the rink boss. This underscored that Miln, rather than the committee, was really in charge.

The speedy Walter Hayes "Midget" Mercer was a horse trainer by profession. Known more as a playmaker and back-checker than a goal scorer, Wally found his arrival in Toronto contested by his former employer in Guelph.

This postcard features the Torontos' Edouard Cyrille Lalonde. While he got his nickname working in a newspaper plant as a youth, Newsy rarely had much to say in the press. He did, however, speak loudly on the ice—with his skills *and* his fists.

Miln's team arrived in Berlin as the definite underdog. The Dutchmen were coming off a loss at Brantford, but they seldom lost on their own ice and had not dropped two straight within anyone's memory. The nearly 2,000 who turned out at the Auditorium were giving odds of three or four to one for the home club.

Toronto got out to an early lead, and although the game was close, the visiting team never trailed. Nevertheless, with a minute and a half left and Mercer serving a penalty, Berlin evened the match at 5–5 off a goalmouth scramble. The Torontos vigorously disputed that tally, without success. As was the custom of the era, the goal umpire who upheld the ruling was replaced.

Another tradition of the time—one inherited from the amateur code—was the frowning upon of tied results. The teams therefore played a ten-minute overtime. Lalonde notched his sixth goal of the night in the first minute, after which the Torontos played defensively and, while the Dutchmen pressed hard, held on to win.

It was now clear that the Queen City seven could prevail against the best. Although Berlin had had an edge in the play, the Pros were good for the win. Tyner was a solid goalie who more than compensated for any weakness in the team's defence. With Lalonde up front, the fast forward unit was now also able to produce when the going got heavy. Even without Morrison, the Torontos were a contender.

Next up would be Brantford. The first of two games was scheduled for Mutual on Saturday, February 1. In other words, as early as 1907–08, a great and durable Toronto tradition was taking shape: the big-league Saturday-night hockey game.

By game day, the Braves had a marginal lead in the OPHL race at three wins and one loss. Toronto and Berlin were half a game back at 3–2. Guelph was down to 1–5 and rapidly falling out of contention. Any game among the other three was now a big one.

The good news for the Garnet and Grey was that Morrison, returned from his stint in Montreal, would finally be back in the lineup. As he was the faster skater and Lalonde the natural sniper, it made sense to leave Newsy at centre and move Bert to rover. Young and Corbeau were pushed back a slot, and Lambe reverted to spare.

The choice of Corbeau at point over Lambe had been a tough one. Hugh had played much better than anticipated, while Con was so far a disappointment. His offensive contribution had been limited and, though tough defensively, he was frequently dirty and heavily penalized.

There were almost 3,000 in the building that night, including 300 from Dykeville. With the largest crowd ever, there was barely room to breathe in the old Caledonian Rink. These patrons would be exposed to the OPHL's first big display of on-ice violence.

It was probably the roughest game ever seen in Toronto. Corbeau took on Brantford's Walter Miller. Young dropped gloves with Brown. Mercer tangled with Taylor. And Morrison mixed it up with John Mickus, the Braves' goalie. However, none of it compared to the vicious battle between Newsy Lalonde and Brantford cover Cap McDonald.

———

Both players were known to be capable of dirty play, and there was bad blood between them from the outset. Finally, just before the midpoint of the second half, Lalonde chopped McDonald hard across the arm. Cap retaliated by taking the lumber to the side of Newsy's head, rendering him unconscious on the ice. For this, referee Fred Waghorne gave McDonald fifteen minutes in penalties, after which Cap chose not to return to the rink—for his own safety. Lalonde got five minutes, but, despite having regained consciousness, was finished for the night.

Paradoxically, this incident could have turned the game in Brantford's favour had it happened sooner. Toronto was just starting to pull away at 7–3 when it occurred. Shorthanded, Brantford held its own. With both Lalonde and McDonald out, the visitors had a definite advantage when the teams were at even strength. Nevertheless, the Pros held on to win 10–7, all the Toronto skaters but Corbeau adding to the offence.

Ten days later, the rematch took place at Brantford's Burnley Rink. By then the Braves were rid of McDonald, although it was not clear whether he had been expelled by the league for his dirty play or merely cut from the roster. In either case, his penalties had been killing his club.

There was also a big crowd in the Telephone City. This included about a hundred coming down on a special train from the provincial capital. They represented an official Torontos fan club set up by friends of Tyner and Young at the University of Toronto. Those two were just returning from a brief stint in Montreal, where they had been hired by the Wheelers to play against Morrison and the Shamrocks.

It was a clean and brilliant contest. The Torontos were down 6–4 at the half, but dominated the second and went on to win 11–8. Ridpath and Young were said to be the stars, but once again, everyone pitched in. The Pros had shown that, no matter how Brantford played, they could beat them.

Only Berlin now stood between Toronto and the league championship. While the Pros were recording their two wins against Brantford, the Dutchmen had also defeated the Braves as well as racking up another one against Guelph. With Brantford reduced to 3–4, Toronto and Berlin were now tied for the league pennant at 5–2.

As one local reporter succinctly observed, "Berlin is now the team to beat."[4]

———

The coming Saturday contest at Mutual—February 15 with Berlin—was the professional team's biggest game yet. The winner would move ahead in the season series and take the undisputed lead in the Ontario race.

Despite mild weather and soft ice, the rink was again packed. Five hundred supporters of the Dutchmen came in for the big match, which was a fast, hard game. The Torontos had the edge in play, but Berlin goalie Charlie "Punch" Ellis had kept it close all through.

Then came the dramatic conclusion.

Late in the contest and leading 5–4, the homesters got into significant penalty trouble. With Morrison and Corbeau both off, the Dutchmen moved six men up for a frantic assault on Tyner's net. The locals responded by surrounding their goal like a "citadel."[5] It held the attackers off until Gross took a penalty and the visitors' momentum was lost.

DISGRACEFUL ASSAULT AT THE PRO. HOCKEY GAME

McDonald of Brantford Knocked Lalonde of Toronto Senseless With His Stick.

Toronto defeated Brantford by 10 goals to 7 in a professional hockey match at the Mutual Street Rink on Saturday night before the largest crowd of the season, the rink being jammed to the doors. The locals led all the way, the half-time score being 6 to 3. The ice was like glass, and the game very fast in spots, but was spoiled by the frequent delays and the unwillingness of some of the visiting team to abide by the referee's decisions. To their credit it must be said that the Toronto team obeyed without hesitation, which made the actions of the visitors very unpalatable to the spectators.

A Disgraceful Assault.

Overshadowing the game itself was

game again expostulating with the presiding official. With one man on the fence Brantford scored, Marks doing the rushing and Ward the necessary work in front of goal. Toronto 4, Brantford 3.

Corbeau hit Mickus with a wrist shot from the other end of the rink. Brown dashed back with the puck, and Taylor and Marks kept Tyner busy. McDonald got into the fray, and Lalonde handed him a crack, but escaped the referee's notice. Corbeau tried half a dozen long distance shots on goal, and Brown returned in kind. Once Marks and Brown nearly knocked the puck in the net trying to clear too quickly. McDonald cracked Morrison and got away with it. Young and Mercer were right inside, and from a scrimmage in the corner Mercer scored. Toronto 5, Brantford 3.

McDonald was ruled off again for slashing, and a moment later Brown and Young were benched for fighting. This left Brantford without a defence, Taylor played point, and saved several times. McDonald came back on the ice, and he and Ridpath clashed on the boards, both being put off. The teams were now playing five a side. Lalonde carried the puck down into the corner, wiggled out in front to get a

"NEWSY" LALONDE
The Toronto pro. hockey player, who was assulted by McDonald of Brantford at Saturday night's game.

On this occasion, the Toronto papers had every reason to be appalled.

Lalonde had again led the Toronto attack, scoring two and being constantly dangerous around the net. The playmaking Ridpath, whose speed and stickhandling just kept getting stronger, was the game's selfless star, his play and demeanour adored by the fawning crowd. The Torontos were now widely acknowledged as a solid seven from goal to left wing, with an ever-improving team game. Tyner had been a bit soft that night, but it was not a real concern.

On the other hand, Morrison was a worry. As each game passed, there was ever more pointed coverage in the local papers of his listless play. Hopping trains back and forth to play with the Montreal Shamrocks, he looked visibly tired to many. The Berlin game had been his fourth in five nights, all in different cities. However, this criticism may have been rooted as much in resentment of Bert's divided loyalties as in his actual performance, since his scoring stats—for both Toronto and the Shamrocks—remained healthy.

TORONTOS BEAT BERLIN IN SPECTACULAR GAME

Game Tied Up Three Times—
Kaisers Check Close All
the Way.

Lalonde............Center ... . Knell
Mercer............R. wing ... ..Dumart
Ridpath...........L. wing .... Schmidt
　Toronto scored first, but Berlin got the next two. Then Toronto evened, but a moment later Berlin again forged in front. Then the home team evened up and cinched it by two in a row just

After this close win over the Dutchmen, the Professionals would never look back.

Exactly one week after taking the OPHL lead, the Toronto Professionals hosted the Guelph Royals. The Royals' downward spiral was accelerating. The year before, they had taken four of their five exhibition games, losing only narrowly to the Montreal Wanderers. By now, however, the Speed River club was in turmoil.

Buck Irving's management errors were beginning to add up. Each loss seemed to be followed by wholesale changes to player personnel and pay arrangements. This sense of panic undermined both employee and fan loyalty. Irving's perpetual trick of getting spectators out through the false promise of a big new star was also wearing thin. Interests connected to the old Guelph Nationals were said to be actively looking for an alternative to Buck's team.

As they reached Toronto, though, the Royals were coming off their second win of the season—another surprise defeat of Brantford—and they gave the overconfident Torontos a bit of a scare. Early in the game, Guelph shot out to a 4–1 lead. Alas, although the visitors continued to play hard, the home squad gradually got untracked and eventually coasted to a 10–7 victory. Robertson's *Tely* characteristically alleged a pro conspiracy, noting that "some were uncharitable enough to remark that they were playing for a close score."[6]

Lalonde added yet another five goals, ably set up by Ridpath with two of his own. The usually unheralded Corbeau and Mercer, who were returning from a stint as ringers in the Temiskaming league, got some plaudits. In fact, the point man scored his first of the season. Morrison also got two goals—as well as more biting criticism of his play.

The following Tuesday, the Torontos were on their way to Berlin and another hugely important match against the Dutchmen. They were now holding a commanding lead in the OPHL race with seven wins and two losses. A road victory would virtually clinch the title for the Professionals.

Berlin was a good team, and every game against Toronto had been a contest. Its record of five wins and four losses was also closer to the leaders than it sounded. A recent narrow loss to Brantford had been overturned by the league due to the Braves' "borrowing" of a Guelph player. Thus, if the Dutchmen could win this one, they would have the same number of official defeats as the Torontos—and still be in it.

Two and a half thousand people came to Berlin that night from all across southwestern Ontario. "Tumultuous applause"[7] greeted Mayor Allan Huber as he dropped the puck wearing a silk hat, brand new for the occasion. The atmosphere was as tense as the stakes were high.

Besides the tight race, there was ill feeling between the teams. Berlin's star cover, Uncle Gross, had had a running feud with the Torontos—especially with his counterpart, Rolly Young—all season. However, Young, a Waterloo native, was ably supported by rooters from both his hometowns.

It turned out to be the Berliners who had nothing to cheer about. The Dutchmen were given "an unmerciful drubbing,"[8] on the losing end of a 9–1 score. The Torontos won in every category, including the battle with Gross. Young fought Gross "hammer and tongs"[9] all night long, aided by partner Corbeau. Con at one point picked up a wooden plank that had (somehow) fallen onto the ice and hurled it at the Berlin player. Near the end, the banged-up Dutchman finally retired for the evening.

For once, Morrison got grudging praise from the Toronto press. His six goals—including one with a two-man disadvantage—had earned him at least a bit of acclaim. More plaudits went to Ridpath, Young and Lalonde, who had done much of the playmaking. Berlin's successful attempt to shut down the French Canadian centre had served only to shift the team's attack to its rover.

While technically still in it, Berlin was, for all practical purposes, now finished. Toronto would have to lose both their remaining games, including one to Guelph. The Dutchmen would have to win both theirs, as well as a replay against Brantford. After that, they would have to beat the Torontos in a tiebreaker—hardly likely after this thrashing.

Recriminations were already beginning in Berlin, with some alleging that the team's abysmal performance was a consequence of being out of condition and "too intimate with the booze."[10]

The Torontos would anticlimactically lock up the championship a mere two nights later at Guelph. Although it was too late to make any difference, the Royals were starting to improve. They held the leaders to a five-all tie in the first half before finally succumbing 8–5. Lambe replaced the travelling Morrison in what was a rough and dirty game. No fewer than five players were laid out on the ice during the contest.

CHAMPION TORONTO PROS. CHALLENGE FOR THE CUP

Bert Morrison Taking the Rest Cure, So Hugh Lambe Played Last Night Against Guelph and Helped Toronto to Win by 8 Goals to 5—Royal City Team to Disband.

The Torontos, finishing the season with ten straight victories and wrapping up the first OPHL championship, were already looking ahead.

The Professionals' last game of the regular season was at home against Brantford on February 29. It would be a testament to the growing popularity of the team. Clearly, it was a nothing contest. As well, Roy Brown was notorious for his tedious delaying tactics against a fast opponent. The house was nevertheless packed to the rafters that Saturday night.

The game was a testament on the ice as well—to the rising Toronto powerhouse. Even with their goaltender playing well, the Braves were demolished by a score of 12–3. Lalonde led the way with eight goals and a fight. His brawl with Brantford right winger Jack Marks ended only when the police finally came on the ice—a first for the Queen City.

The reviews were stellar nonetheless. Billy Hewitt's sports pages at the *Star*, usually so skeptical, declared that "the local 'pros.' never showed up in Toronto so well as they did Saturday night."[11] Some reports even praised Morrison's play. With their tenth-straight victory, the Torontos' OPHL campaign could not be ending on a higher note.

At the same time as the Toronto Professionals were wrapping up the provincial championship, they were also lodging a Stanley Cup challenge with the trustees. Alex Miln contacted P. D. Ross and William Foran[12] in his capacity as president of the Ontario league, and they awarded his team a two-game, total-goals series set for March 14 and 16, conditional on the Montreal Wanderers successfully defending against the Winnipeg Maple Leafs on March 10 and 12.

Miln picked up Donald Smith from Portage la Prairie of the Manitoba league. Donny was from Cornwall, where he had played on the forward line with Reddy McMillan and the late Bud McCourt.

Considering that Miln's team had existed for less than a year and a half, the Mutual Street manager had every reason to savour the moment. Almost immediately, however, there was a serious complication. The trustees issued a decree barring from Cup competition all those who had played for more than one team during the season—an unprecedented intervention prompted by the rampant shifting of men and the hiring of ringers. After the outcry around moves by the Kenora Thistles and Montreal Wanderers in March 1907, Ross and Foran told the senior leagues that restrictions had to be put in place.

The trustees explained their actions in a public statement condemning "the promiscuous buying and selling of players" and "dishonorable [*sic*] violations of contracts." Further, they decried that "the present condition of hockey points to the Stanley Cup becoming merely a gate-money asset to the club executive which is willing to gamble highest and most shamelessly in the purchase of players."[13]

Unfortunately, every Toronto Professional except Ridpath and Lambe had played for another squad during the year. So, no sooner had the Wanderers wrapped up the ECAHA title than they filed a protest against the participation of Toronto players Mercer, Morrison, Tyner and Young in the Stanley Cup series.[14] The trustees backtracked significantly, but still banned Morrison, who had played a game with the Montreal Shamrocks even after the OPHL challenge had been accepted.

Notwithstanding the constant press criticism, Bert's absence from the Torontos' lineup would leave a significant hole to fill—he was the club's second-highest scorer. Acting again on Jimmy Murphy's advice, Miln secured Cornwall's Donald Smith to play rover. At a reputed 130 pounds soaking wet, Smith was small even for his era. However, word was that his speed and skill more than compensated.

Three days before the first Cup game, the Torontos would have the opportunity to test out the new man. It would be in an "all-star game." The Pros, it was announced, would face a team collected from the other three OPHL clubs.

Like all-star games before and after, the affair was a soft, high-scoring one. Referee E. J. "Eddie" Livingstone—a man destined for both fame and infamy on Toronto's pro hockey scene—had little to do. The permanent club rolled over the Ontario All-Stars 16–10, Smith showing up very well with five goals.

The team was scheduled to depart for Montreal the next morning. By then, assessments of its chances were coming in fast and furious. Not surprisingly, the most negative were found in Toronto's OHA newspapers, John Ross Robertson's *Tely* being the harshest:

> For the quintessence of gall commend us to this aggregation of false alarm hockey statesmen, who have wired a challenge for the Stanley Cup: to wit and namely the Toronto professionals. There can be no doubt but that the Wanderers upon receiving the wire last night laughed themselves to sleep. Surely the pros. have no idea they can hope to win, so that we may put this proposed trip down more to pot hunting than the glory of Canada's great winter sport.[15]

More balanced assessments of the challengers—including from Montreal's own observers—were consistent. The Torontos were judged to have as strong, fast and cohesive a forward unit as any, although, except for Lalonde, it was a bit on the small side. The challengers' weakness was in their back end—heavy, but lacking in consistency and teamwork. Corbeau contributed little on offence while Young was erratic defensively. Tyner was thought to be a fine goalkeeper, but had been mediocre in the latter half of the season.

John Joseph "Jack" Marks was one of the OHA's involuntary professionals, but he became a consummate one—big and tough, but also clean and hardworking both ways. At one time a minor-league baseball player, the Brantford winger had previously performed in the Federal, Maritime, International and Western Pennsylvania hockey leagues.

Miln had a few options to shore up his club. The spare man, Lambe, could be used on defence. Yet, despite fan preference for the local player over Corbeau, there seemed little prospect of a switch. Given the risk that Morrison might stay out, Alex decided he also needed an additional spare forward.

The manager's solution was to ask all-star Jack Marks to come east with the team. Besides being a solid player, Marks had some Stanley Cup experience. He had scored two goals for the New Glasgow Cubs in their losing effort back in 1906. Still, what Miln really wanted was neither Smith nor Marks, but to get Morrison back in the lineup where he played best: on the large ice surface of the Montreal Arena.

Miln had been paying close attention to the Wanderers' grumbling about the Stanley Cup playoffs. Frustrated by numerous challenges, the champs had been complaining there was too much work and not enough money in holding the mug. Wanderer president William Jennings even claimed that "most of us feel inclined to send the cup to Toronto, and let them have it, and be done with it."[16]

More than a century later, with the Stanley Cup perhaps the most revered trophy in the sporting world, such a comment seems incomprehensible to hockey fans.

Miln shrewdly figured out the real story. There was no way the Wanderers actually wanted to part with the Cup. Even then, being in the playoffs was gravy for a professional team. In truth, the problem was that the second game of the Toronto series conflicted with the Redbands' plans for their annual—and lucrative—barnstorming pilgrimage to the States.

The Wanderers were slated to take their Montreal Shamrock rivals to New York for a St. Patrick's Day match. Following that, they would play a "World Championship" against the winners of the Pittsburgh league. Cleveland's brand-new artificial-ice rink would be their final stop.

With this knowledge, Alex wired the Cup trustees. He had previously refused the Wanderers' request for a sudden-death game. However, through Foran and Ross, he now offered the Wanderers a one-game series in exchange for permission to play Morrison. The Montreal club's options being limited, they took what was a reasonable deal. Morrison was back in the Torontos' lineup.

Bert was already in Montreal and joined the team and a small band of supporters watching the final game of the Winnipeg Maple Leaf challenge. The Torontos were not discouraged by their look at the champions. Despite losing badly, the Leafs delivered a full load of physical punishment to the victors. Montrealers bemoaned:

> If the Toronto professionals are human . . . they must have chortled with glee last night when the Maple Leaf lot hammered, slashed, and thrust at Wanderer players. The net result of the affair was this: Wanderer won by the substantial score of nine goals to three; but practically every player of the cup team left the ice marked, and two of them, Cecil Blachford and Walter Smaill, carried off liberal loads of adhesive plaster as facile [sic] ornaments.[17]

Whether it was from having Morrison playing or the Cup champions hurting, Alex Miln was getting into a confident frame of mind. His encounters with the press in the rotunda of the Windsor Hotel, where he was renting a palatial suite, became increasingly cocky. Dismissive of key

Wanderer stars, he rated his team as, man for man, equal to the champs and even better on offence. And he bragged:

> I haven't managed championship teams for nothing. Every man I've taken in hand has won a championship, and every one has been a good one. Our boys are all good, can skate, stick handle and shoot, and I'll be the sorest man in America if we don't win out.[18]

This was certainly not the consensus. The betting pools leading up to game time had the Wanderers as 3–1 favourites. Odds were 2–1 that they would double the score on the Ontario representatives.

THE TORONTO PRO TEAM.
—Photographed specially for The Montreal Star.
Young had not arrived when the picture was taken. Reading from right to left, top row—E. Lalonde, C. Corbeau. Bottom row—B. Morrison, B. Redpath, Alec Milne, manager, C. Tyner, J. Mercier.

The now-defunct *Montreal Star* printed this rare photograph of the Toronto Professionals' starting lineup, absent Rolly Young, on the eve of their Stanley Cup appearance. The misspellings betray how poorly the players were known in the champions' hometown.

On the evening of Saturday, March 14, 1908, the big rink at the corner of St. Catherine Street and Wood Avenue opened its doors to an eager crowd. When the Toronto Professionals took the ice to polite applause from the half-full stands, it marked the moment when hockey had come full circle. It had been some twenty years since the sport had first been played in Toronto. Now Canada's upstart commercial centre was taking on Montreal's best at its own game. Back home, fans waited patiently at the Mutual Street Rink for the wires from the Montreal Arena. Local sentiment was rallying around the pro team—with the notable exception of Robertson's *Tely*.

If the fans in Toronto were wound up, the same could hardly be said for Montreal. It was clear from news coverage that the locals did not take the Ontario champions seriously. Still, the crowd of about 3,000, if hardly a sellout, was better than expected. However, it was also readily apparent that the ice was in awful shape. The mild weather had created vast pools—mini-lakes, actually—on large parts of the slushy playing surface.

The Montreal Wanderers—Stanley Cup holders for most of the past three years—had lined up a cast replete with future Hall of Famers. William "Riley" Hern occupied the nets with Art Ross and Walter Smaill forming the defence in front of him. Frank "Pud" Glass would play rover behind centre Ernie Russell, while captain Cecil Blachford and Ernie "Moose" Johnson filled right and left wing respectively.

The challengers—Chuck Tyner, Con Corbeau, Rolly Young, Bert Morrison, Newsy Lalonde, Walter Mercer and Bruce Ridpath—were comparatively young, inexperienced and relatively unknown. All the same, if the challengers from Toronto were intimidated, they did not show it. The hometown fans were stunned as the Torontos came out fast and aggressive. Only three minutes into the game, Ridpath fired a quick shot that eluded Hern. Hockey-savvy Montrealers, instantly recognizing a future star, gave Bruce "a lusty cheer."[19]

The early lead did not last. Only a minute later, Russell finished a Montreal rush by putting a hard one past Tyner. Toronto disputed, albeit weakly, whether the puck had actually gone in before returning to centre ice for the faceoff.

Although the Wanderers continued to be noticeably outplayed, they stayed even with the Torontos throughout the half. With just four minutes left, Ridpath made an end-to-end rush—the best individual play of the night—but it ended when Hern handled his shot comfortably.

Almost from the outset, the horrid ice conditions started to become a major factor in the game. Opposing players bogged down into scrums as they tried to control the puck and force it through the water. They were drenched from head to toe, as were the fans on the rails. At such close quarters, offsides were frequent, numerous penalties incurred and even more fouls committed as tempers grew short. Russell and Mercer had the first scrap of the night.

The first big controversy took shape just near the end of the half. Russell went down, favouring a knee. The Redbands immediately sought to substitute Bruce Stuart, younger brother of the late Hod and a star in his own right. But even the local fans were not buying the authenticity of the injury. They shouted "incredulous remarks"[20] as Russell left the ice. Toronto protested against the use of Stuart. He was not allowed into the game, and Toronto's Mercer went off to even up the sides.

After the halftime break, during which frantic efforts were made to soak up some of the water, the dispute immediately resumed. Stuart again came on the ice. This time, referee Frank Patrick and judge of play Russell Bowie permitted the change. They argued that the intermission constituted the ten-minute break necessary before substitution for injury could be made under eastern rules.

The Torontos were irate at the decision. Not only did they disagree with the ruling, but they did not believe Russell was hurt. The Wanderers, they were convinced, wanted only to replace a player whose performance had been subpar. The Professionals even threatened to leave the ice, but compromised when they got to make a substitution of their own. Jack Marks was moved in for Mercer, who, though playing adequately, was fighting a cold and favouring an ankle.

From the beginning of the second, the Queen City started getting into penalty trouble. Both Young and Corbeau were off when Glass broke the tie off the top. He banged the puck in after a faceoff directly in front of Tyner.

The Torontos came right back. Only two minutes later, Ross lost the puck while trying to clear it. Lalonde managed to dig it out of the slush in front of the Montreal goal and evened the score at two apiece.

Only one minute after that, the Toronto challengers went ahead for the second time in the evening. Young joined the forward line on a rush. Taking control of the puck behind the Wanderer goal, he swept out in front and scored. The Montreal fans were beginning to contemplate the real possibility of losing the Stanley Cup—and losing it to an unheralded new team from . . . *Toronto*. In a haze caused by smoking and warm temperatures, the atmosphere was becoming very intense.

Again, however, the Pros got into penalty trouble. Ridpath was still in the box, with Young and Lalonde just returning, when Glass took a pass from Johnson to tie the game once more. In the contest, the Torontos would take thirty-eight minutes in penalties to only twenty-six for the Wanderers, a differential that opened up almost entirely in the second half. Young, despite being credited with a very strong two-way game, was singled out six times and served fourteen minutes on the fence.

Ironically, power plays were not as big a factor in the game as might be thought. Toronto had a three-man advantage shortly after the count became 3–3, yet the score would stay that way for ten full minutes. In the tough slogging, lopsided manpower was no assurance of goals or even scoring chances.

Nevertheless, the play was beginning to shift Montreal's way, with Tyner increasingly keeping his team in it. Whereas the Torontos had at first seemed less bothered by—and more accustomed to—the poor conditions, the Wanderers' superior weight was beginning to tell. Stuart's presence had also given their attack some spark. Yet the Ontario champs were still getting their opportunities. Morrison in particular missed a couple of good ones.

The Wanderers finally broke the tie. After a strong offensive thrust, Montreal captain Blachford did the trick, fishing the puck out of water during a wild scramble in front of Tyner. The Torontos were again just returning to even strength.

Then came the most unusual event of the evening. After the go-ahead goal, Ridpath was down on the ice. It was later revealed he had received a butt-end to the groin. The injury was serious enough for Riddy, once on his feet, to leave the game for good. Glass was taken off to compensate.

Referee Patrick then proceeded to blow the whistle at centre ice to resume play. For reasons that are unclear, the Redbands showed no sign of heeding the call to action. In frustration, the ref finally dropped the puck in front of Lalonde, the lonely and momentarily startled Toronto centre.

Hern and the other Wanderers had been chatting to admirers at the boards. Suddenly seized with their predicament, they fled towards their

The Wanderers, also known as the Redbands, were one of early hockey's great dynasties.

positions. But Newsy, now realizing what was happening, stepped back and drilled the puck high from centre ice, towards the empty net. With the outstretched arms of the goalie still yards away, the disc dropped in and the umpire's hand went up to signal a goal.

The sudden-death match to decide the Stanley Cup was now tied at four with less than a quarter of the game left to be played. The action became increasingly rough. Smaill was hurt and Marks went off to even up. Without Ridpath, however, the Torontos' attack was fading and the Wanderers were forcing the play to their end. Then, yet again, defence-men Corbeau and Young were penalized.

The Wanderers now outnumbered the Torontos five men to three—counting the goaltenders. Lalonde and Morrison valiantly ragged the puck for a couple of minutes. Finally, Johnson got control and shovelled it in for a 5–4 Redbands lead.

Only about twelve and a half minutes were left in the match. In due course, the penalized players returned, as did Smaill and Marks.

Morrison had a fight with Ross, but this time it was the Wanderers who began to fall into penalty trouble.

With this opportunity, the Torontos launched something of a counter-offensive. Morrison pressed towards the Montreal goal. Lalonde had a clear shot at a partly open net—but it went over the crossbar.

At last, with less than two minutes to go in the contest, the Wanderers broke out and carried the puck down to the Torontos' end. Smaill took a good, hard shot from the side. The rebound off Tyner landed in the pool in front of the challengers' net. The defence attempted to clear, but Stuart managed to poke it in.

It was all over, the champs winning 6–4. In the process, they had confirmed their reputation as great finishers. This had been the club's trademark ever since their first Stanley Cup win over the Ottawas two years earlier.

Finishing their third straight season in possession of the Cup, the Montreal Wanderers would be immortalized as one of early hockey's great dynasties. The Toronto Professionals, their incredible brush with eternity terminated by the final bell, would be a mere footnote in the mug's history.

But on that Saturday night, it could have gone either way.

CHAPTER NINE

THE PROS IN RETREAT

The Garnet and Grey Hit Cracks in the Ice

———◆———

Five or six hundred [Guelph] rooters were out ... vigorously and vehemently declaring that the Torontos were "dogs," "fat lobsters," "cattle," "horses," "wooden men," and other things equally complimentary. [1]

—*Toronto News*

Having come within a whisker of taking the Stanley Cup, the Toronto Professionals had emerged as the toast of the hockey world. They had managed to impress virtually all observers of the big game. Rabid Montreal followers admitted their Wanderers had just scraped through. And even John Ross Robertson's *Tely* heaped praise on the play of Alexander Miln's men, conceding, "it is a big thing for the Mutual street pros to have got within hailing distance of the cup." [2]

To a man, the players also received rave reviews. The defence, normally the weak point, had performed admirably after Miln brought in Jimmy Murphy to do some rearguard coaching. Bruce Ridpath, who had never been seen before on eastern ice, had stunned the men with his speed and skill and charmed the women with his clean-cut good looks. General opinion was that the Torontos had a bright future. "If they can be kept together [they] will be a strong factor in the fight for the Stanley

Cup next season," predicted the *Montreal Star*.[3] The result had some side benefits for Toronto management, too. Miln and sidekick Teddy Marriott had taken many bets against the Wanderers doubling the score. They were coming home with their pockets full—reportedly to the tune of two and a half thousand dollars.

TORONTOS MADE GREAT SHOW
WANDERERS GIVEN SCARE

Stanley Cup Game Turned on Hair in Saturday Night's Play at Montreal

LOOKED LIKE THE LOCAL PROS.

Score Tie at Half-Time and Half Way Through Second Period—Play not up to Standard Because of Water on Ice.

(From Our Own Correspondent.)

Montreal, March 15.—The Toronto Professionals came very near beating the Wanderers on Saturday night. Had their team been as well trained

vere and men were ruled off liberally.

Finally Johnson broke the deadlock again and within ten minutes of the finish made the score five to four in favor of Wanderers.

POLITE GAME.

A lesson in hockey politeness was given by Ross and Young, who collided and apologized in due fashion. Smaill was ruled off shortly before the end. Young was next man. Lalonde came close to evening the score again, while Wanderers were short in numbers. Stuart finally clinched the matter by making it six to four in favor of Wanderers by a fine side shot.

LALONDE ACTIVE.

Lalonde grabbed the puck on the face-off and combined with Morrison right into the Wanderer net, where Lalonde and Ridpath each directed fast, accurate shots at Hern, who stopped. Corbeau took the puck down, and could not get back in time to stop a Wanderer rush, but the whistle sounded for an offside just in time to prevent a shot on Tyner from about six feet out. Morrison and Ridpath

Even the *Tely* was impressed by the Garnet and Grey's performance in the big game.

Yet the close, coarse and controversial sudden-death Stanley Cup match had concluded with none of the good cheer of the old amateur days. Neither club had much good to say about the other. Both claimed they would have won decisively on good ice. The Wanderers' president, William Jennings, dismissed the scare the champs had received. He offered instead a quip about the watery ice surface: "Our fellows are bad swimmers."[4]

Notwithstanding the plaudits and the profits, the Torontos were very bitter in defeat. They complained about every aspect of the refereeing. The eastern officials, they alleged, had failed to understand the Ontario offside rule and had called their plays back frequently. The challengers had also been on the long end of the penalties. The failure to impose one when Ridpath was injured and the allowing of a Wanderer player substitution—the big turning points of the match—had them particularly angry.

Some—though clearly not all—commentators thought the Torontos had a point. It did not help when judge of play Russell Bowie, a Montrealer, opined that "the better team won."[5] Miln's brief postgame statement was as pointed and undiplomatic as his 1902 speech in Winnipeg had been expansive and generous:

We lost on account of the ice. If there had been less water on it, and the officials had been more impartial, there was no reason why we should not have beaten Wanderers. We had them going all the game. I think that they were lucky to win.[6]

Maybe it was the foul mood, but the Toronto Professionals began a downward trend almost as soon as they left Montreal. As was the practice of the day, both teams headed out to finish the season with some exhibition matches. The Wanderers were off to New York, taking Bert Morrison and the Shamrocks with them. The Torontos had their own three-game excursion planned for Ontario, in the hopes of promoting their league—as well as earning some extra cash.

The Torontos' exhibition schedule was to start with the Dutchmen at the Berlin Auditorium on the following Friday night, March 20. The Berlin club likely needed the extra home revenue because Guelph had failed to show there for the final league game.

Right from the outset of the trip, pulling together a lineup was proving to be a challenge. Besides Morrison, the Torontos would also be missing Rolly Young, who was off doing his studies. Guelph's Harvey Corbeau was brought in at cover. Brantford's Jack Marks was retained to play right wing. Walter Mercer was moved to Morrison's position at rover.

With the teams playing for a $500 bet, the game was bound to be intense. Before a crowd of 1,200 Berliners, the home side went up 5–0 before Toronto managed to score. With the half ending 6–1, the play got increasingly rough. No fewer than six players were down at various times. Only the ever-reliable Ridpath was a bright light for the Stanley Cup challengers in the decisive 8–4 loss, while Ezra Dumart and Nelson Gross starred for Berlin.

Matters quickly turned worse. The following night, the Toronto team was even more patched up as they prepared to meet Guelph. Inexplicably, somewhere on the train ride from Berlin, Chuck Tyner and Ridpath had apparently jumped off. This now left only Con Corbeau, Newsy Lalonde and Mercer from the regulars. Berlin goaltender Charlie Ellis and utility man Jim McGinnis were added to Marks to beef up the squad. Guelph also borrowed from Berlin—in the person of Goldie Cochrane—and also put just six men on the ice.

The incomplete, makeshift cast was only the tip of the iceberg. The game was characterized in terms ranging from "burlesque" and "farcical"[7] to just plain "weird."[8] The *Globe* summarized it as "a game of shinny and fighting, with the spectators piling in occasionally."[9] The local paper gave more expansive descriptions of the spectacle:

> It was an exhibition of hockey tag, where one player got the puck and held it as long as he could, despite the interference of friend or foe . . . a free for all scrap . . . however, no one was hurt and, like the game, the whole matter ended in a laugh . . . Bert Booth [Guelph's goalie] helped to sustain the interest of the spectators by occasionally rushing.[10]

If this was the Royals' attempt to relaunch themselves after the dismal season in Guelph, it certainly failed. Only a couple of hundred turned out. Toronto won 12–6—according to the few who were counting.

The last exhibition game—and the second against Berlin—was set for Monday night in the neighbouring town of Galt (now part of the city of Cambridge). There had been unhappiness with the OHA and talk of pro hockey in that burg for some time. By bringing in its two best clubs, there can be no doubt the OPHL was scouting the site for the next season.

Alas, this final chapter to the 1907–08 season was another step in the postseason descent. The contestants again presented the public with improvised rosters falling a man short. This time, the Torontos borrowed Booth and Corbeau from Guelph to supplement their remaining core and Jack Marks. They won convincingly, 9–4. However, with the ice quickly disappearing, the game was nothing to write home about, let alone to waste much space in the sports pages over.

There was no denying that the road trip from Montreal to Galt had been a very odd anticlimax to a great season. The Toronto Professionals had assembled a top-notch, disciplined aggregation and stuck with it all the way through to a near miss at the Stanley Cup. Observers had universally christened them a future contender. Then the club had finished off with cobbled-together lineups and halfhearted efforts.

It would be a sign of things to come.

———

For now, it was but a small example of the growing turmoil within the professional sporting bodies that had risen up in rebellion against the rigid order of amateur athletics. And none was facing greater challenges than the organization that advocated the coexistence of amateur and professional athletes: the Amateur Athletic Federation of Canada. It was gradually but inexorably losing its civil war with the ideologues of the Canadian Amateur Athletic Union. Events between the hockey seasons of 1908 would seal its fate.

Colonel John Hanbury-Williams, secretary to Governor General Grey, had finally, after several false starts, secured his Olympic compromise. The Montreal-based Federation and the Toronto-based Union had been arm-twisted into an uneasy agreement on the structure of a Canadian Olympic Committee. In essence, the two feuding amateur bodies agreed to waive their various rules and injunctions against each other's athletes for the purposes of the London Summer Games only.

A temporary truce had thus been reached in the Athletic War. There would be a Canadian team at the Olympics after all. There was no sense, when the Canadians set sail for Britain, that the pact was soon to blow up in spectacular fashion.

The source of the confrontation lay in the alliance between the AAFC and the American Amateur Athletic Union. The U.S. body had severed its links to the CAAU over a number of issues, including that of Tom

Longboat. American sports authorities were convinced that the stellar Onondaga runner was a professional. In their eyes, he was therefore ineligible for the Olympic marathon, which he was also the clear favourite to win following his remarkable performance the year before in Boston. The split between the American and Canadian unions had given the Federation the advantage in any cross-border athletic endeavour.

Yet the Federation badly overplayed its hand. Egged on by its Yankee ally, the Montreal-based organization decided to support a U.S. protest against Longboat's entry in the Olympic marathon just ten days before the event was to take place. The CAAU and the COC publicly joined in support of Longboat. The challenge was ultimately rejected, but Canadian unity had been shattered before an international audience.

The 1908 London Olympic marathon begins on the East Terrace of Windsor Castle on July 24. Tom Longboat—the favourite to win— can be seen in the back third of runners, beside another Canadian runner wearing a hat and maple leaf jersey.   .

Longboat ran, and indeed, he held the early lead as the runners set out from Windsor Castle. However, he began to struggle in the middle third of the race and, near the twenty-mile mark, collapsed and was unable to finish. The race was marred by controversy. In extremely hot conditions, Italy's Dorando Pietri came first into the Great Stadium but fell several times and, seemingly disoriented, began moving in the wrong direction. He was set right by the intervention of British officials and was all but carried across the finish line. The Americans protested, and U.S. runner Johnny Hayes was ultimately awarded the gold. As for Longboat, the theories were rampant: heat exhaustion, drugs—even that he had been drunk.[11]

Mr. Public: Will you gentlemen kindly consult this eminent specialist as quickly as possible. I am very tired of this nonsense!

The Athletic War was never popular with the Canadian public, whose disgust was now palpable.

Back in Canada, however, the public was outraged. The actions of the AAFC in joining with the Americans to try to block Longboat were widely seen as dishonourable and disloyal. In truth, it was hard to view them any other way.

Ironically, within a few short months, Longboat announced his intention to go openly professional after all. But it did not matter—the Federation's support, even in its home centre of Montreal, had been shattered.

The reality was that the Toronto-centred Union had won more than just the war of public opinion. It had aggressively and massively outorganized the Federation over the previous two years. By its 1908 annual fall meeting, the CAAU had grown from just thirty-six clubs to more than 900, with 60,000 members and provincial branches in every part of the country. It had also adopted a more flexible approach, sometimes offering readmission to those bodies that had dabbled in professionalism.

Conversely, the Federation seemed convinced of its superiority simply by virtue of being based in Montreal. With only token efforts at national recruitment, it remained limited to that city's environs in Quebec and eastern Ontario. Equally important, the AAFC had also failed to advance its core agenda. While professional sport was more and more in the open, professionals and amateurs were mixing less and less. In an era when many athletes played more than one sport competitively, the Union was able to effectively threaten cross-sport bans on pro participants and organizations. Thus, players, clubs and leagues going professional tended to do so without qualification—and outside the Federation—further lessening the Montreal organization's sway.

Nowhere was the division between professionals and amateurs as increasingly stark as in hockey. In the lead-up to the 1908–09 season, the country's leading league finally went fully and officially professional. Following the example of the National Lacrosse Union three years before, the organization dispensed with the word "Amateur" to become simply the Eastern Canada Hockey Association.

Coincident with the rechristening of the ECHA was the departure of two of its historic clubs, Montreal's Victorias and Wheelers. The defection of the latter was a sure sign that the Montreal Amateur Athletic Association—the backbone of the Federation—was preparing to capitulate in the Athletic War. Almost immediately, the two teams would help form a new, major league of amateur hockey, the Interprovincial Amateur Hockey Union. It was clearly intended to parallel the CAAU's "Big Four" rugby football league. The two Montreal clubs would be joined by two from Ontario: the Ottawa Cliffsides and the Toronto Athletics. The four teams would be a high-calibre, purely amateur grouping. Professional hockey had no equivalent cross-regional circuit.

Sir Hugh Montagu Allan was one of Canada's most prominent business leaders. His new trophy would be the national amateur alternative to Lord Stanley's chalice.

Indeed, amateur hockey, with a much more extensive infrastructure in place than the pro game, was regrouping across the country. In Manitoba, the Winnipeg Victorias were leading the re-establishment of a provincial amateur league. The CAAU's provincial wings were likewise linking to amateur hockey associations in their respective jurisdictions. Of course, John Ross Robertson's Ontario Hockey Association, despite the growth of pro hockey in the province, remained the country's largest and most deeply organized hockey body.

In other words, the advocates of amateurism were living by the apparent sports (and life) dictum of Robertson: "If you can't beat 'em, don't join 'em." Unable to stop professional hockey, they were undertaking a second-best alternative—forming their own, parallel structures. But the most important long-term move for the amateur game that year was made by Sir Hugh Montagu Allan, not by the OHA boss.

Soon after the 1908–09 season began, the honorary president of the MAAA announced the presentation of a new national challenge trophy for Canada's winter sport. It had been at first rumoured that the mug would be donated by the governor general. In the end, however, it was to be the Allan Cup, not the Grey Cup, that would serve amateur hockey. It would quickly galvanize coast-to-coast competition just as the Stanley Cup had done for the pros.

Meanwhile, the problems of professional hockey showed no sign of abating. In reality, the pro scene had been built up far too quickly for its foundations to have been well laid. Its rapid growth in the past couple of seasons had clearly been an overexpansion.

Players' salaries were rising faster than revenue streams—far faster. Managers pleaded for the need to control salaries at the same time as they agreed to bigger contracts. And even as they raised ticket prices, they were literally bleeding money. In short, it was the same woeful owners' tale, in microcosm, that hockey fans would be hearing a century later.

Not only was the Eastern Canada Hockey Association shrinking, but so were the circuits around it. The Renfrew Creamery Kings joined the struggling Federal league after its Upper Ottawa Valley group returned to the amateur ranks. The Temiskaming league had lost Latchford the previous year and was now just an isolated three-town association.

In Manitoba, the professional organization—one of the country's most important—completely imploded. The league had lost two of its five teams to financial problems the previous season, including the once-mighty Kenora Thistles. Shortly after 1908–09 began, its three teams became two. By midseason, only the Winnipeg Shamrocks remained.

The Alberta-Saskatchewan association had also become a one-team league. In December, its Edmonton club finally got its first shot at the Stanley Cup. A team loaded with stars—Tom Phillips, Lester Patrick, Didier Pitre, Fred Whitcroft—went down to the defending champion Montreal Wanderers. This would not be the last time an all-star aggregation would fail to defeat a balanced, quality team. In the process, however, the outcry against the hiring of ringers and against players jumping contracts would reach new heights.

Yet the salary wars and shrinking ranks of the commercial game seemed to be of little concern to the Ontario Professional Hockey League. At the November 13 annual meeting, held at Toronto's King Edward Hotel, the league adopted a salary cap of $25 per player per week. Of course, this was a limit that no one intended to honour. More importantly, the organization decided to expand to six teams, the two newcomers being Galt and St. Catharines.

The OPHL had been eyeing Galt since its inception. Alex Miln and Buck Irving had visited the industrial town the previous fall, trying to place a franchise, against a backdrop of continuing local fallout over the charges Irving had levelled against the OHA in January 1907.

During the 1907–08, season the relationship between Galt and the OHA, which had long been tenuous, had soured completely. The local paper charged that "the frothings" of John Ross Robertson and his underlings had led to "a successful professional league that is tearing the vitals out of the O.H.A." [12] Such a ripe audience for the OPHL explains why Toronto and Berlin had held their postseason exhibition in the town known as Little Manchester.

Norman Edgar Irving's big ambitions—and his antics—would make him the most important figure in the history of the Ontario Professional Hockey League.

Interestingly, the Galt franchise was eventually granted to none other than Buck Irving himself. This gave Irving a role in two of the league's six clubs. While the Guelph team was officially taken over by local former pro baseball player Jimmy Cockman, Buck's father, Thomas Irving, kept the franchise in the family orbit through his ownership of the Royal City Rink. Nonetheless, the focus of the younger Irving's escapades shifted to his new team.

Irving immediately set off on his familiar routine of loud self-promotion. He dropped the names of some big potential signings and hinted at others. However, Buck was not repeating his Guelph mistake. He began to recruit realistically and aggressively—and in the process started to create tensions with other league owners.

St. Catharines also had an unhappy history with the OHA. A bastion of lacrosse, its hockey program had been devastated by Robertson's 1904 take-no-prisoners ban on players of the summer game. Two years after that, a hockey team sponsored by the local power company had played a visiting IHL pro team, leading to the breakup of the local amateur league.

With an eye on OPHL membership, the Athletic Lacrosse Club of St. Catharines had formed a pro hockey team during the previous season. The squad had played one exhibition game. It was against Hamilton's pros, a rival also organized by lacrosse players. St. Kitts won decisively and thus prepared to establish a permanent club.

At the outset of the season there was some doubt, however, whether the Ontario capital itself would continue to compete against these other provincial towns. After their strong showing in the Stanley Cup game, rumours swirled around the Toronto Professionals' possible admission to the ECHA. These continued until late November, when Miln was said to have finally rejected a written offer from the Eastern league.

The Eastern teams no doubt wanted Toronto to make up for the defections to the Interprovincial and to blunt the competitive threat the new circuit represented. This time, Miln seems to have been tempted. In the end, though, he came to the same conclusions he had in the past. The Mutual Street Rink lacked the seating capacity to finance the transportation costs involved. The Ontario league represented smaller, but closer markets and was easy on the budget. And, of course, he still did not have that new rink.

With fans' appetite for the pro game so whetted by the Stanley Cup challenge, local opinion was distinctly disappointed by Miln's decision. The clear desire of Toronto fans was to be in a "big league" with Montreal. Worryingly for Miln and the Professionals' supporters, such a rivalry is what the amateur game, with its new Big Four league, would offer Toronto hockey fans.

The local Interprovincial entry, sponsored by the Toronto Amateur Athletic Club, set up shop at the Excelsior Rink on College Street. Percy Quinn and Eddie Livingstone—two hockey men of whom much would be heard in the years to come—were among the team's management. The TAAC, in bright crimson uniforms decorated with a large white *T*, also liked to use the name "Torontos."

The challenge was not subtle.

———

For the Toronto Pros, the first order of business was to re-sign their roster. The players having scattered during the post-Cup exhibition tour in March, this was no easy feat. As well, competition for good players remained intense despite the smaller number of pro employers. Even Eastern league interests, having seen the Torontos up close in Stanley Cup play, were approaching some of the club's best men.

Local opponents tried to make much of rumours that the championship men would head to Pittsburgh. Corbeau, for one, did suit up in the

Smoky City. However, the truth was that those who went did so only to get in shape by playing on artificial ice during the preseason. The Western Pennsylvania league could no longer afford to lure quality players from Canada for the main campaign. In fact, this would be its last year of operation.

Ironically, the most problematic approaches came from within the OPHL itself. The other clubs—especially Berlin—made determined efforts to sign the members of the Torontos. Flagrantly ignoring the $25 salary limit, they were driving up Miln's payroll in the process. The Queen City manager would be successful in signing his core men—Corbeau, Lalonde, Morrison, Ridpath and Tyner. He did allow Mercer to be taken back by Guelph.

The biggest loss was Young—in an affair that got quite complicated. The Toronto cap-

Herbert Frederick Birmingham was an accomplished cross-country runner, but on skates, he was neither fast nor big. He did have a touch around the net.

tain had long had an uneasy relationship with the game. Despite the money earned and modest success on the ice, Rolly's real desire was to become a medical doctor. After the Stanley Cup match, he had mused about retiring and did not accompany the team on its postseason Ontario swing.

Despite declaring in the fall that he was finished, Young was later talked into inking a fat contract by Berlin president Oscar Rumpel and manager W. G. "Pop" Williams. Rolly realized almost immediately, however, that the new twenty-game OPHL schedule was too intense for his studies at the U of T. He asked to be released to play part-time in Toronto instead. Berlin refused and, after a great deal of haggling and threatened retirement, Young decided to stay with the game—but it would have to be in the Dutchmen's lineup.

With Young gone, the Toronto captaincy passed to Newsy Lalonde. Though only twenty-one years of age, the intense French Canadian was showing an increasing interest in leadership and a strong commitment to the franchise. He had, for example, helped get fellow Cornwall man Don Smith to fill in for Bert Morrison at the end of 1907–08.

Miln picked up youngster Erskine Rockcliffe "Skene" Ronan from Pittsburgh to fill the hole created by the departure of Rolly Young. It became immediately evident that he was a performer of great promise.

As captain, Lalonde now had a hand in player recruitment. This was fortuitous. With the Federal league gradually fading, Lalonde's old stomping grounds in eastern Ontario were a good place to look for new talent. Lalonde knew the best players and had the contacts. Miln smartly sent Lalonde on the road east, where his first convert was Zina Runions. Another fellow Cornwall man, Runions was hired to take Mercer's place at right wing. Originally a goalkeeper, his résumé included the infamous March 1907 brawl against the Ottawa Vics that had resulted in the death of Bud McCourt.

Miln also re-signed Hugh Lambe as a spare defenceman and Herb Birmingham, a proven goal scorer, as a spare forward. Birmingham's contract meant that, of the 1904–05 OHA champion Toronto Marlboros, all the regulars had now gone pro except Edgar Winchester. And virtually all had signed at one time or another with the local Professionals.

The real catch was the netting of one Erskine "Skene" Ronan. The Ottawa lad had been a junior sensation before turning pro. Corbeau, returning from the West Penn league, had confirmed the rookie's talent. Although Ronan had been on the wings for the Pittsburgh Bankers, Miln intended to play him in Young's place at cover point.

The club now had five Stanley Cup regulars and good new men. Queen City opinion on the season's prospects was pretty optimistic. The *News* was the most unequivocal: "It looks as if the team would be even better than last year's, when they won the championship."[13]

The Ontario Pro league began its 1908–09 campaign with an aggressive preseason schedule. Its clubs played in no fewer than nine exhibition matches. Two of these would involve the Torontos.

The first was a road game against the Berlin Dutchmen. Last season's runners-up had succeeded in strengthening themselves through their frantic recruiting efforts. Besides Young from Toronto, they had also lured Billy "Lady" Taylor from Brantford, Art Serviss from Portage la Prairie and goalie Hugh Lehman from Pembroke of the Upper Ottawa Valley league. However, they had lost star cover Goldie Cochrane, signed by Buck Irving for Galt.

The Torontos had been training hard for the Christmas Day encounter, both on dry land and some early-winter ice. They were, however, without Runions and Ronan, who were still a couple of days away from relocating to Toronto. Birmingham, a natural centre, was pressed into service at right wing. At cover, the team borrowed Brantford bad boy Cap McDonald, who had returned from Pittsburgh. The presence of such bitter rivals as McDonald and Lalonde on the same side reminded fans that pro allegiance is a fleeting thing.

The Torontos had a decided advantage over Berlin, playing its second game that day. The

Alfred Ernest McDonald was the stereotypical dirty, violent International Hockey League veteran. The previous season's incident appeared forgiven when Cap joined Newsy Lalonde in a Toronto uniform for the Christmas 1908 exhibition against Berlin.

Dutchmen had beaten Galt on the road, but fell behind the Professionals early and stayed that way most of the game. Nevertheless, they fought back to tie 5–5 before time expired. Toronto then wisely declined Berlin's offer to play off the draw.

The game was considered a good one, but a rough one. Young's performance had mixed reviews, but his defection only accentuated the bad blood between the clubs. Again, Uncle Gross was at the centre of the battles, this time principally with Corbeau. Lalonde and Ridpath picked up where they had left off in leading the Toronto offence.

The Torontos' home opener would be the only one of the preseason exhibitions not to feature two OPHL teams. It originated with Miln's attempts to get the Edmonton Seniors to come to Toronto. Those plans went awry when the recent Stanley Cup challenger started to break up shortly after its loss in Montreal. Fortunately, Manager Miln was able to snare the Ottawa Hockey Club in the meantime.

The match between the Toronto Professionals and Ottawa Silver Seven was a real coup. These two teams were widely considered the principal threats to the Montreal Wanderers' hold on the Cup. The Ottawas had bolstered themselves through the replacement of some aging veterans, in particular by luring Bruce Stuart from the Redbands.

As it happened, Stuart was either hurt or ill (depending on the report) and did not dress that Saturday evening, January 2, at the Mutual Street Rink. Still, the Ottawas lined up an impressive septet: Percy LeSueur, Fred Lake, Fred Taylor, Edgar Dey, Marty Walsh, Billy Gilmour and Hamby Shore. Cyclone Taylor's return to Toronto was his first since the OHA junior final of 1903–04.

With ticket prices hiked for the occasion—fifty cents for general admission, $1 for reserved seating—the teams did not disappoint. The encounter was fast and hard, with the Torontos matching the legendary dirty play of the Ottawas blow for blow. Lalonde put Gilmour out of the game with a cross-check to the mouth. Morrison was assigned to check Taylor, and the two went at each other all night.

In fact, the Professionals—their full lineup in place—were more than a match for the Ottawas, winning 5–4. Despite a clearly weaker defence, the hard skating and checking of their forwards slowed and frequently reversed the attack of the husky visitors. Walsh got three goals for Ottawa, but Taylor was held scoreless, while Morrison got two. Tyner equalled the renowned LeSueur at every turn.

For a club setting out to capture the Stanley Cup, it was a brilliant start to the year. Even the *Globe*, one of the harshest critics of the Pros, was impressed:

> It is not intended to detract from the abilities of the great seven from Ottawa, but the Torontos were just as good, and a little better, and would repeat the victory in three games out of four.[14]

Impressive as the Toronto Professionals had been, they would begin their regular season with a significant hole in their lineup. Bert Morrison would not dress for the OPHL opener the following Tuesday in Berlin. He had apparently been hurt in the Ottawa game, though the nature of the injury was not disclosed. In the interim, Birmingham took his place at rover. The Ottawa exhibition had also featured the appearance of another new player. Albert "Dubbie" Kerr had replaced Runions at right wing halfway through the game. Recruited from Pittsburgh just in time for the season, his play had been exceptional. However, as the club hit the road, he was becoming the centre of controversy.

Kerr had been negotiating with both Toronto and Berlin. While it was claimed he signed first with the Professionals, the Dutchmen had paid for his transportation to Canada. An angry manager Williams bluntly told the press: "Kerr accepted and used our transportation and he's our man. Why, his trunk is here at the station." [15]

Miln had barely arrived at his hotel when he was loudly accosted by Berlin's senior people. The yelling continued until the game was supposed to start, and then some. The home team finally consented to allow Dubbie to play, but only under protest to the league executive.

Albert Daniel "Dubbie" Kerr had been a teammate of Con Corbeau's in Pittsburgh before Christmas. The object of a vicious contract dispute between Toronto and Berlin, the "Brockville Cannonball" proved to be a player worth fighting for.

The dispute only heightened the increasingly bitter rivalry between the two clubs. With both sides running the goalies, a good half-dozen scraps filled the night. The main event was between the former defence partners, Corbeau and Young.

It was also an exciting, seesaw game. In better condition thanks to longer preseason ice, Berlin eventually pulled through by a count of 8–7. As for Kerr, despite the loss, opinion was clearly that "he is a player worth fighting for." [16]

The same lineup would get another chance—this time at home on Saturday against Guelph. The Royals' new management had not cured the club's problems. Uncertainty over financing had led to the abrupt dismissal and rehiring of its personnel around Christmas.

By the time the visitors arrived in Toronto, however, things were looking up somewhat. Guelph had come off a 2–2 preseason with some decent newcomers in uniform. Walter Mercer was back at right wing, rejoining Herb Fyfe at centre. Alex Miln believed the new rover, Howard Manson, to be "the fastest man in the league."[17]

Although the game was entertaining, the Royals proved no match for the Torontos. The local Pros pulled ahead early on power plays and won handily by a score of 15–8. At one point, they even managed to score while short two men. All the forwards had helped run up the count.

With a win and a near win, the club was satisfied with the season's first week on the ice. There was even more reason to celebrate at the box office. The Saturday-night game had gone head to head with the TAAC's Interprovincial match—and it was no contest. Nearly 2,000 turned out to see the professional Torontos at Mutual. The amateur version got clobbered by the Montreal Wheelers 14–7 before a small crowd at the Excelsior.

The Torontos headed into a busy second week with some storm clouds gathering around their lineup. Morrison remained out and was now said to be suffering from an "illness."[18] Lalonde had received a bad gash to the foot in the season opener, leading to his early exit when it was reinjured against Guelph. As well, rumours had the other owners siding with Berlin in the Kerr dispute. There were further reports that, frustrated with the situation, Dubbie was about to jump at an offer from Ottawa.

On Monday night, the team travelled to Brantford and managed to put both Newsy and Dubbie on the ice just the same. It was a good thing. Brantford was widely rated as Toronto's most dangerous competitor. Notwithstanding the loss of Taylor and the retirement of Roy Brown as a player, the Braves had strengthened overall, especially with the addition of forwards Tommy Smith and Art Throop from Pittsburgh. This season's games with Brantford, much like the previous year's with Berlin, would prove to be the critical turning points of the campaign.

This first one was another well-attended, wildly entertaining and hard-fought match, but with the Torontos again coming up short. All the players—with the exception of Birmingham—were judged to have played well. Unfortunately, the Braves had the edge and pulled ahead in the final minutes to win 9–6.

It was a big loss on the ice, followed by bigger ones off the ice. Kerr defected to the Ottawas almost as quickly as the final bell sounded. The later, bizarre decision of the league to award him to neither Toronto nor Berlin, but instead to Guelph, only confirmed the personal wisdom of his move. Lalonde was also lost, at least temporarily. Shortly after the game, he was confined to bed, as, apparently, was Morrison. Newsy had a serious case of blood poisoning. He was hospitalized just in time, the attending physician judging him fortunate to have avoided the amputation of his foot.

Lawson Whitehead put in a good effort against Galt, but most reviews indicated he struggled to keep pace. This picture of the local lacrosse player was taken much later— in 1926.

With the club badly hobbled, it headed back to Mutual Street for a game on Wednesday against Buck Irving's new Galt club. Runions moved back into Kerr's place at right wing. The surprise was on defence. Corbeau, Ronan and Birmingham were all moved up a slot, while Lawson Whitehead was tried out at point. Whitehead was a star with Toronto's Tecumseh Lacrosse Club and had been trying to get a place on the pro hockey team since its inception.

Galt had a solid lineup, much of it recruited from the other OPHL clubs. It included Goldie Cochrane and his brother, Marsh, on the forward line. Bob Mercer, brother of Walter, was in the nets. Despite some contract scraps with key players, "Irving's Indians"[19] were undefeated in the league race and doing reasonably well at the box office.

Again the Torontos lost a close affair, this time 5–4. It was a game in which rough play was as common as "samples of Red Rose tea at a country fair."[20] The hosts were judged the worse offenders. It ultimately cost them due to a key call against goalie Chuck Tyner. Tyner had again played a solid game, but he took a late penalty. That allowed Galt to score the eventual winner while Corbeau was left guarding the cage. Chuck tried valiantly to compensate by joining the rush in the closing moments. For the visitors, the surprise had been Pete Charlton. Playing point at the age of thirty, he had been one of the best performers on the ice.

Having lost three key players, the Torontos were now a fairly ordinary lot (excepting, of course, the sensational Ridpath). Miln had promised to spare no expense to retain the championship, but with just one win in four league games, the club was beginning to fall back. Although opinion thus far was that he deserved "sympathy rather than criticism,"[21] pressure was on the manager to make good.

The next game—at St. Catharines on Friday night—would be a must-win.

———

St. Kitts had a very weak team. Winless in four (counting one exhibition), the Athletics[22] had not been close in a single game. Their predicament was deepened by management's insistence on being the sole OPHL club to stick to the $25-a-player salary cap. By now their starting goaltender, 1906–07 Toronto Pro Mark Tooze, had quit in favour of Clarence Gorrie of the stillborn 1905–06 squad. More general turmoil was setting in, with some of their better players jumping ship and returning to Pittsburgh.

Miln was also making changes. He ended the Whitehead experiment by bringing the club's old reliable, Hugh Lambe, back at point. He also dumped Runions for good. Although tough, the right winger was judged to be otherwise inadequate. He would be replaced by Fred Young, little brother of Rolly.[23] Fred had played the previous season in Pittsburgh, where the reviews had been fairly good.

The revamped squad played reasonably well and won 7–4 in front of a fairly large crowd. The Torontos had fallen behind 3–1 early on, relying on Tyner to keep it close. After that, the visitors had gradually overpowered a home side filled out with local intermediates.

While Toronto's lineup holes were challenging, it was Brantford who evoked the sympathy that second week. Heading home from a Wednesday game at Guelph, the Braves were involved in a terrible train wreck on the Grand Trunk line. Most badly injured was right winger Jack Marks. Marks had played with the local club in last year's Cup game and postseason. By all accounts, his extensive injuries would mean the end of his career. The *Star* gave unusual praise to a professional, calling Marks "a faithful and skilful player, who always gave his best efforts to his employers."[24]

The big gaps in Brantford's roster would mean even more intense competition for Miln in his efforts to shore up his team. But the manager was not letting up. For the next game, Monday, January 18, in Toronto, he would bring in yet another new defenceman and right winger. The first was "Stoke" Doran of the Pittsburgh Bankers. Husky, though often awkward on his skates, he resembled rearguard partner Con Corbeau enough to be mistaken for him. The second was Harold McNamara, one of three hockey-playing brothers from Sault Ste. Marie. McNamara was one of the former Edmontons who had gone his own way after the Cup challenge.

James Doran, like Kerr, was a Miln recruit originally from Brockville. Almost identical in appearance to Corbeau, "Stoke" wore a blue cap on the ice to distinguish himself from Con.

Interestingly, the constant changes and frequent defeats had not yet put even a dint in local fan interest in the Toronto Pros. Close to 3,000—some of whom took the train from Berlin—packed the Mutual Street Rink that evening. Despite missing the injured Gross, the Dutchmen were off to a strong start at four wins and one loss, and were a close second to Brantford in the standings.

The supporters of both teams were treated to a great game. Even the most hostile observers deemed it one of the best pro games yet played. The action was intense from the outset, with the Torontos utterly dominating. Excitement so rocked the old building that, after a goal by Ronan, a section of bleachers collapsed, heaving its cheering spectators onto the ice.

The Torontos may have carried the play, but Berlin goalkeeper Hugh Lehman carried the day. The goalie displayed just the combination of brilliance and luck necessary to produce a 5–4 upset. The *Star* was the most colourful in its analysis, alleging Lehman "had a rabbit's foot in each pad and horseshoes all over the net rail." [25] At the other end, Tyner had uncharacteristically let in a couple of long shots.

Although the Torontos now had only two wins in six games, local sympathy remained on the side of the "hard-luck outfit." [26] With only a

Harold McNamara and his brothers. While equally giant siblings George (right) and Howard (left) were tough defencemen, the well-travelled Harold "Hal" McNamara (middle) was a stylish forward.

break here or there, all four losses could have gone either way. Nevertheless, the club was falling back further. It was well behind Brantford (five wins and one tie), Berlin (just one loss) and Galt (a loss and a tie). Avoiding another loss on Wednesday against Guelph would thus be essential.

The Royals, though not as bad as St. Kitts, were also a winless squad. Rumours of the two clubs' imminent demise were circulating wildly in both centres and their morale was plunging. By comparison, the Toronto champs looked remarkably strong, although they would again be facing lineup changes.

Despite a strong performance, McNamara would not be back. Miln had signed him for only one game. Hal was aiming to get on with the Montreal Shamrocks, where his brothers were playing. Besides, the trustees' anti-ringer rule meant he would not be eligible for Cup competition with Toronto. Fred Young, whose play had received passing grades, was pressed back into service at right wing.

At this point, however, it appears the constant changes began taking their toll on the Professionals. Lacking any teamwork, they fell 6–4 before 500 remaining Royals' supporters. Only Tyner and (once again) Ridpath had shone during the contest. The Guelph crowd jeered them mercilessly, "declaring that the Torontos were 'dogs,' 'fat lobsters,' 'cattle,' 'horses,' 'wooden men,' and other things equally complimentary."[27]

Less than a year after the Toronto Professionals were being praised as a legitimate Stanley Cup contender, they were being laughed off the ice.

And their problems were only beginning.

CHAPTER TEN

THE TRIUMPH OF THE AMATEURS

The End of the Toronto Professionals

———•◦•———

It is not often that amateur hockey can chase the pro. article out of a city the size of Toronto. But that's what has happened here . . . It means that hockey in Toronto is on a healthy foundation, that O.H.A. supervision is universally satisfactory and that the future of the game is assured.[1]

—*Toronto Telegram*

Sport is the ultimate reality show. Try as some might to write its script, the drama has a way of finding its own, unpredictable path. That was certainly true in the case of the Toronto Professionals' 1908–09 season. The humiliating loss at Guelph had been a devastating finish to the team's third week of action—putting a seeming end to any shot at the Ontario title, let alone a second challenge for the Stanley Cup. And yet, no sooner had the Guelph defeat been recorded than a spectacular series of events would befall the Ontario Professional Hockey League. While all of them were bad from the league's standpoint, they would combine to give the stumbling champions a new lease on life.

As soon as Guelph registered its first victory, the club announced its breakup. A second losing season was killing attendance. The disastrous St. Catharines outfit threw in the towel shortly thereafter. Rumours swirled around Galt's departure as well, but Irving managed to pull through by convincing the owners of the smallish local rink to cut their rent.

In effect, the problems afflicting pro hockey everywhere had hit the OPHL with a vengeance, revealing its early-season expansion as foolish. It all confirmed that the commercial game had grown far too quickly for its foundations to have been well laid. These, combined with ordeals of the local Professionals, greatly delighted John Ross Robertson and his OHA followers. This comment from Frank Nelson's *Globe* was typical:

> Professional hockey in such places as St. Catharines, Galt and Guelph
> in western Ontario, and Renfrew, Smith's [*sic*] Falls and Cornwall, in
> the east, must of necessity be either a joke or an imposition. In most
> of the places named it partakes of the character of both.[2]

ST. KITTS PROS. QUIT THE GAME

The Five Consecutive Defeats Put Them Out of Business and They Disbanded To-day.

GUELPH ALSO TO GIVE UP

No Chance for the Championship, and It's Only Throwing Good Money After Bad.

The St. Kitts pro. hockey team gave up the ghost to-day, and the two or three outside players who were on the line-up went to their respective homes. Donald Smith went through to-day to his home in Cornwall, where he will finish the season.

With the loss of two clubs, the ailments afflicting pro hockey had hit the OPHL.

Yet in Toronto, the crafty Alexander Miln would respond rapidly to the challenges. In fact, he took quick advantage of the situation by scooping up the best player from each of the collapsing OPHL franchises. These were Howard Manson of Guelph and Donald Smith of St. Kitts, both originally from Cornwall. For Smith, it was his second stop in Toronto. He had been retained as a substitute in the run-up to the previous season's Cup challenge.

Toronto also benefited from the curious league decision to count all games against the defunct teams, regardless of outcome, as victories for the surviving ones. The "dogs" and "fat lobsters" defeated 6–4 in Guelph were now said to have won that game. Indeed, the Torontos, having been the only club to have lost to either the Royals or the Athletics, were the only beneficiaries of the ruling. It was a small step up, but one that gave them some hope of regaining the championship.

Miln's fortune was not all good, however. He was the victim of growing raids on the OPHL by the Temiskaming league. One night after practice, Skene Ronan and Con Corbeau took their gear from trainer Frank Carroll, left the rink, quickly packed their bags and secretly slipped out of town for a train ride to Haileybury.

The loss of Ronan and Corbeau was a real blow. Skene, who had been moved up to centre in recent matches, was getting noticeably better with each outing. Con was maturing into a quality defenceman and team leader, acting as unofficial captain while fellow French Canadian Newsy Lalonde was on the injury list.

Corbeau later tried to explain to Toronto fans how he could have broken his contract and run off to Haileybury for the princely sum of $75 a week:

We were honestly sorry to leave Toronto ... Manager Alex. Milne [sic] is the straightest man who ever managed me. He is a good fellow in every way, and we were sorry to leave him. But what could we do? No fair-minded man would blame us under the circumstances.[3]

Corbeau was either being facetious or naive. The loyal Torontos' supporters blamed him. They felt betrayed. So, too, did the Ontario league, which banned both Corbeau and Ronan for life. However, given the

competitive pressures on pro clubs to recruit constantly, players knew
that such sanctions were meaningless.

AU REVOIR "CON" AND ALSO RONAN

Money Bug Hit Toronto Pros. But the Team is Still a Fighting Machine

More troubles!
And still the Toronto professional
hockey team is on its pins. If Galt
doesn't find them a set of winners this
very night it will be passing strange.
The unexpected has happened—Corbeau and Ronan have departed.
The clink of Haileybury silver was
too much for the pair, and last night
they beat it for the mines.
Haileybury has been after Lalonde,
Corbeau and Ronan for the last couple
of weeks, and they all declined to go.
But yesterday Mr. Solomon, a Hailey-

The OPHL's problems seemed to be of some benefit
to Toronto. However, the defections of Corbeau and
Ronan to the Temiskaming league were an ominous
sign.

For Toronto's manager, there also remained the questions surrounding his disabled stars. Word was that Newsy Lalonde was out of hospital,
practising and ready for action. Yet Bert Morrison, according to reports,
remained stricken with his vague "illness." Last season, he had been
the target of constant press criticism; this year, the same writers had not
ceased talking about the damage done by his absence. Nonetheless, any
expectation of his return gradually—and strangely—slipped away as the
season progressed.

Now, with a surplus of forwards to choose from, Miln made the
decision to cut Herb Birmingham. The twenty-seven-year-old veteran

lacked the weight to check back and no longer had the speed to keep pace. Herbie had been averaging two goals a game for the Torontos, but the decision was not controversial. There was no outcry from either fans or press. This underscores just how lightly goal scoring was taken as a measure of offensive prowess during this era.

A general thaw throughout southern Ontario delayed the Torontos' next match until Wednesday, January 27, at the Galt Rink. The made-over Professionals included only three players from their previous game. Chuck Tyner in goal and Bruce Ridpath on left wing had been the two constants throughout the season. Stoke Doran at cover was still a relative newcomer.

The reconstituted offence looked very good on paper. Lalonde was back at centre, while Smith took his natural place at rover and Manson was moved to the right side. However, with Hugh Lambe behind Doran, the defence looked slow and suspect. The club had no spare rearguard, Fred Young being the only extra player still under contract. For this contest at least, the weakness did not matter. When the defence proved inadequate, Tyner more than compensated with his goaltending. Lalonde, with four markers, led an offence that rolled over the Indians 7–3. He also took his team through the tough stuff, bettering the home side's Angus Dusome in the main bout.

Galt, previously tied with Brantford in the standings, had lost for only the second time, and Little Manchester's fans did not take it well. A couple of hundred locals waited outside the rink to confront the visitors after the game. In the end, however, they turned largely passive, reserving "a few warm hisses"[4] for the referee.

Miln now wanted an opportunity to show his new powerhouse offence to Torontonians. He decided to schedule a postponed game with Brantford for that Saturday night at the Mutual Street Rink. Almost immediately there was an uproar. The Toronto Amateur Athletic Club had its Interprovincial home game scheduled for the same time at the Excelsior. The amateur Torontos clearly were not relishing the competition for fans, as they threatened to cancel their future OHA bookings at the old Caledonian if the head-to-head manoeuvres of Miln and his Professionals continued.

For the pro Torontos, Brantford would be the real test. That club was again in first in the OPHL race. The Braves had kept on winning despite

An accomplished stickhandler as well as a fast skater, tall, lean Howard Manson had played for the Ottawa Victorias in their January 1908 Stanley Cup challenge against the Montreal Wanderers. His play in Toronto was consistently rated as good.

the personnel losses sustained in the recent train crash. Interestingly, the replacement for Jack Marks at right wing had turned out to be none other than former Toronto Pro Wally Mercer, picked up when Guelph dissolved.

The Pros' manager decided to shore up his defence for the encounter. He relegated Lambe to the substitution list, put Doran back at point, and brought in a new cover. This would be yet another Cornwall player, Hank Smith. Hank was a cousin of Donald, and he came directly from the Factory Town's Federal league club.

There was yet another packed house that evening in the Queen City. And the fans were not disappointed. The offence, with Manson and Donny Smith swapped, more than lived up to its billing. Even Robertson's *Tely* was in awe of its performance:

> The whole four passed and re-passed the disc, bandied it about with the surety of wizards, never faltering, seldom failing, and slipping along past their opponents like shadows.[5]

The born-again Torontos proved they were for real, literally crushing the front-runners. The 15–10 score was deceptive. The locals had gone up by a wide margin early, Brantford narrowing it somewhat only after the matter had become hopeless. Three hundred Dykeville supporters who had come down on the train grew silent as the "cakewalk"[6] continued. The spectacular Ridpath, with seven goals that night, looked as if he could have beaten them single-handedly.

The Professionals had also again bettered their amateur competition at the gate. The Toronto Athletics had faced the famed Montreal Victorias and their legendary star, Russell Bowie. The amateur squad was trounced in front of a small gathering at the Excelsior. Toronto hockey fans seemed to be in complete ignorance of the increasingly savage coverage of the professional league in most of their local newspapers. When ticket sales were stopped at Mutual, there remained a lineup stretching fifty yards down the street.

Nonetheless, after four weeks of the OPHL season, the Torontos still found themselves in last place. However, their prospects had definitely improved. Including the eight defaulted games each team was credited against Guelph and St. Catharines, the official league standings were now:

	W	L	REMAINING[7]
Brantford	11	2	7
Galt	11	2	7
Berlin	11	3	6
Toronto	10	4	6

The revitalized Professionals would face their next test almost immediately—on Monday, February 1, at Berlin. For that occasion, the Dutchmen would not feature Rolly Young. The former Toronto captain's hesitancy about hockey had spilled over into the regular season. After debating whether he would play at all, his performance in Berlin had gone steadily downhill. Young had refused to practise between games and, as a consequence, he put on weight. Never fast to begin with, Rolly lost both a step and the edge to his physical game. He also failed to bring support from his Waterloo home over to his new club. Management finally decided to cut him. While he was rumoured to be interested in returning to the Ontario capital, Miln also decided to pass.

———

The Berlin game was a rough, crude affair—something increasingly common in the OPHL that season. A raft of penalties finally culminated in a free-for-all. When Edward "Toad" Edmunds slashed Don Smith,

Yet another recruit from Cornwall's Federal league club, cover point Howard "Hank" Smith was studying to be a marine engineer.

Lalonde went after him. Then Uncle Gross came in, followed by Doran, and soon every player was part of a "tumbling, slugging pile."[8] It ended only when the police finally intervened.

With the flow of the game destroyed, the Torontos' offence was broken up. Without a strong attack—and periodically bogged down in penalties—the Professionals' weak defence became their downfall. Berlin took it 6–3. Big Ezra Dumart shone in the tough going and scored a hat trick for the winners. As they rolled to victory, the hometown fans chanted their song, "Oh the Dutch companee is the best companee!"[9]

The Torontos headed back home, banged up and with their confidence shaken. Teddy Marriott declared that the players had performed "1,000 per cent worse"[10] in Berlin than in their previous outing. They were thus eager to show the Mutual gallery that the recent run had been no fluke. The awaited opposition would be Galt, which had slipped into first place in a razor-thin race between the three country teams.

After two games with the same roster, the Pros seemed almost overdue for a lineup change. This became necessary when Hank Smith returned to Cornwall to prepare for his exams for the marine service. Lambe was brought back in at point.

By the time Thursday night came, the homesters had their form back. The offence opened the scoring with five unanswered goals en route to a 6–2 win on poor ice. In front of the usual big crowd, the visiting Indians were totally outplayed both ways.

Lalonde led the offence, but all the forwards contributed. Lambe and Doran had unusually strong games on defence. Tyner also played well, but it did not really matter. As one writer wryly observed:

The only excitement of the evening was caused by a couple of female rooters from Galt, who were stationed in the gallery, and who had many verbal encounters with male fans of the big city.[11]

A disappointing season for the Toronto HC had now concluded its fifth week. While the usual critics of pro hockey had become bolder, the club still enjoyed significant goodwill among its many fans. Attendance had remained large and enthusiastic at all home games—even with play that had frequently been either rough or uninspired.

The revolving door of the dressing room had also been largely accepted. With unfortunate injuries and unforeseen defections, Miln's many player movements had generally been regarded as bold and necessary. There was also increasing excitement and confidence in the team's new lineup. The *World* flatly declared that the win over Galt "again demonstrated that the Toronto team have no license at the bottom of the league and with any share of luck they should even now tie Brantford for the championship."[12]

In retrospect, however, the elements of a deep disillusionment were beginning to take shape. Fan patience was being pushed very close to a precipice. A couple of events would soon edge it over. Foremost was the reality that the championship was virtually out of reach, notwithstanding the wishful thinking of the *World*. It did

HE MADE THEM SIT UP

BRUCE RIDPATH,
The fast forward of the Toronto professional team, who accepted big money to go to Cobalt. He played a wonderful game against Haileybury, when the two teams met last Wednesday.
Bruce will be back in Toronto with his team for the game against Brantford next week.

Initial reports on Ridpath's departure suggested that he would be back. This article includes a rare picture of the Professionals' 1908–09 jersey.

not matter how good the team had become or how many games they had almost won. The closeness of the race was exaggerated by OPHL standings typically showing eight free wins for each team against their defunct rivals. In reality, with five losses in what was now effectively a twelve-game schedule (with their three remaining competitors), Toronto's chances of finishing or tying for first were mathematically very slim.

All this was being noticed by some—but most significantly by Bruce Ridpath. On Monday, February 8, a spreading rumour was confirmed: Riddy had signed with the Cobalt Silver Kings of the Temiskaming league. Bruce, who maintained a sporting goods store on Yonge Street, said he would be willing to come back to Toronto when available. However, he was being paid $500 to help settle the northern league's tight race. Any return to the Queen City club therefore seemed like wishful thinking.

It is hard to overstate the magnitude of the blow Ridpath's loss dealt the franchise. A local boy, he was the team's founder, key playmaker and most popular player. Since becoming a senior with the Marlboros in 1904–05, he had been miles away the city's most exciting performer when at full throttle. The *Star* captured a sense of this, recounting a recent match when "a stentorian-voiced rooter made the rafters ring with, 'Go it, you little rat, go it!' "[13] as Riddy repeatedly led the attack.

But now Ridpath was gone to hockey's newest land of opportunity, the cash-rich mining towns of northeastern Ontario. It was not his first adventure into the Temiskaming Hockey League. He had, after all, gone there late in the 1905–06 season, when he had joined teammates Rolly Young and Harry Burgoyne to play under assumed names for New Liskeard against Haileybury. That infamous excursion had shattered the amateur Marlboros and paved the way for the formation of the Professionals.

The Toronto papers, ever loyal to the OHA, had claimed that there had been deep revulsion in the north country against ringers as a consequence of the scandal. They could not have been more wrong. Indeed, the Temiskaming league began taking hockey "tourism" to levels never seen before or since. Lineups changed nonstop as players were literally hired game to game. On occasion, the personnel of clubs from other leagues were recruited in their entirety to substitute for local talent.

International Hockey League teams had been willing renters of their lineups to the Temiskaming clubs. However, the U.S.-based league was the ultimate loser in this dubious practice. Just as the IHL had once lured away promising Canadian prospects with the big bucks of the Michigan mining country, it then faced the same sort of competition in reverse. Northeastern Ontario was experiencing a mining boom in everything from cobalt to gold. Its hockey clubs quickly became key Dominion competitors in the economic struggle that eventually finished the IHL.

Filled with well-paid young men lacking wives and mortgages, Canada's booming mining communities had lots of money to spend on hockey. Huge gates fuelled runaway player salaries. For example, in the home opener of Ridpath's new club, there were reportedly 4,000 rooters present—and Cobalt was a town of just 5,000 people. Yet the sum spent on tickets was only a small part of the cash haul. Wagers were plentiful and often very large. The total gambling in Riddy's first home-and-home series against Haileybury was in the range of $50,000. Robertson's *Telegram* was not exaggerating all that much when it claimed "up north they bet real money on hockey, and keep the mining stocks to sell to their friends."[14]

Miln sought James Irwin Mallen to help fill the hole created by the departure of Bruce Ridpath. Ironically, "Kid" Mallen was Ken's older brother.

None of this should imply that the hockey played in the Temiskaming league was farcical—far from it. From 1906 on, the circuit's calibre grew steadily. By 1909, increasing numbers of established stars were being pilfered permanently from the clubs of big-city leagues like the ECHA and OPHL. Even before Ridpath's recruitment, the Silver Kings had beaten the Stanley Cup champion Montreal Wanderers 6–4 in an exhibition match earlier that season. Yet, because of progressively stricter residency rules in place for Cup competition, the bush league had virtually no chance of playing for Lord Stanley's chalice.

Miln, however, had apparently not given up on the championship. On the contrary, he again had his wires out and acted with speed and skill in frantic efforts to replace the hole left by Ridpath. Alex first elected to dump Fred Young, whom he had relegated to being a goal umpire. He then recruited Jimmy Mallen. Mallen, on his way out of the dissolving West Penn League, was from good stock. His brother, former Toronto Pro Ken Mallen, was a widely sought-after performer.

Mallen was not available for the game to be played the following evening, so Miln also brought in Herb Fyfe. This refugee from Guelph was a steady performer who had practised with the Torontos in the 1907–08 preseason. In the end, though, it would not matter who took Riddy's place on left wing.

The contest was another of the year's key turning points involving Brantford. Fittingly, the showdown would take place at its address on Waterloo Street. The Torontos went down by a score of 12–4. However, they did not just lose big—they lost ugly. It all unravelled when Newsy Lalonde's hypercompetitive nature got the better of him.

Toronto had been outplayed in the first half and trailed 4–2. The young captain sensed the season was slipping away. So, when Brantford goal judge Charles Carson allowed a dubious fifth marker early in the second, Lalonde simply lost it. He went after Carson with his fists, causing a mad rush of players, fans and police officers to enter the melee. Although not thrown out of the game, Newsy's heart was not in it after that—and thus the blowout began.

It was clear that Lalonde would be facing charges from the Brantford authorities. No matter how much roughness was sometimes tolerated in hockey in those days, the line had always been drawn at attacks on officials. More critically, Lalonde's image had shifted. Newsy had always been a tough—and occasionally dirty—hockey player. As a star scorer who spent much time near the goalmouth, it was an occupational requirement. However, his behaviour had been borderline before—for example, he once pummelled a Galt fan who had attempted to interfere with the on-ice play. Toronto may not have been as pure about hockey violence as the OHA pretended, but fans did draw a distinction between an on-ice "policeman" and a thug.

So the fan favourite was gone. The captain was under a cloud. Team play had largely been lost through the constant shuffling. And the championship was now unequivocally out of reach. The Torontos were approaching a point of no return.

Before resuming league play, however, the club would take the train to London for an exhibition contest that Friday. This OPHL expedition, canvassing a potential new market after the loss of two franchises, was certainly going against the grain. The Garnet and Grey met up with Galt and lost 7–4. A well-filled Princess Rink witnessed a lacklustre effort on both sides—hardly a move to inspire interest in a London franchise. If nothing else, though, the match did confirm that the Miln-Irving business partnership remained intact despite the league's boardroom battles.[15]

The following Tuesday, February 16, the Torontos went on to Galt itself, where they again lost, the final count being 16–11. At this point, Lalonde seems to have embarked on a score-settling campaign. His aggressive play led to another fight with Dusome. This followed his appearance earlier that day in front of a police magistrate in Brantford. There, the Toronto centre got off with a fine for assault and abusive language.

Newsy's reign of terror moved back to Mutual Street on Thursday night. In a contest marked by the terrible refereeing of Buck Irving— who was generally known to be a terrible referee—Lalonde took after Berlin's Edmunds and Gross with vicious stickwork. The hometown fans loudly jeered him when he was finally thrown out of the game. The *Globe* observed the seriousness of the situation:

BURLESQUE IN THE PRO. LEAGUE

Berlin Defeated Toronto in a Joke Encounter at the Mutual Street Rink.

LALONDE USES HIS STICK

Chops Down a Couple of Berlin Players, and Is Hooted Off the Ice by Spectators.

There have been some mighty poor games at the Mutual street rink this season, but last night's encounter between Berlin and Toronto pros. was absolutely the worst. It was not even up to the quality of poor intermediate hockey, and to make matters worse "Newsy" Lalonde interjected a lot of deliberate rough-house tactics that will probably end his usefulness as a hockey player in Toronto.

The headlines were getting ever worse. In particular, captain Newsy Lalonde's rough play was making him increasingly unpopular with Toronto fans.

> When a local crowd hisses and hoots the captain of the local team for brutal attacks on opposing players, the same captain having been fined a few days ago in the Brantford Police Court for beating a goal umpire, his usefulness in promoting the game of hockey seems to have reached the limit.[16]

Unfortunately for the Professionals, the bad news did not end there. They had again lost—this time 8–5—and had played very poorly. The

crowd was a small one, and even those fans were dissatisfied. The reviews were universally bad, the following being typical: "If the players
received real money for playing a hockey game, they got it under false
pretences. It wasn't even shinny. Alex Miln, himself, admitted that."[17]

To compound matters, some serious local competition to the pro team
was emerging. It was not from the Interprovincial Union, where the Toronto Amateur Athletic Club had finished the season winless, but from
the good old Ontario Hockey Association. The TAAC's entry in the old
association was having a decent season, but the new senior club from
St. Michael's College was doing even better. For the first time in several
years, the possibility of a senior championship was generating real amateur hockey excitement in Toronto.

Queen City fans were also being reminded daily of their departed pro
celebrities. Reports from the mining country heaped praise on the exploits of Bruce Ridpath, now the darling of Cobalt, lifting his team ahead
of Haileybury's Skene Ronan and Con Corbeau to take the local championship. And Dubbie Kerr was emerging as a new star of the Ottawas,
hot on the trail of the Eastern league title.

The Toronto Professionals' final game of the season would be at Mutual on Tuesday, February 23—and it would be another seminal moment
against Brantford. By now, the Torontos were merely limping towards
the finish line, both on the ice and at the box office.

The events of that evening would make things far worse for the organization.

———

Despite the previous three losses, the Torontos' lineup was starting to
come back together. Lambe had been returned to spare status while
Lalonde was moved to the cover point position. This had allowed forwards Mallen, Manson, Smith and Fyfe—all decent hockey players—to
be put on the ice as a unit. The team again had a solid attack, while Tyner
in goal and an improving Doran at point covered the back end.

Indeed, the Torontos did look like the better team against Manager
Roy Brown's outfit that evening. Yet every time they appeared ready to
roll ahead, the players seemed to either pull back or permit a soft goal.

In the end, they let Brantford turn a 7–6 deficit into a 9–7 victory. The few hundred diehards present were vocally displeased.

It is evident from all reports the next day that many suspected the game had been thrown, if not rigged outright. Even the *News*, the club's most sympathetic organ, testified that "there were those at the rink who said openly that the locals wouldn't take it as a gift."[18] John Ross Robertson's *Telegram*, which regularly implied that pro hockey was fixed, gleefully proclaimed "professional hockey got a bad black eye in last night's game."[19]

The criticism focused on two players: Lalonde and Tyner. Lalonde was unusually passive and, very uncharacteristically, failed to score. Tyner let in an abnormal number of soft ones. According to nasty but widely circulating rumours, the pair, after deliberately losing the game, were going to play for Brantford to help them overtake Galt in the homestretch.[20] Miln was even said to be in on the scheme.[21]

THE ONTARIO PRO. SEASON IS OVER

Galt are the Undisputed Champions—Defeated Berlin at Berlin 4 to 2.

FISHY GAME PLAYED HERE

Fans Cry That Local Game Was Sold — Brantford Won 9 Goals to 7.

The Ontario professional season is over, and Galt are the undisputed champions. If there was any doubt about the location of this year's championship, Galt settled it last night at Berlin, where they laid the Dutch away to the dirge of 4–2. Brantford defeated Toronto in Toronto 9–7.

The Berlin game, which was played on pretty fair ice, considering the weather, was a good, keen contest in the initial half, but in the second half Galt had it on the German crew at all stages, and won by farther than the score indicates. Not even the most

The Torontos' last game was a public-relations disaster. They were widely suspected of throwing it—confirming the worst stereotype of professional athletes.

There can be no doubt that this conspiracy theory, combined with events on the ice that night, did real damage—but was it true? Maybe Chuck, who had been inconsistent all season, just had an off game? Maybe Newsy did not score because he was playing defence? Was the public not demanding he rein in his aggressiveness anyway? In the end, Tyner and Lalonde never did suit up for the Braves, as the Indians coasted to the pennant in the closing games.[22]

For Lalonde, the criticism must have been especially wounding.

The captain, whatever his faults, had been a consistent competitor. He had stuck with the club despite the offer of big money from the mining league up north. He had also thrown himself into recruiting work as the club struggled with defections. This partly explains why so many new-comers had come from Cornwall and other parts of eastern Ontario.

In any case, professional hockey was ending the local season at a new low—just as the amateur game was on the rise. In the weeks that followed, St. Mike's took the senior OHA championship and the John Ross Robertson Cup. The Queen City was on top for the first time since the Marlboro title of 1904–05. Although it turned out to be too late to challenge for the Allan Cup, the prospect of genuine national honours was capturing the public's imagination.

Both the amateur and professional hockey champions of Canada were, for now, to be found in the nation's capital. The Allan Cup was first held—albeit briefly—by the Ottawa Cliffsides, who had taken the Inter-provincial title. Ottawa's Silver Seven had won the Eastern crown and thus had finally taken the Stanley Cup back from the Montreal Wanderers.

With the Toronto Professionals' season in tatters, it was understandably forgotten that they had beaten the new Stanley Cup champions just two months before. How quickly—and completely—things had changed.

Still, despite the disastrous end to the 1908–09 season, the Torontos had managed to complete their schedule. The club had not disbanded and there were no reports that it would do so. Indeed, as the city entered the fall, there were clear expectations that the Professionals would ice a squad in 1909–10. Supporters were already speculating that it would be a comeback year.

One warning sign, however, was the apparent lack of star players. Professional recruiting promised to be as competitive as ever. Alex Miln claimed to have a line out to several pro veterans, including defectors Dubbie Kerr and Bruce Ridpath. Yet fan favourite Riddy had spoken highly of his experiences in the north country and was showing no sign of returning.

The one top performer who had stuck with the club through thick and thin the past season was Newsy Lalonde. The malicious rumours that he would be a ringer for Brantford at season's end being false,

the much-maligned captain had instead travelled to Montreal. There,
he had played on a hastily formed
French Canadian all-star team. Reports had him staying with a Francophone club, likely the Montreal
Nationals.

In early November, rumours
about the club's future began to circulate for the first time. These were
sparked by Miln's failure to appear
at an OPHL meeting scheduled for
Brantford. The reason was not clear,
but the stories suggested the Toronto
manager was again looking at taking
his club into the ECHA.

Miln finally did show up at the
league meeting that had been re-
scheduled for November 19. There,
he stunned observers by wielding
the axe. He was stepping down as
president of the Ontario Pro league
and withdrawing his club from the
circuit. However, it was not joining
any other league.

Hockey
TORONTO SEVEN IS WITHDRAWN

This City Will Not be in the Professional League.

TOO MANY AMATEUR TEAMS

Mutual Street Rink Would Not Support Both Brands of Hockey at
the Same Time.

Special to The Mail and Empire.
Brantford, Ont., Nov. 19.—Only four
teams will comprise the Ontario Professional Hockey League this year, the Toronto professional team being formally
withdrawn at the annual meeting of the
league here to-night, by Alex. Miln, of
the Mutual Street Rink. Eight senior
amateur teams already had applied for
playing dates at the Mutual Street Rink.

The final curtain for the Torontos
came as somewhat of a surprise.
Alex Miln would henceforth re-
fuse to associate with pro hockey.

Three days short of its third birthday, the Toronto Hockey Club was
no more.

The Mutual Street Rink manager went further. Noting that he was
receiving numerous applications—professional and amateur—for the
coming season, "Mr. Miln was of the opinion that the two brands of
hockey did not mix, and he was desirous of giving the preference to the
amateur clubs." [23] In other words, the boss of the former pro team was
endorsing the separation principle of the amateur purists. More than
that, he was saying professionals and amateurs could not mix, *even in the
same facility*. It was a stunning and devastating rebuke of the commercial
game from Toronto's chief promoter of professional hockey.

Little is known about why Miln made such a sudden about-face without warning. There was nothing new about much demand for ice time at Mutual Street—it happened every year. Money doubtless had more to do with it. Miln suggested that, by drawing the big gates, the pro club had taken the profits out of local amateur hockey. Meanwhile, reports indicated the pro club itself had lost at least $1,500 in 1908–09. In truth, leaving aside the March 1908 Stanley Cup gambling takes, the Toronto Hockey Club probably did not make money on hockey operations in any of its three seasons.

Whatever Miln's reasons, the advocates of amateurism were ecstatic. John Ross Robertson's organ was the most eloquent:

> It is not often that amateur hockey can chase the pro. article out of a city the size of Toronto. But that's what has happened here. So many senior O.H.A. teams are in line that the pros. are crowded off Mutual street rink . . . The rush of amateurs is the healthiest sign any sport can show. It means that hockey in Toronto is on a healthy foundation, that O.H.A. supervision is universally satisfactory and that the future of the game is assured.[24]

Such self-congratulatory commentary underscored a sense of triumph among Toronto's amateurs that was total. Just as victory was inexorably moving their way in the long Athletic War, so too had the battle for control of hockey in the Queen City. The field had been vacated. The professionals had been expelled, never to return.

At least that's what John Ross Robertson and his followers wanted to believe.

CHAPTER ELEVEN

THE OLD ORDER RESTORED

The Era of Amateurism Returns to the Queen City

———•◦•———

They learned nothing and forgot nothing.

—TALLEYRAND[1]

The 1909–10 Toronto hockey season was opening not just without the professionals, but also amid a genuine renaissance in the amateur game. The OHA champions, St. Michael's College of Toronto, had their eyes set on the national glory of the Allan Cup. At the provincial level, there would be as many as ten local senior amateur clubs crowding the Mutual Street Rink, and, proclaimed the *Tely*, "still the list of aspirants for the J. Ross Robertson Cup grows."[2]

In fact, amateurism was ascendant everywhere. Led by the revived Olympic Games of Pierre de Coubertin, its purists were gaining a world-wide reach. The London Games had particularly captured the public's imagination, despite a controversy during the opening ceremony when American flag bearer Ralph Rose refused to dip his colours before King Edward VII. The Games had lasted more than six months—the longest in Olympic history—thanks to the addition of four figure-skating events held later in the year. All in all, they were widely hailed as a great success for amateur sport.

CAAU president
James Merrick spoke
magnanimously
about the merger
with the Federation.
However, there was
little doubt the Union
had won the Athletic
War.

Canadians' most poignant memory, however, had been the disastrous showing of Tom Longboat in the marathon. And yet, even that was a blessing to the amateur ideologues, for it had marked the beginning of the end for the pragmatists.

In the spring of 1909, this was confirmed when the Montreal-based Amateur Athletic Federation of Canada came to the Toronto-based Canadian Amateur Athletic Union seeking peace. The Union, by now rid of its most intransigent leaders, responded positively to the Federation's overtures. The country's three-year-long Athletic War was coming to a surprisingly amicable conclusion.

On Labour Day, the two bodies officially established the new Amateur Athletic Union of Canada. It would be led by CAAU president James G. Merrick, a Toronto disciple of John Ross Robertson. Montreal men were also given positions of prominence. In particular, the AAFC would form the basis of the AAUC's Quebec branch. Merrick declared the battle over with quintessential Canadian diplomacy:

> The Federation, as represented by the Montreal Amateur Athletic Association, the proudest and most powerful club in Canada, was perfectly sincere in its idea of amateurism in sport, and just as ready to jealously guard it as we are. With both bodies working for pure amateurism it was only a matter of time until the points of difference were satisfactorily adjusted, and the schism bridged.[3]

A bit of flexibility had been shown on the amateur definition. A broad amnesty on past bans was instituted. Transitional measures were put in place for hockey and lacrosse. As well, a few athletes—golfers, cricketers and bowlers—would be allowed to play against professionals. Nonetheless, there was no illusion about who had won this Canadian civil war.

Exceptions were just that. Going forward, an ironclad, no-mixing amateurism would generally apply, just as John Ross Robertson would have wished.

The "peace, order and good government" of Canadian athletics would be under the AAUC, with Toronto, not Montreal, as the national capital of amateur sport.

———

The advocates of amateur purity were also in the process of creating their own parallel national structures. The Mann Cup was introduced to displace the Minto Cup in lacrosse, just as the Allan Cup aimed to upstage the Stanley Cup. Of course, the separation of amateur and professional athletics was already in effect in hockey. With professionals now gravitating towards purely professional leagues, this led to significantly fewer eligibility conflicts in organizations like the Ontario Hockey Association. It only further convinced Robertson and his cohorts that their approach had been the right one all along.

There were, however, a few early warning signs.

Professionalism was hardly disappearing. On the contrary, in some sports it was emerging as not only a separate, but also a higher, tier. For instance, it was already noted that amateur running meets were becoming a training ground for those aspiring to be the next Tom Longboat. The aboriginal runner was now achieving great success in his new career as an open professional. In a rematch of the London Olympics staged at Madison Square Garden, Longboat easily prevailed. In 1909, again in New York City, he won another contest that declared him "Professional Champion of the World."[4]

The first evidence of the same phenomenon could also be seen in hockey. There was, for example, talk in Ottawa that hockey's Cliffsides would amalgamate with the Senators'[5] second squad. This would, in effect, make them a pro farm team, even if their players remained officially amateur.

Yet, in the fall of 1909, it was the future of the stand-alone world of professional hockey that was very much in doubt. Merrick, and amateur leaders like him, had long predicted that the paid game could not survive detached from its amateur roots. With pro leagues and teams folding faster than new ones could spring up, many thought he was right.

Alex Miln had suddenly and surprisingly joined these growing ranks of pro hockey doubters. Faced with the prospect of another unprofitable season in the Ontario Professional Hockey League, he had decided to fold his Toronto Professionals rather than take a gamble by joining the premier big league, the Eastern Canada Hockey Association. Looking at the high travel costs of the Eastern league, the small markets of the Ontario one, and rising player salaries everywhere, he may well have concluded that pro hockey simply could not be viable. With an unprecedented commercial crisis about to beset the ECHA, Miln's decision looked prescient.

A direct descendant of the original Amateur Hockey Association of Canada, the ECHA and its predecessors had always been the country's top league. Its most recent victors, the Ottawa Senators, were Stanley Cup champs and kings of the pro hockey world. Indeed, the league had almost always held the trophy.

Below the surface, however, it was a deeply troubled organization.

Pro hockey continued to be racked by contract jumping, unruly on-ice behaviour, unresolved off-ice battles and, especially, escalating payrolls. However, the ECHA had a unique problem. Since the return of the Montreal Wheelers and Montreal Victorias to the amateur ranks, the imbalance of the remaining four-team league had become glaring. The Eastern league had only two real contenders: the champions from Ottawa and the Montreal Wanderers. The Montreal Shamrocks and Quebec Bulldogs were increasingly poor also-rans. It meant the championship would invariably boil down to the games between the two elite clubs. Such predictability was not a recipe for commercial viability. Even as winners of the Stanley Cup—long considered the golden goose of the box office—the Ottawas had lost money in 1908–09.

As the 1909–10 season approached, these pressures began to unwind the long-standing business alliance between the Ottawas and the Wanderers. The clubs agreed changes in the league needed to be made, but could not arrive at a consensus as to how. The proverbial stuff really hit the fan, however, when the Redbands decided to move to a newer but smaller rink, the Jubilee Arena. The other teams believed this would cut into their dwindling gates. Led by Ottawa, they began to plot against the Wanderers.

Finally, on November 25, the Senators, Shamrocks and Bulldogs withdrew from the ECHA and formed a new league, christened the Canadian Hockey Association. The CHA promptly admitted two new clubs. The Montreal Nationals were brought in to appeal to the Francophone market. A new English organization named All-Montreal was recruited to replace the stranded Wanderers.

EASTERN CANADA HOCKEY
WANDERERS WERE FROZEN OUT

French-Canadian Team Admitted Under Name of Nationals at Last Night's Meeting

DISSOLVED AND FORMED ANEW

Hockey Po'itics in Pro. Circuit at Montreal Settled Into Something Definite

(From Our Own Correspondent.)

Montreal, Nov. 26.—The Wanderers are out in the cold, that is as far as the principal senior hockey body is concerned, but they will have the roof of the Jubilee Rink over their head and considerable financial backing, it is said, to keep the wolf from the door.

FRENCH GET FRANCHIE.

It was a question of Wanderers or Nationals, and it was decided that an "All French-Canadian" team with the name "Nationals" would be a bigger money maker than the Wanderers.

HENDRY AND MCMASTER.

(From Our Own Correspondent.)

Mitchell, Ont., Nov. 26.—President McKeand to-day appointed Dr. Hendry, of Toronto, and Phil. Mc Master, of Montreal, to referee the big Canadian Rugby championship final between Varsity and Ottawa at Toronto to-morrow.

ED. BARROW IS MANAGER

TAKES HOLD OF MONTREAL.

Arrived There This Morning and at Once Signed Up to Lead Ball team.

(From Our Own Correspondent.)

Montreal, Nov. 26.—Ed Barrow is here to-day in the capacity of new manager of the Montreal Baseball Club. After much dickering, he agreed to act and he is getting a big salary for it. When he arrived this morning it was not long before the document installing him as head of the team was signed. He has a free hand to do so

The other eastern pro clubs may have decided they did not want the Wanderers, but it was not a judgment the Redbands were prepared to accept.

However, if any club knew how to play the game of league hopping, it was the Redbands. They would almost immediately enter into talks with the leagues up in the northern "bush." Although run by wealthy interests, those towns' Cup ambitions had long been frustrated by anti-ringer rules and forced exclusion from the "big-league" circuit. It was not surprising that the principals of the Temiskaming league—businessmen like Noah Timmins of Haileybury and T. C. "Tommy" Hare of Cobalt—wanted their clubs in the upper echelon of hockey.

They were backed by an even bigger player: Michael John O'Brien of Renfrew.

———

M. J. O'Brien was an increasingly rich and powerful railroad and mining baron, with holdings in various parts of the country. His hometown Renfrew Creamery Kings had long been the rulers of the Upper Ottawa Valley league. The previous season, they had moved into a reinvigorated Federal league, where they were also champions. These organizations shared the Temiskaming league's entrepreneurial hockey culture and played regularly against its clubs.

M.J.'s aspiring hockey-manager son, John Ambrose O'Brien, and his partner, J. G. Barnett, had been making ever more serious attempts to get into hockey's big time. The established interests of the ECHA were making it just as obvious that they were not interested, despite the league's deep financial trouble. As its clubs conspired to expel the Wanderers, it also made the young O'Brien sit in the lobby of Montreal's Windsor Hotel—rejecting his application without even the courtesy of hearing him out. It would turn out to be a mistake of historic proportions.

The O'Briens' wrath was about to alter the world of professional hockey forever.

Ambrose did not simply leave the building as the ECHA thought he would. Instead, he continued to patiently wait and ended up intercepting the furious, cursing bosses of the ostracized Wanderers as they left the meeting. And so they began to commiserate with each other.

The two sides quickly discovered a natural partnership. The Wanderers needed a league; the O'Briens needed the Montreal market. Thus, a mere week later, the Wanderers combined with the Federal champion Renfrew Creamery Kings, the Temiskaming champion Cobalt Silver Kings and their close rival, the Haileybury Comets, to form the National

Hockey Association. To compete with the CHA among Francophones, Ambrose created a new franchise for the NHA—to be called *les Canadiens*.

HON. MICHAEL JOHN O'BRIEN
The Man who built it

JOHN AMBROSE O'BRIEN
Vice-President, M. J. O'Brien, Limited, Ottawa, Ont.

The O'Briens, father (Michael John) and son (John Ambrose), were becoming one of Canada's most powerful families. Shunned by the sport's establishment, their rival league, the National Hockey Association, would lay the foundation for the modern pro hockey business.

The NHA was set up by outcasts who hailed mainly from small towns. Nevertheless, it was the basis for today's pro hockey order—and it spawned "a new club," the Montreal Canadiens.

From rooms only a few doors apart in Montreal's Windsor Hotel, the NHA and CHA began planning for all-out war. In fact, the split in the ECHA would be followed by the most rapid rise of salaries in hockey history. The two pro associations went after key players with vengeance and desperation. The most spectacular signings were made by Renfrew, an organization soon to be famously dubbed the Millionaires. Powered by the O'Briens' virtually limitless bankroll, Renfrew sought the best players in the country. Their recruiting efforts made the infamous spending of the Edmonton pros look like small change. They lured the game's biggest star, Fred "Cyclone" Taylor, from Ottawa for a reputed salary of $5,250[6]—close to triple what top players had previously been earning. The deal made him, on a per-game basis, the highest-paid athlete in the world.

Overall, the new league was pulling ahead in the recruiting sweepstakes. Led by the Taylor signing, Renfrew was out-recruiting Ottawa—although the Senators did pull Bruce Ridpath from Cobalt. The Wanderers were generally holding their lineup against All-Montreal. And, after court battles over broken contracts, the Canadiens succeeded in stealing the best French players, including Newsy Lalonde, from the Nationals.

All observers agreed that this was a fight to the death—and that it could not last long. The *Globe*, for one, confidently predicted that "there is not the slightest probability that they [the NHA and CHA] will go through the season they have mapped out in their schedules."[7] It was particularly noted that the central war zone of Montreal had five professional clubs competing for fans.

The Montreal market was actually saturated well beyond this commercial conflict. The two pro groupings would also be competing for fans with three amateur associations of Allan Cup calibre: the Interprovincial, Intercollegiate and a new entry, the St. Lawrence. All told, the city was now home to ten senior-level hockey teams.

It was the Stanley Cup champions who blinked first. The Ottawa Senators came to the NHA, looking for an armistice. On January 16, after some brief negotiations, the new league admitted them and the Montreal Shamrocks. What remained of the competing circuit was not viable, and the CHA folded.

This historic battle, fought between the traditional, middle-class hockey managers of the CHA and the rising industrialists behind the NHA, had been no contest. The power of the bankroll had trumped the vaunted legacies of the older organization and its clubs. After twenty-four years (under various names) as Canada's most prestigious hockey league, the CHA was no more.[8]

Professional hockey increasingly looked like a wreckage yard. All that remained of pro hockey in western Canada was a fledgling new league in Saskatchewan and a declining club in Edmonton. In Ontario, there were just two associations—one in the southwest, the other in the northwest—and both were small groups of modest-sized towns. The commercial game was still in its infancy in the Maritimes, and Doc Gibson's pro ranks had vanished entirely from the United States. Even worse, the war with the CHA had left the new big league, the NHA, weighed down by unsustainable costs.

While the pro hockey war of 1909–10 was an eastern phenomenon, its effects were felt elsewhere. Indeed, the elevated level of instability had ramifications throughout Canada. In Ontario, for example, the money-losing OPHL was further squeezed by the high salaries offered during the CHA–NHA showdown. Also, amateur Toronto, the war's "western front," was, ironically, the site of some minor skirmishes during the professional hostilities.

The truth was that, while the Toronto Professionals had died fairly quietly, they had not done so in complete silence. Some voices had decried—and resisted—the club's demise. As well, eastern pro hockey barons had begun looking at the prosperous, heavily populated Ontario capital as a potential marketplace.

Teddy Marriott was always willing to bet on a hockey game, his winning ways being legendary. The veteran hockey manager—who also served as Miln's assistant—wanted to keep pro hockey in Toronto. He was, however, the sort of fellow the business was leaving behind.

Even within the Toronto Hockey Club itself, Miln's decision to embrace Simon-pure amateurism had not been uncontested. Foremost among the dissenters was Teddy Marriott, the second-in-command at both the Mutual Street Rink and its pro club. Marriott proposed to run the OPHL squad himself and was putting out feelers to the local veterans. Miln remained adamant that he would not allow a professional team in his building.

A more determined attempt to keep the club alive was made by former player Herb Birmingham and his brother Hilliard. The Birminghams were a powerful political family of well-connected provincial Conservative organizers. Herb and Hilliard were leading a players' consortium that aspired to move the team into the ECHA. The trouble was that they also lacked a rink to play in.

To this obstacle, the Birminghams had a rather unique solution. They proposed to put a large canvas tent over the open-air National Rink on Brock Avenue. This rink was located on a large baseball field that would provide plenty of space to build a permanent facility later. The short-term cost was reckoned at just $2,000.

The idea attracted howls of laughter from the local press. "Any circus stunts to be done in the Eastern Pro. Hockey League will be done in Montreal and Ottawa, not in Toronto,"[9] wrote Billy Hewitt's *Star*. Nevertheless, the Eastern Association seemed ready to at least give them a listen.

To most observers' genuine surprise, the Birminghams got their franchise. It was not for the tent scheme, however, which was judged too shaky. Instead, on the condition they build a new indoor rink, the ECHA granted Toronto a franchise for 1910–11. When the ECHA evolved into the CHA, it extended the same terms. Of course, that possibility died with the league.

Seeing the CHA attempting to corner the prospective Toronto market, the NHA moved quickly to do the same thing. Its leaders arranged a meeting with Miln, but were also unable to dissuade him from his opposition to any new pro venture. The league then acted swiftly to find other partners.

These turned out to be pro baseball men E. J. "Eddie" McCafferty of Montreal and Lawrence "Lol" Solman of Toronto. McCafferty, who had connections to the Wanderers, was also

The NHA first granted a Toronto franchise to Lawrence "Lol" Solman, an entrepreneur involved in sponsoring local sports since the heyday of his brother-in-law, Ned Hanlan. A big businessman with big facilities, he was the kind of person who would control high-level hockey in the future.

the NHA's secretary-treasurer. Solman's Toronto Baseball and Amusement Company had myriad other sports and entertainment interests, including the Toronto Island ferry franchise and the Tecumseh Lacrosse Club.

The NHA offered this group the same terms as the CHA had to the Birminghams: a Toronto franchise in 1910–11, conditional on a new rink.

With the conclusion of the CHA–NHA war, talk of pro hockey in Toronto all but died for the rest of the season. In its place, shinny attention in the city focused on St. Michael's. Under the direction of Jimmy Murphy, St. Mike's would repeat as OHA champions and, this time, capture the Allan Cup.

With the amateurs having finally brought the Queen City a national hockey crown, the Ontario capital now appeared utterly in their grip. It is hard to overstate the hold that John Ross Robertson's Ontario Hockey Association had taken over the city's hockey culture. Professional hockey was covered in the local papers, but usually with reminders from OHA leaders that the chaotic competition for the ringer-infested Stanley Cup had become a "joke." [10]

Even the once-independent *Toronto News* had now become a disciple of Robertson's amateur puritanism—for example, castigating Bruce Ridpath when the former Toronto Pro idol made remarks suggesting that clandestine pay had long existed in the OHA. [11]

That same Ridpath had sold his Yonge Street sporting goods store in December 1909. He was moving to Ottawa permanently. For Toronto professional hockey, all hope seemed lost.

John Ross Robertson was almost too busy to savour his seemingly total victory. If the suffragette movement had been a distraction and an annoyance, there were now far larger issues to concern the publisher and his powerful newspaper. He was, after all, a man of principle dedicated to the propagation of a firmly developed worldview. Robertson might have united Toronto editorial opinion on the question of amateurism in sports, but there were greater battles to fight. And if they divided his sports allies, then divide them he would.

The most volatile split was between Joe Atkinson's (and Billy Hewitt's) *Star* and Robertson's *Telegram* over the question of Canada's war readiness. The *Star* could see no threat of war coming. Atkinson attacked the "jingoism" of the British press and declared that "this whole German scare is simply a nightmare." Germany, the *Star* believed, was "a nation now wholly [*sic*] friendly."

Robertson's *Telegram*, on the other hand, viewed the German naval buildup as a "danger to humanity, to liberty, to everything." Both the *Star* and Frank Nelson's *Globe* argued that if Canada must build up its naval power, it must be the Dominion's own, as Prime Minister Sir Wilfrid Laurier preferred. Robertson aligned his paper with Opposition leader Robert Borden, saying Canada should build battleships for the Empire and its Royal Navy. [12]

Yet, while they debated such weighty affairs, all the Toronto papers continued to pontificate on the evils of professional hockey. They would sometimes take the argument even further. It was not just that pro hockey should not exist; rather, as the Queen City had demonstrated, it was that it really *could not* exist.

Robertson's *Tely* was, predictably, the most vociferous, postulating that the commercial sport had a fatal logic that could never be overcome. The clubs engaged in professional hockey, it argued, were inexorably faced with a no-win choice: "to decide between paying big salaries, in which event the players would take all the gates, and then some, or paying small salaries and having no gates worth mentioning to pay them with."[13]

In March ·1910, James A. Murphy took St. Michael's College to Toronto's first national hockey championship. A coach and advisor to Alex Miln's Professionals, he was better known as the former boss of the Toronto Lacrosse Club and future president of the National Lacrosse Union.

As the 1910–11 season approached, even some in the NHA must have wondered if this was indeed true. It had won the war with the CHA, but at a price it could not continue to afford to pay. Indeed, the preseason began with the loss of three of its seven previous clubs. The Montreal Shamrocks, in over their financial heads, took advantage of the AAUC's transition rules and returned to the amateur ranks. And the O'Briens, bathing in red ink as the backers of four of the league's teams, decided to unload some of their franchises.

First, the Renfrew group managed to transfer their Cobalt Silver Kings to Quebec City. This allowed the Bulldogs to re-enter top-level hockey. Then they had to deal with George Kennedy (né Kendall), the owner of Montreal's Club Athlétique Canadien. Kennedy was threatening to sue them for stealing his trademark when the NHA's Canadiens had been created.

From the outset, it had been the O'Briens' intention to secure local French-Canadian ownership for their Montreal club. In a sense, the arrival of Kennedy on the scene was a blessing. However, for reasons unknown, the franchise the O'Briens sold to Kennedy before the 1910–11 season was Haileybury's, not the Canadiens'. True, Kennedy got control of the name and signed most of the Montreal club's players, but the O'Briens retained legal ownership of the original Canadiens entity.[14] This was to have some implications later. For now, the Renfrew owners opted to keep the original Canadiens franchise dormant, putting all their money into another attempt at getting the Stanley Cup for their Millionaires.

When the dust had settled, the NHA was left with five operating teams. They were, however, saddled with the salary expectations created by the prior year's bidding war. In truth, this sort of thing had been a recurring problem since the days of the International league. Ideally, it had long been claimed, hockey would set up a national commission to enforce contracts, limit salaries, schedule playoffs and regulate player movements between leagues and clubs, as baseball had done in the United States. The rival pro hockey organizations had periodically discussed such an arrangement, but had never been able to nail anything down.

The National Hockey Association, now clearly dominant in the pro hockey world, decided to act unilaterally. It launched a number of reforms, including a highly disputed salary cap. No club could have a payroll exceeding $5,000—less than half what most had spent the year before. In short order, the pro association had an employee rebellion on its hands.

The workers, led by stars Art Ross and Bruce Stuart, threatened their own, long-rumoured scheme: the formation of a players' union. As this "insurgency" spread it became more elaborate. Most of the leading NHA performers signed on to an attempt to establish an alternative, player-run *league*. Failure to secure an arena in Montreal ultimately scuttled the project, but deep divisions between management and players—and among the players themselves—persisted throughout the year.

While some clubs doubtlessly cheated, the salary cap did have an impact. Payrolls came down considerably, though to levels still historically quite high. At the same time, the NHA's infighting helped breathe some life back into rival pro leagues.

As alternatives for the players, the Saskatchewan and New Ontario circuits trudged along. An Interprovincial group sprang up in the Maritimes. And the struggling OPHL also seemed briefly to revive, establishing a new division east of Toronto.

The ongoing financial challenges of the NHA kept it from drifting to the Queen City, at least for the time being. Yet it would have been a logical development. In that other big national sport, lacrosse, the precedent had already been established. After emerging as the biggest pro circuit in the country, the Montreal-based National Lacrosse Union had secured good markets—both home and away—by expanding into Toronto in 1906.

However, the Queen City in 1910–11 remained its own, isolated hockey realm, under the restored order of Simon-pure amateurism. The city had seven senior teams in the Ontario Hockey Association that season, including the defending Allan Cup champions. Local matches were well attended and rivalries were keen. And the OHA view of the world remained the position of virtually all Toronto media.

The amateur advocates did sometimes still worry that pro hockey could have a future in Toronto. They knew that the exploits of departed OHA stars—Bruce Ridpath, Cyclone Taylor, Dubbie Kerr, Marty Walsh and the like—were followed closely by the city's hockey fans. A quiet elation swept the town as Ridpath and company helped the Senators regain the Stanley Cup from the Wanderers in 1910–11. The *News* even admitted ruefully that "although the N.H.A. has nothing to do with Toronto, local fans are immensely interested in the doings down East." [15]

The OHA's propaganda, of course, had effectively killed any possibility of a return to Toronto by its immediate competitor, the Ontario Professional Hockey League. The OPHL's 1910–11 expansion into eastern Ontario proved to be an unqualified failure. By the end of the campaign, it was apparent that even its established western clubs might soon give up the ghost.

In reality, ever since the departure of its flagship Toronto club, the OPHL's remaining towns had struggled in their compact circuit of southwestern Ontario. Writers from the provincial capital had constantly and mercilessly ridiculed this so-called "Trolley League." [16] Locked out of the big-city market, the Ontario Pro league became even less competitive in the hunt for the best pro players. Its champions, likewise, became even less convincing as contenders for the Stanley Cup.

The OPHL's image was not helped by the antics of Buck Irving. It has been said of Irving that "the league's father he may have been; but if it had been actual paternity involved, the Children's Aid would have declared him an unfit parent."[17] Buck hopscotched from Guelph to Galt to Waterloo to Belleville and finally to Brantford. His bravado efforts to establish a viable pro hockey club became increasingly less credible and less welcome.

WILL BE A COSTLY STRUCTURE

The new Arena Gardens had long been planned for the site of the Mutual Street Rink. By the time it came to pass, however, a whole new consortium—minus Alexander Miln—would be in charge.

Thus, the attention of the Toronto hockey community remained focused where the OHA papers told them it should be: on the OHA. Each spring after the demise of the Professionals, crowds of up to 3,000 would pile into the creaking old Mutual Street Rink for the association's biggest games. In 1911, it would crown a new senior champion, which in turn promised to bring the Queen City the Allan Cup.

This winner of the John Ross Robertson trophy would, sadly, serve only to remind Torontonians that the restored amateur order had neither forgotten nor learned from any of its earlier absurdities.

The team was the Toronto Eatonias. It was the creation of the Eaton's Athletic Association, a group of employees of the city's famous department store, also one of its largest employers. The Eaton's club repeated as OHA senior champions the following season, 1911–12, playing for, but failing to capture, Sir Montagu's mug.

There would be no third Ontario championship for the Eatonias, however. Prior to the 1912–13 season, the titleholders were expelled by the OHA. The reason? No, they had not been found guilty of professionalism; they had not really even been accused of playing for pay. Nonetheless, because they were linked to a commercial entity—the department store—they were deemed to be *potentially* professional.

Whereas decisions like this might have once caused a firestorm, they did no more. The OHA's annual meetings had become highly scripted, lightly attended affairs where the association's permitted business would still be authored by the Three White Czars—John Ross Robertson, perennial secretary W. A. Hewitt, AAUC representative Francis Nelson—and a handful of their followers. Virtually all the offices went routinely uncontested. Besides, the executive rarely met, leaving most important business to Robertson's "subcommittee."

Instead, delegates would be treated to Robertsonesque orations from the OHA president of the day. These spoke of the glory of Canada's national winter sport, comparing it with—you guessed it—the grandeur of the OHA itself. Welland newspaperman and former Olympian Louis Blake Duff gave one of the most eloquent in his 1910 address:

Today, after these score of years, we find the domain of the OHA reaching to the uttermost West of Old Ontario, east to within hailing distance of Montreal, north to the edge of civilization and south to the edge of winter—a domain that would make a dozen European principalities.

The game has taken a tremendous hold upon the interests of the Canadian people, and it is not strange, for it typifies wonderfully the sturdy pluck, the courage, the stamina, the resolution, the dash and go, that is lifting this country up to the heights of splendid achievement ... The hockey stick struck a responsive chord in the breast of young Canada, and in the breast of Canada that is not so young.

John Ross Robertson was saving his own speeches—and his enormous energies—for the biggest issues of the day. As 1911 progressed, this was clearly the proposal of the Laurier government for "reciprocity"—i.e., free trade—with the United States. It was not hard to predict what the *Telegram* would think of the idea of letting the protective walls of the Canadian Dominion come down against the ravenous encroachment of the American Republic. Robertson's right-hand man, *Tely* editor John "Black Jack" Robinson, declared that free trade was "the enemy of Toronto" and that the streets of the city would be soon covered over in grass if a deal with the United States went ahead.[18]

Robertson had spent part of the summer in Great Britain, but had returned in early September to launch his own campaign against free trade. Speaking in Montreal, the proprietor of the *Telegram* told his audience that "the people of the great province of Ontario have not changed their party allegiance. They are simply voting almost as one man against the reciprocity agreement the government has concluded with the United States."

His province, Robertson claimed, was aroused as it had not been since the people rose up and threw out the corrupt provincial government of Premier G. W. Ross in 1905 following allegations of vote buying in the previous election. Ontario, he predicted, would vote in overwhelming majority for the opposition in the federal election that would be held the following week.[19]

"Ontario is Awake," proclaimed the *Gazette* headline over the Montreal newspaper's account of Robertson's speech. And the old man was right—the Laurier government and reciprocity were indeed trounced at the polls. Still, as Robertson celebrated another great victory, he seemed oblivious to the fact that his earlier one was beginning to slip away.

Back in Toronto in the late spring, J. J. Palmer had sold most of his share in the Caledonian properties to a larger consortium. This land, which was substantially larger than the area occupied by the Mutual Street Rink, had been intended for the famous "new rink." His manager,

Alexander Miln, had long promised such. In fact, in the fall of 1910, Miln had returned from New York with plans for precisely such a modern, steel structure. Building materials had even appeared at the site.

Maybe Robertson thought the whole thing of no consequence. After all, Miln's opposition to any professional tenant in a Mutual Street building was well known. However, Miln was away in England at the time of the sale. The new principals—who hailed from both Toronto and Montreal—promptly removed him and put a new man in his place.

The new manager also had connections to both Toronto and Montreal. He was a Toronto businessman and a former star player in Montreal hockey. He was W. J. Bellingham, the first man to have attempted to form a Toronto professional hockey club back in the fall of 1903.

And this time, the powerful interests behind Bellingham were determined that pro hockey would come to Toronto to stay.

CHAPTER TWELVE

THE REVENGE OF HISTORY

A New and Stronger Toronto Hockey Club Emerges

———•••———

Toronto could do with pro hockey of the best brand, though it rather turns up its nose at the kind that loses championships to Galt, Berlin and other rural constituencies.[1]

—*Toronto Telegram*

In his occupational heart, John Ross Robertson always remained a journalist. As such, he sometimes mixed the two motives that animate his vocation. Believing events to be important, he wanted to shape them as much as report them. And, regardless of his own worldview, he wished to demonstrate objectivity and insight into what was transpiring. The quote above, from the *Telegram*, may be both. No doubt it was motivated by the ongoing desire of Robertson and his amateur colleagues to denigrate the Ontario Professional Hockey League. In the process, however, it betrayed an understanding that Torontonians' hockey aspirations were not exactly in line with the ideals of Robertson's Ontario Hockey Association.

The amateur zealots of the OHA and its Toronto papers had also fundamentally misjudged the recent developments in professional hockey. As commercial clubs and leagues came and vanished with increasing and shocking rapidity, they saw what, in an amateur environment, would be only disorder and disunity. Yet, in the world of enterprise, what was occurring was the conquest of weaker participants and networks by competitors that were growing ever stronger. A solid group of essentially volunteer organizations surrounded the Allan Cup. However, out of the apparent chaos of Stanley Cup competition, far more powerful structures were emerging. As amateur leaders celebrated their segregated existence, pro hockey was quietly laying the groundwork for its longer-term supremacy in the sport.

The purchase of the old Caledonian properties by the 1911 consortium was one step in this progression. The group, headed by Toronto's Sir Henry Pellatt—the man who brought hydroelectricity to the city and was using his enormous wealth to build Casa Loma—also included Montreal interests. These Quebec owners were closely connected to the National Hockey Association.

The NHA intended to rip the old Mutual Street building down, construct a big new rink and place a franchise in Toronto. A modern artificial-ice arena would ensure a viable commercial season for the full length of Toronto's unreliable winters. The new rink would also serve a range of other public functions, including selling ice to the populace in the summer.

Important as it was, the planned arrival of big-time eastern pro hockey in Toronto in 1911–12 was just one in a series of historic developments in the sport that season. The fall of 1911 is the moment when, in retrospect, the era of the professional domination of hockey began to first take shape. And its most significant events that year took place on the West Coast.

That's where the Patricks—later to be christened "Hockey's Royal Family"—had just relocated.

———

Joe Patrick had been in the lumber business in Quebec and Ontario before moving his family to Nelson, British Columbia, in 1907. Joe's eldest son, Lester, had been born in Drummondville, Quebec, in 1883; younger brother Frank came along two years later in Ottawa. They would learn the game in the East, but they would *own* the game in the West, both figuratively and literally. The Patricks' effect on the sport would be nothing short of profound.

The Patrick boys were already well known as superb hockey players. A third brother, Ted, was expected to do just as well, but had any such dreams cut short when he lost his right leg in a sledding accident.[2] Ted played anyway, anchoring his peg—at the age of nineteen, he switched to an artificial wooden leg—to the ice while pivoting. He was said by family members to have been good enough to play professional hockey but for his handicap.[3]

Lester and Frank, who both played at McGill University, went on to become professionals. Lester famously performed for the Montreal Wanderers in their Stanley Cup days, including the March 1907 exhibition encounter at Mutual against Alex Miln's Professionals. More recently, both had suited up with Renfrew's Millionaires in 1909–10. Convinced that pro hockey had a bright future, they persuaded their father to invest the proceeds from the sale of the lucrative family enterprise in their idea for a new league.

The Patrick family's Pacific Coast Hockey Association would be a league unlike any other. What made the PCHA unique was that the professional sport had, to date, evolved largely through the conversion of the amateur game's top level. Conversely, the Pacific Coast league was a completely novel and wholly commercial organization. Its rise was an unmistakable sign that the pro game was creating its own structures and, in the process, fundamentally altering the nature of the sport.

The first big difference was the character of the PCHA entries. The association's Vancouver, Victoria and New Westminster squads would not be built around any pre-existing entities and would all be owned by the Patricks. In fact, Frank would play for, coach and manage the team in Vancouver, while Lester would do the same for the one in Victoria. The purists thus derided the PCHA as mere "syndicate hockey," by which they meant that its component organizations had no membership, no history, no tradition, no real existence in the conventional sense. They were *teams*, not clubs—mere franchises of the syndicate that ran the league.

While the critics were entirely correct about hockey's heritage, it was the Patricks who had grasped its future. Unlike its amateur forerunner, pro hockey was a commercial business, not a network of gentlemen's clubs. As a business, the profitability of the venture would ultimately depend upon the soundness of the enterprise as a whole. The league, not the club, had to be the ultimate focus if the undertaking were to succeed.

The National Hockey Association had stumbled upon the "syndicate hockey" concept when it established the Montreal Canadiens in 1909. The Canadiens were, in effect, the first purely "manufactured" big-league franchise in hockey history. They had been similarly denounced, only to quickly earn the highest loyalty of the French Canadian hockey fan. The PCHA's uniqueness, however, went beyond its complete syndicate nature.

The PCHA franchises would be located in what was a spectator, rather than a player, environment. B.C.'s Lower Mainland and Vancouver Island were the only parts of Canada where hockey had been essentially a foreign sport. It could be sustained in the West Coast climate only through artificial ice. The Patricks were therefore building the country's first such rinks: the 10,500-seat Denman Street Arena in Vancouver, then the largest in the country, and the 3,500-seat Willow Arena in Victoria. Pro hockey, it was being discovered, did not depend on player pools or indigenous institutions, but on modern facilities and the urban markets that could sustain them.

The new league was distinct in yet another way: the Patrick brothers' view that they could rewrite the rules of the sport to sell it as a commercial product. For years, they had brainstormed on how to open up the game and make it more exciting. Their proprietary league would be employed to test-market these theories.

The NHL official rule book contains some twenty-two entries that can be linked to Frank's innovations—the creation of the blue line, which divided the rink into three zones, being the most notable. The Patricks are credited with inventing the forward pass, the penalty shot, delayed calls, line changes, a playoff format and, finally, a rule allowing goaltenders to leave their feet to make a save.[4]

Such innovations are as legendary as the Patrick name itself.

———

While most of the Patrick rule changes were still some years off, it was the NHA that introduced the seminal changes of 1911–12. Foremost was the announcement that the league was shifting to six-man hockey. The rover would be eliminated from the game.

The reason for the disappearance of the rover—until then the key man in the lineup—is still somewhat of a mystery. No explanation was ever made public, although it was alleged the NHA needed to cut rosters to deal with ongoing salary pressures. However, once the position was eliminated, the game flowed more quickly and the innovation gradually became more popular. Along with the rover, the positions of point and cover point withered away, with defencemen tending increasingly to "left" and "right" positions. The "T" formation inexorably gave way to the more familiar triangle configuration.

The NHA also introduced on-ice substitutions and, consequently, player numbers. Combined with the switch from two halves to three periods and two intermissions—unveiled the previous season—the pace of the action was stepped up, as performers rested in the dressing room or on the bench instead of on the ice. All this also had the effect of prolonging the careers of star veterans entering their thirties. They could now conceivably go the distance against twenty-somethings at the peak of their physical prowess.

All these changes were interrelated. No rover meant more room on the ice and a faster game. A faster game led to a need for rest and substitution, which produced bigger lineups and therefore numbers to identify the players. Of course, all this would seem to disprove the allegation that the rover was eliminated to reduce payroll.

Yet the NHA's most anticipated change for the fall of 1911 was its expected expansion to Toronto. Almost immediately after its consortium got control of the Mutual Street properties, the association sold a franchise to interests connected with the Toronto Lacrosse Club, including Percy Quinn and Frank Robinson. Percy, the brother of league president Emmett Quinn, was most noted in hockey circles as a referee. He had initially been named ref of the Wanderers–Torontos Stanley Cup match of 1908, although he was ultimately unavailable. He had also emerged as an executive member of the Interprovincial Amateur Hockey Union through his connection to the Toronto Athletics.

Percy Quinn had been an executive with the Toronto Lacrosse Club, the Toronto Amateur Athletic Club and the Interprovincial Amateur Hockey Union. However, it was his connection to his brother Emmett, president of the NHA, that secured the new Toronto Hockey Club franchise for Percy.

It is interesting to note that the franchise sold to Quinn and company—for the modest sum of $2,000—was the O'Briens' original *les Canadiens*. This meant, in effect, that two NHA teams now traced their roots to that franchise. One was the new Toronto club, its legal heir, while the other was evidently the team using the name Montreal Canadiens.

The Toronto Lacrosse Club's crosstown rival, the Tecumseh Lacrosse Club, was rather unhappy about the NHA's favouritism towards Quinn and his organization. It demanded a team of its own. The league hummed and hawed for a while, but ultimately had no choice in the matter. Lol Solman, the managing director of the new arena company, was also the proprietor of the Tecumsehs. He reminded the association he had been granted a franchise back in 1909. With Solman to be in control of Toronto's new arena, the NHA was obliged to live up to that promise.

The Tecumsehs were then managed by Charlie Querrie. Querrie had long been the lacrosse club's boss and star performer. Once a decent hockey player, he had desired to play professionally. He was, however, past his prime when the original Torontos came to town in late 1906.

What finally allowed the Tecumsehs to enter the NHA was the preseason decision by the O'Briens to sell their hometown Renfrew club, the last of their hockey holdings. They got $2,500 the second time round. Still, it was not enough to compensate for the Millionaires' two seasons of red ink with no Stanley Cup to show for them.

The death of Renfrew's Cup pursuit was yet another example of the failure to build a championship team out of exclusively star performers. It was also the historic end of small-town competition for the national professional championship. As the amateur advocates of the OHA had long claimed, small-market clubs were gradually being squeezed out by the economics of the pro game. Those few, smaller pro leagues that continued to exist increasingly had the feel of a "farm system" to them.

Yet the amateur ideologues had again missed the big picture. If it was true that Ontario's smaller centres could not support major-league hockey, then it was just as likely that Toronto could. In a matter of a few months, the Queen City's hockey order had undergone a remarkable transformation. After a seemingly total victory for the amateurs, the pros were back with a vengeance. The city had gone from being a professional wasteland to having not one, but two franchises in the sport's biggest commercial association.

This link of the new Toronto franchises to lacrosse clubs was not coincidental. The leaders of professional lacrosse and professional hockey were increasingly found in the same circles, pursuing the same business models. In fact, the National Lacrosse Union would also soon drop its smaller-market clubs, morphing into the new Dominion Lacrosse Association. The DLA, like the NHA, would find itself mired deep in a recruiting war with a league on the Pacific coast. It was the creation of one Conrad "Con" Jones, a western sports tycoon—the lacrosse parallel of the hockey Patricks and their PCHA.

Unlike the PCHA clubs, however, Toronto's new NHA teams were firmly anchored in the city's sports culture. The lacrosse-sponsored Toronto Hockey Club even had some echoes of its professional predecessor. Jimmy Murphy, now president of the NLU, had been an advisor and sometime coach of Miln's outfit while he was manager of the Toronto Lacrosse Club. The perennial hockey spare man of 1906–09, Hugh Lambe, had long been a star defenceman on the same lacrosse team.

The most visible resemblance between the two clubs was, of course, in their jerseys. The new Torontos quickly became known by the moniker of their lacrosse parent, the "Blue Shirts" (sometimes in hyphenated form).[5] However, they too would be at times referred to as the Professionals.[6]

————

The strongest connection to the past was yet to come: in October, Bruce Ridpath, founder of the original Torontos, was named playing manager of the NHA team.

In leading Ottawa to the Stanley Cup the previous season, Ridpath had emerged as one of the league's premier forwards. Incidentally, his change of residence was not entirely amicable. Despite having granted Riddy permission to go back to his hometown, the Senators would periodically demand compensation from his new bosses.

Ridpath was certainly worth it. Quite simply, he was the best hockey player Toronto had ever produced. Almost three years since his departure, he was still the hero of the city's hockey fans.

Riddy was also quite literally a hero, having saved a life the previous summer. It happened while he was competing in the Canadian Canoeing Association championships on Ottawa's Rideau River in early August. The junior-four crew capsized near the press stand. "The boat overturned as the Valois paddlers acknowledged greetings from their friends," reported the *Citizen*, "and for three minutes Hamilton, who cannot swim, was in grave danger of going under . . . Ridpath seized a row boat and pulled Hamilton into it, just as he was on the verge of collapse."[7]

Ridpath's homecoming—a huge coup for the new club—was eagerly anticipated. However, it would soon be eclipsed by a terrible tragedy. On November 2, 1911, Ridpath was the victim of a near-fatal accident. Getting off a streetcar on Yonge Street near Alexander Street, Bruce walked behind the trolley and began to cross the road to meet a younger brother. Startled by the dimly lit headlights of an oncoming motor vehicle, he was hit and thrown back. The hockey star ended up under the car with severe head injuries, just barely alive.

The Montreal *Gazette* reported that an "automobile containing a party of men and women came down Yonge Street and Ridpath was struck down [and was] thrown to the side of the street with great force, as the automobile was travelling fairly fast." The driver, Colin A. Campbell, stopped and carried Ridpath to a nearby drugstore before running for medical help. "Two doctors worked over Ridpath, but could not restore consciousness, and he was taken to the hospital in the ambulance."[8] Campbell followed the ambulance to the hospital and then went and found Ridpath's brother, informing him of the accident. Shortly after midnight, he was arrested, "charged with causing grievous bodily injury, and lodged in cells."[9]

The Ridpath story was huge news in the hockey world throughout Canada. Though initially given almost no chance of surviving, daily news briefings from St. Michael's Hospital began to note some improvement in his condition. After a few days, Bruce began to sporadically regain consciousness. A month after that, he left the hospital. Nevertheless, Bruce suffered from severe head pain and memory loss, and there was no possibility that he would play in 1911–12.

BRUCE RIDPATH IS HIT BY AUTO AND MAY NOT RECOVER

Famous Canoeist and Hockey Player Apparently Puzzled by Shadow in Leaving Car.

RUSHED TO HOSPITAL IN SERIOUS STATE

Colin A. Campbell, Owner of the Automobile, Does All He Can to Help.

IS HELD WITHOUT BAIL

Patient Has Internal Hemorrhage During Night and Remains in Unconscious Condition.

Bruce Ridpath, the well-known canoeist, hockey player, and hockey manager, was struck on Yonge street just south of Alexander street by an automobile driven by Colin A. Campbell of 62, Havelock street, at 7.40 last night, and at nine o'clock this morning he was still unconscious in St. Michael's Hospital, suffering from an injury at the base of the skull, concussion of the brain, and bruises on face and arms.

BRUCE RIDPATH.

during the night, and is still unconscious. His condition is bad. In fact, his recovery is doubtful, although not hopeless. He has some minor injuries on the body. There is no fracture at the base of the skull, but he has concussion of the brain."

Says Campbell Was Careful.

Mr. Campbell was taking a friend of Mrs. Campbell's home, and, so far as the police had heard this forenoon, the auto was not moving rapidly.

"Campbell is an excessively careful driver," said C. G. McGill, the surety for the automobilist, to The Star. "I drive a car, and I know that he is careful and considerate of pedestrians and persons alighting from street cars. He has had a car since spring, and he handled an auto often before he owned one.

"Now, there is a natural feeling against motors and motorists, but

Bruce Ridpath had been the most important on-ice figure during the life of the original Torontos. Had this tragedy not ensued, he would have undoubtedly played the same role with their successor.

The accident was more than just a personal tragedy. In Toronto, it heightened a growing backlash against the automobile. Though still relatively rare on city streets, cars were becoming common enough to provoke a growing number of pedestrian injuries. Incidents of drinking and driving caused particular anger. Action was demanded by the citizenry. Mayor Geary proclaimed it outrageous that cars "should travel around at twenty miles an hour and keep citizen [sic] dodging them all the time to escape being killed or maimed."[10]

In high-profile cases like Ridpath's, charges were being laid and the proceedings were intensely followed in the papers. Campbell had to post bail in the amount of $5,000—a substantial sum at the time. Also, for months to come, debate raged over speed limits, driver credentials, road lighting,[11] signalling, mandatory crosswalks, the size of fines and prison terms, and even possible bans of the new mechanical menace. One writer pointedly asked, "how are the aged and infirm to escape when the most vigorous and alert fail to do so?"[12]

Surprisingly, Ridpath bore the man who had nearly killed him no malice. When he could finally speak to the press, he assigned no blame. Bruce told them that "his injury was due to 'nothing more than an unfortunate accident.'" He said the vehicle had its lights on, that there was no speeding involved and that the driver, Campbell, had had no chance to avert the accident.[13]

The recovering Riddy was not forgotten. An immensely popular figure wherever he had performed, he had benefits held for him in Cobalt, Ottawa and Toronto over the course of the season. The largest was a Massey Hall extravaganza organized for May 2, 1912. Attended by all the city's dignitaries and sports personalities, it featured tributes, musical entertainment and a free airing of a film featuring Bruce's canoe exploits—a hit of Toronto's early cinema years.

Toronto's Ridpath benefit had a significance, however, well beyond its charitable purpose. It showed how quickly and completely the cultural values of the sports world were shifting. The affair had been spearheaded by the city's amateur athletic clubs, out in force with their colours on display. Try as the amateur bosses might, the star professional athlete was no longer an outcast to his amateur brethren. On the contrary, he was in an elite category to which most of them aspired.

The loss of Ridpath was obviously a huge blow to the fledgling new Torontos. To temporarily take his place, Quinn hired as manager his fellow referee Chaucer Elliott—one of the men associated with the efforts to organize a Toronto pro hockey club in 1905–06. Percy also made lacrosse star Eddie Powers the team's captain.

Soon, however, both the Toronto Hockey Club and the Tecumseh Hockey Club were in serious jeopardy. Their entire season depended on a new arena, and that facility showed few signs of being ready.

Toronto was experiencing a historic boom in construction activity, with intense competition for approvals and crews. Demolition of the old Caledonian building itself did not begin until August. No sense of nostalgia would greet the landmark's death. The *Star* even went so far as to proclaim: "Good-bye, old Mutual Street Rink! Farewell! At last! At last! We are going to have a real hockey rink!"[14]

When the structure finally came down, the architects were dumbfounded by what they found. So decayed were the stonework and woodwork of the foundation, it was a miracle the old barn had not just collapsed of its own accord. Indeed, during demolition some parts did, injuring several workers.

Once work began, it seemed to just crawl along—with seemingly one serious accident after another. In mid-November, the NHA released its schedule, which had the Blue Shirts and Tecumsehs on the road until well into January. By then, the clubs were frantically looking for backup plans. They were checking out rinks in Toronto and neighbouring Ontario cities. They briefly toyed with the notion of playing the entire season out of Montreal or even Boston.

Finally, on December 16 at a league meeting in Montreal, the NHA dropped the Torontos and Tecumsehs for the 1911–12 season. The league went further, seizing their $500 deposits as a fine for the inconvenience caused. Quinn and Querrie were furious. Coming on the heels of the Tecumseh dispute over their franchise and the (ongoing) Blue Shirt one over Ridpath's rights, bad blood was already developing between the pro association and its Toronto clubs. The consortium building the new artificial-ice arena was said to be contemplating the formation of an

The successful manager of the Tecumseh Lacrosse Club was initially in charge of the hockey team as well. However, Charlie Querrie ended up on the outside when the NHA returned to Toronto in the fall of 1912.

alternative "International League," with similar ventures in the northeast United States.

In spite of the lack of a permanent facility, the two Toronto clubs did not give up entirely in 1911–12. They decided to move over to the Excelsior Rink and began to look around for other options. However, with the OPHL gone, there were no plausible leagues to play in. They then looked to barnstorm, but soon had to face the fact there were no other pro clubs at any reasonable distance.

The two organizations were thus left with just each other. So they decided they would meet in a "city professional hockey championship" of three games. Even that, in due course, got whittled down to a single match.

For that match, the Torontos and Tecumsehs would have to come up with players. However, the few name players signed had already moved elsewhere. Only Edwin "Mag" McGregor, an OPHL veteran and the interim Tecumseh captain, had opted to stay. His decision was not hockey-related—he was studying at the city's dental college.

Because neither the Blue Shirts nor the "Indians" had ever been significant hockey powers, they now had to create on-ice squads mainly from their lacrosse teams. Strangely, the Tecumseh lineup did not include either Lawson Whitehead or Harry "Sport" Murton. These two lacrosse men were both good enough to have tried out for Miln's old team, with Whitehead having played in one game. Conversely, the Torontos rehabilitated a former Professional, thirty-year-old Jack Carmichael, as a link to the past. In goal, they placed local amateur star Harry Holmes, who would prove to be their connection to the future.

Thus, on January 25, 1912, the two clubs entered the Excelsior Rink with a collection of marginal players, untested on the ice and discernibly out of condition. To kick off this new professional era, the teams played

NHA-style six-man hockey in three periods. The Toronto Blue Shirts beat the Toronto Tecumsehs, 5–3. The Indians had the overwhelming margin of the play, but goalkeeping was the determining factor. The game was anything but pretty.

Although hotly contested, the match was severely limited by the deficiencies of its participants. Unable to play quality hockey, the lacrosse rivals became increasingly aggressive. Referee Lou Marsh—another journalist deeply imbedded in the sports he covered—seemed incapable of containing the escalating violence. The *News*, marvelling that no one was seriously hurt, gave a taste of the evening:

> McGregor was all but put out of business by what looked like a deliberate cross-check by Morrison. Six teeth fell out of his mouth when he was bumped like peas out of a pod, but he picked up the gold one and skated off the ice. He showed his gameness by returning, but his real reason for coming back apparently was to get "even." [15]

Despite the irony of poor toothless McGregor studying to be a dentist, there was, in all this, a silver lining to be found. The long-standing lacrosse rivalry between the island Tecumsehs and the mainland Blue Shirts had sustained their supporters' interest in the contest.

When the gong had finally rung, the fans went home looking forward to next season.

———

Some question remained as to what that next season would look like. While an off-season reconciliation took place between Quinn and the NHA, Querrie continued his war of words with the association throughout the spring and summer of 1912. His threatened International league did not look entirely idle.

This conflict was doubtlessly egged on by the virulent anti-NHA campaign of the local OHA-controlled newspapers. John Ross Robertson and his allies had by no means given up their battle against professionalism in the city. Story after story complained about the NHA's treatment of the Ontario capital. The press also bemoaned its "bobtailed" (or "curtailed") six-man game. This innovation appears to have been genuinely unpopular in both Toronto and Ottawa—Ridpath being one of the leading critics. Most seriously, amateur interests alleged that match fixing was common in the professional league.

The rigging accusations seem to have been based on nothing more than the fact that the 1911–12 NHA season had been a close one. The suggestion was vigorously denounced by respected hockey man Jack Marshall. The veteran—a member of the aborted Toronto pro practice squad of 1905–06—was spending much time around town. The official reason was to referee local matches, as he had all but retired as an active player.

In any case, by the fall of 1912, the NHA had managed to patch things up with the owners of the new arena. Solman helped smooth things over by authorizing the transfer of the Tecumseh Hockey Club to Billy Bellingham and Eddie McCafferty, leaving Querrie out in the cold when the International scheme fell through. But this would not be a relationship built on love. The spats of 1911–12 foreshadowed almost constant tension between the association and its Toronto interests over the subsequent five years. In the meantime, both the league and its local owners decided their shared interests lay in a secure plan for use of Toronto's new hockey shrine.

Quite a palace it was. While the Arena Gardens is now remembered as the inadequate old place eclipsed by Conn Smythe's Maple Leaf Gardens, it was one of the continent's top facilities in its day. An amphitheatre capable of seating more than 7,000, with numerous contemporary amenities, eastern Canada's first artificial-ice rink was an impressive monument. The steel-and-brick structure covered a significantly larger area than its wood-and-stone predecessor. Yet it soon picked up a colloquial designation almost identical to that of the old Caledonian building: the "Mutual Arena."

While the purpose of the Arena Gardens had always been to house professional hockey, its owners were under no illusion about the high level of local support for the OHA. After all, the old association still had most of the city's newspapers in its hip pocket. The arena thus granted the use of the facility to no fewer than eight amateur clubs that first year. They were also handsomely rewarded at the box office for doing so. The amateur bosses, after a miserable year split between the Excelsior and west-end Ravina Rink—where Teddy Marriott now toiled as the icemaker—no longer had any qualms about this sort of "mixing."

Also, as much as the local papers liked to run down the NHA and its Toronto clubs, press coverage at the end of 1912 began to shift as surely as snow started to cover the fallen leaves. Stories of boardroom battles and rumours of inevitable implosion were giving way to reports on the race to sign players. A recovering Bruce Ridpath was back in the saddle as manager of the Torontos and in the thick of the hunt. So was his Tecumseh counterpart, veteran goalie Billy Nicholson.

Ridpath and Nicholson missed getting Fred "Cyclone" Taylor by a whisker. The Queen City clubs had bid the highest amount of money, but, because the NHA continued to designate the superstar as Wanderers' property against his wishes, Cyclone left for the West Coast. In going to British Columbia, Taylor secured the status of the PCHA as a second "big league" for many years to come. However, with salaries again rising because of the bidding war, the number of circuits continued to diminish. Only the Maritime league seemed to (at least temporarily) buck the trend. The Saskatchewan League finally closed up shop, as did the New Ontario one. They had been raided out of existence by the stronger bodies.

THE TORONTO PROFESSIONAL HOCKEY TEAM

The team which gave the fast Canadiens of Montreal such a lively struggle Christmas night in the N.H.A opening league game in the Arena. Right to left, standing: Holmes, Wilson, Neighbor, Jopp, Percy Quinn, president of the club; Tom Humphrey, coach; McLean, McGiffin, Doherty, Stanyon, Frank Carroll, trainer. Sitting: Davidson, Randall, Cameron, Foyston, Walker. In front is Bruce Ridpath, the manager of the team.

The Toronto Blue Shirts were still occasionally known by the same moniker as Alex Miln's club. Manager Ridpath, who had still not practised since the accident, appears in skates, but not in uniform.

In mid-December, the two local teams began their tryouts. Montreal's pro clubs also got into the act, coming up from Quebec to get some early-season practice on the new artificial ice surface. On December 21, the Wanderers and Canadiens even played an exhibition match in Toronto to show off the more open six-man game. It was a fast, spirited contest before a big crowd, with the French team featuring former Professionals Donald Smith and Newsy Lalonde. The latter was conspicuously at the centre of yet another violent confrontation, this time leading to charges against Wanderer tough guy Sprague Cleghorn.

The Montreal Canadiens launched the modern hockey rivalry with Toronto on Christmas 1912. Newsy Lalonde and Don Smith returned to Mutual Street as visitors.

At last, on December 25, 1912, the reborn Toronto Hockey Club played its first game in the National Hockey Association. The team lost 9–5, but that would prove to be incidental. It had played before a gathering 4,000 strong and in a first-class facility. It had done so as part of Canada's leading league, which pitted the country's biggest cities against each other in pursuit of the highest prize in the game.

An important step was taken that Christmas night at the Arena Gardens. A Toronto team in blue faced a Montreal team wearing the *tricolore*. One of the clubs even wore the maple leaf that evening. Ironically, it was the visitors.

Both teams, as has been noted, were descended from the very same franchise Ambrose O'Brien had created in 1909. More important, they had a common future, now over a century old. While it was far from obvious at the time, Toronto's greatest hockey rivalry—the struggle with the Montreal Canadiens—had begun.

CHAPTER THIRTEEN

THE NEW ORDER IN HOCKEY'S SECOND CITY

The Blue Shirts Take the Stanley Cup

———•—•———

Little chance of any great hockey developing in this game.[1]

—*Toronto Telegram*

On Christmas Day 1912, the Toronto Hockey Club re-emerged as part of an established sports organization, housed in a modern rink and playing in a stronger league. That league included a crosstown competitor and clubs in Montreal, Toronto's great national rival. Yet despite the large and enthusiastic crowd that had turned out, the pros still had ahead of them a serious battle for support and survival in the Queen City.

The amateur game in the Ontario capital retained its big traditional following, its powerful media allies and a strong national symbol in the Allan Cup. In the winter of 1911–12, the city had been transfixed by the (ultimately doomed) Toronto Eatonias and their run at the Canadian championship. In comparison, the professional encounter between the Torontos and Tecumsehs had been a pathetic competitor.

But Toronto's amateur hockey order had a persistent Achilles' heel. Much as John Ross Robertson and the other Ontario Hockey Association moguls might protest otherwise, the greatest prize in the game was still the Stanley Cup, and it was contested by professional teams.

The Stanley Cup had not become a trophy for professional hockey because its trustees were committed to the principles of playing for pay. On the contrary, they had been reluctant converts. However, given that the original viceregal gift had come with no stipulation that the Cup be awarded solely to amateurs, the trustees had decided that the winner would be the very best team and players, regardless of how they were organized. As trustee William Foran explained, "The Stanley Cup is not hung up for either amateur or professional hockey in particular but for the best hockey."[2]

If Toronto wanted one thing, it was to be the best. And being best, of course, meant being better than archrival Montreal, which could claim sixteen Cup titles since Lord Stanley's trophy was first awarded back in 1893.[3] That was what its pro managers, the Tecumsehs' Billy Nicholson and the Blue Shirts' Bruce Ridpath, told the fans they would get. To win the Stanley Cup, they would set out on diametrically opposite recruitment strategies for their first National Hockey Association season.

The Tecumsehs aimed to build their winner from established professional ranks. In fact, it was this club, not the new Torontos, that offered openings to veterans of Alexander Miln's original pro squad. In the course of their December tryouts, Herb Birmingham, Harry Burgoyne, Con Corbeau, Charlie Liffiton and the elusive Bert Morrison all fought for places in the lineup.

Of these, only Corbeau was successful, although Ezra Dumart also returned to the Queen City during the course of the season. Dumart had played a single match for the old Toronto Professionals—their March 1907 exhibition against the Montreal Wanderers. As a longtime fixture on the Berlin Dutchmen, he was, though, the top goal scorer over the four-year history of the Ontario Professional Hockey League.

Naturally, the Tecumsehs' hunt for veterans did not confine itself to Toronto. Gradually—indeed, at a shockingly slow pace—the team began to ink contracts with a number of familiar pro journeymen and the occasional former star. These regulars would ultimately include Horace Gaul (originally from Ottawa), Ernie Liffiton (brother of Charlie, from Montreal), George and Howard McNamara (brothers of former

Toronto Pro Harold, from the Canadian Soo), Harry Smith (Ottawa), Art Throop (Ottawa), Steve Vair (Barrie) and Nicholson himself (Montreal).

It is interesting to note that Ridpath took a pass on his old teammates from the original Torontos. In fact, the only holdover from the old Mutual Street Pros was the trainer, Frank Carroll, who had at one time been a boxer of some note, winning the Canadian welterweight championship in 1906. Bruce did, however, give tryouts to the Blue Shirts' one-game "city championship" team of the previous season—the gang that had been drawn from the ranks of the Toronto Lacrosse Club. Of those men, Ridpath signed only goalkeeper Harry "Hap" Holmes, previously a comer on the local amateur hockey scene. Among those he dropped was forward Ed Longfellow, who then landed a place as a spare with the Tecumsehs.

The bigger surprise was Riddy's decision to forgo almost entirely any attempt to sign known professionals (excepting, of course, Cyclone Taylor). Most of his regulars would be players only two years out of the junior ranks. They included Allan "Scotty"

TORONTO TEAMS WILL BE WEAK

Ottawa Pro. Hockey Experts Do Not Think Very Highly of Queen City Prospects

Lehman and Lalonde Not Wanted In The East at Salaries They Demand

Ottawa, Nov. 7.—Developments continued yesterday in the professional hockey situation. It was announced from Cornwall that "Newsy" Lalonde had decided to remain in the East, and that he would be found with George Kennedy's Canadien team, but Kennedy came through last night with an emphatic denial, in which he declares that Lalonde's price is far in excess of what the Canadien club can possibly give him. Lalonde is evidently playing one league against the other, but according to intimate friends he will honor the contract which he has with the Patrick syndicate.

Hugh Lehman has sent word to Sam Lichtenhein that he intends to go West again. Lichtenhein understood that Lehman wanted $600 for the season, but when it came to sign Lehman demanded that a thousand be stacked up beside the six hundred, and Lichtenhein passed him up.

The Ottawa and Toronto clubs are fighting hard for the restoration of seven man hockey in the N. H. A., but the Wanderers, Canadiens and Quebec want the six man game, and President Quinn is evidently with them. The Wanderers have given Ottawa until Saturday night to accept their offer of Taylor for Ronan, but there is no possibility of it being accepted.

Local amateurs say that the Toronto clubs actually offered them $25 per week on trial. As this is about one-quarter of what the teams in the East are paying it looks as if Toronto would have two very weak aggregations.

The OHA-centric Toronto press spared no ink in predicting that new NHA teams would be uncompetitive disasters.

Davidson (a Kingston graduate playing in Calgary), Frank Foyston (of the dissolving Eaton's team), Roy "Minnie" McGiffin (of Teddy Marriott's Simcoes), and Carol "Cully" Wilson (Winnipeg). Bruce also grabbed youngsters Harry Cameron and Frank "Dutch" Nighbor from Port Arthur—part of the NHA raids that finished off the New Ontario pro league. This left just Archie "Sue" McLean, enticed away from the Pacific Coast Hockey Association, as the only previous big-leaguer among the new Torontos' starters.

As the Tecumsehs inched forward and the Blue Shirts recruited unknowns, the reaction of the Queen City's OHA-controlled newspapers was predictably negative. Story after story talked about teams of "bushers" being built "on the cheap."[4] It was claimed that the other NHA clubs feared the league's Toronto expansion was turning into a fiasco. Rumours were spread of emergency plans to come to the rescue of the uncompetitive fledgling entities. And any unsuccessful attempt to sign a local amateur player was quickly reported and immediately ridiculed.

To this pro catastrophe, a solution was conveniently offered: OHA senior hockey. Toronto had a number of good clubs playing at the Arena Gardens that season, even if the champion Eatonias, deemed "professional" because of their connection with the department store, would not be among them. One was certainly the St. Michael's College team. The Allan Cup champions of 1910 were always in the hunt. Another was, conveniently, a new amateur "Torontos."

The original amateur Torontos had been the Toronto Amateur Athletic Club. Back in the days of Alex Miln's Torontos, the TAAC had used the same moniker and had also adopted dark red as their colour. Now, with the arrival of the NHA Torontos, the TAAC had reorganized. In the fall of 1912, under the leadership of Eddie Livingstone, they became the "Toronto Rugby and Athletic Association." The TR&AA chose as the colours for these new "Torontos" none other than blue and white.

The Blue Shirts had to have been worried about this amateur competition and the possible confusion around the team name and colours. Of the two Toronto pro clubs, the Tecumsehs, with their known players, certainly sounded the stronger. They also had an intimidating defence, anchored by the "Dynamite Twins," the heavy-hitting McNamara brothers, and supplemented by spare rearguard Corbeau and goalkeeper Nicholson. Each of the quartet was said to tip the scales at almost 200 pounds.

Conversely, the Indians' forwards appeared decidedly slow in their preseason workouts. That was certainly not the case for Ridpath's boys. Whatever the OHA papers claimed, the "railbirds" who took in their practices at the Arena came away saying the Blue Shirts looked surprisingly fast and skilled for a bunch of no-names.

TECUMSEH'S BIG FOUR

Stalwart defence of the Indian Pro. Team. In the above group are: Nicholson, goal-keeper and Manager, 198 lbs.; G. McNamara, point player, 188 lbs.; Con. Corbeau, defence, 190 lbs., and H. McNamara, cover-point, 192 lbs.

In fact, both Queen City pro clubs came out of the starting gate better than the local hockey powers had predicted. The Tecumsehs won three of their first five games and challenged for the league lead early in the campaign. Yet, while the rookie Torontos were generally competitive in their contests, they had only one victory in their first six.

The young Blue Shirts seemed to have all the talent and energy in the world, but little team play, finish or confidence, especially in the tough going. Ridpath's coaching was most commonly cited as the problem. He was said to be overusing the substitute rule—that is, changing players too frequently and often at the wrong times. Riddy was also reputed to be temperamental on the bench.

In fairness, Ridpath acted quickly to address the issue. Shortly after the season began, he retained a respected veteran to help him coach the team. It was none other than Jack Marshall, the referee of the Blue Shirts'

December 25 home opener. While Marshall immediately brought a greater sense of stability to the bench and to practice, the team at first still failed to win.

The club's biggest problem was really Bruce Ridpath's absence from the ice. Notwithstanding periodic rumours of his return, the after-effects of his accident—vision problems, unsteadiness—led him to quickly nip such reports in the bud.

Toronto's starters, with Bruce Ridpath looking more like a manager than a player.

What were the Blue Shirts to do? Marshall publicly observed after the Christmas game that the Torontos had the makings of a solid team. He said they needed just one veteran on the ice to steady them. As it became apparent that Ridpath was never going to play, Marshall then offered a solution: himself.

It was not an obvious choice. True, Marshall had at one time been a force on the ice. Indeed, back in 1902, he was the original "Little Man of Iron," leading the Winged Wheelers of Montreal to their surprise Stanley Cup win over the Winnipeg Victorias. In fact, Marshall had played for a Vics Cup team even before that. When the Wheeler champions defected to the Wanderers, Jack had gone with them and had won Lord Stanley's mug with that club, too. Alex Miln had also tapped him to be a key man when he was putting together the aborted Toronto pro club of 1905–06.

All of that, however, was now many years in the past. Since then, Marshall had added dozens more scars and wrinkles to his battle-hardened face—one of which represented a serious injury that had caused the loss of some vision in one eye. On top of all that, "Jawn" was now thirty-five years old.

None of it mattered. The moment Marshall stepped on the ice in a Torontos uniform—January 15, 1913—it was as if he had discovered the fountain of youth. Just four days earlier, the Blue Shirts had been beaten convincingly by the Tecumsehs, 5–2. This time, with that one veteran to steady them, the contest was no match, and the Indians went down to a 6–1 defeat.

"The cause of the startling reversal in form: not far to seek—Jack Marshall's brains and Jack Marshall's grit,"[5] was how the *Star* succinctly put it. Marshall had anchored the defence and occasionally contributed to the attack. More important, in his foghorn voice he had quarterbacked the lineup and called out the plays. It was a commanding performance.

An outstanding athlete in virtually every sport, Jack Marshall was spending more and more time around Toronto. He refereed the Blue Shirts' first game in the NHA, observing that, with just one veteran to steady the young team, they would be hard to beat.

That game was the turning point of the season. The Tecumsehs soon plateaued and then began to falter. Rather than looking big, they started to look just slow. Instead of looking experienced, they became old. Beyond a strong defence corps, there really was not much. Their scoring became anemic. Nicholson's goaltending, never great to start with, became chronically weak.

On the other side, the Blue Shirts began to come together as a team. There were still ups and downs, but the trend line was unmistakably pointing skyward. With Marshall in the lineup, the youngsters would win eight and lose just five. The indispensability of the ageless rearguard was shown in the one game he subsequently missed owing to a death in the family: the young Torontos got shellacked 11–2 at home by Quebec City's Bulldogs.

How totally it had all turned around was demonstrated on the last night of the season. On March 5, the hapless Tecumsehs were beaten at the Mutual Street Arena 10–3 by the Montreal Wanderers and finished in the cellar of the six-team league. At the same time, in Montreal, the Blue Shirts bested the Canadiens 6–2 to end up third. They finished well back of Quebec, who had just won eleven straight games to take their second consecutive Stanley Cup, but the result was good enough for most local fans to proclaim, "Wait until next year."

———

All in all, it was a pretty successful year for the professional Torontos. When the dust settled, the club had almost broken even. The loss of a mere $300 represented a decent first-year bottom line for Montrealer Frank Robinson, Torontonian Percy Quinn and their fellow investors. The fine showing after such a shaky start, however, was not quite enough for them to leave management alone.

In truth, the manager should have seen what was coming. As the season wore on, there had been a growing tendency in reports to see every Blue Shirts' victory as the coach's. Yet, when they lost, accounts talked about the coach's boss. In other words, it was Marshall's men who won hockey games, but "Ridpath's roustabouts"[6] who went down to defeat. Given Jack's complete command of the squad, this was perhaps not surprising. Nonetheless, it was Bruce who had assembled them all—Marshall included.

In any case, when the Toronto Hockey Club assembled at the King Edward Hotel for its annual meeting on November 6, 1913, Marshall had become both manager and coach. Ridpath had quietly vanished. Oddly, though, he did turn up in December for the Blue Shirt tryouts. To everyone's surprise, Bruce was trying to make a comeback as a player. Press reports of his performance were, for a few days, quite positive, even noting Riddy's strong performance in scrimmages. Then, just as quickly, his name again disappeared from the dailies. No explanation was ever offered.

More than just Bruce Ridpath would depart the Toronto pro hockey scene prior to the 1913–14 season. So would the Tecumseh Hockey Club. With attendance plummeting near the end of the previous year, the Indians had lost $2,500—not an enormous amount, but substantial just the same. W. J. Bellingham had had enough, and he unloaded the organization.

The Tecumsehs' problems at the gate underscored a difficulty for the NHA in Toronto. Amateur advocates claimed the Queen City was simply not a pro town. There may have been a grain of truth there, but attendance figures do not entirely bear the argument out. Both the Blue Shirts and Tecumsehs had played before big crowds—even at prices substantially higher than for the OHA—for much of the season. The latter's attendance really tailed off only once the team fell hopelessly out of contention.

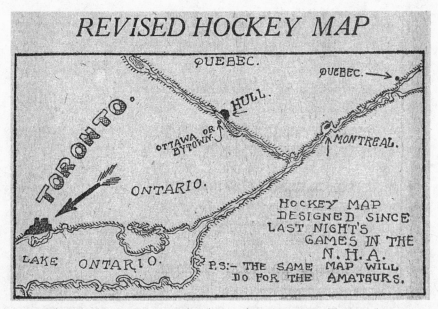

Though the amateurs might claim otherwise, many Torontonians were persuaded that the NHA franchises had put them in the big leagues.

This was not a problem for Toronto's OHA clubs. Whereas the NHA teams played a twenty-game schedule, the amateur "regular season" consisted of small round-robins of just four to eight games. After that, the winners of the various groups participated in a series of two-game, total-goals playoffs until only the champion remained standing. In short, an OHA team never really had to sustain fan support over a losing season. Any such campaign ended very quickly.

What this pattern did highlight was the importance of winning for Toronto's pro clubs. If they were not winning, their campaigns at least had to generate some intensity. This may have been what the NHA had in mind when the Tecumsehs were sold, although it would not have been immediately evident.

The franchise was bought by Tom Wall, a Montrealer who was manager of Spalding's Canadian operations. With no longer even a tenuous link between the NHA team and its Tecumseh Lacrosse Club namesake, Wall decided a rebranding was in order. Thus, the Indians became the Ontario Hockey Club. To run it, Wall brought in one of his Toronto business partners, the famous Jimmy Murphy.

———

Jimmy Murphy was renowned in hockey as the longtime coach of St. Michael's College. Under his direction, St. Mike's had captured the senior OHA championship in 1908–09 and 1909–10. In the latter year, they had also taken the Allan Cup, giving Toronto its first national hockey title. A few observers might also have remembered Murphy's even earlier life as a sometime advisor and coach to Alex Miln's Toronto Professionals.

A more intriguing part of Murphy's background was on the lacrosse side. Murphy was president of the National Lacrosse Union. Before that, he had been manager of the Toronto Lacrosse Club. When that team's ownership changed, he had been replaced by Percy Quinn, who had gone on to run the Dominion Lacrosse Association after its split from the NLU.

Thus, the relationship between the Queen City's two pro hockey clubs had morphed. The Torontos–Tecumsehs version had been based on a crosstown lacrosse rivalry. The one between the Torontos and Ontarios was also a lacrosse feud, but it was internecine, rooted in two factions originating within the Toronto Lacrosse Club itself. With members of each group surrounding Quinn and Murphy respectively, the newspapers predicted a heated relationship between the two shinny organizations.

A stormy battle for local pro hockey supremacy in 1913–14 may have been expected, but it was not to be. The Ontarios were no match for the Blue Shirts. It soon became evident that the Ontarios were worse than their predecessor, the Tecumsehs, had been the previous season.

In hindsight, Billy Nicholson's failure as a manager should not have been a surprise. Nothing in his background indicated any obvious special talent for the role. Also, frankly, the goaltender's position is not an ideal one from which to organize and coach a team—especially in the heat of a game.

In the case of Jimmy Murphy, however, greater things were genuinely anticipated. He began the year by, quite expectedly, retaining only three previous regulars: Steve Vair and the McNamara brothers. After that, his recruitment strategy seemed to strangely mirror Nicholson's. He ever so slowly gathered a number of unsigned pro veterans, most of whom were well into the back nine of their careers.

A couple of Murphy's signings were good men. Jack McDonald of Quebec, recovered from the PCHA, was a perennially reliable scorer. Fred Lake had at one time been a star defenceman in Ottawa and still had some goods to sell. Nonetheless, beyond these it was largely a collection of has-beens and never-weres.

The sum total was an Ontarios lineup that again had a fair back end but a pathetic offence. They did not merely lack scoring punch; they regularly came up short on what the papers then called "ginger"—i.e., aggressiveness—whether on the attack or backchecking. The team was simply old, heavy and slow—just like the year before.

The Ontarios were consistently lacklustre and on their heels. Despite some competitive games early in the season, they lost seven of their first eight. They then rallied to win three in a row before going into a slow descent for the rest of the campaign.

After nine more consecutive losses, their 4–16 record was again the worst in the NHA—and three games worse than the Tecumsehs had finished the year before.

By contrast, the Torontos picked up where they left off. They entered training camp with virtually the same roster. The only changes were Sue McLean and Frank Nighbor. McLean had been dropped the year before once Marshall became a regular. Nighbor, though a solid young forward throughout the previous season, had been lured away to British Columbia.

The loss of Nighbor was more than compensated for by the return of Jack Walker. Walker was another prospect who had been recruited the previous season from Port Arthur. He had, however, gone to the Maritime league after just one game with the Blue Shirts.

MONSTER CROWD CHEERED TORONTOS ON TO VICTORY OVER HUSTLING SENATORS

Blue Shirts Demonstrated All Round Superiority Over Leaders in Strenuous Contest—Winning Goal Scored in Last Minute of Play

THERE have been hockey games and hockey games, but none for sheer down right bare-to-the-bone excitement as that which was played last night at the Arena between Ottawa and Toronto. It was a desperate duel from the time that Referee Pulford blew his whistle until the final gong, which rang exactly fifty seconds after Cully Wilson had registered the goal which meant a first place tie and victory for Marshall's speedsters.

General Sherman at one time placed himself on record with a remark descriptive of the horrors of war, but he never saw a pro game. If he has there is no doubt but that he would have substituted another word for war. They did everything but bite or gouge last night. Donnybrook was a May time festival or a Tango tea compared with the contest. Hooking, jabbing, slashing, tripping, in fact everything that could be done to stop an opponent was indulged in and the officials were kept busy picking out the offender. It was particularly brutal at times and though none of the participants were seriously injured, it is a safe bet that very few of them escaped unscratched.

Fan interest in the Blue Shirts built steadily in 1913–14.

Reading the reports from the season, one is struck by the degree to which hockey was changing. A contender like the 1913–14 Toronto Hockey Club would very much resemble a top team of future eras, and presented a striking contrast to the game of just a decade before.

For example, the Blue Shirts were not wedded to old theories about complex patterns of "combination" offence. They kept their passes short and sparse. They were fast, but they used their speed as much for checking as for attack. Their forwards bore directly in on the net, rarely circling in mid-ice. They harassed and hit the opposition relentlessly, keying on its main men. And they were not afraid to take penalties as long as they were a consequence of tough, hard work.

The team also had magnificent balance—great stars and solid role players. Holmes kept maturing as a reliable, consistent goaltender. Cameron was the flashy, rushing defenceman. In Davidson there was a power forward and with Foyston a quiet, classy centre. Walker was simply sensational as both an offensive threat and a persistent forechecker. For reliable relief, the team could call on Wilson as a utility man.

And then there was McGiffin.

Roy "Minnie" McGiffin—his nickname was said to be short for Minerva, the goddess of warfare—was the most controversial member of the club. Hockey histories now tend to describe him as the original "goon." More accurately, he was the prototypical "agitator." Minnie was actually quite small, at a reputed 127 pounds, but he was always willing to mix it up.

Though in fact Minnie rarely fought, he was regularly penalized. At his worst, he took dumb, dirty and retaliatory penalties—or undeserved ones imposed by old-fashioned refs who just wanted him off the ice. At his best, he checked ferociously and energetically, driving opposing players to distraction, lifting his teammates and notching the odd marker himself.

Behind it all—indeed, often barking instructions to the boys—was old Jack Marshall. At thirty-six, he tended to play back, but he still occasionally led the charge. As Cameron spent much of the season fighting a separated shoulder, Marshall recruited a couple of old hands to help him. One of these was Con Corbeau, the former Toronto Professional who was secured from the Ontarios just before the campaign started. The other was George McNamara, sold for cash by the irrelevant Ontarios in midseason. The truth was that Toronto now had only one team that mattered—and they had the big white "T" on their blue sweaters.

These Toronto Blue Shirts had a great season—and a lucrative one—but it was no cakewalk. The Montreal Canadiens (with ex–Toronto Pros Newsy Lalonde and Donald Smith) and Ottawa Senators (with ex–Toronto Pro Skene Ronan) also had very good teams and were contenders most of the way. The defending champion Quebec Bulldogs (with ex–Toronto Pro Jack Marks) likewise seemed always close behind and threatening. The Blue Shirts were usually at the top, but rarely alone in that position.

That began to change on February 21. On that Saturday night, the Blue Shirts edged the Canadiens 3–2 at the Arena Gardens to assume sole possession of first place. The next Wednesday, they blew past the Ontarios by a count of 6–1. The small crowd was actually paying more attention to the out-of-town scoreboard, which showed the Senators, who had been fading in recent games, surprising the Canadiens 6–5 in overtime at the national capital.

The victory seemed to put the Blue Shirts over the top, adding to the city's growing excitement. Even Billy Hewitt's *Star* seemed to be shunting aside its amateur adherence. The appearance of the legendary amateur Princeton star Hobey Baker in Canada that month[7] could not compete with its focus on the Toronto pros. Almost from the beginning of the campaign, its coverage of the team it dubbed the "Blue Streaks" had been expanding. Now it was unreservedly jumping on the bandwagon, proclaiming, "Torontos Sure of Championship."[8]

After all, with a two-game lead in the NHA race, just two games left to play and a favourable remaining schedule, what could go wrong?

———

So confident was Toronto of the NHA championship and the resulting Stanley Cup title that talk inside and outside the dressing room turned to the coming Cup defence against the Victoria Aristocrats. Before the season, the National, Pacific and Maritime associations had agreed to set up the long-contemplated "hockey commission" to regulate player rights, enforce contracts and schedule Stanley Cup games. Lester Patrick's Victoria team had recently wrapped up the PCHA championship. They were already planning the trip east, bringing their wives and their Vancouver rivals with them.

Nobody seemed much troubled when the Blue Shirts lost their next game in Quebec. They had played reasonably well on poor ice, and after all, the Bulldogs were the reigning champs. However, the Canadiens edged out the Wanderers in an overtime struggle at Montreal to move within a game of the leaders.

So, for the Torontos, it all came down to their home match against the Wanderers. In fact, the fifth-place Redbands were coming to Mutual Street with excessively low expectations. Long a Cup contender, their season had been ruined by multiple injuries to key players. All of these had returned, though, and the Montreal club was again playing in top form.

On March 4, the Wanderers did not just beat the Blue Shirts—by a score of 7–5—they completely outplayed their hosts. Truth be told, the Torontos stunk out the joint. With Holmes holding them in it, their play became increasingly feeble as the game progressed. Meanwhile the Canadiens, seeing the scores flash from the Queen City, made an extra push and overcame the Ontarios, 5–3. The race for the NHA regular-season crown had finished in a tie, with each of the leaders posting thirteen wins and seven losses.

The Torontos' supporters were furious about this turn of events. Particular anger was directed at Davidson, whose performance had progressively declined in the last half of the season. The *Star* was the bluntest: "Davidson was, to use the fans' own picturesque phraseology, 'absolutely putrid.'"[9] The newspapers repeated widely circulated rumours about breaks from training and sobriety by Scotty and his young Blue Shirt teammates.

But there was an even more serious charge: that the Torontos had thrown the game.

The hypothesis was that the club wanted an extra gate from a home-and-home final with the Canadiens. The accusation was said to be pouring off the lips of the 4,000 streaming out of the Arena after the match.

THE N.H.A. RACE TIED UP BY LAST NIGHT'S RESULTS

Wanderers Trounce Torontos—Ontarios Gave Canadiens a Run— Blue-Shirts Very Much Off Color Here.

TIE TO BE SETTLED BY HOME-AND-HOME GAMES

Four thousand disgruntled—almost disgusted—pro. hockey fans piled out of the Arena last night anthematizing the Torontos for an hour's dopey play. Two hours previously the Blue Streaks looked like cinch champions, but the near-tail-enders, Sammy Lichtenhein's Wanderers, handed them the short end of a 7 to 5 score, and as Ontarios failed to come through with a victory over Canadiens at Montreal the Torontos and the Torontos are now tied for the N.H.A. title, and play home-and-home games Saturday and Wednesday to break the deadlock.

Blue Streaks?

Blue Molds, you mean!

Jack Marshall's squad fell down woefully last night. They hadn't anything from goal out on the regular squad, and got a sound trouncing. Indeed, the only real hockey playing done by a Blue Shirt all evening was that of "Cully" Wilson, who was used as a substitute. Holmes in goal was off color, the defence was weak offensively, though Marshall and Cameron did some nice rushing, while on the forward line, Davidson was, to use the fans' own picturesque phraseology, "absolutely putrid." He was very erratic on his skates, played—or, rather, tried to play—all over the ice, and did absolutely no back or body-checking. At one time Davidson was one of the bright and shining stars of the team, but after half a dozen good games the froth of public acclaim went to his head and he became, to say the least, careless. He has played more than one bad game for Torontos this season, but last night's was absolutely his worst, and he lost a host of friends by his exhibition. He looked as if he had forgotten what training meant.

tured an artery in his foot, and he finished the game with a great effort.

The line-up:

Canadiens—Goal, Vezina; defence, Laviolette and Dubeau; centre, Scott; wings, D. Smith and Berlinquette.

Ontarios—Goal, Hebert; defence, McNamara and F. Lake; centre, Hunt; wings, McDonald and Lowery.

The Summary.

First Period.

1. Ontarios.........McNamara 9.20

Second Period.

2. Canadiens......Payan 3.55
3. Canadiens......Payan 8.55

Third Period.

4. Ontarios......Hunt 3.40
5. Ontarios.......McDonald 2.40
6. Canadiens......Payan 1.45
7. Canadiens......Scott 7.15
8. Canadiens......Scott 4.15

OTTAWA BLANKED.

The champion Quebec team handed Ottawas a 10—0 lacing last night and cinched third place in the N.H.A. final reckoning. The ice was slow and watery. Ottawa never had a peek in. Joe Hall was presented with a "popular player" cup.

The line-up:

Quebec—Goal, Moran; defence, Hall, Mummery; centre, T. Smith; wings, Malone, Crawford.

Ottawa—Goal, Benedict; defence, Merrill, Gerard; centre, Ronan; wings, Darragh, Broadbent.

Referee—Leo Dandurand. Judge of play—Riley Hern.

Summary.

First Period.

1. Quebec........Smith 1.30
2. Quebec........Hall 13.30

Second Period.

3. Quebec........Hall 8.12
4. Quebec........Crawford 08

The Blue Shirts' unexpected loss to the Wanderers would lead to a torrent of fan anger and accusations.

Many in the media did question the conspiracy theory. Would the team really have thrown the game that would have clinched the NHA championship and the Stanley Cup just so that they could earn an extra gate? And why would anyone potentially squander an entire Stanley Cup series—the pending PCHA challenge—by deliberately putting the NHA title at risk? Nevertheless, the papers repeated the charge ad nauseam. As they did, the Blue Shirts' Queen City survival suddenly seemed endangered by the same ghosts that had driven the old Toronto Professionals out of Mutual Street in 1909.

The Blue Shirts organization had to be conscious of how dangerous this situation was. It would not take much to turn the fans back to pure amateur loyalty—particularly because the amateur Torontos were about to wrap up another senior provincial championship. For the second year running, Eddie Livingstone's TR&AA had taken the John Ross Robertson trophy and was musing about a challenge for the Allan Cup.

In reality, by backing themselves into the tiebreakers with the Canadiens, the Blue Shirts were taking a huge gamble. The "Flying Frenchmen" were definitely coming on. Montreal also promised to have Newsy Lalonde—who had missed a considerable chunk of the season with shoulder problems—back in their lineup for the series.

Four years since his departure from the Ontario provincial capital, Newsy remained the player the fans loved to hate. His every appearance at the Arena Gardens was followed by accounts of his poor play. The following editorial comment in the midst of a midseason game report was typical: "Lalonde was the slowest man on the ice . . . Any hustling young player has 'Newsy' beaten nowadays before he starts; so much for a reputation."[10]

On the ice, Lalonde's performance was consistently described as sluggish. His frequent scoring was attributed to "loafing" ahead of the play. His competitive spirit was dismissed as nothing more than crudeness. Periodic episodes of violent confrontation—most notably with Quebec's "Bad Joe" Hall—were greeted with wagging fingers and shaking heads.

Lalonde's apparently inexplicable success in hockey was usually chalked up to his manoeuvrings off the ice. In an era of unrestrained commercial competition, he had proven to be the ultimate master at playing leagues and owners off each other for his services. Even the new hockey commission had not stopped him. By cross-negotiating his contract as a star lacrosse player, Newsy still managed to attract competing bids. In 1913–14, as in many seasons before and after, he was the highest-paid athlete in Canada.

Nonetheless, the opinion of Toronto fans was clear. Except for being the highest-paid, often highest-scoring performer in the business, Newsy Lalonde was not much of a hockey player. Other than being one of the fiercest, most effective leaders on the ice, he added little to his team.

The two-game, total-goals series to decide the NHA championship and the Stanley Cup did not begin well for the Blue Shirts. In Montreal for game one, the Torontos lost 2–0 on mushy, water-covered ice. They simply could not keep pace with the bigger Frenchmen under such conditions. Lalonde, playing with what was reported after the series as a partially separated shoulder, had not been much of a factor, but he did bring confidence to his club.

Returning to Toronto, the Blue Shirts thus became definite underdogs. Despite a healthy demand for tickets, betting was strongly against the home side on that fateful night of March 11, 1914. Almost a hundred fans had come up from Montreal. Indeed, it was widely suggested that it would take only one goal to bring the Queen City crowd behind the Canadiens.

Whether that was true or not, the hypothesis never got tested. On the cold, hard artificial ice, the Torontos came out flying. And the Canadiens made an age-old mistake: playing defensively and sitting on the 2–0 lead they had brought with them from Montreal. With no more than two French forwards ever moving up, the Blue Shirts' defence joined the rush. After two periods of relentless attack, they had the series tied at 2–2.

Finally, early in the third, Marshall confidently carried the puck up the ice and deep into the Montreal end. As the Canadiens' attention shifted to him, he faked a pass to Walker and then sailed it over to Davidson. The big forward blasted the rubber into the net, the 6,000 present exploding into bedlam with the series lead.

The Canadiens tried to turn up the heat on offence. However, trying to reverse the flow at this point only caused their game to collapse into chaos. By the time it was over, the Blue Shirts had whipped them 6–0 (for an aggregate score of 6–2), giving Toronto its first national professional hockey championship.

The *News*, reflecting the city's sense of triumph, proclaimed that "Torontos settled all argument last night as to their superiority."[11]

The Stanley Cup, twenty-two years after it had first been presented, had finally come to the Queen City.

The Blue Shirts had been rehabilitated. Although it was Toronto's first Stanley Cup, the mug was not presented that night. It was still in

Quebec City, awaiting transportation. For now, the players had to be content to hoist the O'Brien Trophy, emblematic of the NHA championship. Besides, unless the Torontos dealt successfully with the upcoming challenge from Victoria, they would not be champions for very long.

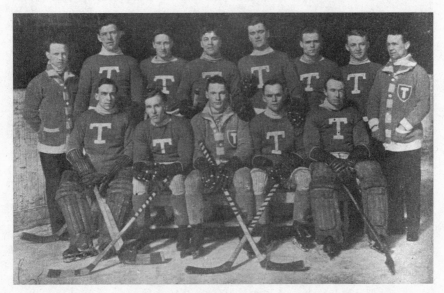

The Toronto Hockey Club, Stanley Cup champions of 1913–14. The young club, assembled by former manager Bruce Ridpath, was thought to have a great future ahead of it.

The best-of-five playoff between the NHA and PCHA was the subject of considerable hype in Toronto—the "World's Series," no less. That moniker was rather at odds with trustee William Foran's recent declaration that he would not allow any club outside Canada to play for the Stanley Cup; all the same, there seemed to be great interest. Fans flocked to the Arena Gardens to watch the western outfit practise.

The Victoria team consisted largely of well-known and well-regarded veterans. Patrick himself and Walter Smaill were old Wanderer champions. Dubbie Kerr was remembered as a Toronto Professional and Ottawa Senator. Of course, no one could forget Bobby Rowe, the Barrie player at the epicentre of the OHA crisis of 1906 and, more recently, one of Renfrew's Millionaires. Most unusual was spare forward Jack Ulrich, probably the first deaf man to play hockey at such a high level.

PHENOMENAL INTEREST IN STANLEY CUP GAME TO-NIGHT

As a Sporting Proposition the Public Is Aroused, But Not With the Same Keen Excitement Manifested in the Senior O.H.A. Finals—Australian Cricketer Sues for Libel.

REGINA'S VICTORY IN THE ALLAN CUP CONTEST

The interest in the Stanley Cup series between Torontos, the N.H.A. champions, and Victorias, the Pacific Coast champions, is phenomenal. It is not quite so keen as that which marked the St. Michael's-T.R. and A.A. senior O.H.A. final, because that series brought out two teams of local boys, nearly all of whom have been playing here for years, and who each had a strong individual following of admirers. In addition, there was a certain amount of extraneous rivalry of an intangible nature which divided the hockey fans of the city into two huge camps.

In the Stanley Cup series the interest is almost purely sporting. Two teams of professional players are meeting. The British Columbia team is almost entirely strange to Toronto fans. Some have seen Dubbie Kerr when he was with the old Toronto pros in the forerunner of the Trolley League, and some know Lindsay, a Toronto boy, personally. Bobby Rowe, the Barrie veteran, has a few friends here, and Walter Small, Dunderdale, and Lester Patrick are not unknown, but they have not the personal drawing powers of the Meekings, Dissette, Laflamme, Heffernan, and Gooch, and the rest of the amateur stars. The Toronto players, of course, have their friends. Harry Holmes and Roy McGiffin are Toronto boys, and Frank Foyston, of Barrie, and Allan Davidson, of Kingston are old O.H.A. friends and they have a good personal following.

Harry Cameron, Jack Marshall, Cully Wilson, Con Corbeau, George McNamara, and the rest of them have made friends in their two winters' sojourn here, and Jack Walker, the "poke-check" impresario, has made a host of friends in his one season, but still take it all in all there is less personal interest about this series than there was about the O.H.A. final, and so there is less sporting ferment.

However, the full measure of the sporting interest is measured by the demand for seats of the big series which has inundated the Arena box office and the office of the local club. Hundreds of fans are coming in from the country, and to-day all sorts of wires are being pulled to obtain tickets. Speculation is going on, but the care with which tickets were handled prohibits much of this sort of profit-taking.

While Torontos should win to-night's game because N.H.A. rules are in vogue, the defeat of Ottawa and Quebec by Vancouver, the Western runners-up, in games played half under each rule, indicates that the Western champions are a distinctly dangerous proposition.

The Blue Shirts were winning again, and even the *Star* was on board—up to a point.

The enthusiasts who turned out at the Mutual Street warm-ups were impressed by what they saw. It was true the Aristocrats were not as fast as the Blue Shirts; they were, however, highly skilled, disciplined and diligent. In workouts, they displayed team play that was far more developed than anything the Blue Shirts had shown.

That was, as they say, in practice. The Torontos simply skated past the Victorias, 5–2, in the first game on Saturday night, March 14. According to the local papers, the match was neither close nor interesting. The winners, they said, had triumphed even while playing noticeably below par.

No one could quite say what was wrong with Lester's men. They were certainly well trained and well rested. Yet the contest had been lopsided enough for the referee to publicly declare the Blue Shirts certain to win the series.

This referee was none other than the famous Montreal hockey man Russell Bowie. It was Bowie who had similarly declared the Wanderers the better team after their 1908 Cup match against the Toronto Professionals. This time, though, Bowie was rendering a prediction on games yet to be played, in which he would be the referee. No wonder complacency set into the city, causing attendance for the series to begin to slide.

Those who stayed away from the rink probably should not have, because Victoria had a marked advantage in game two. According to the agreement between the leagues, the even-numbered matches would be fought under Pacific Coast rules. That meant, first and foremost, seven a side on the ice, with the return of the rover. Yet the young Blue Shirts had played the older style fairly recently and did not anticipate much problem in adapting to this wrinkle. In fact, the NHA had used seven-man hockey in the middle of the 1912–13 season, after its Ontario teams insisted the experiment was essential to their box-office survival. The Tecumsehs and Torontos were locked in an intense competition for fans with the OHA, which had preserved the rover. Very quickly, however, the rule change proved to be wildly unpopular in Montreal and Quebec City, while Toronto and Ottawa patrons appeared at worst indifferent. After little more than a week, the NHA had gone back to six men once and for all.

The Patricks' other changes—on offsides and penalties—were much more problematic for the Torontos. That season, the PCHA had brought in the blue lines—and with them, unlimited forward passing in the neutral zone. This was something no Toronto player had ever seen. On the other hand, the western league's penalty system was more traditional, meaning time in the box for infractions. The NHA used what the OHA papers ridiculed as the "wig-wag"[12] system for misdemeanours. The offender received a fine, ranging anywhere from $2 for a minor to $25 for a match and expulsion. McGiffin had led the league with $116 worth of sanctions, the Torontos being a heavily penalized team. In short, the Blue Shirts were a physically aggressive bunch, yet unaccustomed to power plays or shorthanded situations at the professional level.

To top it all off, the Torontos had some health issues. Cameron had dressed but not played a single shift in the first encounter. In addition, Davidson had been consigned to bed by the doctor after the game, suffering from a bad cold that had developed into influenza.

That second match, the following Tuesday, proved to be the key to the series. Befuddled by all the rule modifications and novel situations, the Blue Shirts fell behind for most of the game. Yet they refused to let up, skating hard and checking persistently throughout the contest. While Holmes kept them in it, the Torontos pecked away. In the third period, they came back from two goals down to tie it up at 5–5.

Then came the heroics.

The unlikely star was McGiffin. All night, he had followed Marshall's instructions and zeroed in on Victoria defenceman Bobby Genge, a dominating two-way player. Genge was also big, at nearly 200 pounds. McGiffin bounced on and off him all night like a dog off a bear. Finally, the larger man slammed and butt-ended Minnie, knocking him out cold.

Despite this, in overtime, McGiffin came back out on the ice. Battered, bruised and with blood still streaming down his face, he at last managed to get a hold of the puck. Eighteen minutes in, he shot it into the net for the winner. It was his second of the game and the crowd went wild.

The Aristocrats were finished. Entering game three on Thursday, Patrick even talked as though he knew it was over. Still, the veteran club did not lie down. In one of the most physical, violent games ever seen in Toronto, the Pacific champions fought for dear life. At one point, a punch-up between Genge and Davidson (who were actually first cousins) nearly became an all-out brawl. That brought the police into the dressing rooms, warning the players they were close to being charged.

In the end, the Torontos held on to win 2–1. They had swept the western contenders in three straight to hold the Stanley Cup, technically taking it for the second time in 1914.[13] The Maritime winners, the Sydney Millionaires, decided not to challenge. Thus, on March 19, 1914, before all the key people in professional hockey, assembled there at the Arena Gardens, the Blue Shirts had been declared the undisputed champions of the world.

Toronto was finally on top. Its club not only was the best, but seemed as complete as a team could be. A local panel picked Jack Walker as the most valuable man over the season. Frank Foyston was judged the star of the final series. Along with Cameron, Davidson, Holmes, McGiffin and Wilson, these young Blue Shirts were a group not yet even close to their prime. Only Marshall, the man credited with making it all happen, was looking at the end. Having just celebrated his thirty-seventh birthday, old Jack declared that he had played his last hockey.

———

It seems that most Torontonians were pleased as punch—most, but not all.

John Ross Robertson's *Telegram* remained distinctly restrained in its enthusiasm. While Robertson himself was not quoted, the former promoter Tom Flanagan doubtlessly echoed the boss when he wrote in his column that the professional Stanley Cup was "dragging the national game to the mud."[14]

The *Tely* did not stop there. Its Stanley Cup analysis repeatedly emphasized the skill of the Victoria players and the dirtiness of the local ones. It regularly rolled out commentary like this for the final match: "Little chance of any great hockey developing in this game."[15] Most strikingly, it gradually dropped virtually all reference to Lord Stanley's chalice. Its story about the final game noted only that the Blue Shirts had won what it called "the Inter-League Professional Hockey Series."[16]

Robertson may not even have been in the city when the Blue Shirts made Toronto hockey history. He

TORONTOS CLEAN UP SERIES CHOPPED THEIR WAY TO VICTORY

Last Game of Inter-League Pro Series Was Battle in Every Sense of Word.

FASTEST PRO GAME OF YEAR

Men Tore Up and Down Ice Like Fiends — Every Roughhouse Trick Known Used — Beaten Team Made a Strong Showing in the Final.

All mention of the Stanley Cup championship vanished from the *Tely*'s grudging coverage of the Blue Shirt victories.

had other things on his eclectic mind as 1914 began. Having long since been made a very wealthy man by his publication, he devoted ever more time to the charities close to his heart, especially the Hospital for Sick Children.

The world around Robertson was one of change and contradiction. When King Edward VII died in the spring of 1910, his funeral became "the greatest assemblage of royalty and rank ever gathered in one place."[17] His son, the new king, was a duller but serious man, preoccupied with matters like state honours and grappling with issues of constitutional change. He would definitely reign rather than rule; the victory of the Commons over the Lords in the parliamentary crisis of 1911 ensured that once and for all.

Socialism and organized labour continued to rise, alongside expanding industrialism and mass production. The social purity movement continued to toil away. Women were demanding, and sometimes getting, the vote. Art circles were in a tizzy over an exhibition of Cubism in New York City. Republicanism in Ireland and nationalism in India were gaining strength. More than anything, the power of Germany and its allies was increasingly testing the primacy of Britain and its friends.

In Canada, Robertson was still a giant. The renowned writer and critic Augustus Bridle was researching the book he would soon publish, *Sons of Canada: Short Studies of Characteristic Canadians*, which featured the local legend. While weightier matters preoccupied him, the book made clear that Robertson had not turned his back on hockey. "The genial boss," Bridle wrote, "goes to the games; sits in his fur-lined greatcoat at the rinkside, hawk-eyeing the players of to-day, remembering as in a Homeric dream the experts of long ago."[18]

In the midst of the commotion of any era, it has never been obvious what is truly transformation and what is just fashion. With the triumph in the Athletic War and his OHA about to spearhead the formation of the Canadian Amateur Hockey Association, Robertson no doubt felt the amateur order was secure. He could not have known, and would not have believed, that the Blue Shirts' Stanley Cup was the beginning of something else in hockey's second city. Yet in retrospect, it is clear: Toronto's new order—the professional order—was finally beginning to emerge.

As the new pro Torontos were making their drive for the mug, Robertson and his *Telegram* editor, Black Jack Robinson, travelled together to Britain. People worldwide were speculating ominously on a coming war. In the mother country, Robertson was struck by the military parades and the confident spirit of the people. If hostilities were indeed coming, he predicted, they wouldn't last three months.[19]

He would be wrong on that one, too.

AN ERA FADES AWAY

Livingstone was always arguing. No place for arguing in hockey. Let's make money instead.[1]

—AN NHL FOUNDER

The year 1914 was one of the true watersheds of history. A mere 131 days after the conclusion of the Toronto Blue Shirts' Stanley Cup season, the Great War commenced. The changes it would initiate in the power structures of global politics and the social fabrics of participating countries—not to mention the accompanying lives of millions—are simply too numerous and profound to recount here. Let it simply be said that the world of professional hockey was no different.

The draw of thousands of young contestants to the Western Front profoundly altered the course of their careers and those of the teams and leagues they belonged to. Above all, it created a player shortage that quickly undermined the peace established by the "hockey commission." In fact, as the war dragged on, the fight for existence among the commercial hockey entities became ever more desperate. The third pro partner, the weaker Maritime Professional Hockey League, was finished off very quickly. However, all were affected, including the Stanley Cup champions.

The Blue Shirts lost Allan Davidson to the war effort. Scotty was said to have been the first pro hockey player to volunteer for service. The Torontos suffered from both this departure of their leading scorer and the consistent absence of Marshall, their veteran quarterback. They were unable to fully replace either man, and the team slumped back to finish fourth in the National Hockey Association in 1914–15.

This was the beginning of a rocky road for commercial hockey in Toronto. In spite of the Stanley Cup breakthrough of 1914, it would be almost two decades before the supremacy of the new professional order would be firmly established in Canada's second city. Yet it was not so much the Blue Shirts as that other NHA Queen City franchise that laid the first big potholes on this long path.

In the fall of 1914, a new figure entered Toronto's professional hockey scene: Edward James Livingstone. Livingstone left the OHA champions, the Toronto Rugby & Athletic Association, to buy the troubled Ontario Hockey Club from Tom Wall. He renamed them the Toronto Shamrocks, but that did not much change their luck. The club finished fifth in the six-team association.

Anyone who had followed Livingstone's record in amateur hockey and football could have seen what was coming. "Livvy"—also known as E.J. and Eddie—was a combative, sanctimonious and generally difficult personality. He expected others to live rigidly by the rules while he would skirt their spirit. He regularly denounced those with whom he clashed, while demanding apologies for the thinnest of slights.

While Livingstone's team was a flop on the ice, its owner was a veritable wrecking ball in the boardroom. His elevation to the governing body, already full of men fractious in their own right, was the last thing the struggling pro game needed. Almost from the day he got hold of the Tecumseh/Ontario/Shamrock outfit, his disputes with the other NHA owners, its partner leagues and his employee-players became legion.

The Livingstone issue became double trouble when Eddie bought a second hockey team, the former Stanley Cup champion Blue Shirts, before the beginning of the 1915–16 season. Toronto's marquee team was undergoing devastating raids by the Pacific Coast Hockey Association. Rather than address the issue—and against the wishes of the NHA— Livingstone decided to fold his Shamrocks and use that team's players to fill the depleted ranks of the Blue Shirts.

For scheduling reasons, the weakened NHA had not wanted an odd number of clubs. Thus, for 1916–17, it took Livingstone's second franchise and gave it to an army unit, the 228th Battalion of the Canadian Expeditionary Force, who would also play out of Toronto's Mutual Street Arena. When that team, contrary to the promises of the military, got shipped overseas in midseason, the association dropped both Queen City teams. It wanted a balanced schedule and, it can be fairly presumed, to be rid of the cantankerous Livvy.

E. J. "Livvy" Livingstone was the last owner of the Toronto Blue Shirts. His tenure would transform professional hockey, but not in the way he intended.

With the stroke of a pen, the Blue Shirts vanished from the National Hockey Association.

The man who was increasingly leading the other NHA owners in their moves against Livingstone was a former Montreal sports reporter named Frank Calder. Calder had been named the league's secretary-treasurer in the fall of ·1914. It was fitting that Calder and Livingstone joined the board in the same fall that the "war to end all wars" began. Calder became the association's antidote to the toxic Toronto owner, leading a long business battle that ultimately determined hockey's structure for the century to come.[2]

By the fall of 1917, the NHA was hanging on by a thread because of contract competition from the PCHA and the (literal) wartime bleeding of the players. The quarrelsome and litigious Livingstone was a distraction it could not afford. Calder finally convinced his NHA colleagues they had to get rid of Livvy—at any cost.

To accomplish this, the other owners left the NHA and, on November 26, 1917, formed a new body, the National Hockey League, with Calder installed as its president. The NHL then created a new Toronto franchise under the management of the Arena Gardens. Effectively expropriated by the new circuit, the Toronto Blue Shirts would thus be-

Frank Calder created a business empire for the express purpose of keeping Livingstone out of pro hockey. That empire is the National Hockey League.

come the Toronto Arenas, and then evolving into the Toronto St. Patricks a mere two years later.[3]

Livvy was left on the outside, desperately trying to figure out how to get back in. He was joined in this NHL exile by the original Blue Shirts' boss, Percy Quinn, an associate from his Toronto Athletics days. Meanwhile the Arenas/St. Patricks fell under the management of the Tecumsehs' former kingpin, Charlie Querrie. Ironically, Querrie had been ostracized by the earlier NHA for *his* argumentative ways.

Even as an outcast, Livingstone would prove to be a pivotal figure in the evolution of hockey as a business. His manoeuvring to either get into the NHL or create a rival league progressively transformed the reorganized association. Under the iron control of President Calder, the NHL began to replicate the unified "syndicate" culture of its remaining rival, the Patrick family's West Coast PCHA.

The final piece fell into place when Livvy started to look at big American facilities as a base for his alternative league. The NHL moved pre-emptively to outflank him. Beginning with the creation of the Boston Bruins in 1924, the NHL finally entered the U.S. market. Such a development had been contemplated by the major eastern Canadian hockey leagues for two decades, but only the western PCHA had theretofore actually done it.

With its parallel, syndicate-like organization, combined with larger buildings in far larger markets, the superior power of the NHL was ensured. Given the "natural monopoly" features of pro sports,[4] this quickly led to its domination of the smaller, western wing of the business. The NHL bought out the PCHA's remnants (by then part of the Western

Hockey League) in 1926. Its control of top-level hockey has been occasionally challenged, but has remained unbroken, ever since.

By 1927, these developments were belatedly—but unmistakably— reshaping the hockey world in Toronto itself. That was the year Conn Smythe purchased the St. Pats and rebranded them as the Toronto Maple Leafs. With a skilful and strategic approach to management and marketing, the Leafs created a modern, model pro sports franchise. Four years later, Smythe's Maple Leaf Gardens was built for $1.5 million in a furious six-month span using early-Depression labour.[5] Thus, by 1931, the predominance of the paid men in Toronto was ensured.

This gradual ascent of pro hockey had occurred in complete independence from developments in the amateur hockey world. And this was precisely the way the country's amateur leaders had wanted it. For many years, and to many people, it had seemed as if that decision to sever any and all connection to professionalism had been correct. Yet the slow and often imperceptible rise of pro hockey in Toronto had been paralleled by a similar decline in the amateur game. This was certainly not what the "winners" of the Athletic War had expected.

In that great confrontation, the amateur zealots had fought for the separation principle. By the time the Stanley Cup came to Toronto, they had fully achieved their wish. Commercial shinny was evolving on its own, going through mind-numbing upheavals and restructurings. The stability of the amateur scene appeared a marked contrast. The Interprovincial Amateur Hockey Union may not have lasted for long, but the Allan Cup quickly became a veritable hockey institution.

Competition for the Allan Cup helped inspire the formation of the Canadian Amateur Hockey Association in that fateful year of 1914. The CAHA completed the system of parallel hockey structures the amateur ideologues had put together to counter the development of the professional sport. It would represent Canadian hockey in other avowedly amateur organizations, such as the International Ice Hockey Federation and the Amateur Athletic Union of Canada.

To no one's surprise, the driving force behind both the CAHA and the AAUC had been the Ontario Hockey Association. The OHA remained the great power of Toronto hockey during the First World War. It also continued to be a remarkably progressive body in terms of the evolution of the game on the ice. The OHA's rule changes were still numerous and significant. At the 1913 annual meeting, its three-foot line for goalie rebounds became a ten-foot line and then, in 1917, a twenty-foot line within which forward passing was allowed. This was also a foreshadowing of the modern blue line. In 1915, the association moved to the modern set of three periods. And, at his final OHA gathering, a declining John Ross Robertson struggled to his feet to successfully urge the adoption of six-man hockey.

By then, however, it was no longer the OHA that was pioneering these innovations. They were largely originating in the pro ranks. Indeed, if one looks at the various NHA or PCHA rules during the Blue Shirts' Stanley Cup games of 1914, one can clearly see the outlines of the modern sport (in contrast to the Professionals' Cup challenge only six years earlier). These modifications had been roundly condemned in the amateur circles as "not real hockey"—at least, that is, until the OHA finally endorsed them, typically at the urging of Robertson himself.

Needless to say, one set of changes Robertson never advocated would be to the principles of amateurism. On the contrary, it seemed the OHA was going to ever more extreme lengths to enforce its creed. As Torontonians took in the Blue Shirts' playoff victories against the Canadiens and Victoria in 1914, the OHA debated the idea of making itself the owner of all gate monies throughout the province. How else, Robertson's *Telegram* asked, could the temptations of professionalism truly and forever be removed?

All of this served to underscore the degree to which the former president remained in total control of the OHA. Despite the large membership of the association, its affairs remained dominated by a small clique centred on Robertson and his subcommittee, the Three White Czars. This arrangement allowed Robertson to continue to run the OHA without it absorbing too much of his energies, which were largely devoted to other matters: his newspaper, his hospital and nursing philanthropy, his Masonic duties and his growing collection of historical artefacts.

Nonetheless, time eventually overtakes even the most vigorous among us. Early in 1918, the seventy-six-year-old Robertson fell ill with a heavy cold when he went to Florida. He returned in mid-April suffering badly from asthma. Refusing to rest, he headed for New York and the annual meeting of the American Publishers' Association. Back home, still ill, he finished a campaign that cleared the mortgage on the new Masonic Temple and insisted on touring the unfinished building. A friend thought it was this visit, where he breathed cold, damp air amid the wet plaster and green lumber, that took him.[6] He was diagnosed with pneumonia, and his condition worsened throughout May.

JOHN ROSS ROBERTSON IS DEAD: NOTED PUBLISHER AND BENEFACTOR

Founder of The Evening Telegram, Chief Supporter of Hospital for Sick Children and Prominent as Free Mason

Mr. John Ross Robertson, publisher and proprietor of The Toronto Evening Telegram, Chairman of the Board of Trustees of the Hospital for Sick Children, a former member of Parliament for East Toronto, and one of the most prominent Freemasons of Canada, died yesterday at his residence, 291 Sherbourne street, Toronto, of pneumonia. The end came at 9.30 in the morning after a short illness.

77 Years of Age.

The late Mr. Robertson was 77 years of age, having been born in Toronto in December, 1841. He is survived by Mrs. Robertson and two sons by his first marriage, namely, John Sinclair Robertson and Irving Earle Robertson, both of Toronto, and by nine nephews and nieces, namely, Douglas S. Robertson, London, Eng., correspondent of The Evening Telegram; Irving G. Roberson of the Canadian Expeditionary Force; L. Bruce Robertson and Struan Robertson; Mrs. Stuart Wallace, Major Charles A. and Hector Robertson, and Kenneth and Margaret Robertson. There are also one grandson and one grandnephew. The funeral will be private.

Cold Develops Into Pneumonia.

The late Mr. Robertson spent the winter in Florida and returned to Toronto on April 12, apparently with renewed health and strength. On the journey north he contracted a slight cold, but did not pay much attention to it. He went about his work as usual, and attended the annual meeting in New York of the American Publishers' Association. When he returned home his cold had not cleared up and he decided to stay indoors for a few days. He spent some days in his library, but the work of the Hospital for Sick Children, in which he was so intensely interested, and the campaign to clear the debt of the Masonic Temple demanded his attention. Although he had been unable to shake off this cold he apparently enjoyed his usual strength up till a few days ago, when pneumonia developed. It was on the morning of May 17, just two weeks ago, that he complained of not feeling well. He was quickly taken home and Dr. Crawford Scadding, who was called in, found traces of pneumonia in his right lung.

Aids Hospital in Sickbed.

While he was on his deathbed Mr. Robertson discussed plans for clearing of the debt on the Hospital for Sick Children, and on Monday morning, May 26, he signed his last

The next year he founded his last paper, and his greatest success, The Evening Telegram.

Stick to His Style.

Fifteen years of founding and printing newspapers taught John Ross Robertson, what others had not seen so clearly as he, the amazing revenue that might be obtained by the "want ad," and The Telegram now, as then, uses the front part of its publication for printing small ads, putting the news far in-

up in the early nineties. It was recently announced that Mr. Robertson had himself contributed a total of $150,000 to the support of this institution.

The Island Home.

He also built the Lakeside Home for Little Children at Lighthouse Point, Toronto Island, with an accommodation for 150 patients and a complete hospital equipment. This building was burned two years ago, but the smaller adjacent buildings

were all done under his direction and editing. These books give minutely the early days of Toronto and York to the present time. Possibly more of encyclopedic than of literary value, nevertheless, they are valuable productions, and show to their amazed owners that Toronto has had an entrancing history.

Mr. Robertson was the Past President of the Canadian Copyright Association ; Member, Canadian Institute, Toronto; Fellow, Royal Colonial Institute, London; Vice-President, Clan Donnachaidh (Robertson) Society, Scotland; he was presented by invitation to his Majesty King Edward and her Majesty Queen Alexandra in Westminster Abbey, Coronation Day, 1902.

Gifts to the University.

He gave to the University of Toronto for the dais in Convocation Hall, ten handsomely-carved chairs, each made of historic wood, in connection with the history of Canada.

The late Mr. Robertson was married twice. His first wife was Maria Louise, daughter of E. M. Gilbee, England. She died in 1886. His second wife was Jessie Elizabeth, daughter of G. B. Holland, Toronto. Mr. Robertson was a Presbyterian.

Tribute of Premier.

Sir Wm. Hearst, Prime Minister of Ontario:—"The death of Mr. John Ross Robertson will be severely felt, not only in the city where he has lived so long, but throughout the whole of Canada. A big, generous, patriotic citizen has passed away—a man who has done much for his city and his country. The Hospital for Sick Children will stand as a monument to his energy, his kindly, generous heart and untiring work on behalf of suffering humanity. He was widely known throughout the Province and beyond its boundaries, not only for his connection with the Hospital for Sick Children, but in Masonic and other circles. He will be mourned deeply by all who know him."

R. J. Fleming's Estimate.

Mr. R. J. Fleming, General Manager of the Toronto Railway Co., and former Mayor of Toronto:—"The death of Mr. Robertson is almost an irreparable loss to the community. His interest in humanity and the service which he has rendered to the city by the honest and powerful advocacy daily in his paper of everything he believed to be for the benefit of the community, and his powerful denunciation of everything that he believed to be against the best interests of the community, have placed him, in my estimation, by all odds, our foremost citizen.

"And when you take into consideration his life of unselfish and devoted service to the Hospital for Sick Children, which he became identified with in its early foundation, probably forty years ago, when it had few friends, few contributors and only a handful interested in its work, and realize the work he has done to build up such a magnificent institution, the time he has given to it, making it as much or more his daily business then his own personal affairs, then I think we can, with every citizen, class him as the first citizen of our Dominion."

Wm. Douglas, Business Manager The Mail:—"I have known John Ross Robertson for many years and had a great admiration for him. He was a diamond in the rough. Mr. Robertson had a very high sense of honor; his word was his bond. His work at the Hospital for Sick Children was one of the greatest ever undertaken in Toronto, and I don't know what the hospital will do without him."

Well Known as Publisher.

JOHN ROSS ROBERTSON.

The enormity of Robertson's public stature was reflected even in the obituaries published by his newspaper rivals. His death, however, would not lessen his absolute control over the affairs of the OHA.

One report said, "During the early part of this week he seemed to be on the mend, but his condition became worse yesterday."[7] He died at home on May 31, surrounded by his family. Flags were lowered throughout the Queen City for his funeral, though he had directed that it should be "strictly private, absolutely plain, simple and inexpensive."[8] The mayor and several aldermen came anyway. Tributes poured in from across the province and beyond.

Incredibly, Robertson's iron grip over the Ontario Hockey Association did not loosen with his death. His carefully groomed cadre of activists would provide the OHA with successors for many years to come. Before taking any decision, these men would first carefully reflect upon what John Ross might be thinking in his grave, as if he were still sitting there among them.

Meanwhile, as the amateur leaders retreated into splendid isolation like the emperors of the Forbidden City, professionalism continued to progress. Pro hockey's business structures were consolidating, becoming ever more disciplined and marketing themselves ever more effectively. The professional level was becoming the sport's highest, and was gradually being acknowledged as such. The developmental stages of hockey began to quietly fall under the influence of the commercial side of the game.

By the time that fortress of professional hockey, Maple Leaf Gardens, opened its doors in 1931, the OHA was in desperate retreat. The Great Depression was putting the final nails in the coffin of the once-omnipotent amateur order. The decade's economic ravages, along with the popularity of the pros and the exodus of players, were threatening to bankrupt the old association. In a deathbed conversion, its leaders proclaimed Simon-pure amateurism to be a historic anachronism. In fact, in 1936 the OHA led the CAHA into a financial arrangement that effectively made amateur hockey the farm system of the NHL.

One of the advocates of the OHA's eventual abandonment of John Ross Robertson's creed turned out to be none other than Billy Hewitt himself. "The Long Survivor"[9] of its various internal battles, Hewitt served as secretary of the Ontario Association until 1961—an incredible fifty-eight years. He was also instrumental in the formation of the Canadian Amateur Hockey Association in 1914, and he served as that organization's secretary-treasurer and later as registrar and treasurer, also until 1961.

Hewitt's involvement in Canadian sports during the first half of the twentieth century was nothing short of astonishing. Beyond his incredible career in hockey management at all levels, he played key executive roles in football and horse racing, not to mention sports journalism. In 1925, he joined his son Foster in the world's first broadcast of a horse race. Foster Hewitt would soon establish himself as Toronto's voice of professional hockey. In 1931, Billy himself entered the commercial game when he left the *Star* sports editor's job to become manager of attractions at Maple Leaf Gardens.

Like so many sports journalists of the era, W. A. Hewitt's career was

W. A. Hewitt lived long enough to help finally overthrow the old amateur order and become a prophet of the professional television age.

racked by what we would now see as real or apparent conflicts of interest. At the same time, the diversity of experience that marked his life in the world of sports helped make him a visionary. "I can foresee an era," he wrote in his 1958 autobiography, "when promoters can obtain most of their revenue from selling the television rights to corporations who will channel the scenes only to paying viewers . . . I would predict that during the coming four decades, sports crowds will lessen, but sports viewers will become legion." [10]

In 1947, W. A. Hewitt was inducted into the Hockey Hall of Fame, later to be joined by his favourite broadcasters, son Foster and grandson Bill. [11]

Of course, by the time the age of television arrived, the era of the Athletic War had been long forgotten. In truth, beyond the annual and diminishing competition for the Allan Cup, nothing of it remained. The triumph of the amateur ideologues had been an illusion. The "War" had been a battle—and a Pyrrhic one at that. John Ross Robertson's disciples had followed a path that would prove to be one of history's great dead ends.

This was already clear when the CAHA hoisted the flag of unconditional surrender to professionalism in 1936. After that, the ironies became even richer as the CAHA withdrew from the AAUC. It then became the leading opponent of hard-line amateurism at the international level.

Canada was in constant conflict with the IIHF until the latter body began to relax its restrictions against professionals in the 1970s. Gradually, even the Olympic movement—by then an unholy alliance of European elitists and Soviet communists, who were really marketing nationalism more than amateurism—came to terms with the inevitabilities of paid sport. In 1998, the National Hockey League's top professionals finally played for their countries in the Nagano Winter Games.

Interestingly, the Athletic War and its aftermath had a parallel in Canadian political life. This was, as noted, the free-trade election of 1911, in which the acolytes of Robertson's Toryism had decisively defeated free trade with the United States. The next seven decades would similarly feature the steady erosion and final reversal of that watershed moment.[12]

In this context, the lasting significance of the Athletic War was something else—the victory of Ontario's leading city over Quebec's. It foretold the national shift of power in things generally. After Confederation, Montreal's English establishment went from being the leaders of Canada's largest centre to an isolated elite within a largely French-speaking hinterland. By contrast, Toronto became the biggest city of the Dominion's biggest province.[13]

———

Alas, on the ice, Montreal's dominance has not been broken. This, more than anything, is the real legacy of this tale. Generations of fans have witnessed more than a century of professional hockey, of which the most legendary and enduring rivalry is between Toronto and Montreal. How incomprehensible, then, it would be to the average fan of the Leafs or the Habs to discover that these seemingly eternal adversaries are descended from a common ancestor.

Certainly, nobody mentioned this when the Montreal Canadiens proudly celebrated the centennial of their 1909 birth a few years ago.

Long glossed over is the fact that the original *les Canadiens* franchise became dormant in 1910 and was then sold by the O'Briens in 1911. Nevertheless it is, in strict legal terms, a fact.

More awkward yet is that, while a new Canadiens team was established in 1910 (from the Haileybury franchise), the original entity went to, of all places, Toronto. In other words, the Canadiens were created by the Renfrew family, awarded first to Montreal and then sold to Toronto. It is easy to see why the Habs stick to a simple story—that they are the original Canadiens even if, strictly speaking, they really are not.

Conn Smythe built the Leafs into hockey's most profitable enterprise—and helped erase any history that preceded him.

The more interesting question is why the Leafs pretend not to have the origins they really do.

Some of this relates to the mythology created by Conn Smythe himself. When Smythe purchased the NHL's failing Toronto St. Patricks in 1927, he claimed to have given them a new birth, inspired by a patriotic vision. The Maple Leafs, he declared, were conceived from the insignia on the shoulder of his First World War uniform. The fact that the city already had a successful, long-running professional sports franchise by that name—the Toronto Maple Leaf baseball club—was apparently pure coincidence.

Smythe did, however, truly remake professional hockey in Toronto. Also, to be fair, the Maple Leafs have always recognized their legal link to the St. Patricks and the Arenas before them. What they have never acknowledged is their relationship to the club that bought the original Canadiens and won the city's first Stanley Cup: the Toronto Blue Shirts.

This denial of history is imbedded in the legal manoeuvring that led to the end of the Blue Shirts and the old National Hockey Association.

Since the Arenas and the National Hockey League effectively confiscated the Toronto club from E. J. Livingstone, it has long been official dogma to emphasize the legal break of 1917. Yet, in reality, the NHL's "new" Toronto team used the same players, wore the same jersey and was commonly called by the same names (the "Torontos" and, initially, the "Blue Shirts") as its NHA predecessor.

That the Blue Shirts have been thus orphaned by history is understandable. The Livingstone saga led to almost a decade of court battles that helped undermine the pre-Smythe franchise. That is to say, it is understandable, but it is sad nonetheless.

In truth, Toronto's first Stanley Cup club has been largely forgotten. It remains to this day the only one of the city's pro hockey champions not to have its banner hung in the Air Canada Centre.

———

Forgotten, and yet the players of the original Blue Shirts, collectively and individually, made a considerable mark in the sport.

No fewer than seven members of this championship team belong to the Hockey Hall of Fame. Indeed, most of the young Torontos had professional careers that extended through the 1920s and into the 1930s. Few of these, however, were spent in the Ontario capital.

The notable exception was Harry Cameron. He would be the only one to play on all three pre-Leaf Cup squads: the Blue Shirts of 1914, the Arenas of 1918 and the St. Patricks of 1922.

Although the Blue Shirts franchise faded after 1914, the group arguably did win one more Stanley Cup together. This occurred after Livingstone's club was plundered to stock the PCHA's new franchise, the Seattle Metropolitans, in 1915. Former Blue Shirts Frank Foyston, Hap Holmes, Jack Walker, Cully Wilson and Eddie Carpenter (the replacement for Jack Marshall) all shared in the Mets' championship two years later. This club was also notable as the first U.S.-based team to hold the Cup.[14] The phenomenon of the "Seattle Blue Shirts" (my term) would be replicated nearly eighty years later, when captain Mark Messier led a number of players from his former Edmonton championship team to a Stanley Cup with the Rangers—i.e., the so-called "New York Oilers."

Seattle Metropolitans, 1916–17. Bruce Ridpath's former Blue Shirts were the core of this team, the first U.S.-based Stanley Cup champions.

Speaking of Jack Marshall, old "Jawn" did not quite retire following the 1914 championship after all. He did some spot duty the next season, but knew enough to leave once the Livingstone era began. Returning to Montreal, Marshall played occasionally with the Wanderers until 1917, when he turned forty. He died there in 1965, shortly after his induction into the Hockey Hall of Fame. An obituary stated that Jack never knew about his honour, being by then eighty-eight and "lost in the mists of memory." [15]

Allan Davidson was one of only two Blue Shirt champions who did not have a long hockey career. Scotty was killed in action in Belgium in 1915, reputedly after refusing to retreat during a battle. Despite his relatively brief shinny story, his exploits on and off the ice were recognized with induction into the Hockey Hall of Fame in 1950.

The other man to have a brief presence in the sport was Roy McGiffin. Since his junior days, McGiffin had spent the off-seasons in Dinuba, California, where he was in the fruit business. Leaving hockey after the 1914–15 season, he ended up in the American military during the First World War. In fact, Flight Lieutenant McGiffin was an instructor in aerobatics in the U.S. Army Air Service. A daredevil to the end, he went

Hobey Baker. Ironically, the American amateur hockey legend met with a demise almost identical to that of Canadian professional hockey "goon" Roy McGiffin.

down near the end of the war while looping his aircraft outside Wichita Falls, Texas.

There is quite an irony in a player like McGiffin having a fate similar to the American hockey prodigy Hobey Baker. Baker was, it will be remembered, also killed in a 1918 plane accident while serving in the U.S. air force. One can imagine heaven's hockey rink hosting two of the most radically different characters ever to lace up a pair of skates. We can picture the great Princeton star trying to lead the rush as Minnie hacks, harasses and hotly tests his legendary eternal patience.

And so the Stanley Cup champion Toronto Hockey Club has been largely left to the graces of heaven and history. Yet if it has been for the most part forgotten, its predecessor of the same name—erroneously christened the "Maple Leafs" many decades later [16]—has been utterly so. Even in the accounts of the 1914 playoffs, Toronto papers would sometimes note the previous Cup challenges of the Wellingtons and Marlboros, strangely omitting the (much more competitive) one of Alexander Miln's Professionals.

Some of this may be attributable to Miln himself. The man who directed the original Torontos had renounced his professional past and returned to rabid amateurism not long before pro hockey took hold in the city for good. Pulled down as manager with the demolition of the old Mutual Street Rink, he became a minor figure in the local shinny scene.

Miln remained active in other sports, and by 1915 was a thirty-seven-year-old bachelor employed as Ontario representative of the British-American Bank Note Company. That is when, like so many members of Toronto's elite, he eagerly signed on to fight for the British

Empire in the Great War. Alex rose rapidly through the depleting ranks to become an army major. Younger brother Jack Miln also enlisted and attained the rank of lieutenant.

The tragic death of Major Miln on November 18, 1916, was prominently featured in all the city's dailies. Yet only the *Toronto Star* remembered that the all-round amateur sportsman had once been "manager of the Torontos, champions of the Ontario Professional League."[17]

Miln was not the only one associated with the original Torontos to serve and die in the First World War. The brief Professional and former Marlboro star Herb Birmingham left a clerical job at Toronto City Hall to join the Canadian Expeditionary Force in 1915. Lieutenant Birmingham died from battle wounds on August 10, 1918. He was survived by a wife and numerous family members, including brother Hilliard. The Birmingham family was prominent in politics, his brother and late father being leading Conservative political organizers in the city and the province.

Eight other onetime Toronto Professionals traded hockey jerseys for the uniform of the Canadian Army: Harry Burgoyne, Charlie Ellis, Walter Mercer, Skene Ronan, Zina Runions, Donald Smith, Rolly

MAJOR ALEX. MILN,
of the 75th Battalion, one of the most prominent business and sporting men of Toronto, who was to-day reported killed in action.

MAJOR MILN KILLED

No Details Given of How Well-known Figure Passed.

Major Alex. Miln, who left Toronto in March as a captain in the 75th Battalion, was killed in action Saturday, November 18, according to an official telegram received by his father at 40 Division st. to-day. No details other than the announcement of his death have been received.

The death of Major Miln removes one of the best known men in the sporting, business, and social world of Toronto.

Alexander Miln had long since left the world of pro hockey at the time of his death in the service of his country. His original "Leafs" were already fading from memory.

Young and the man I have called the "elusive" Bert Morrison. While all survived the conflict, Bert must nevertheless be classed as a casualty.

In the case of Morrison, the mystery to be solved was his disappearance early in the 1908–09 season. Vague reports as the campaign progressed had suggested that he was "ill." In the code language of the time, this may have referred to a drinking problem. Unfortunately, a tracing of Bert's military career gives credence to this theory—and more.

Attestation paper of Bertram Clifford Morrison. Bert Morrison might have been a troubled man before enlisting. He certainly was afterward.

Morrison's war story is a sad one, indeed. The saga begins with his enrolment late in 1916. At that point, Bert was a sales representative for his father's brass manufacturing company. Although deemed fit, he was almost thirty-seven years old.

Bert was shipped overseas, but by 1917 had begun forfeiting pay due to various ailments. The following year, he vanished for three weeks, and, when finally discovered, was clearly suffering from a serious breakdown. He was hospitalized for some nine months. His medical records indicate severe mental illness—what we would today label as schizophrenia. Previous alcohol and drug abuse are also suspected in the doctors' reports.

Morrison was released from the military in April 1919. He then spent the better part of the next decade in a London, Ontario, mental institution. Discharged in 1929 to the care of family members, he was subsequently certified as mentally incompetent.

Bert was never able to work again and lived in virtual anonymity in Toronto. Yet the reclusive bachelor remained in generally good physical health. He outlived all his kin, passing away four decades later at the age of eighty-nine.

Walter Mercer's war story is not sad, but it is perplexing. After apparently finishing his hockey career in Brantford in 1910, the right winger of the Professionals' Cup challenge team headed to British Columbia. Yet Mercer still claimed to be a "professional lacrosse and hockey"[18] player when he enlisted there in 1915. Even more oddly, he appears to have falsified his birthdate on his attestation papers, declaring himself to be a full five years younger—twenty-five rather than thirty years of age.

Mercer had a good service record before heading back to B.C. at the end of the conflict. Yet files indicate he maintained the revised longevity for the rest of his life. Thus, when he passed away at Sunnybrook Hospital in 1961, he was said to be in "his 71st year."[19]

Chuck Tyner played with Mercer in Brantford during the 1909–10 campaign, where he was the manager. Like Wally, Chuck exited the game at the end of the season. He also fought in the First World War, though, in getting there, he took a very different path than his teammates did.

For reasons unknown, Tyner left Canada shortly after his days as a

Reverend Charles R. Tyner (1924). This photograph shows Tyner shortly after he took up his mission in Kansas City, Missouri, where he would spend the rest of his life.

professional goalkeeper ended, apparently simultaneously forgoing his ambition to become a medical doctor. He went first to Vermont. By May 1914, Tyner, who was Anglican, had become a graduate of Seabury Theological Seminary in Minnesota. He then headed to Nebraska, where two brothers were also Episcopal ministers, and where his future wife, Mary Sprague, had been born.

Tyner had settled into his theological career for only a few years when, approaching forty and apparently still restless, he took a sabbatical. It was a stint in the U.S. Army after the Americans finally entered the war. Tyner was not a chaplain; he was a full-fledged combatant. Reverend Charles fought hard and became something of a correspondent for his hometown paper in Lincoln, Nebraska.[20]

Tyner returned to the active priesthood in Nebraska after the armistice in 1918. In 1923, he moved to Kansas City, Missouri, to take over St. George's Episcopal Church and stayed there for the remainder of his career, becoming emeritus in 1952.

Canon Tyner passed away in 1967, just before his eighty-eighth birthday. Mary lived until 1980. St. George's went on to become part of St. Mary's Episcopal Church in 1986.

Not surprisingly, Charles Tyner was active in his community. His pastimes included an interest in hockey and skating. He served as timekeeper at local games and was honorary president of the Kansas City Figure Skating Club. His obituary declared that, as a hockey player long ago, he had been "with the Toronto team that won a Stanley Cup."[21] The story, it seems, had improved over the years.

Unlike Tyner, by the time Rolly Young headed to Europe, he had achieved his dream of becoming a physician. After being cut from the Berlin Dutchmen in 1908–09, Young made one brief and final return to the OPHL, with his hometown Waterloo Colts the following season. After that, Young dedicated himself solely to his studies.

Rolly had graduated from McMaster University (then located in Toronto) in 1907. As has been noted, he then studied medicine at the University of Toronto. He finally finished up in 1911.

Dr. Roland W. Young signed up with the British Royal Army Medical Corps in 1914. He served in Malta, Egypt and Macedonia before returning to Canada and joining the Canadian Army Medical Corps. After being demobilized in 1919, he practised medicine in Waterloo, London, Toronto and Bronte, Ontario.

At the age of forty, Young married one Elizabeth Ross Greene, a nurse. Like most of the key Toronto Professionals, he left no descendants.[22] Rolly passed away in 1961 and is buried in the family plot at Waterloo.

———

As has been noted, Young's defence partner, Con Corbeau, was the first of the original Torontos to play again professionally for the Queen City. He was also the first former Professional to drink from the Stanley Cup while wearing a Toronto uniform. The veteran's on-ice career ended the following season with Glace Bay of the dying Maritime pro league.

Corbeau was later a fairly successful coach in the senior amateur game. However, Con died in 1920 at just thirty-eight from heart and kidney disease. Interestingly, his younger brother Bert Corbeau was a prominent NHL defenceman who played his pro hockey in Toronto from 1923 to 1928.

Con Corbeau was one of four Toronto Professionals to play hockey for the Queen City later in their careers. Harold McNamara and Skene Ronan returned in 1915 to join Livingstone's Toronto Shamrocks. Jack Marks would also come back and, like Corbeau, would help bring the Stanley Cup to Toronto.

Marks was the ringer who had substituted in the second half of the 1908 showdown with the Wanderers. He had later accompanied the club on its disastrous postseason road trip. Jack's career was prominently eulogized after the train wreck of 1909, which had presumably ended his playing days. However, not only was he back with Brantford before the end of the season, but he went on to a long and successful pro career. Although it was spent mostly in Quebec City, Marks would serve as a spare forward on the 1917–18 champion Toronto Arenas.

A couple of other erstwhile Toronto Professionals—the Mallen brothers—have Stanley Cup history that is worth mentioning. Of these, Ken was the biggest star and played until 1917. Acknowledged as the fastest skater of his era, he helped the Ottawa Senators hold the Stanley Cup in 1910. He won Lord Stanley's mug a second time with Cyclone Taylor and the Vancouver Millionaires in 1915. However, it remains a mystery why Kenny's name was never engraved on the jug.

Ken had three hockey-playing siblings, including fellow Toronto Pro Jimmy Mallen. Jim had less success in the game, but he does have one notable achievement to his name. In January 1910, Jimmy and Kenny lined up for Galt and Ottawa respectively—the first brothers to ever play against one another in a Stanley Cup final.

Although most of Alex Miln's squad had some presence in the sport after the team folded, one notable who did not was Hugh Lambe. Lambe never played in another professional match, but he did periodically surface in the local news. The club's perennial spare defenceman—and the only man with the team for the entirety of their existence—he was actually one of their most popular players. This fan following really came from lacrosse. Hughie was regarded as one of the best defenders of all time for the Toronto Lacrosse Club.

A 1912 report noted Lambe's marriage to Eleanor Rubidge Barron. Miss Barron was the daughter of Stratford judge John Augustus Barron. Barron, it may be recalled, was captain of the old Rideau Rebels and chaired the founding meeting of the OHA. We know that the marriage, which eventually ended in separation, was troubled due to Hugh's drinking.[23]

Lambe died tragically in 1941 from a fall down the stairs while running to catch a taxi to the railway station. Interestingly, he was then apparently travelling the world as a tea examiner with the Department of National Revenue. Why such an occupation was necessary is not self-evident, but the *Toronto Star* reported that "the position is one which requires years of special training—training possessed by not more than a handful of experts in the whole country."[24]

———

The most significant member of the Toronto Professionals, Bruce Ridpath, also never played another game of hockey. In retrospect, the trajectory of Ridpath's shinny career was already apparent when the modern hockey rivalry between Toronto and Montreal began on Christmas night 1912. The man chosen to be the franchise player of the new Queen City team was behind the bench in street clothes. Bruce was still very much in the early stages of a long convalescence from his near-fatal automobile accident.

Ridpath did, however, eventually return successfully to canoeing, his original claim to fame in sporting circles. It also appears he was able to regain much of his former expertise. In the summer of 1919 an advertisement appeared in the *Toronto World*, stating, "On the lagoon in Jubilee Park the expert canoeist, Mr. Bruce Ridpath, will demonstrate the correct method of steering a canoe, the proper positions for paddling, either with single or double paddle, and safety-first rules."[25]

Riddy kept his youthful looks, but largely lost the fame hockey had brought him. He became a sales representative for a sporting goods company. Bruce also remained a bachelor—it is remarkable how rarely these early hockey stars appear to have married—and ran a summer camp for boys where, naturally, canoeing was a key activity.

Ridpath also never fully shook off the health effects of his head trauma. In the spring of 1925 he suffered a minor stroke while playing cards with friends. A week later, he had a more serious seizure and was taken to St. Michael's Hospital. Bruce never regained consciousness and passed away three weeks later, on June 4. He was only forty-one.

Bound for the Hockey Hall of Fame before fate intervened, Ridpath is the ultimate "forgotten Leaf." His role as the founder and first captain of the original Toronto Hockey Club was washed away as quickly as the memory of that team. So too was his role as the designated captain of the reborn Toronto Hockey Club. This is even more striking in that, as

BRUCE RIDPATH
well known former athlete, who is dead, following his collapse on May 18, while playing cards with friends. He never regained consciousness.

BRUCE RIDPATH DEAD WELL-KNOWN ATHLETE

Collapsed From Stroke on May 18 and Remained Unconscious Until Death

After lying in St. Michael's Hospital in an unconscious condition for over two weeks, Bruce D. Ridpath, one of Toronto's foremost athletes and instructors, died this morning. The exact cause of his death is not known. His body has been removed

Ridpath would almost certainly have been one of two Toronto Professionals in the Hockey Hall of Fame had fate not intervened. As it was, his passing was still of some local note a dozen years after he left the sport.

manager, it was he who, against all conventional wisdom, assembled the Stanley Cup lineup, Jack Marshall included.

And yet, when the Blue Shirts took that historic first Stanley Cup, no mention, let alone credit, was given to Ridpath.

The same anonymity was not in store for the other of the Toronto Professionals' two big stars. As Ridpath stood in street clothes, watching helplessly from the sidelines, Newsy Lalonde stood at centre ice as the captain of the Montreal Canadiens on December 25, 1912. Booed out of Toronto in 1909—and booed in Toronto many times after that—he was by then well on his way to becoming one of the greatest players in the history of the game. On January 5, 1910, he had scored the Habs' first-ever goal. By the spring of 1916, Lalonde would be their playing manager, leading the club to the first of its two dozen Stanley Cup championships.

Newsy Lalonde has been gone for so long that his legendary careers in both hockey and lacrosse have gradually faded from popular culture. Yet it took a long time because, for the first two decades of the twentieth century, he was arguably the single most dominant player in both of Canada's national sports. A true gentleman off the ice, Lalonde established himself as one of the fiercest and roughest competitors the rink has hosted.

Lalonde's various fights and ongoing feuds were epic even for the time. Demanding only the best effort from himself and others in every match he played, he probably dropped the gloves in more circumstances than any other player in history. At various times, Newsy punched out not only opponents, but also fans, officials and even teammates. At least once, as a referee himself in a lacrosse game, he pummelled a player who gave him too hard a time. Still, Lalonde was one of those who lived by a hockey "code," refusing ever to speak or act against an opponent outside the arena.

Newsy also honed his instinct for scoring in a way that would completely overcome his average skating ability. In fact, before the arrival of Maurice Richard, Lalonde was the highest scorer in pro hockey history. He is a member of the Hockey Hall of Fame, Lacrosse Hall of Fame and Canada's Sports Hall of Fame. He was chosen to light the torch for the Sports Hall when it opened in Toronto in 1955. He was a grand old eighty-three when he passed away in 1970.

Not surprisingly, Lalonde was named "Athlete of the Half Century" for lacrosse in 1950. In 1998, *The Hockey News* ranked him thirty-second in a list of "The 100 Greatest Hockey Players." This placed him highest among those who had played prior to the founding of the National Hockey League.

⸻

One other major character to fade only slowly from public memory was the bane of the existence of every Toronto Professional: John Ross Robertson. In 1921, a school was built in his name in the north part of the city. Thereafter, each year in late spring, a delegation of *Telegram* editors and school children would visit the family plot and remember the great man. In 1947, the mythical "father of the OHA" became an early member of the Hockey Hall of Fame.

Yet the pilgrimages to the grave site stopped after 1942.[26] Three decades later, in 1971, the *Tely* itself vanished, having been on the wrong side of too many business decisions, labour disputes and editorial choices.

Lalonde became a hockey legend in Montreal, attending games at the Forum until his death in 1970.

Today, only a few Toronto library archivists and Hospital for Sick Children administrators can recount something of Robertson's life and achievements.

As for his role in hockey, did Robertson actually change the course of the game? Might things today have been different without him? What if the pragmatists had won the Athletic War? Could, as they preferred, an element of the noncommercial ethic have been preserved at the highest level of the national winter sport? Would top-level hockey have evolved on a more community-oriented, less purely commercial basis, perhaps even preserving the National Hockey League and the Stanley Cup as Canada's own?

Those who hold this view sometimes have the Canadian Football League and its Grey Cup in mind.[27] The parallels seem to make sense. The inspiration for the Interprovincial Amateur Hockey Union was the Interprovincial Rugby Football Union—which eventually became the CFL's Eastern Division. Indeed, Earl Grey's mug had originally been conceived, not as a football award, but as the amateur hockey alternative to Lord Stanley's.

These simple similarities ignore some important differences. Unlike hockey, Canadian football is a unique national game, not an international sport. The last time American football seriously tried to enter the country—the Toronto Northmen of the World Football League—it was saved by good old-fashioned government protection, not by the structure of the Canadian sport. And it was ultimately the Americans themselves who, in 1995, thwarted the CFL's own continentalist ambitions.

In other words, while the Athletic War doubtlessly delayed the future, a skeptic must doubt whether it really altered its eventual outcome. After all, at the time, the forces behind amateurism were international in nature. The revived Olympic Games of Pierre de Coubertin gave the amateur purists a worldwide reach. Likewise, commercial forces, rooted in our natural American export market—and deeply imbedded in Western society generally—were already aggressively shaping the business side of hockey. Perhaps, truth be told, the pragmatic "mixers" never had a chance.

On the other side of the argument, it is easy in hindsight to see the Athletic War's victors as nothing more than excessively powerful, old white men fighting for the values of a dying culture that gave old white men excessive power. Yet we still do hear the echoes of these amateur advocates' cry against professional hockey. They told us that one played for either the love of the game or the money. The pros protested that one could do both. Living in the shadow of four NHL labour shutdowns in twenty years—including one lost season and a recent one nearly so—it is no wonder the old doubts remain.

Wage cycles have been a big part of the business story of hockey ever since the professional game was first established over a hundred years ago. On the one hand, there have been periods of intense competition between leagues and players. These have been marked by rapid salary escalation, pools of red ink for management and increasing franchise instability. On the other hand, there have been times of remarkable constancy—most notably the quarter century of the NHL's Original Six. In such eras, the dominance of the market by a tight cartel meant healthy profits for owners and ironclad contracts that reduced players to little more than serfs. The inability of successive collective bargaining agreements to establish equilibrium is only the latest episode in this long story of volatility. Interestingly, the amateur advocates of Robertson's time predicted all of this.

The most recent labour turmoil, some would say, has exposed millionaire players as motivated more by personal greed than by any devotion to the national game. The same critics point at the even wealthier owners, making profits off a ridiculously long season and a largely needless playoff system. Watching it all, they see the fans, living vicariously through the stars rather than playing the sport themselves. Those in the small communities breeding many of the players have long been squeezed out of the game's top echelon. For the rest, team loyalties have been sold as commodities, constant player movements rendering them little more than "cheering for laundry," as Jerry Seinfeld once observed.

That is not the way everyone sees it, but I have no doubt that it is the perspective John Ross Robertson would take. We can even visualize him barging into a sports television studio today to comment on the state of the game and to address the critics of his actions. Yes, he would concede, he now sees he lost the war. All those furious battles were indeed futile assaults against the inevitable.

So, would John Ross Robertson do it all differently if he could? I think he would pause and answer, "A poor man is he who journeys through the mazes of a busy world with no purpose in view, no ambition to serve."[28]

In other words, and without hesitation, he would do exactly the same.

ACKNOWLEDGMENTS

My work on this book began back in 2004 as a distraction from the hectic and obsessive nature of political life. I had become unusually interested in hockey history as a youngster growing up in Toronto. As a studious and rather unathletic boy, this pastime helped to compensate for my conspicuous inability on the ice. Two people deserve some credit for cultivating this interest of mine. First and foremost, my father, Joseph Harris Harper, was himself an avid researcher in many fields and a role model in all things. Some mention is also due to an individual whom my dad much admired, the late W. Harold Rea—the man who also gave me my first ticket to an NHL game.

The Society for International Hockey Research is the foremost organization of its kind and is largely responsible for reviving my attention to this boyhood hobby. Past president Lenard Kotylo, who possesses a wealth of information on all aspects of hockey history, provided a number of documents at the outset of my research. His initial help truly got this project off the ground. Lenard closed the loop by providing an expert review of the final manuscript.

Lenard also connected me with a couple of other walking hockey encyclopaediae, Eric Zweig and Glen Goodhand. Eric also did a thorough review of the final product, finding an embarrassing number of inaccuracies and digging up some good stuff on Bruce Ridpath. As for Glen, his unpublished work on the Ontario Professional Hockey League has long been the only one of substance relating to the Toronto Professionals hockey club. (Kevin Slater's recent opus on the OPHL is now another.) Reverend Glen, through Professor Jo Behrens of the University of Omaha, was also helpful in tracking down information on the theological career of Chuck Tyner. As well, James Milks and Ernie Fitzsimmons of SIHR were helpful on matters relating to the statistical record.

The laborious task of combing through the original news reports of the era was handled by this project's researcher, Greg Stoicoiu. Greg's contribution is significant. An expert in hockey memorabilia, he has solid knowledge of the subjects he was digging into and a good eye for relevant material. That good eye also provided the jersey drawings that colour the inserts. Let me state for the record that Greg was paid by me personally, not by the taxpayers of Canada.

A number of organizations and their people were supportive in tracking biographical information. This includes Ian Wilson, Marthe Seguin-Muntz and Neysa McLeod of Library and Archives Canada. They were particularly helpful for those players who served in the First World War. Patrick Deane, Rick Stapleton and Alexandra Lawson of McMaster University assisted with details of Rolly Young's academic and sports career at that institution. Guy Lauzon, MP, pointed me to Tracy Cameron of the Diocese of Alexandria-Cornwall, David Hill and George and Bev Runions, all of whom provided information on Zina Runions. Reverend Lauren Lyon of St. Mary's Episcopal Church in Kansas City shared a number of pictures and stories of Chuck Tyner's career there. Jim Miln of Winnipeg and Bruce Miln of Victoria supplied some family trees on namesake Alexander. Kevin Shea also provided some useful bits of information on the hockey history of St. Michael's College.

More general sources of information included the Toronto Public Library. Special thanks go to Jane Pyper and a number of people whose assistance she procured, including Nancy Marshall, Linda Mackenzie, Mary Rae Shantz, Bill Hamade and Christopher Coutlee. They were especially accommodating in reproducing articles and photographs from the local newspapers of the era. Craig Campbell of the Hockey Hall of Fame deserves special mention for opening its files and photographs collections. A similar thanks is owed to Chuck Puchmayr and the Canadian Lacrosse Hall of Fame in New Westminster.

I know that Greg would also like to convey some additional appreciation to those who helped him. The folks at the Calgary Public Library, the University of Calgary McKinney Library and the Glenbow Museum and Library were of great assistance in getting newspapers on microfilm and navigating genealogical information. Suzanne Plouffe and Janet Seally of the Waterloo Public Library and Crystal Williamson of the Ontario College of Physicians and Surgeons were eager to aid in tracking down Rolly Young's later life story. Finally, Jim Woodland assisted Greg in getting some local information while spending time in Toronto.

After seven years of slow but steady progress, I finished the first version of this work some two years ago. It was then that I began the process of seeking a publisher. That led me to my dedicated agent, Michael Levine—a veteran expert who literally knows everyone—and ultimately to the good people at Simon & Schuster.

Simon & Schuster retained Roy MacGregor to be my principal editor. What an experience and a pleasure it has been to work with him. Roy would admit that he wrote very little of the revised product, but he did provide copious commentary and advice. At his suggestion, elements of the narrative were reordered, its timeline extended (from December 1912 to March 1914), and key characters and their great moments filled out (but not fictionalized). The result is a book that, while in some ways not very different, is at the same time a great deal better. So here's a big thanks to journalist and writer Roy MacGregor, who once again demonstrated the superiority of the consummate professional to that of the aspiring amateur.

It was also largely Roy who dealt with the publisher. I know he and I want to thank Kevin Hanson, Phyllis Bruce, Brendan May and Lloyd Davis. This is a great team from top to bottom—one that has been supportive (and patient) every step of the way.

I tried to ensure this project had minimal impact upon my staff; nevertheless at various times Myles Atwood, Alison Barrett, Ranelle Massey and Dennis Matthews put through phone calls and obtained documents from the Library of Parliament and the internet. Myles, Sean Speer, Andrew MacDougall, Carl Vallée and also the Rt. Hon. David Johnston offered to read the manuscript and provided many good suggestions. Nigel Wright similarly assisted with advice and liaison with Ethics Commissioner Mary Dawson, whose office was forthright and constructive.

At last, I would be more than remiss if I did not thank Laureen, Ben and Rachel for their patience during this project and their love and support in all things. It is an understatement to say I would not have completed this book—or much else in life—without them.

One final note: to all these people and organizations I owe considerable credit, while reserving to myself any responsibility for this work's errors and deficiencies.

NOTES

INTRODUCTION: FACING OFF

1 "Remarked on the Side," *Toronto Telegram*, March 5, 1908.

2 "Snap Shots on Sport," *Toronto Telegram*, December 1, 1906.

3 The *Toronto Star* cited the *London Advertiser* to make its point. See "Latest Hockey Notes From Star Exchanges," *Toronto Star*, January 3, 1907.

4 "Snap Shots on Sport," *Toronto Telegram*, December 4, 1907.

5 "Edward Hanlan," *Toronto Globe*, January 4, 1908.

6 "Hockey on Bare Floor," *Toronto News*, January 6, 1908.

7 "Berlin Wins Great Game from Torontos—Score 3 to 0," *Toronto World*, January 6, 1908.

8 As far as I am aware this error originates with Charles Coleman's seminal work on the history of the Stanley Cup. See Charles L. Coleman, *The Trail of the Stanley Cup: Volume 1, 1893–1926*, 1964, pp. 162 & 610.

9 Mike Ozanian. "The Business of Hockey: Team Values Hit All-Time High," Sports Money, *Forbes*, November 30, 2011. As of November 2011, *Forbes* estimated the value of the Toronto Maple Leafs at $521 million, followed by the New York Rangers at $507 million and the Montreal Canadiens at $445 million.

CHAPTER ONE: THE OLD ORDER IN HOCKEY'S SECOND CITY

1 Richard M. Sherman and Robert B. Sherman, "The Life I Lead," from *Mary Poppins* (Burbank, CA: Walt Disney Productions, 1964).

2 Sir Wilfrid Laurier, Canadian Club of Ottawa, January 18, 1904.

3 These newspapers represent the vast majority of information available on pre–First World War hockey in Toronto.

4 The exception in this period was the year 1907, which witnessed a brief recession throughout the Canadian economy.

5 "Star for Burlesque," *Toronto News*, January 2, 1909.

6 Interestingly, smoking tobacco was already commonly viewed as bad for one's health, especially for an athlete. For example, see "No Cigarettes for Lindsay Hockey Players," *Toronto News*, October 24, 1906, and the advertisement "Tobacco Kills," *Toronto Star*, March 13, 1909. Even the first book ever written on hockey warns players of the dangers of cigarette smoking. See Arthur Farrell, *Hockey: Canada's Royal Winter Game* (Montreal: C.R. Corneil, 1899), p. 59.

7   "More than Double in West Toronto," *Toronto News*, June 24, 1911.

8   John Irwin Cooper, *Montreal: A Brief History* (Montreal: McGill-Queen's University Press, 1969), p. 130.

9   Cooper, p. 131.

10   Mariana Valverde, *The Age of Light, Soap & Water: Moral Reform in English Canada, 1825–1925* (Toronto: McClelland & Stewart, 1991).

11   The view that Montreal is the birthplace of hockey as an organized sport, though contested, is widely shared. It is, for example, the position of both the Society for International Hockey Research and the International Ice Hockey Federation that a match played on March 3, 1875, is the first fully recorded, formally organized game. Although arranged by a native of Halifax, James G. A. Creighton, the contest was played on Montreal's Victoria Skating Rink. From this game one can trace subsequent developments. However, some observers believe this history should be turned on its head. That is to say, it is not a question of modern hockey having been established in Montreal, which just happened to be Canada's power centre. Rather, the organized sport traces its origins to Montreal *because* it was the country's most influential city at the time. According to this argument, the emergence of a formal sport like ice hockey out of a collection of folk games could—due to the rationing of space and time—occur only in the context of an urbanizing, industrial society. The society's leading locale and its elites would then invariably set the rules—just as hockey's "McGill Rules" squeezed out the alternative, perhaps even older, "Halifax Rules." See Richard Gruneau and David Whitson, *Hockey Night in Canada* (Toronto: Garamond Press, 1993), pp. 45–46; Bruce Kidd, *The Struggle for Canadian Sport* (Toronto: University of Toronto Press, 1996), pp. 16–17; and Michael McKinley, *Putting a Roof on Winter* (Vancouver: Greystone Books, 2000), pp. 15–19.

12   The five teams in the league, the Amateur Hockey Association of Canada, were Ottawa, Quebec, Montreal, Victoria and Crystal (later Shamrock), the last three of which were based in Montreal. I mention this because it is important to understand that, in the pre–First World War era, hockey clubs really had only one name. The practice of designating a hockey club by two terms—a place name followed by a team name—came about gradually and for two reasons. The first reason was the intercity game. For example, the Victoria Hockey Club of Montreal really only became known as the "Montreal Victorias" when they later played against the Victoria Hockey Club of Winnipeg (the "Winnipeg Victorias") for the Stanley Cup. (It seems every city had a "Victoria Hockey Club" back then.) The second reason was the conversion of nicknames to official or near-official status. The Ottawa Hockey Club had then, as its usual nickname, the "Generals." After 1900, the "Silver Seven" arose and, eventually and most commonly, the "Senators." The Quebec

Hockey Club was long nicknamed the "Bulldogs," with a mascot to match. In this book, I have tended to use two-name versions of club names for the ease of the modern-day reader. This is challenging where such names were uncommon. For example, the Montreal Hockey Club, when not called just "Montreal," would have been designated "Montreal HC" or "Montreal AAA" (after its sponsor, the Montreal Amateur Athletic Association). In such instances, I have tended to use more genuine nicknames. I have also tended more to the shortened forms of those nicknames. In this case, for instance, I have chosen to use "Montreal Wheelers" more than "Montreal Winged Wheelers," both of which came from the team's symbol (which originated in its bicycle club).

13   See the advertisement "New Caledonian Rink Mutual Street," *Toronto News*, December 10, 1885.

14   I reluctantly name the children because different sources cite different names. In Lord Stanley's recent biography by Kevin Shea and John Jason Wilson, Edward, Victor and Arthur are mentioned as playing on or practising with the Rebels, although only Arthur did so regularly. These were the three eldest of Stanley's eight (living) children. However, the book also implies that all the Stanley children played hockey. Algernon is mentioned in one passage as having some connection to the Rebels. This is possible, although he was only nineteen when the family left Canada in 1893. If he played with them, then it is likely older brothers Ferdinand ("Ferdy") and George did also. The youngest brother, William ("Billy"), is mentioned as a very good player, but he would have been only fifteen when the family left Canada. Interestingly, daughter Isobel also played hockey. She played on the Government House ladies' team and performed in the first women's hockey game ever recorded, in 1889. See Kevin Shea and John Jason Wilson, *Lord Stanley: The Man Behind The Cup* (H. B. Fenn and Company Ltd., 2006), pp. 348–386.

15   "The Granites Defeated," *Toronto Mail*, February 10, 1890.

16   "The Vice Regal Team Will Play Two Games Here," *Toronto Mail*, February 7, 1890.

17   "The Granites Defeated." Ibid.

18   "The Visitors Beaten by the St. Georges," *Toronto Mail*, February 10, 1890.

19   Barron was a controversial politician. The Liberal MP was one of only thirteen cross-benchers who had defied their leadership and voted in favour of urging Lord Stanley to disallow Quebec's Jesuit Estates Act. The measure was one of a series of disputes that pitched French and Catholic against English and Protestant during the later years of John A. Macdonald's government. The "Devil's Dozen" or the "Noble Thirteen" (depending on one's political perspective) were ultimately unsuccessful in persuading the governor general to intervene.

20   "The Granites Defeated." Ibid.

21 "Hockey Clubs in Toronto," *Toronto Mail and Empire*, December 21, 1897.

22 This is taken from the *Toronto Mail*, "The Toronto Hoggy Association," December 7, 1893.

23 Numerous sources agree that amateurism was rooted in the history of the class structure. For perhaps the most comprehensive review of this from an Anglo-Canadian perspective, see Frank Cosentino, "A History of the Concept of Professionalism in Canadian Sport," Ph.D. Thesis, University of Alberta, 1973.

24 A proscription on remuneration would also have been completely consistent with the original class criteria, given that aristocratic-military society was explicitly noncommercial. For a broad discussion of this question, see Jane Jacobs, *Systems of Survival*, 1992.

25 For a hypothesis on the role of religion in amateurism, see Alan Metcalfe, *Canada Learns to Play*, 1987, pp. 24–26. Metcalfe views the Christian version of "Hellenic dualism" (the noble mind, the sinful flesh) as an integral part of the social values behind amateurism. However, while an explanation rooted in social structures and one based on theological assumptions may be compatible, they are certainly distinctive.

26 This is taken from Richard Gruneau and David Whitson, *Hockey Night in Canada*, 1993, pp. 46–47.

27 Scott Beckman, *Ringside: A History of Professional Wrestling in America* (Westport, CN: Praeger Publishing, 2006), p. 26.

CHAPTER TWO: THE RISE OF "THE PAPER TYRANT"

1 "Hockey: The O.H.A. Annual Meeting," *Toronto Globe*, December 7, 1903.

2 Ron Poulton, *The Paper Tyrant* (Toronto: Clarke Irwin, 1977).

3 *Murdoch Mysteries*, "Murdoch Night in Canada," Episode no. 64, first broadcast August 21, 2012, by CityTV. Directed by Gail Harvey and written by Lori Spring.

4 Scott Young, *100 Years of Dropping the Puck* (Toronto: McClelland & Stewart, 1989), p. 46.

5 "Thirteenth Annual Convention of Ontario Hockey Association," *Toronto News*, December 6, 1902.

6 Young, p. 46.

7 "Annual Meeting of Hockeyists," *Toronto Mail and Empire*, December 5, 1898.

8 Poulton, p. 13.

9 Poulton, p. 95.

10 Poulton, p. 14.

11 "Annual Meeting of Ontario Hockeyists," *Toronto News*, December 5, 1898.

12 Ontario Hockey Association, *Constitution, Rules of Competition and Laws of the Game: As Amended December 1, 1900*, p. 27.

13 See "The Address of the O. H. A. President," *Toronto News*, December 5, 1903.

14 Shea and Wilson, pp. 89–108.

15 Andrew C. Holman, "Playing in the Neutral Zone: Meanings and Uses of Ice Hockey in the Canadian-U.S. Borderlands 1895–1915," in *American Review of Canadian Studies* (Spring 2004), pp. 38–39.

16 "Hockey: The O.H.A. Annual Meeting," Ibid.

17 "Note and Comment," *Toronto World*, December 25, 1907.

18 "Review of the O.H.A. Convention," *Toronto Star*, November 22, 1909.

19 "Thirteenth Annual Convention of Ontario Hockey Association," *Toronto News*, December 6, 1902.

20 Ibid.

21 W. A. Hewitt, *Down the Stretch* (Toronto: Ryerson Press, 1958), p. 185.

22 This was, of course, also the nickname of the first Duke of Wellington, Arthur Wellesley, the late British prime minister and vanquisher of Napoleon, after whom the hockey club itself was named.

23 Note that this means the Wellington champions of 1900–01 did not meet the Cup champion Victoria Club of Winnipeg until 1901–02. This was not unusual. The hockey season was quite short in the era of natural ice. Even in the coldest cities, it did not start before mid-December and did not go much beyond mid-March. Ideally, Stanley Cup challenges would be played between league champions at the end of the season—that is, in February or March. However, given the shortness of the season and the difficulty of interprovincial travel, Cup contenders would often play off early in the next season—that is, in December or January.

24 "First Stanley Cup Game To-Night," *Toronto News*, January 21, 1902.

25 "Wellingtons' Departure," *Winnipeg Tribune*, January 25, 1902.

26 Ibid.

27 "Wellingtons Will Arrive To-morrow," *Toronto News*, January 27, 1902.

28 "Wellingtons' Home-Coming," *Toronto Globe*, January 29, 1902.

29 Ibid.

30 Because winter begins earlier in Winnipeg than in Toronto, the Wellingtons were bound to be in poorer game shape than the Victorias. However, unseasonably mild weather in the early part of that Toronto winter had further complicated the situation for the Iron Dukes.

CHAPTER THREE: THE ENEMY IN THE OPEN

1 Copyright 1970 Okefenokee Glee & Perloo, Inc. Used by permission.

2 J. W. (Bill) Fitsell, "Doc Gibson: The Eye in the IHL," *Hockey Research Journal*, Volume 8 (Fall 2004), p. 5.

3 It should be noted that the official spelling of the western Pennsylvania city was actually "Pittsburg" during this period. Apparently, in 1896, it had been

decided that the *h* was an aberration. However, the change never caught on and was reversed in 1911. In this work, the conventional spelling of Pittsburgh is maintained throughout.

4   In this work, I have tended to refer to the Ottawa Hockey Club as the "Silver Seven" rather than the "Senators," before 1910 although, of the two, the latter was clearly more common at the time. The problem is that there was also an officially named Senator Hockey Club—Ottawa's entry in the Federal league during 1908–09. For a detailed discussion of the nicknames of the Ottawa HC, see Paul Kitchen, "They Weren't the Silver Seven," *Hockey Research Journal*, Volume 5 (2001), pp. 21–22.

5   This should not be confused with an earlier Montreal amateur club called the Wanderers that had existed in the late 1800s. See John Chi-Kit Wong, *Lords of the Rinks: The Emergence of the National Hockey League, 1875–1936* (Toronto: University of Toronto Press, 2005), pp. 18 and 183.

6   "The Address of the O.H.A. President," *Toronto News*, December 5, 1903.

7   "The O.H.A. Annual Meeting," *Toronto Globe*, December 7, 1903.

8   Baseball Almanac, "World Series Gate Receipts and Player Shares," http://www.baseball-almanac.com/ws/wsshares.shtml.

9   "With the Hockey Players," *Toronto News*, November 7, 1903.

10 Andrew Podnieks, *Canada's Olympic Hockey Teams: The Complete History 1920–1998* (Toronto: Doubleday Canada, 1997), p. 4.

11 In his autobiography, Hewitt claimed he and Nelson invented the goal net for hockey. The latter had apparently returned from a trip to Australia with two large fishing nets that he believed could be adapted to the winter sport. He shipped them to Montreal after Hewitt arranged for their use in an 1899 game between the Victorias and the Shamrocks. There is, however, evidence of limited use of goal nets prior to the Nelson-Hewitt story. What cannot be disputed is that Hewitt's *Herald* and Nelson's *Globe* were active proponents of the innovation. See W. A. Hewitt, *Down the Stretch: Recollections of a Pioneer Sportsman and Journalist* (Ryerson Press: Toronto, 1958), p. 33, and Paul Kitchen, "The Early Goal Net: Hockey Innovation and the Sporting Page, 1896–1912," in Colin D. Howell, ed., *Putting It On Ice, Volume 1: Hockey and Cultural Identities*, 2002, pp. 35–46.

12 Howell, p. 37.

13 "Mr. Cox's Amateur Principles," *Toronto Globe*, February 20, 1904.

14 The Marlboros were named after John Churchill, first Duke of Marlborough, the renowned British military commander and statesman of the late seventeenth and early eighteenth centuries, and ancestor of Sir Winston Churchill. The Marlboros were thus nicknamed the "Little Dukes," although simply the "Dukes" was more common. As already noted, the Wellingtons were nicknamed the "Iron Dukes," which, in contrast, was never shortened.

15 "A Record Crowd Saw Hockey Match," *Toronto News*, January 18, 1904.

16 "Marlboros and the Cup," *Toronto Globe*, February 18, 1904.

17 It should be mentioned that the McGee family was quite prominent. Thomas D'Arcy McGee, the assassinated Father of Confederation, was Frank's uncle. His father, John Joseph McGee, was clerk of the privy council during the Silver Seven's championship years. His older brother, Jim, also played for the team before his untimely death in a horse-racing accident in May 1904.

18 "Ottawa Led at the Finish," *Toronto Globe*, February 24, 1904.

19 "Slugged and Bodied into Submission," *Toronto Star*, February 24, 1904.

20 "Ottawas Win First Stanley Cup Match," *Ottawa Citizen*, February 24, 1904.

21 "Stanley Cup Holders Outclass Marlboros," *Ottawa Citizen*, February 26, 1904.

22 Ibid.

23 See "Ottawa Won First Stanley Cup Match," *Toronto News*, February 24, 1904, and "Ottawa Won Easily," *Toronto News*, February 26, 1904.

24 "Hockey is Not Ping-Pong," *Toronto News*, February 29, 1904.

25 See "Sporting Note and Comment," *Belleville Intelligencer*, February 26, 1904. This was far from an isolated opinion. For example, in "Puckerings" (*Cornwall Freeholder*, March 4, 1904), a similar argument is made about the difference between Ping-Pong and hockey, noting Toronto's reputation as "squealers."

26 This is taken from Charles L. Coleman, *The Trail of the Stanley Cup: Vol. 1* (Montreal: National Hockey League, 1966), p. 132.

27 "The O.H.A.'s Fine Record," *Toronto Globe*, March 14, 1905.

28 "Snap Shots on Sport," *Toronto Telegram*, February 19, 1904.

29 "Stanley Cup Holders Outclass Marlboros," *Toronto Telegram*, February 19, 1904.

30 Hewitt, *Down the Stretch*, p. 189.

31 Eric Zweig has pointed out to me that "there were lots of stories after the first Rat Portage-Ottawa Stanley Cup game in 1905 that the ice was salted before game two. It is therefore very possible Hewitt was just mixing up these events all those years ago." Still, the partisanship of Hewitt's *Star* for the Marlboros is beyond doubt.

32 See "President Robertson's Note," *Toronto Globe*, November 5, 1904. This was written before the annual meeting, no doubt to undermine the campaign of his lesser-known rival. Robertson did, however, present the same theory in his presidential address a month later.

33 Ibid.

CHAPTER FOUR: THE ROAD TO WAR

1 "Pure Amateurism in O.H.A. the Main Theme," *Toronto Star*, December 3, 1904.

2 See Eric Whitehead, *Cyclone Taylor*, 1977, p. 31. The author says that the calls between Hewitt and Taylor began in October 1903. If that is so, then Hewitt had been in touch with Taylor for a year.

3 Whitehead, pp. 32–33.

4 A recent high-profile rendition of the story can be found in the Canadian Broadcasting Corporation–sponsored work by Michael McKinley, *Hockey: A People's History* (Toronto: McClelland & Stewart, 2006), pp. 39–41.

5 Eric Zweig, "Setting Cyclone's Story Straight," *Hockey Research Journal*, vol. 11 (2007), pp. 47–50.

6 See W. A. Hewitt, *Down the Stretch* (Toronto: Ryerson Press, 1958), p. 214. Hewitt did, however, vividly remember Taylor's professional career and considered him one of the greatest players of all time.

7 "The O.H.A. Convention," *Toronto Globe*, December 5, 1904.

8 For examples of this label, see "Puckerings," *Toronto Globe*, December 11, 1907, and "Bruce Ridpath's Trip Abroad," *Toronto Star*, December 11, 1907.

9 "The Marlboros Have a Good Lead," *Toronto News*, February 20, 1905.

10 "A Good Hockey Season," *Toronto News*, November 11, 1905.

11 Ibid.

12 Hewitt, *Down the Stretch*, p. 186.

13 "A Good Hockey Season," *Toronto News*, November 11, 1905.

14 This is taken from Paul Kitchen, *Win, Tie, or Wrangle* (Manotick, ON: Penumbra, 2008), p. 133.

15 "Is the O.H.A. a Purely Philanthropic Body?" *Toronto News*, January 30, 1906.

16 Ibid.

17· "Darroch and Rowe Case," *Toronto Telegram*, March 20, 1906.

18 "Injunction Made Permanent," *Toronto Globe*, February 22, 1906.

19 "Last Stages of Hockey," *Toronto Telegram*, March 26, 1906.

20 The *Tely* cited the *London Free Press* to advance its argument. See "New Ontario Ambitions," *Toronto Telegram*, March 9, 1906.

21 "Jack at Play," *Toronto Globe*, March 8, 1906.

22 See Don Morrow, "A Case Study in Amateur Conflict: The Athletic War in Canada 1906–08" in *British Journal of Sports History*, Volume 3, September 1986, p. 178.

23 "The O.H.A. Convention."

CHAPTER FIVE: THE REBELLION BEGINS

1 "Snap Shots on Sport," *Toronto Telegram*, December 1, 1906.

2 This is taken from Kitchen, *Win, Tie, or Wrangle*, p. 152.

3 The ECAHA would require its clubs to publish the names of their professional players. Whether these lists were entirely accurate or not, it did show

that there was still some discomfort with professionalism even among the managers who were now openly embracing it.

4 "Pro. Idea in Canada," *Toronto Telegram*, January 30, 1907.

5 "The O.H.A. Annual," *Toronto Globe*, November 17, 1906.

6 "Jack at Play," *Toronto Globe*, November 17, 1906.

7 Although Spanner appears in the team picture of 1906–07, I have never found a single reference to him in news reports that season.

8 "Can Be Nominated for Only One Office in O.H.A.," *Toronto News*, October 31, 1905.

9 This is inferred from Miln's membership in the Albany Club.

10 "Mutual Street Ice Surface," *Toronto Star*, February 19, 1906.

11 Some in Toronto, even then, were suggesting the climate was warming, thus necessitating an artificial-ice rink. See the following, written during an unusually mild period after New Year's: "Will Toronto Have an Artificial Ice Rink?" *Toronto News*, January 3, 1906.

12 "Odds and Ends of Current Sport," *Toronto Star*, November 22, 1906.

13 "Snap Shots on Sport."

14 "Canadian Soo and Torontos," *Toronto Globe*, December 28, 1906.

CHAPTER SIX: THE UPRISING SPREADS

1 "Guelph 9, Toronto 4," *Guelph Mercury*, January 31, 1907.

2 Kevin Slater, *The Trolley League*, Online Publications, p. 198.

3 Many rinks provided musical entertainment by bands—usually military bands—during interludes. However, this does not seem to have been the case for the Toronto Professionals' home games at the Mutual Street Rink.

4 "Canadian 'Soo' Blanked Torontos," *Toronto Mail and Empire*, December 29, 1906.

5 "Canadian Soo Blanked Locals," *Toronto Star*, December 29, 1906.

6 The *Star* cited the *London Advertiser* to make its point. See "Latest Hockey Notes From Star Exchanges," *Toronto Star*, January 3, 1907.

7 The terms "American Soo" and "Michigan Soo" were used interchangeably, the latter being more common. However, the "Canadian Soo" club appears to have never been called the "Ontario Soo."

8 The nickname "Wolverines" was the term used by the local newspaper, the *Soo Evening News*, for the American Soo team of the International Hockey League, although "Indians" (which I have not seen at the time) is used in more modern references. See Daniel Scott Mason, "The Origins and Development of the International Hockey League and its Effects on the Sport of Professional Ice Hockey in North America," M.A. Thesis, University of British Columbia, 1994, p. 75.

9 "Young the Star of a Great Game," *Toronto News*, January 18, 1907.

10 "Toronto Pros. Beat Soo," *Toronto Globe*, January 18, 1907.

11 Rat Portage had changed its name to Kenora in 1905.

12 It should be noted that the Winnipeg Victorias' trip to Toronto in February 1895 was not actually part of a quest for the Stanley Cup, but rather just an exhibition tour. Their first Stanley Cup trip east occurred in February 1896, during which they defeated the Montreal Victorias for the championship.

13 "Kenora To-morrow Night," *Toronto Mail and Empire*, January 24, 1907.

14 It should be noted that the Thistles played their home games on an under-sized rink in Kenora, so this experience was not new to them. However, their speed was obviously more suited to a larger ice surface.

15 "Guelph 9, Toronto 4."

16 "Smoky City Team Beaten by Locals," *Toronto Mail and Empire*, February 5, 1907.

17 It should be noted that this intervention by the trustees was unprecedented. Until the Thistle–Wanderer series, the trustees had satisfied themselves with simply judging the qualifications of challengers. Once a challenge was accepted, they generally left the details of the arrangements to the clubs themselves. By beginning to intervene on player eligibility, Ross and Foran were indicating they still held some reservations about professionalism, at least at its extremes. However, I would observe that such rulings on this occasion and in the future only seemed to work against challengers from outside the Montreal–Ottawa hockey power corridor.

18 "Dutchmen Beat the Local Pros.," *Toronto News*, March 2, 1907.

CHAPTER SEVEN: THE PROS ON THE MARCH

1 "Snap Shots on Sport," *Toronto Telegram*, December 4, 1907.

2 "Fastest Marathon Ever Run Won By Longboat: Record Clipped by Indian Youth," *Boston Globe*, April 20, 1907.

3 See "Snap Shots on Sport," *Toronto Telegram*, January 15, 1908. References to Longboat's aboriginal ethnicity were routine. As his heroic status wore off, they descended into racial slurs.

4 "Temporary Truce is Declared for Next Year's Olympic Games," *Toronto Star*, December 2, 1907.

5 "President Discusses Football Once More," *San Francisco Call*, December 5, 1905.

6 The relative passivity regarding sports violence shown by authorities in Canada versus the United States is perplexing—as is the wider sports culture. The Canadian national winter and summer sports are hockey and lacrosse, while their American counterparts are basketball and baseball. How do we explain the violent and chaotic favourite sports of the "peaceable kingdom" and the serene and orderly ones of the "revolutionary republic"? Preston Manning

told me many years ago that he thought this made perfect sense, saying, "People engage in sports as leisure, as a break, so wouldn't we expect a society's preferences to be the opposite of its character?"

7   Poulton, *The Paper Tyrant*, p. 131.

8   Poulton, pp. 126–130.

9   The OPHL executive consisted of the league officers and a delegate from each club. Toronto's delegate was one J. C. Palmer. We have found no definitive information on this man, but suspect he was the son of the owner of the Mutual Street Rink, J. J. Palmer.

10 "Clubs are Clamoring for Space at Mutual St. Rink," *Toronto News*, November 14, 1907.

11 "Snap Shots on Sport," *Toronto Telegram*, December 4, 1907.

12 Although it had a slender OHA record, the Simcoe Hockey Club of Toronto had long been the home club of John Ross Robertson. As previously noted, when he was a boy, the president had called his neighbourhood shinny team the Simcoes. It is unclear whether it was named after his hero John Graves Simcoe, first lieutenant governor of Upper Canada (Ontario), or Simcoe Street, where the Robertson family home was located. Interestingly, the club of which Marriott was manager counted both Robertson and Alexander Miln among its patrons. See Ron Poulton, *The Paper Tyrant*, p. 16.

13 "Edward Hanlan," *Toronto Globe*, January 4, 1908.

14 "Hockey on Bare Floor," *Toronto News*, January 6, 1908.

15 "Berlin Wins Great Game from Torontos—Score 3 to 0," *Toronto World*, January 6, 1908.

16 I have chosen to use the term "Braves" as the moniker for Roy Brown's team. However, unlike the Dutchmen of Berlin and the Royals of Guelph, no nickname seems to have consistently attached to Brantford's professional hockey club. Although "Indians" has been used in various OPHL histories, I have never seen the term in contemporary reporting. Conversely, Braves, Brants, Mohawks, Dykers and the generic Professionals all appeared. For this use of Braves (though without a capital), see "Brants. Beat Dutch.," *Toronto Telegram*, January 8, 1909. For similar uses in the Brantford papers, see Kevin Slater, *Trolley League*, pp. 96 and 273.

17 "Torontos Again Down," *Toronto Telegram*, January 11, 1908.

18 Some, though not all, game reports list Toronto's point man as "Gamble." This player was clearly Lambe, whose name somehow became scrambled after an added "G."

19 "Guelph Defeated 4–3 in Sensational Game," *Guelph Mercury*, January 14, 1908.

CHAPTER EIGHT: A BRUSH WITH ETERNITY

1 "Remarked on the Side," *Toronto Telegram*, March 5, 1908.

2 "Guelph Lost to Toronto in a Poor Exhibition," *Guelph Mercury*, January 20, 1908.

3 Ibid.

4 "Berlin Here To-morrow," *Toronto Mail and Empire*, February 14, 1908.

5 "Toronto Pros Beat Berlin," *Toronto World*, February 17, 1908.

6 "Toronto Pros. Careless," *Toronto Telegram*, February 24, 1908.

7 "Torontos Walloped Berlin," *Toronto Globe*, February 26, 1908.

8 Ibid.

9 "Dutchmen Were Easy for Toronto 'Pros.' Last Night," *Toronto Star*, February 26, 1908.

10 "The Little German Band No Match for Torontos," *Toronto News*, February 26, 1908.

11 "Brantford 'Pro' Team was Easy for the Fast Torontos," *Toronto Star*, March 2, 1908.

12 Foran had been appointed as a trustee by Ross to succeed his original partner, Sheriff John Sweetland, who stepped down in early 1907 due to ill health.

13 "Stanley Cup Trustees Issue Statement," *Toronto Telegram*, February 29, 1908.

14 It is interesting to note that the Wanderers did not protest either Lalonde or Corbeau. Although they had also played for other clubs during the season, they had not played against ECAHA teams. This would imply that the trustees' ban, which was reported to be against all who had performed for more than one team, was actually much narrower. It was likely only against players who had already performed in a series involving the Stanley Cup champions. It also explains why Miln had no hesitancy in signing particular new players to the Toronto Professionals after the ban was announced.

15 "Remarked on the Side."

16 "May Surrender Cup," *Montreal Gazette*, March 12, 1908.

17 "N-E-X-T!" *Montreal Star*, March 13, 1908.

18 "Will Only Play One Cup Game," *Toronto Mail and Empire*, March 14, 1908.

19 "Wanderers Held on to the Stanley Cup in Rough and Ready Match," *Montreal Star*, March 16, 1908.

20 "Torontos Almost Lift Stanley Cup," *Toronto Mail and Empire*, March 16, 1908.

CHAPTER NINE: THE PROS IN RETREAT

1 "Guelph Defeats Toronto Before Saying Good-Bye," *Toronto News*, January 21, 1909.

2 "Snap Shots on Sport," *Toronto Telegram*, March 16, 1908.

3   "Wanderers Held on to the Stanley Cup in Rough and Ready Match," *Montreal Star*, March 16, 1908.

4   "Close Call for Champions and Cup," *Montreal Gazette*, March 16, 1908.

5   "Opinions on the Game," *Toronto Mail and Empire*, March 17, 1908.

6   Ibid.

7   "A Burlesque at Guelph," *Toronto Globe*, March 23, 1908.

8   " 'Pro' Rough House at the Royal City," *Toronto Star*, March 23, 1908.

9   "A Burlesque at Guelph."

10   "The Last Game of the Season and the Worst by Long Odds," *Guelph Mercury*, March 23, 1908.

11   "Legacy of the 1908 Olympics involves a Canadian connection," Matthew Fisher, *National Post*, July 31, 2012.

12   "Editorial Notes," *Galt Reporter*, January 25, 1908.

13   "Alex. Miln's Team Now Ready," *Toronto News*, December 22, 1908.

14   "Ottawa Not Invincible," *Toronto Globe*, January 4, 1909.

15   "Kerr is Protested," *Toronto News*, January 6, 1909.

16   "Berlin Beat Toronto," *Toronto Globe*, January 6, 1909.

17   "Guelph Here To-Night," *Toronto Globe*, January 9, 1909.

18   See "Torontos Won Easily," *Toronto Mail and Empire*, January 11, 1909. This report, like others around this time, indicated that Morrison's return was imminent.

19   Although no nickname has been applied to the Galt professional hockey club in various OPHL histories, the term "Irving's Indians" was consistently used during 1908–09. It had also been occasionally used to describe Buck's organization in Guelph the previous season. However, there are some indications that the term "Indians" was genuinely employed as the unofficial moniker for the Galt team, at least in the Toronto papers. See "Hard to Keep Men Together," *Toronto News*, January 20, 1909, and "Gossip of the Pro. Hockey Players," *Toronto Star*, January 21, 1909, as well as "Irving's Indians Invincible," *Galt Reporter*, February 26, 1909.

20   "Galt Win by 5 to 4 Over Toronto Pros," *Toronto World*, January 14, 1909.

21   "Snap Shots on Sport," *Toronto Telegram*, January 14, 1909.

22   Again, no nickname has been applied by historians to the St. Kitts team that played in the OPHL in 1908–09. I have used the term "Athletics" because this was the name of the lacrosse club that founded the local pro team late in the previous season. However, St. Catharines papers are very spotty during the period in which the organization belonged to the league. It is thus hard to know whether this or any other term took hold locally.

23   Some, though not all, reports of the Torontos' game at St. Catharines record Fred Young's name as "Borden." These are clearly one and the same person, yet there is no readily apparent explanation for the confusion.

24 "Observations on Current Sport," *Toronto Star*, January 15, 1909.

25 "Toronto Pros. Lose a Hard Luck Game to the Germans," *Toronto Star*, January 19, 1909.

26 "Torontos Outplay Berlin but Lose," *Toronto Mail and Empire*, January 19, 1909.

27 "Guelph Defeats Toronto Before Saying Good-Bye."

CHAPTER TEN: THE TRIUMPH OF THE AMATEURS

1 "Snap Shots on Sport," *Toronto Telegram*, November 23, 1909.

2 "Puckerings," *Toronto Globe*, January 21, 1909.

3 "Pros. Hated to Leave," *Toronto News*, February 9, 1909.

4 "Torontos in Great Form Easily Vanquish Galt," *Toronto News*, January 28, 1909.

5 "Torontos Beat the Leaders, Brants Swept off Feet," *Toronto Telegram*, February 1, 1909.

6 "Torontos Downed the Brantfords," *Toronto Mail and Empire*, February 1, 1909.

7 It had been agreed that the tied game between Brantford and Galt on January 5 would be played off before the end of the season. It is thus excluded at this point.

8 "Berlin Doubled Toronto's Score," *Toronto Mail and Empire*, February 2, 1909.

9 "Lack of Team Work Causes Downfall of Toronto Pros.," *Toronto News*, February 2, 1909.

10 Ibid.

11 "Galt Easy for Toronto Pros," *Toronto Star*, February 5, 1909.

12 "Torontos Trim Galt," *Toronto World*, February 5, 1909.

13 "Toronto Pros. Lose a Hard Luck Game to the Germans," *Toronto Star*, January 19, 1909.

14 "Snap Shots on Sport," *Toronto Telegram*, February 8, 1909.

15 There is some uncertainty about who played left wing for the Toronto Professionals in the London exhibition. The limited extant reports of the contest list the man as "Carl." However, no player by this name is known to have performed anywhere in this region during this era. The available evidence suggests that this was the first OPHL-circuit game for Jimmy "Kid" Mallen. Mallen would have been completely unknown to local reporters, who had initially thought that Bruce Ridpath might be playing for the Torontos.

16 "Jack at Play," *Toronto Globe*, February 20, 1909.

17 "Burlesque in the Pro. League," *Toronto Star*, February 19, 1909.

18 "Torontos Lose Slow Game," *Toronto News*, February 24, 1909.

19 "Brants Beat Toronto," *Toronto Telegram*, February 24, 1909.

20 The standings between the other three teams were very tight. In particular, the January 5 tied game between Brantford and Galt, which would be played off after all other scheduled regular-season games, was thought to be key to the championship.

21 See "Brantford Gets Tyner," *Toronto Globe*, February 13, 1909. This is one of the first reports (in the anti-professional papers) claiming that Toronto would directly aid Brantford's bid to win the championship. Although the article indicated that Miln had said as much, it did not actually quote him. Were it true, such action would have been decidedly unethical and clearly contrary to league policy.

22 In fairness, the final game between Brantford and Galt on February 25 was ultimately irrelevant. By beating Berlin on February 23 (the night Toronto lost to Brantford), the Indians wrapped up the championship even before beating the Braves. There was, however, some contradictory information in the press about the standings, as some reports failed to understand that a January 28 victory of Brantford over Galt was an exhibition match, not a regular-season game.

23 "No Pros. For Toronto," *Toronto Globe*, November 20, 1909.

24 "Snap Shots on Sport," *Toronto Telegram*, November 23, 1909.

CHAPTER ELEVEN: THE OLD ORDER RESTORED

1 This quotation has been attributed to the diplomat Charles Maurice de Talleyrand-Périgord, it being his rueful observation after the restoration of the Bourbon monarchy in France.

2 "Two More Senior O.H.A. Teams, Eurekas and St. Paul's Up," *Toronto Telegram*, November 30, 1909.

3 "Athletic Peace Treaty Sept. 6," *Toronto Star*, September 3, 1909.

4 Jack Batten. *The Man Who Ran Faster than Everyone: The Story of Tom Longboat* (Toronto: Tundra Books, 2002), p. 6.

5 With the passing of the Senators Hockey Club of the Federal league at the end of 1908–09, this moniker would henceforth be used solely by the Ottawa Hockey Club. I have thus adopted it from this point forward in the text.

6 Eric Zweig notes that this was Cyclone Taylor's recollection of his salary many years later. News reports at the time suggested somewhat lower amounts although, considering the "position" that came with the hockey contract, the total is not implausible. See Eric Zweig, "Setting Cyclone's Story Straight," in *Hockey Research Journal*, Volume 11 (2007), pp. 47–50.

7 "Jack at Play," *Toronto Globe*, December 29, 1909.

8 Just to be clear on this twenty-four-year timeline, the Amateur Hockey Association of Canada was formed in 1886. In 1898, its existing clubs reorganized as the Canadian Amateur Hockey League after a dispute over new members. In 1906, most of the CAHL's clubs joined with the Federal league's Montreal

Wanderers and (returning) Ottawa Silver Seven to form the Eastern Canada Amateur Hockey Association. In 1908, the ECAHA dropped the word
"Amateur" and its Montreal AAA and Victoria clubs. Of course, in 1909, it
attempted to reorganize without the Wanderers as the Canadian Hockey Association, leading to its final demise in 1910.

9   "Reflections on Sporting Topics," *Toronto Star*, November 25, 1909.

10   This was the clear and repeated position of the *Tely*. For example, see "Snap
       Shots on Sport," *Toronto Telegram*, January 4, 1908, and "Snap Shots on
       Sport," *Toronto Telegram*, February 1, 1909.

11   "Bruce Ridpath's Foolish Talk," *Toronto News*, January 19, 1911.

12   Poulton, pp.134–135.

13   "Snap Shots on Sport," *Toronto Telegram*, November 4, 1909.

14   The disposition of the O'Brien franchises, including the original *Les Cana-
       diens* entity, is laid out in Frank Cosentino, "From Millionaires to Maple
       Leafs: Exploring Toronto's Roots in Renfrew," in *Hockey Research Journal*,
       Volume 6 (2002), pp. 19–20. In my reading of the press reports of the time,
       I have seen nothing to contradict Cosentino's summary of these events.

15   "With the Puck Chasers," *Toronto News*, December 10, 1910.

16   Contrary to many conventional histories, the OPHL was not referred to as
       the "Trolley League" in its first two seasons, during which the Toronto Pro-
       fessionals were members. See "Toronto Out of the Pro. League," *Toronto Star*,
       November 20, 1909, for the first appearance of this nickname. The article
       notes that the OPHL "is now a Trolley League" *because of* the withdrawal of
       Toronto. For this reason, references to Alexander Miln's club as the "Toronto
       Trolley Leaguers" (as appear, for example, in the history section of NHL.com)
       are obviously incorrect.

17   Glen R. Goodhand, *A History of the Ontario Professional Hockey League 1908–
       1911*, Unpublished, p. 2.

18   Poulton, p. 134.

19   "Political Notes: Ontario is Awake," *Montreal Gazette*, September 20, 1911.

CHAPTER TWELVE: THE REVENGE OF HISTORY

1   "Snap Shots on Sport," *Toronto Telegram*, November 24, 1909.

2   Eric Whitehead, *The Patricks: Hockey's Royal Family* (Toronto: Doubleday,
       1980), p. 13.

3   Travis Paterson, "100 Years of Hockey in Victoria," *Victoria News*, Decem-
       ber 30, 2011.

4   Ibid.

5   The "Blue Shirts"—or sometimes "Blue-Shirts"—are referred to as the
       "Blueshirts" in most modern-day publications. However, I have not seen the
       one-word version of the name in reports of the era.

6   For example, see the photograph "Six of the Toronto Professionals," *Toronto News*, January 4, 1913.

7   "Rideau Tandem Swamped," *Ottawa Citizen*, August 6, 1910.

8   "Bruce Ridpath Badly Injured," *Montreal Gazette*, November 3, 1911.

9   Ibid.

10   "Motorist Must Remain in Jail," *Toronto News*, October 6, 1911.

11   See "Streets Illuminated for First Time by Civic Hydro-Electric Service," *Toronto News*, November 2, 1911. Ironically, this took place the night before Ridpath's automobile accident. It indicates that, even with this historic improvement, lighting was still quite dim by today's standards.

12   "Pedestrian's Right of Way," *Toronto World*, November 4, 1911.

13   "Not Driver's Fault Said Ridpath," *Toronto World*, January 12, 1912.

14   "The Passing of Mutual St. Rink," *Toronto Star*, August 12, 1911.

15   "Was a Farce," *Toronto News*, January 26, 1912.

CHAPTER THIRTEEN: THE NEW ORDER IN HOCKEY'S SECOND CITY

1   "Three Straight for Torontos, Should Beat Victoria Again," *Toronto Telegram*, March 19, 1914.

2   This is taken from Frank Cosentino, *The Renfrew Millionaires* (Burnstown, ON: General Store Publishing, 1990), p. 13.

3   *National Hockey League Official Guide & Record Book 2013*, p. 242. (There is some ambiguity in the early years concerning what constituted a Stanley Cup win.)

4   For example, see " 'Bushers' for Toronto Pro Hockey Team," *Toronto News*, October 30, 1912, and "New Ontario Stars Laughed at Low Offers of Toronto Clubs," *Toronto News*, November 12, 1912.

5   "Torontos Play Real Hockey and Smother the Indians," *Toronto Star*, January 16, 1913.

6   "Ridpath's Roustabouts Were No Match For Champions," *Toronto News*, February 13, 1913.

7   Baker actually played his final game for Princeton in Canada. It was at Ottawa's Dey Rink on February 28, 1914. Princeton lost to Ottawa College 3–2.

8   "Torontos Sure of Championship," *Toronto Star*, February 26, 1914.

9   "The N.H.A. Race Tied Up By Last Night's Results," *Toronto Star*, March 5, 1914.

10   "Ontarios and Torontos Beat Montreal N.H.A. Teams," *Toronto Star*, February 2, 1914.

11   "Torontos Played Superb Hockey and Outclassed Canadiens in Final Game," *Toronto News*, March 12, 1914.

12   "Wig Wag System Used For Denoting Penalties in N.H.A.," *Toronto News*, December 20, 1912.

13 It should be noted that there was some uncertainty during the Toronto–Victoria matches as to their bearing on possession of the Stanley Cup. During the series, reports appeared saying that the trustees would not recognize the games because the leagues' "hockey commission" had not asked their formal approval for the challenge. However, the matter appears to have been ironed out by the time it was all concluded. The Blue Shirts are thus now recognized as having successfully defended their Cup title after first gaining it with the NHA championship.

14 "Flanagan on Current Sport," *Toronto Telegram*, March 17, 1914.

15 "Three Straight For Torontos, Should Beat Victoria Again."

16 For example, see "Inter-League Hockey Pros Second Game at the Arena," *Toronto Telegram*, March 17, 1914.

17 Barbara Wertheim Tuchman, *The Guns of August* (New York: Macmillan, 1962), p. 1.

18 Augustus Bridle, *Sons of Canada: Short Studies of Characteristic Canadians* (Toronto: J.M. Dent & Sons Ltd., 1916), p. 26.

19 Poulton, *The Paper Tyrant*, p. 138.

OVERTIME: AN ERA FADES AWAY

1 This is attributed to Tommy Gorman of the old Ottawa Senators. See Morey Holzman and Joseph Nieforth, *Deceptions and Doublecross: How the NHL Conquered Hockey* (Toronto: Dundurn, 2002), p. 24.

2 I admit that my take on the Calder–Livingstone rivalry is close to the traditional NHL-authorized view of history. For an interpretation more sympathetic to Livingstone, see Holzman and Nieforth.

3 This whole episode was actually quite complex. The Arenas initially contracted with Livingstone for the temporary use of his players. However, they never did pay the required sums and eventually turned the men over to the St. Patricks rather than returning them.

4 This is discussed in detail in Walter C. Neale, "The Peculiar Economics of Professional Sports," *Quarterly Journal of Economics*, vol. 78 (February 1964), pp. 1–14.

5 "Maple Leafs Gardens Contract Goes to Local Firm," *Toronto Globe*, May 30, 1931.

6 Poulton, *The Paper Tyrant*, p. 173.

7 "Great Toronto Newspaperman Has Passed Away," *Morning Leader*, June 1, 1918.

8 Poulton, p. 172.

9 This is the title of the chapter about Hewitt in Scott Young's OHA history. See Scott Young, *100 Years of Dropping the Puck: A History of the OHA* (Toronto: McClelland & Stewart, 1989), pp. 62–74.

10   Hewitt, *Down the Stretch*, pp. 238–39.

11   Technically, only W. A. Hewitt and Foster Hewitt are members of the Hockey Hall of Fame. Bill Hewitt is, however, a recipient of the Hall's Foster Hewitt Memorial Award for broadcasting.

12   My observation here originates in the comments of Bruce Kidd, *The Struggle for Canadian Sport* (Toronto: University of Toronto Press, 1996), pp. 35–36, although my perspective is somewhat different.

13   As above, my observation here grew out of that of Kidd, *The Struggle for Canadian Sport*.

14   The U.S.-based Portland Rosebuds attempted to claim the Stanley Cup one year earlier, in 1916. They had won the PCHA championship against, among others, the reigning Cup holders, the Vancouver Millionaires. However, after 1914, the trustees did not recognize a Cup champion until all interleague play-offs were completed at the end of the season. Nevertheless, Portland engraved its name on the Cup, to this day the only non-winner to appear on the chalice.

15   "Marshall Was Last of Famed Ice Squad," *Montreal Star*, August 9, 1965.

16   An obvious question is why Charles Coleman ascribed the "Maple Leafs" moniker to the 1908 Toronto Stanley Cup contender. As noted, just before the Montreal Wanderers met Alex Miln's Professionals, they defeated a challenge from the Winnipeg Maple Leafs. As these two series reported on the same page, the nickname may have originated simply as a transposition error. See Charles L. Coleman, *The Trail of the Stanley Cup: Volume 1, 1893–1926* (1964), p. 162.

17   "Another Hockeyist Killed in Action," *Toronto Star*, November 24, 1916.

18   "Attestation Paper No. 443780," MERCER, WALTER, Regimental Number: 443780, Reference: RG 150, Accession 1992–93/166, Box 6122–28.

19   Obituaries of Walter Hayes Mercer in the *Toronto Globe and Mail*, *Star* and *Telegram*, May 30, 1961.

20   "Rev. Tyner, of Lincoln, in Front Line Trenches, Describes Conditions on Fields Where Americans are Fighting," *Lincoln Star*, April 21, 1918.

21   "Rev. Charles R. Tyner," *Kansas City Times*, March 13, 1967.

22   This is a fact I am at pains to explain, but it is a fact nonetheless. It appears that Bruce Ridpath, Con Corbeau, Bert Morrison, Alexander Miln and Teddy Marriott never married. Chuck Tyner and Rolly Young wed late and had no children. Only Newsy Lalonde, Hugh Lambe and Walter Mercer produced offspring. Looking at the team's lesser lights whom I have been able to obtain information on, the same pattern appears. A notable exception is Ezra Dumart. His son, Woody Dumart, starred with the Boston Bruins from the late 1930s to the early 1950s and is a member of the Hockey Hall of Fame.

23   Some discussion of Hugh Lambe's married life can be found in "Dunsford Family," *Ancestry.ca*.

24   "Hugh Lambe Killed by Fall on Stairs," *Toronto Star*, May 7, 1941.

25   "For the Would-Be Paddler," *Toronto World*, July 9, 1919.

26   Poulton, *The Paper Tyrant*, p. 173.

27   Various elements of this argument can be found in Kidd, *The Struggle for Canadian Sport*, pp. 42 and 265–70; Alan Metcalfe, *Canada Learns to Play* (Toronto: Oxford University Press, 1987), pp. 223–224, and Don Morrow, "A Case Study in Conflict," in *British Journal of Sports History* (September 1986), pp. 185–86.

28   John Ross Robertson, *Talks with Craftsmen and Pencillings by the Wayside: Thoughts for Those Who Are Earnest in a Work that Serves a Noble End and Binds the Hearts of a Great Brotherhood in the Golden Chain of Faith, Fellowship, and Fraternity* (Toronto: Hunter, Rose, 1890), p. 6.

BIBLIOGRAPHY

Aiken, Mike et al. *Kenora Thistles: Our Hockey Heritage*. Kenora: Bowes Publishers, 2006.

Batten, Jack. *The Man Who Ran Faster than Everyone: The Story of Tom Longboat*. Toronto: Tundra Books, 2002.

Beekman, Scott. *Ringside: A History of Professional Wrestling in America*. Wesport: Praeger Publishing, 2006.

Blight, Jim, pub. *Kenora Thistles: Our Hockey Heritage*. Kenora: Bowes Publishers, 2006.

Boileau, Ron and Philip Wolf. "The Pacific Coast Hockey Association: Innovative Pioneer League Took Top Hockey West" in Dan Diamond, ed., *Total Hockey: The Official Encyclopedia of the National Hockey League, Second Edition*. New York: Total Sports, 2000, pp. 51–54.

Brown, Robert Craig and Ramsay Cook. *Canada 1896–1921: A Nation Transformed*. Toronto: McClelland & Stewart, 1974.

Cauz, Louis. *Baseball's Back in Town: From the Don to the Blue Jays, A history of baseball in Toronto*. Toronto: Controlled Media Corp., 1977.

Clark, Donald M. "Early Artificial Ice: The Development of Refrigeration Allowed the Game to Spread" in Dan Diamond, ed., *Total Hockey: The Official Encyclopedia of the National Hockey League*, New York: Total Sports, 1998, pp. 564–65.

Coleman, Charles L. *The Trail of the Stanley Cup: Volume 1, 1893–1926*. National Hockey League, 1964.

Cooper, John Irwin. *Montreal: A Brief History*. Montreal: McGill–Queen's University Press, 1969.

Cosentino, Frank. "A History of the Concept of Professionalism in Canadian Sport," Ph.D. Thesis, University of Alberta, 1973.

———. *The Renfrew Millionaires: The Valley Boys of Winter 1910*. Burnstown: General Store Publishing House, 1990.

———. "From Millionaires to Maple Leafs: Exploring Toronto's Roots in Renfrew," in *Hockey Research Journal*, Volume 6, 2002, pp. 19–20.

———. "*Les Glorieux*: Canadiens, Canadians, Habs or Habs Not" in *Hockey Research Journal*, Volume 6, 2002, pp. 21–22.

Currie, Gordon. *100 Years of Canadian Football*. Don Mills: Pagurian Press, 1968.

Diamond, Dan, ed. *The Official National Hockey League Stanley Cup Centennial Book*. Toronto: McClelland & Stewart, 1992.

Dryden, Ken. *The Game: A Thoughtful and Provocative Look at Life in Hockey*. Toronto: Macmillan of Canada, 1983.

Duplacey, James. "Legends and Facts: The First Presentation of the Stanley Cup," in *Hockey Research Journal*, Volume 2, 1994, pp. 13–15.

Farrell, Arthur. *Hockey: Canada's Royal Winter Game*. Montreal: C.R. Corneil, 1899.

Field, Russell. "Profits, Playoffs, and the Building of Maple Leaf Gardens, 1931," in Colin D. Howell, ed., *Putting It on Ice*, Volume I: Hockey and Cultural Identities, 2002, pp. 47–58.

Filichia, Peter. *Professional Baseball Franchises: From the Abbeville Athletics to the Zanesville Indians*. New York: Facts on File Incorporated, 1993.

Fitsell, J. W. (Bill). *Hockey's Captains, Colonels and Kings*. Erin, ON: Boston Mills Press, 1987.

———. "How Hockey Got Its Kick Start" in *Hockey Research Journal*, Volume 1, 1993, pp. 36–39.

———. "Is Windsor the Birthplace of Hockey?" in *Hockey Research Journal*, Volume 2, 1994, pp. 3–4.

———. "The Rise and Fall of Ice Polo: The Roots of Hockey" in Dan Diamond, ed., *Total Hockey: The Official Encyclopedia of the National Hockey League*, New York: Total Sports, 2000, pp. 5–7.

———. "The Halifax Rules: Fact or Fiction?" in *Hockey Research Journal*, Volume 5, 2001, pp. 9–11.

———. "Marks on Hockey's Face," in *Hockey Research Journal*, Volume 5, 2001, pp. 32–37.

———. "Doc Gibson: The Eye in the IHL," in *Hockey Research Journal*, Volume 8, 2004, pp. 5–7.

———. "When Mascots Were Barefaced," in *Hockey Research Journal*, Volume 11, 2007, pp. 71–73.

Fitzsimmons, Ernie. "Early Pro Leagues: The First Days of Play-for-Pay Hockey" in Dan Diamond, ed., *Total Hockey: The Official Encyclopedia of the National Hockey League*, New York: Total Sports, 2000, pp. 32–36.

———. "Early Professional, Early Senior, WHA and Modern Minor Professional League Standings" in Dan Diamond, ed., *Total Hockey: The Official Encyclopedia of the National Hockey League*, New York: Total Sports, 2000, pp. 414–32.

———. "IHL Players: The Professional Pioneers," in *Hockey Research Journal*, Volume 8, 2004, pp. 8–11.

———. "Pittsburgh: The Cradle of Pro Hockey," in *Hockey Research Journal*, Volume 13, 2009, pp. 5–8.

Garton, Harold. *Hockey Town in Canada*. Carp, ON: Creative Bound, 1992.

Goodhand, Glen R. *A History of the Ontario Professional Hockey League 1908–1911: Berlin (Kitchener)—Brantford—Galt—Guelph—St. Catharines—Toronto—Waterloo*. Unpublished Manuscript.

————. "Is Necessity the Mother of Invention: The Evolution of Hockey Equipment," in *Hockey Research Journal*, Volume 2, 1994, pp. 9–12.

————. *Hockey's Historic Highlights*. Haworth: Saint Johann Press, 2010.

Goyens, Chrys and Frank Orr. *Blades on Ice: A Century of Professional Hockey*. Markham: TPE, 2000.

Green, R. Wayne. "John Ross Robertson: Hockey Czar and Humanitarian," in *Hockey Research Journal*, Volume 8, 2004, pp. 12–14.

Gruneau, Richard and David Whitson. *Hockey Night in Canada: Sport, Identities and Cultural Politics*. Toronto: Garamond Press, 1993.

Harley, E. Gay. "Of Cultural Identity and Creation Myths: The Subject of 'Beginnings' and The Writing of Hockey History," in Colin D. Howell, ed., *Putting it on Ice*, Volume I: Hockey and Cultural Identities, 2002, pp. 1–5.

Hewitt, Foster. *Hockey Night in Canada: The Maple Leafs' Story, Second Edition*. Toronto: Ryerson Press, 1961.

Hewitt, W. A. *Down the Stretch: Recollections of a Pioneer Sportsman and Journalist*. Toronto: Ryerson Press, 1958.

Holman, Andrew C. "Playing in the Neutral Zone: Meanings and Uses of Ice Hockey in the Canadian-U.S. Borderlands 1895–1915," in *American Journal of Canadian Studies*, Spring 2004, pp. 17–29.

Holzman, Morey and Joseph Nieforth. *Deceptions and Doublecross: How the NHL Conquered Hockey*. Toronto: Dundurn Press, 2002.

Howell, Nancy and Maxwell L. Howell. *Sports and Games in Canadian Life: 1700 to the Present*. Toronto: Macmillan of Canada, 1969.

Jacobs, Jane. *Systems of Survival: A Dialogue on the Moral Foundations of Commerce and Politics*. Toronto: Random House, 1992.

Jenish, D'Arcy. *The Montreal Canadiens: 100 Years of Glory*. Toronto: Doubleday Canada, 2008.

Kemmett, Leighton. "The Life and Times of Frank McGee Synopsis," in *Hockey Research Journal*, Volume 4, 1999, pp. 22–24.

Kerr, John. *Curling in Canada and the United States: A Record of the Tour of the Scottish Team, 1902–3, and the Game in the Republic and the Dominion*. Edinburgh: G.A. Morton, 1904.

Kidd, Bruce. "In Defence of Tom Longboat," in *Canadian Journal of History of Sport*, Volume 14, May 1983, pp. 34–63.

————. *The Struggle for Canadian Sport*. Toronto: University of Toronto Press, 1996.

King, George. *Hockey Year Book*. Toronto: G. King, 1924.

Kitchen, Paul. "From Dey's Rink to Bryden's Palladium," in *Hockey Research Journal*, Volume 4, 1999, pp. 18–21.

————. "Before 'The Trail of the Stanley Cup': The Amateur Hockey Association of Canada 1886 to 1892 Inclusive" in Dan Diamond, ed., *Total Hockey: The*

Official Encyclopedia of the National Hockey League, New York: Total Sports, 2000, pp. 8–15.

———. "They Refused the Stanley Cup: Anatomy of a Controversy" in Dan Diamond, ed., *Total Hockey: The Official Encyclopedia of the National Hockey League*, New York: Total Sports, 2000, pp. 20–24.

———. "Early Goal Nets: The Evolution of an Idea," in *Hockey Research Journal*, Volume 5, 2001, pp. 12–14.

———. "They Weren't the Silver Seven: The Search for Ottawa's Nickname," in *Hockey Research Journal*, Volume 5, 2001, pp. 21–22.

———. "The Early Goal Net: Hockey Innovation and the Sporting Page, 1896–1912," in Colin D. Howell, ed., *Putting It On Ice*, Volume 1: Hockey and Cultural Identities, 2002, pp. 35–46.

———. *Win, Tie, or Wrangle: The Inside Story of the Old Ottawa Senators 1883–1935*. Newcastle, ON: Penumbra Press, 2008.

Kitchen, Paul et al. "SIHR 'Origins' Report: Looking into the Claim of Windsor, N.S.," in *Hockey Research Journal*, Volume 6, 2002, pp. 1–14.

Kotylo, Leonard. "The History of Hockey in Toronto: From Granite Club to Air Canada Centre" in Dan Diamond, ed., *Total Hockey: The Official Encyclopedia of the National Hockey League*, New York: Total Sports, 2000, pp. 27–29.

———. "Cyclone Taylor: The View from the Pacific Coast," in *Hockey Research Journal*, Volume 10, 2006, pp. 16–17.

———. "Aspects of Hockey That Give the Game International Appeal," in *Hockey Research Journal*, Volume 11, 2007, pp. 1–4.

Lalonde, Newsy. *Personal Scrapbook*. Unpublished Collection.

Lappage, R. S. "The Kenora Thistles' Stanley Cup Trail," in *Canadian Journal of History of Sport*, Volume 19, December 1988, pp. 79–100.

Lorenz, Stacy L. and Geraint B. Osborne. "Brutal Butchery, Strenuous Spectacle: Hockey Violence, Manhood, and the 1907 Season" in John Chi-Kit Wong, ed., *Coast to Coast: Hockey in Canada to the Second World War*, Toronto: University of Toronto Press, 2009, pp. 160–202.

Mason, Daniel Scott. "The Origins and Development of the International Hockey League and its Effects on the Sport of Professional Ice Hockey in North America," M.A. Thesis, University of British Columbia, 1994.

———. "The International Hockey League and the Professionalization of Ice Hockey 1904–1907," in *Journal of Sport History*, Volume 25, Spring 1998, pp. 1–17.

McFarlane, Brian. *The Story of the Stanley Cup*. Toronto: Pagurian Press, 1971.

———. *Legendary Stanley Cup Stories*. Bolton: Fenn Publishing, 2008.

McParland, Kelly. *The Lives of Conn Smythe: From the Battlefield to Maple Leaf Gardens, A Hockey Icon's Story*. Toronto: Fenn-McClelland & Stewart, 2011.

McKinley, Michael. *Putting a Roof on Winter: Hockey's Rise from Sport to Spectacle*. Vancouver: Greystone Books, 2000.

————. *Hockey: A People's History*. Toronto: McClelland & Stewart, 2006.

Metcalfe, Alan. *Canada Learns to Play: The Emergence of Organized Sport 1807–1914*. Toronto: McClelland & Stewart, 1987.

————. "Power: A Case Study of the Ontario Hockey Association, 1890–1936," in *Journal of Sports History*, Volume 19, Spring 1992, pp. 5–25.

Mickowski, Howard. *Hockeyology: Digging Up Hockey's Past*. Tchuti Press, 1999.

————. "Being a Hockey Fan in 1900: A Chilly Rink Through a Smoky Haze" in Dan Diamond, ed., *Total Hockey: The Official Encyclopedia of the National Hockey League*, New York: Total Sports, 2000, pp. 25–26.

Milks, James, ed. *Pucklore: The Hockey Research Anthology Volume 1*. Fox Music Books, 2010.

Morrison, John and Doug McLatchy. *A Year in the History of the Toronto Blue Shirts a.k.a. the Torontos: The NHL's First Stanley Cup Champions 1917–1918*. Stouffville: Hockey Information Service, 1996.

Morrow, Don. "A Case Study in Amateur Conflict: The Athletic War in Canada 1906–08," in *British Journal of Sports History*, Volume 3, September 1986, pp. 173–190.

Mott, Morris K. "The Problems of Professionalism: The Manitoba Amateur Athletic Association and the Fight Against Pro Hockey" in Elise A. Corbet and Anthony W. Rasporich, eds., *Winter Sports in the West*, Calgary: Historical Society of Alberta, 1990, pp. 132–42.

Neale, Walter C. "The Peculiar Economics of Professional Sports," in *Quarterly Journal of Economics*, Volume 78, February 1964, pp. 1–14.

O'Hanley, Don. "From Steel Rails to Jet Trails" in Dan Diamond, ed., *Total Hockey: The Official Encyclopedia of the National Hockey League*, New York: Total Sports, 2000, pp. 87–88.

————. "Why the Trolley League?" in *Hockey Research Journal*, Volume 4, 1999, pp. 42–47.

Owen, Gerald. "The Origins of 'Hockey': Behind the Dictionary Definition" in Dan Diamond, ed., *Total Hockey: The Official Encyclopedia of the National Hockey League*, New York: Total Sports, 2000, pp. 3–4.

Oxley, J. Macdonald. "Midwinter in Canada," in *Christian Union*, Volume 45, January 30, 1892, pp. 196–97.

Paddick, Robert J. "Amateurism: An Idea of the Past or a Necessity for the Future?" in *Olympika: The International Journal of Olympic Studies*, Volume 3, 1994, pp. 1–15.

Patterson, Charles. "Hockey: A National Winter Game," in *Outing: An Illustrated Monthly Magazine of Recreation*, Volume 41, February 1903, pp. 622–27.

Pope, S. W. "Amateurism and American Sports Culture: The Invention of an Athletic Tradition in the United States 1870–1900," in *International Journal of the History of Sport*, Volume 13, 1996, pp. 290–309.

Poulton, Ron. *The Paper Tyrant: John Ross Robertson of the Toronto Telegram*. Toronto: Clarke, Irwin, 1971.

Purcell, John W. "English Sport and Canadian Culture in Toronto 1867 to 1911," M.P.E. Thesis, University of Windsor, 1974.

Reddick, Don. "The Genesis of Dawson's Stanley Cup Challenge," in *Hockey Research Journal*, Volume 4, 1999, pp. 63–69.

Roche, Wilfrid Victor (Bill), ed. *The Hockey Book*. Toronto: McClelland & Stewart, 1953.

Roxborough, Henry. *The Stanley Cup Story: Revised Edition*. Toronto: McGraw-Hill Ryerson, 1971.

Selke, Frank J. with Gordon Green. *Behind the Cheering*. Toronto: McClelland & Stewart, 1962.

Shea, Kevin and John Jason Wilson. *Lord Stanley: The Man Behind the Cup*. Toronto: Fenn Publishing, 2006.

Shields, Norman. "James George Alywin Creighton (1850–1930)," Historic Sites and Monument Board of Canada Report Number 2008–01.

Shubert, Howard. "The Changing Experience of Hockey Spectatorship: Architecture, Design, Technology, and Economics," in Colin D. Howell, ed., *Putting it on Ice*, Volume I: Hockey and Cultural Identities, 2002, pp. 59–63.

Slater, Kevin. *Trolley League: The Complete History of the Ontario Professional Hockey League 1908–1911*. Online Publication.

———. "Rivalry and Ringers: The Temiskaming Senior Hockey League, 1905–1907," in *Hockey Research Journal*, Volume 15, 2011, pp. 11–15.

Smythe, Conn with Scott Young. *If You Can't Beat 'Em in the Alley: The Memoirs of the Late Conn Symthe*. Toronto: McClelland & Stewart, 1981.

Sproule, Bill. "Houghton: The Birthplace of Professional Hockey," in *Hockey Research Journal*, Volume 8, 2004, pp. 1–4.

———. "The Allan Cup: Hockey's Second-Oldest Trophy," in *Hockey Research Journal*, Volume 14, 2010, pp. 17–21.

Stevens, Julie. "The Development of the Canadian Hockey System: A Process of Institutional Divergence and Convergence," in Colin D. Howell, ed., *Putting it on Ice*, Volume II: Internationalizing "Canada's Game," 2002, pp. 51–64.

Sullivan, Jack. *The Grey Cup Story*. Toronto: Pagurian Press, 1971.

Urquhart, M. C., ed. *Historical Statistics of Canada*. Cambridge: Cambridge University Press, 1965.

Valverde, Mariana. *The Age of Light, Soap & Water: Moral Reform in English Canada, 1825–1925*. Toronto: McClelland & Stewart, 1991.

Vigneault, Michel. "The Montreal Hockey Tradition," in *Hockey Research Journal*, Volume 1, 1993, pp. 8–9.

———. "Montreal Ice-Hockey Rinks 1875–1917," in *Hockey Research Journal*, Volume 3, 1997, pp. 8–14.

Vincent, Guy R. "North Skates South: North American Professional Hockey Throughout the Twentieth Century," in Colin D. Howell, ed., *Putting it on Ice*, Volume II: Internationalizing "Canada's Game," 2002, pp. 1–10.

Warren, H. D. "Hockey in Ontario," in *Dominion Illustrated Monthly*, Volume 2, February–September 1893, pp. 99–108.

Whelan, James. "Kings of the Ice," in *The Beaver*, February–March 1994, pp. 28–36.

Whitehead, Eric. *Cyclone Taylor: A Hockey Legend*. Toronto: Doubleday Canada, 1977.

Wiebe, Gary. *Hockey in Berlin*. Kitchener: Centre Ice Hockey News, 1997.

Wilson, George, Manson, Lyall and Lily Worrall. *Down the Lane (Again): Volume 2*. Cornwall: Stormont, Dundas, & Glengarry Historical Society, 2005.

Wilton, Peter. "Pioneer Executive W. A. Hewitt: Hockey's Rapid Growth in the Early 1900s Challenged the Game's Organizers" in Dan Diamond, ed., *Total Hockey: The Official Encyclopedia of the National Hockey League*, New York: Total Sports, 2000, pp. 29–31.

Wise, S. F. "Sport and Class Values in Old Ontario and Quebec" in W. H. Heick and Roger Graham, eds., *His Own Man: Essays in Honour of Arthur Reginald Marsden Lower*, 1974, pp. 93–117.

Wise, S. F. and Douglas Fisher. *Canada's Sporting Heroes*. Don Mills: General Publishing Company, 1974.

Witmer, James. *The Berlin Professional Hockey Club*. Self-published, 1993.

Wong, John Chi-Kit. *Lords of the Rinks: The Emergence of the National Hockey League 1875–1936*. Toronto: University of Toronto Press, 2005.

———. "Boomtown Hockey: The Vancouver Millionaires" in John Chi-Kit Wong, ed., *Coast to Coast: Hockey in Canada to the Second World War*, 2009, pp. 223–57.

Wong, John, and Michel Vigneault. "An English Team in a French Environment: The Rise and Fall of Professional Hockey in Quebec City, 1911–1920," in Colin D. Howell, ed., *Putting it on Ice*, Volume I: Hockey and Cultural Identities, 2002, pp. 17–23.

Young, Scott. *100 Years of Dropping the Puck: A History of the OHA*. Toronto: McClelland & Stewart, 1989.

Young, Scott and Astrid Young. *O'Brien*. Toronto: Ryerson Press, 1967.

Zukerman, Earl. "McGill University: The Missing Link to the Birthplace of Hockey" in Dan Diamond, ed., *Total Hockey: The Official Encyclopedia of the National Hockey League*, New York: Total Sports, 2000, pp. 16–19.

Zweig, Eric. "Kenora vs Brandon: The Small Town Series that Disappeared," in *Hockey Research Journal*, Volume 5, 2001, pp. 17–20.

———. "P. D. Ross: How He Came to be a Stanley Cup Trustee," in *Hockey Research Journal*, Volume 10, 2006, pp. 4–6.

———. "Setting Cyclone's Story Straight," in *Hockey Research Journal*, Volume 11, 2007, pp. 47–50.

————. "Torontos Defeat Victorias: How the *Toronto Star* Saw It," in *Hockey Research Journal*, Volume 12, 2008, pp. 53–55.

FILMS AND TELEVISION

Hockey: A People's History, 2006
Mary Poppins, 1964

INSTITUTIONAL PUBLICATIONS

Census of Canada
Episcopal Church Diocesan Bulletin
McMaster University Monthly
Ontario County Registries
Ontario Hockey Association Constitution and Rules
Toronto City Directories
Upper Canada College Times
Veterans Affairs Canada Service Records

NEWSPAPERS

Belleville Intelligencer
Berlin Telegraph
Calgary Albertan
Calgary Herald
Cornwall Freeholder
Cornwall Standard
Cornwall Standard-Freeholder
Edmonton Bulletin
Edmonton Capital
Edmonton Journal
Edmonton News
Galt Reporter
Guelph Mercury
Hamilton Spectator
Houghton Mining Gazette
Kansas City Times
Lincoln Star
London Free Press
Montreal Gazette
Montreal Star
Orillia Times
Ottawa Citizen
Ottawa Journal
Pittsburgh Gazette

Sault Ste. Marie Star
St. Catharines Standard
Strathcona Chronicle
Strathcona Plaindealer
Toronto Globe
Toronto Globe and Mail
Toronto Mail
Toronto Mail and Empire
Toronto News
Toronto Star
Toronto Telegram
Toronto World
Vancouver Sun
Winnipeg Free Press
Winnipeg Telegram
Winnipeg Tribune

WEBSITES

Ancestry Canada
Angus Carroll Blog
Archives of Ontario
Canada GenWeb Project
Canadian Great War Project
Canadian Football Hall of Fame
Classic Auctions
Copper Country Hockey History
FAQ Archives
Find A Grave
Habs Eyes on the Prize
Hockey Hall of Fame
Kansas City Public Library
Library and Archives Canada
McCord Museum
National Hockey League
RootsWeb
Society for International Hockey Research
Sports Card Forum
St. Catharines Athletics Lacrosse History
Waterloo Region Generations
Wikia
Wikipedia

ILLUSTRATION CREDITS

Page 82   *Toronto News*, November 23, 1906, p. 10. Courtesy of Toronto Public Library.

Page 83   *Toronto News*, November 15, 1906, p. 10. Courtesy of Toronto Public Library.

Page 84   *Toronto News*, January 18, 1907, p. 8. Courtesy of Toronto Public Library.

Page 85   Hockey Hall of Fame.

Page 86   *Toronto News*, January 6, 1904, p. 8. Courtesy of Toronto Public Library.

Page 87   *Toronto Globe*, January 22, 1902, p. 10. Courtesy of Toronto Public Library and *The Globe and Mail*.

Page 89 (top) John Kerr. *Curling in Canada and the United States*. Toronto: The Toronto News Co., Ltd., 1904, p. 327.

Page 89 (bottom) John Kerr. *Curling in Canada and the United States*. Toronto: The Toronto News Co., Ltd., 1904, p. 327.

Page 98   *Toronto Globe*, December 28, 1906, p. 8. Courtesy of Toronto Public Library and *The Globe and Mail*.

Page 100 *Toronto News*, December 7, 1906, p. 10. Courtesy of Toronto Public Library.

Page 101 *Toronto Globe*, December 22, 1903, p. 10. Courtesy of Toronto Public Library and *The Globe and Mail*.

Page 102 *Toronto News*, January 26, 1907, p. 20. Courtesy of Toronto Public Library.

Page 103 *Toronto Star*, January 3, 1907, p. 10. Reproduction courtesy of Toronto Public Library.

Page 104 *Toronto News*, January 19, 1907, p. 20. Courtesy of Toronto Public Library.

Page 105 Hockey Hall of Fame.

Page 107 *Toronto News*, January 28, 1907, p. 8. Courtesy of Toronto Public Library.

Page 109 *Toronto News*, January 26 1907, p. 20. Courtesy of Toronto Public Library.

Page 111 Society for International Hockey Research.

Page 112 Hockey Hall of Fame.

Page 113 Hockey Hall of Fame.

Page 114 Hockey Hall of Fame.

Page 119 "Tom Longboat, the Canadian Runner, standing with trophy besides him," April 22, 1907. Library and Archives Canada/Credit: Charles A. Aylett/Canadian Intellectual Property Office fonds/C–014090.

Page 123 Hockey Hall of Fame.

Page 126 *Toronto Star*, November 13, 1907, p. 10. Reproduction courtesy of Toronto Public Library.

Page 127 *Toronto Star*, March, 16 1908, p. 9. Reproduction courtesy of Toronto Public Library.

Page 128 Hockey Hall of Fame.

Page 129   Michigan Technological University Archives and Copper Country Historical Collections.

Page 131   *Toronto News*, December 28, 1907, p. 9. Courtesy of Toronto Public Library.

Page 132   Hockey Hall of Fame.

Page 133   Kevin Slater. *Trolley League: The Complete History of the Ontario Professional Hockey League*, p. A30.

Page 134   Hockey Hall of Fame.

Page 139   *Toronto Star*, February 24, 1908, p. 8. Reproduction courtesy of Toronto Public Library.

Page 140   Image courtesy of Classic Auctions.

Page 143   *Toronto Star*, February 3, 1908, p. 10. Reproduction courtesy of Toronto Public Library.

Page 144   *Toronto Star*, February 17, 1908, p. 9. Reproduction courtesy of Toronto Public Library.

Page 146   *Toronto Star*, February 28, 1908, p. 12. Reproduction courtesy of Toronto Public Library.

Page 147   Society for International Hockey Research.

Page 149   *Toronto Telegram*, January 15, 1909, p. 8. Courtesy of Toronto Public Library.

Page 151   *Montreal Star*, March 14, 1908, p. 22.

Page 155   Hockey Hall of Fame.

Page 158   *Toronto Telegram*, March 16, 1908, p. 12. Courtesy of Toronto Public Library.

Page 162   Photo sourced from *Maclean's*.

Page 163   *Montreal Star*, September 1, 1908, p. 2.

Page 165   *An Encyclopedia of Canadian biography. Containing brief sketches and steel engravings of Canada's prominent men (July 1904)*. Montreal: Montreal Canadian Press Syndicate, 1904, p. 17.

Page 167   Hockey Hall of Fame.

Page 169   *Toronto Globe*, December 18, 1903, p. 10. Courtesy of Toronto Public Library and *The Globe and Mail*.

Page 170   *Toronto News*, January 22, 1909, p. 8. Courtesy of Toronto Public Library.

Page 171   Society for International Hockey Research.

Page 173   *Toronto News*, January 15, 1909, p. 8. Courtesy of Toronto Public Library.

Page 175   Photo courtesy of Athleticslacrosse.com (St. Catharines Athletics Lacrosse).

Page 177   *Toronto News*, January 23, 1909, p. 8. Courtesy of Toronto Public Library.

Page 178   Courtesy of Harold McNamara via Glen Goodhand.

Page 182   *Toronto Star*, January 20, 1909, p. 9.

Page 184   *Toronto News*, January 27, 1909, p. 8. Courtesy of Toronto Public Library.

Page 186 *Toronto Star*, January 7, 1910, p. 15. Reproduction courtesy of Toronto Public Library.

Page 188 *Toronto News*, January 30, 1909, p. 8. Courtesy of Toronto Public Library.

Page 189 *Toronto News*, February 15, 1909, p. 8. Courtesy of Toronto Public Library.

Page 191 Hockey Hall of Fame

Page 193 *Toronto Star*, February 19, 1909, p. 12.

Page 195 *Toronto Star*, February 24, 1909, p. 12.

Page 197 *Toronto Mail and Empire*, November 20, 1909, p. 9. Courtesy of Toronto Public Library and *The Globe and Mail*.

Page 200 *Toronto News*, November 5, 1906, p. 8. Courtesy of Toronto Public Library.

Page 203 *Toronto Telegram*, November 26, 1909, p. 8. Courtesy of Toronto Public Library.

Page 205 (top) Arthur George Racey, M20111.82, McCord Museum.

Page 205 (bottom) Arthur George Racey, M20111.42, McCord Museum.

Page 206 *Toronto Mail and Empire*, December 6, 1909, p. 9. Courtesy of Toronto Public Library and *The Globe and Mail*.

Page 208 *Toronto News*, January 9, 1905, p. 8. Courtesy of Toronto Public Library.

Page 209 *Toronto News*, March 2, 1907, p. 24. Courtesy of Toronto Public Library.

Page 211 *Toronto News*, March 7, 1908, p. 8. Courtesy of Toronto Public Library.

Page 214 *Toronto News*, April 29, 1911, p. 15. Courtesy of Toronto Public Library.

Page 224 *Toronto News*, December 26, 1912, p. 9. Courtesy of Toronto Public Library.

Page 227 *Toronto Star*, November 3, 1911, p. 14. Reproduction courtesy of Toronto Public Library.

Page 230 *Toronto News*, February 29, 1912, p. 8. Courtesy of Toronto Public Library.

Page 233 *Toronto Star*, December 27, 1912, p. 12. Reproduction courtesy of Toronto Public Library.

Page 234 Hockey Hall of Fame.

Page 239 *Toronto News*, November 7, 1913, p. 9. Courtesy of Toronto Public Library.

Page 241 *Toronto News*, December 18, 1912, p. 9. Courtesy of Toronto Public Library.

Page 242 *Toronto News*, January 4, 1913, p. 8. Courtesy of Toronto Public Library.

Page 243 Hockey Hall of Fame.

Page 245 *Toronto News*, January 23, 1913, p. 8. Courtesy of Toronto Public Library.

Page 248 *Toronto News*, February 5, 1914, p. 8. Courtesy of Toronto Public Library.

Page 252 *Toronto Star*, March 5, 1914, p. 8. Reproduction courtesy of Toronto Public Library.

Page 255   Hockey Hall of Fame.

Page 256   *Toronto Star*, March 14, 1914, p. 20. Reproduction courtesy of Toronto Public Library.

Page 259   *Toronto Telegram*, March 20, 1914, p. 20. Courtesy of Toronto Public Library.

Page 263   Hockey Hall of Fame.

Page 264   Hockey Hall of Fame.

Page 267   *Toronto Globe*, June 1, 1918, p. 11. Courtesy of Toronto Public Library and *The Globe and Mail*.

Page 269   Hockey Hall of Fame.

Page 271   Hockey Hall of Fame.

Page 273   "The Seattle Metropolitans—Stanley Cup winners in 1916–17." Library and Archives Canada/The National Hockey League/AMICUS 26950055/p. 29.

Page 274   Hockey Hall of Fame.

Page 275   *Toronto Star*, November 23, 1916, p. 1. Reproduction courtesy of Toronto Public Library.

Page 276   "Morrison, Bertram Clifford, SPR, Regimental Number 1096070." Library and Archives Canada/RG 150/accession 1992–93/166, box 6400–30.

Page 278   Missouri Valley Special Collections, Kansas City Public Library, Kansas City, Missouri.

Page 282   *Toronto Star*, June 4, 1925, p. 1. Reproduction courtesy of Toronto Public Library.

Page 284   Imperial Oil—Turofsky/Hockey Hall of Fame.

Insert page 1   C 11-142, D. B. Dick's architectural drawings of the Queen's Hotel in Toronto, Ontario (1877–1901) Lithograph, K-70 F006673.

Insert page 2 (top left)   Michigan Technological University Archives and Copper Country Historical Collections.

Insert page 2 (bottom)   Library and Archives, Heinz History Center.

Insert page 3 (top)   Image courtesy of Peel's Prairie Provinces (http://peel.library .ualberta.ca), a digital initiative of the University of Alberta Libraries.

Insert page 3 (bottom right)   *Toronto Mail and Empire*, January 22, 1896, p. 2. Courtesy of Toronto Public Library and *The Globe and Mail*.

Insert pages 4–5   "Exhibition Building," March 1903, Ottawa, Ontario Library and Archives Canada/Credit: William James Topley/Topley Studio fonds/ PA-009125.

Insert page 6 (top)   City of Toronto Archives, Series 330, File 228 Item 0029.

Insert page 6 (bottom)   Michigan Technological University Archives and Copper Country Historical Collections.

Insert page 7   Courtesy of Bibliothèque et Archives nationales du Québec.

Insert page 8 (top left)   Greg Stoicoiu.

Insert page 8 (top right) Greg Stoicoiu.

Insert page 8 (bottom left) Greg Stoicoiu.

Insert page 8 (bottom right) Greg Stoicoiu.

Insert page 9 *Toronto Star*, January 5, 1909, p. 13. Reproduction courtesy of Toronto Public Library.

Insert page 10 (top) Pittaway Postcard, 1910.

Insert page 10 (bottom) "The Arena, Dey's Rink," February 10, 1908, Ottawa, Ontario Library and Archives Canada/Credit: G.A.E. Chapman/George Arthur Emerson Chapman fonds/PA-203558.

Insert page 11 (top left) *Logansport Reporter*, July 2, 1908, p. 6. Reproduction courtesy of Indiana State Library.

Insert page 11 (bottom) Carnegie Library of Pittsburgh. All rights reserved. Unauthorized reproduction or usage prohibited.

Insert page 12 (top left) Greg Stoicoiu.

Insert page 12 (top right) Greg Stoicoiu.

Insert page 12 (centre left) Greg Stoicoiu.

Insert page 12 (centre right) Greg Stoicoiu.

Insert page 12 (bottom) Greg Stoicoiu.

Insert page 13 (top left) Greg Stoicoiu.

Insert page 13 (top right) Greg Stoicoiu.

Insert page 13 (bottom left) Greg Stoicoiu.

Insert page 13 (bottom right) Greg Stoicoiu.

Insert page 14 "Renfrew Hockey Team 1909–10," Renfrew, Ontario Library and Archives Canada/Harry Hinchley fonds/C-015278.

Insert page 15 (top middle) Hockey Hall of Fame.

Insert page 15 (top right) Hockey Hall of Fame.

Insert page 15 (centre left) Hockey Hall of Fame.

Insert page 15 (centre middle) Hockey Hall of Fame.

Insert page 15 (centre right) Hockey Hall of Fame.

Insert page 15 (bottom left) Hockey Hall of Fame.

Insert page 15 (bottom middle) Hockey Hall of Fame.

Insert page 16 "Boys choosing sides for hockey on Sarnia Bay," December 29, 1908, Sarnia, Ontario Library and Archives Canada/Credit: John Boyd/John Boyd fonds/PA-060732.

STATISTICAL RECORDS, 1906–1909

PRO HOCKEY STANDINGS 1906–1907

Ontario Pro Hockey Exhibitions*

TEAM	GP	W	L	T	GF	GA
Guelph Royals	5	4	1	0	28	19
Berlin Dutchmen	5	2	2	1	32	28
Toronto Professionals	8	2	5	1	49	64
Belleville Red & Whites	1	0	1	0	2	6
Barrie Professionals	1	0	1	0	4	12

* Including games against outside teams

Eastern Canada Amateur Hockey Association

TEAM	GP	W	L	T	GF	GA
Montreal Wanderers	10	10	0	0	105	39
Ottawa Silver Seven	10	7	3	0	76	54
Montreal Victorias	10	6	4	0	101	70
Montreal Wheelers	10	3	7	0	58	83
Quebec Bulldogs	10	2	8	0	62	88
Montreal Shamrocks	10	2	8	0	52	120

Federal Amateur Hockey League

TEAM	GP	W	L	T	GF	GA
Montreal Montagnards	11	8	1	2	74	53
Cornwall HC	11	6	4	1	58	39
Ottawa Victorias*	11	6	4	1	43	54
Morrisburg HC	11	0	11	0	25	54

* Awarded championship after Montagnard and Cornwall withdrew

Upper Ottawa Valley Hockey League

TEAM	GP	W	L	T	GF	GA
Renfrew Creamery Kings	8	6	1	1		
Pembroke Seniors	8	2	4	2	SCORING	
Arnprior HC	8	2	5	1	N/A	

Temiskaming Hockey League

TEAM	GP	W	L	T	GF	GA
Cobalt Silver Kings						
Haileybury Comets		STANDINGS				
Latchford HC		N/A				
New Liskeard HC						

Manitoba Professional Hockey League

TEAM	GP	W	L	T	GF	GA
Kenora Thistles	6	4	2	0	38	19
Brandon Wheat Cities	10*	4	2	0	53	41
Portage la Prairie HC	10*	3	3	0	37	36
Winnipeg Strathconas	10*	1	5	0	38	70

* Games not involving Kenora counted in pairs

International Hockey League

TEAM	GP	W	L	T	GF	GA
Hougton Portage Lakers	24	16	8	0	102	102
Sault Ste. Marie Algonquins*	24	13	11	0	124	123
Pittsburgh Pirates	25	12	12	1	94	82
Sault Ste. Marie Wolverines**	24	11	13	0	103	88
Calumet Miners	25	8	16	1	96	124

* "Canadian Soo"

** "American Soo"

STANLEY CUP PLAYOFFS 1906–1907

FINAL*

Montreal Wanderers (Eastern) vs New Glasgow Cubs (Nova Scotia)

| December 27, 1906 | New Glasgow Cubs 3 | at Montreal Wanderers 10 |
| December 29, 1906 | New Glasgow Cubs 2 | at Montreal Wanderers 7 |

MONTREAL WANDERERS win total-goals 17–5

FINAL*

Montreal Wanderers (Eastern) vs Kenora Thistles (Manitoba)

| January 17, 1907 | Kenora Thistles 4 | at Montreal Wanderers 2 |
| January 21, 1907 | Kenora Thistles 8 | at Montreal Wanderers 6 |

KENORA THISTLES win total-goals 12–8

LEAGUE

Kenora Thistles (Manitoba) vs Brandon Wheat Cities (runner-up)
March 16, 1907   Brandon Wheat Cities 6   vs Kenora Thistles 8
March 18, 1907   Brandon Wheat Cities 1   vs Kenora Thistles 4
KENORA THISTLES win best-of-three 2–0

FINAL

Kenora Thistles (Manitoba) vs Montreal Wanderers (Eastern)
March 23, 1907   Montreal Wanderers 7   at Kenora Thistles 2
March 25, 1907   Montreal Wanderers 5   at Kenora Thistles 6
MONTREAL WANDERERS win total-goals 12–8

SEMI-FINAL**

Ottawa Victorias (Federal) vs Renfrew Creamery Kings (Upper Ottawa Valley)
December 27, 1907   Renfrew Creamery Kings 1 at Ottawa Victorias 4
December 30, 1907   Ottawa Victorias 1 at Renfrew Creamery Kings 3
OTTAWA VICTORIAS win total-goals 5–4

FINAL**

Montreal Wanderers (Eastern) vs Ottawa Victorias (Federal)
January 9, 1908   Ottawa Victorias 3   at Montreal Wanderers 9
January 13, 1908   Ottawa Victorias 1   at Montreal Wanderers 13
MONTREAL WANDERERS win total-goals 22–4

* Series brought forward from 1905–1906

** Series held over to 1907–1908

TORONTO PROFESSIONALS RECORD 1906–1907

DATE	SCORE	H/A	OPPONENT
December 28	0–7	vs	Sault Ste. Marie Algonquins
January 17	8–7	vs	Sault Ste. Marie Wolverines
January 25	8–9	vs	Kenora Thistles
January 30	4–9	at	Guelph Royals
February 4	9–5	vs	Pittsburgh Pirates
February 26	7–7	at	Berlin Dutchmen
March 1	3–8	vs	Berlin Dutchmen
March 11	10–12	vs	Montreal Wanderers

PLAYER	GP	GF(GA)
Bruce Ridpath	8	16
Jack Carmichael	8	11
Rolly Young	8	5
Hugh Lambe	8	1
Mark Tooze	8	(64)
Charlie Liffiton	5	13
Frank McLaren	4	0
Harry Burgoyne	3	3
Joe Ouelette	2	0
Howard Gee	1	0
Bert Brown	1	0
Ezra Dumart	1	0

PRO HOCKEY STANDINGS 1907–1908

Ontario Professional Hockey League*

TEAM	GP	W	L	T	GF	GA
Toronto Professionals	12	10	2	0	88	55
Berlin Dutchmen	11	6	5	0	57	49
Brantford Braves	12	5	7	0	65	79
Guelph Royals	11	2	9	0	3	60

* Actual results, ignoring one game defaulted by Guelph to Berlin

Ontario Pro Hockey Exhibitions*

TEAM	GP	W	L	T	GF	GA
Toronto Professionals	4	3	1	0	41	28
Berlin Dutchmen	4	2	2	0	21	22
St. Catharines Athletics	1	1	0	0	12	2
Brantford Braves	1	1	0	0	10	6
Guelph Royals	3	1	2	0	15	21
Ontario All-Stars	1	0	1	0	10	16
Hamilton Tigers	1	0	1	0	2	12

* Including games against outside teams

Eastern Canada Amateur Hockey Association

TEAM	GP	W	L	T	GF	GA
Montreal Wanderers	10	8	2	0	63	52
Ottawa Silver Seven	10	7	3	0	86	51
Quebec Bulldogs	10	5	5	0	81	74
Montreal Shamrocks	10	5	5	0	53	49

| Montreal Victorias | 10 | 4 | 6 | 0 | 73 | 78 |
| Montreal Wheelers | 10 | 1 | 9 | 0 | 53 | 105 |

Federal Hockey League

TEAM	GP	W	L	T	GF	GA
Ottawa Victorias	4	2	2	0	32	22
Cornwall HC	5	2	3	0	22	44
Brockville Invincibles	1	1	0	0	12	0

Upper Ottawa Valley Hockey League

TEAM	GP	W	L	T	GF	GA
Renfrew Creamery Kings	4	4	0	0	33	16
Pembroke Seniors	4	2	2	0	20	22
Arnprior HC	4	0	4	0	15	30

Temiskaming Hockey League

TEAM	GP	W	L	T	GF	GA
New Liskeard HC	8	6	2	0		
Haileybury Comets	8	6	2	0	SCORING	
Cobalt Silver Kings	8	0	8	0	N/A	

New Ontario Hockey League

TEAM	GP	W	L	T	GF	GA
Fort William Wanderers	11	8	3	0	47	29
Port Arthur Lake Cities	9	4	5	0	47	38
Port Arthur Thunder Bays	9	4	5	0	35	39
Fort William Arenas	5	1	4	0	6	29

Manitoba Professional Hockey League*

TEAM	GP	W	L	T	GF	GA
Winnipeg Maple Leafs	17	11	6	0	110	89
Portage la Prairie HC	15	8	7	0	76	73
Winnipeg Strathconas	16	6	10	0	108	113
Brandon Wheat Cities	1	0	1	0	0	4
Kenora Thistles	1	0	1	0	1	16

* Actual results, ignoring defaulted games

Interprovincial Hockey League

TEAM	GP	W	L	T	GF	GA
Edmonton Seniors	10	7	2	1	70	51
Strathcona HC	9	4	4	1	43	48
North Battleford HC	9	2	7	0	53	67

Western Pennsylvania Hockey League

TEAM	GP	W	L	T	GF	GA
Pittsburgh Bankers	19	12	4	3	81	59
Pittsburgh Lyceums	17	11	5	1	77	49
Pittsburgh Pirates	17	5	10	2	59	70
Pittsburgh Athletics	17	3	12	2	41	80

STANLEY CUP PLAYOFFS 1907–1908

LEAGUE

Montreal Wanderers (Eastern) vs Ottawa Silver Seven (runner-up)
February 29, 1908   Ottawa Silver Seven 2   at Montreal Wanderers 4
March 4, 1908   Montreal Wanderers 6   at Montreal Shamrocks 4
MONTREAL WANDERERS win key game (February 29) and clinching game (March 4)

FINAL

Montreal Wanderers (Eastern) vs Winnipeg Maple Leafs (Manitoba)
March 10, 1908   Winnipeg Maple Leafs 5 at Montreal Wanderers 11
March 12, 1908   Winnipeg Maple Leafs 3 at Montreal Wanderers 9
MONTREAL WANDERERS win total-goals 20–8

FINAL

Montreal Wanderers (Eastern) vs Toronto Professionals (Ontario)
March 14, 1908   Toronto Professionals 4   at Montreal Wanderers 6
MONTREAL WANDERERS win sudden-death game

FINAL**

Montreal Wanderers (Eastern) vs Edmonton Seniors (Interprovincial)
December 28, 1908   Edmonton Seniors 3   at Montreal Wanderers 7
December 30, 1908   Edmonton Seniors 7   at Montreal Wanderers 6
MONTREAL WANDERERS win total-goals 13–10

** Series held over to 1908–1909

TORONTO PROFESSIONALS RECORD 1907–1908

DATE	SCORE	H/A	OPPONENT
January 4	0–3	vs	Berlin Dutchmen
January 10	6–7	at	Brantford Braves
January 13	4–3	at	Guelph Royals
January 18	7–2	vs	Guelph Royals
January 24	6–5	at	Berlin Dutchmen (OT)
February 1	10–7	vs	Brantford Braves
February 11	11–8	at	Brantford Braves
February 15	5–4	vs	Berlin Dutchmen
February 22	10–7	vs	Guelph Royals
February 25	9–1	at	Berlin Dutchmen
February 27	8–5	at	Guelph Royals
February 29	12–3	vs	Brantford Braves
March 11	16–10	vs	Ontario All-Stars
March 14	4–6	at	Montreal Wanderers
March 20	4–8	at	Berlin Dutchmen
March 21	12–6	at	Guelph Royals
March 23	9–4	at	Berlin Dutchmen (game played in Galt)

PLAYER	GP	GF(GA)*
Con Corbeau	17	3
Bruce Ridpath	15	12
Chuck Tyner	15	(79)
Newsy Lalonde	14	56
Walter Mercer	14	14
Rolly Young	14	12
Bert Morrison	10	20
Hugh Lambe	5	0
Jack Marks	4	9
Ken Mallen	3	2
Harvey Corbeau	2	0
Donald Smith	1	5
Howard Gee	1	0
Jim McGinnis	1	0
Bert Booth	1	(4)
Charlie Ellis	1	(6)

* Including estimates when scorers unknown

PRO HOCKEY STANDINGS 1908–1909

Ontario Professional Hockey League*

TEAM	GP	W	L	T	GF	GA
Galt Indians	16	12	3	1	110	81
Brantford Braves	16	9	6	1	113	103
Berlin Dutchmen	15	9	6	0	96	72
Toronto Professionals	15	5	10	0	105	111
Guelph Royals	6	1	5	0	28	56
St. Catharines Athletics	6	0	6	0	29	58

* Actual results, ignoring defaults assigned to Guelph and St. Catharines

Ontario Pro Hockey Exhibitions*

TEAM	GP	W	L	T	GF	GA
Berlin Dutchmen	7	3	2	2	36	34
Galt Indians	8	3	4	1	43	45
Brantford Braves	2	2	0	0	27	11
Guelph Royals	4	2	2	0	15	18
Toronto Professionals	3	1	1	1	14	16
St. Catharines Athletics	1	0	1	0	3	13

* Including games against outside teams

Eastern Canada Hockey Association

TEAM	GP	W	L	T	GF	GA
Ottawa Silver Seven	12	10	2	0	117	63
Montreal Wanderers	12	9	3	0	82	61
Quebec Bulldogs	12	3	9	0	78	106
Montreal Shamrocks	12	2	10	0	56	103

Federal Hockey League

TEAM	GP	W	L	T	GF	GA
Renfrew Creamery Kings	6	6	0	0	93	25
Ottawa Senators	6	3	3	0	37	38
Smiths Falls HC	6	2	4	0	34	71
Cornwall HC	6	1	5	0	30	60

Temiskaming Hockey League

TEAM	GP	W	L	T	GF	GA
Cobalt Silver Kings	8	6	2	0	64	32
Haileybury Comets	8	5	2	1	53	42
New Liskeard HC	8	0	7	1	24	67

New Ontario Hockey League

TEAM	GP	W	L	T	GF	GA
Port Arthur Thunder Bays	12	8	4	0	55	42
Fort William Forts	12	7	4	1	54	42
Fort William Wanderers	12	6	5	1	44	40
Port Arthur HC	12	2	10	0	36	65

Manitoba Professional Hockey League

FIRST HALF

TEAM	GP	W	L	T	GF	GA
Winnipeg Maple Leafs	4	4	0	0	37	21
Winnipeg Shamrocks	4	1	3	0	22	29
Winnipeg Winnipegs	2	0	2	0	13	22

SECOND HALF

TEAM	GP	W	L	T	GF	GA
Winnipeg Shamrocks	5	4	1	0	48	35
Winnipeg Maple Leafs	5	1	4	0	35	48

Interprovincial Pro Hockey Exhibitions

TEAM	GP	W	L	T	GF	GA
Edmonton Seniors	10	10	0	0	95	37

Western Pennsylvania Hockey League

TEAM	GP	W	L	T	GF	GA
Pittsburgh Bankers	15	9	4	2	56	49
Pittsburgh Duquesnes	15	9	5	1	63	48
Pittsburgh Athletics	14	2	12	0	46	74
Pittsburgh Lyceums	8	4	3	1	31	25

STANLEY CUP PLAYOFFS 1908–1909

LEAGUE

Ottawa Silver Seven (Eastern) vs Montreal Wanderers (runner-up)
March 3, 1909   Montreal Wanderers 3   at Ottawa Silver Seven 8
OTTAWA SILVER SEVEN win clinching game (March 3)

FINAL**

Ottawa Silver Seven (Eastern) vs Galt Indians (Ontario)
January 5, 1910   Galt Indians 3   at Ottawa Silver Seven 12
January 7, 1910   Galt Indians 1   at Ottawa Silver Seven 3
OTTAWA SILVER SEVEN win total-goals 15–4

FINAL**

Ottawa Silver Seven (Eastern) vs Edmonton Seniors (Interprovincial)

| January 18, 1910 | Edmonton Seniors 4 | at Ottawa Silver Seven 8 |
| January 20, 1910 | Edmonton Seniors 7 | at Ottawa Silver Seven 13 |

OTTAWA SILVER SEVEN win total-goals 21–11

** Series held over to 1909–1910

TORONTO PROFESSIONALS RECORD 1908–1909

DATE	SCORE	H/A	OPPONENT
December 25	5–5	at	Berlin Dutchmen
January 2	5–4	vs	Ottawa Silver Seven
January 5	7–8	at	Berlin Dutchmen
January 9	15–8	vs	Guelph Royals
January 11	6–9	at	Brantford Braves
January 13	4–5	vs	Galt Indians
January 15	7–4	at	St. Catharines Athletics
January 18	4–5	vs	Berlin Dutchmen
January 20	4–6	at	Guelph Royals
January 27	7–3	at	Galt Indians
January 30	15–10	vs	Brantford Braves
February 1	3–6	at	Berlin Dutchmen
February 4	6–2	vs	Galt Indians
February 9	4–12	at	Brantford Braves
February 12	4–7	at	Galt Indians (game played in London)
February 16	11–16	at	Galt Indians
February 18	5–8	vs	Berlin Dutchmen
February 23	7–9	vs	Brantford Braves

PLAYER	GP	GF(GA)*
Chuck Tyner	18	(127)
Newsy Lalonde	14	33
Bruce Ridpath	13	22
Stoke Doran	11	1
Howard Manson	9	12
Donald Smith	9	8
Con Corbeau	9	1
Herb Birmingham	8	16
Skene Ronan	8	4
Hugh Lambe	6	0

Jimmy Mallen	4	8
Dubbie Kerr	4	7
Herb Fyfe	3	4
Bert Morrison	2	2
Zina Runions	2	1
Fred Young	2	0
Hank Smith	2	0
Cap McDonald	1	0
Lawson Whitehead	1	0
Harold McNamara	1	0

* Including estimates when scorers unknown

TORONTO PROFESSIONALS CLUB HISTORY

SEASON	GP	W	L	T	GF	GA
1906–1907	8	2	5	1	49	64
1907–1908	17	13	4	0	133	89
1908–1909	18	6	11	1	119	127
TOTAL	43	21	20	2	301	280

PLAYER	GP	GF(GA)*
Bruce Ridpath	36	50
Chuck Tyner	33	(206)
Newsy Lalonde	28	89
Con Corbeau	26	4
Rolly Young	22	17
Hugh Lambe	19	1
Walter Mercer	14	14
Bert Morrison	12	22
Stoke Doran	11	1
Donald Smith	10	13
Howard Manson	9	12
Herb Birmingham	8	16
Jack Carmichael	8	11
Skene Ronan	8	4
Mark Tooze	8	(64)
Charlie Liffiton	5	13
Jack Marks	4	9
Jimmy Mallen	4	8
Dubbie Kerr	4	7
Frank McLaren	4	0

Herb Fyfe	3	4
Harry Burgoyne	3	3
Ken Mallen	3	2
Zina Runions	2	1
Joe Ouelette	2	0
Howard Gee	2	0
Harvey Corbeau	2	0
Fred Young	2	0
Hank Smith	2	0
Bert Brown	1	0
Ezra Dumart	1	0
Jim McGinnis	1	0
Cap McDonald	1	0
Lawson Whitehead	1	0
Harold McNamara	1	0
Bert Booth	1	(4)
Charlie Ellis	1	(6)

* Including estimates when scorers unknown

TORONTO PROFESSIONALS PLAYER REGISTRY

PLAYER	BORN	TOWN	RETIRED	DIED
Herb Birmingham	1881	Toronto	1909	1918
Bert Booth	N/A	N/A	1910	N/A
Bert Brown	1884	Belleville	1907	N/A
Harry Burgoyne	1884	Belleville	1911	1937
Jack Carmichael	1881	Alliston	1912	N/A
Con Corbeau	1885	Penetanguishene	1912	1920
Harvey Corbeau	1881	Sault Ste. Marie	1911	1952
Stoke Doran	1884	Brockville	1915	N/A
Ezra Dumart	1882	Zurich	1913	1954
Charlie Ellis	1884	Bridge Post	1917	N/A
Herb Fyfe	1886	Acton	1909	N/A
Howard Gee	1883	Markham	1908	1963
Dubbie Kerr	1888	Brockville	1920	1941
Newsy Lalonde	1887	Cornwall	1928	1970
Hugh Lambe	1882	Toronto	1909	1941
Charlie Liffiton	1878	Montreal	1910	1941
Jimmy Mallen	1881	Morrisburg	1914	1954
Ken Mallen	1884	Morrisburg	1917	1930
Howard Manson	1885	Cornwall	1912	N/A

Jack Marks	1882	Belleville	1920	1945
Cap McDonald	1877	Mattawa	1914	1955
Jim McGinnis	1882	Port Dalhousie	1909	1970
Frank McLaren	1880	Perth	1907	N/A
Harold McNamara	1889	Randolph	1917	1937
Walter Mercer	1885	Port Hope	1910	1961
Bert Morrison	1880	Toronto	1909	1969
Joe Ouelette	1884	Ottawa	1911	N/A
Bruce Ridpath	1884	Lakefield	1911	1925
Skene Ronan	1889	Ottawa	1919	1937
Zina Runions	1888	Cornwall	1909	1962
Donald Smith	1887	Cornwall	1920	1959
Hank Smith	N/A	Cornwall	1909	N/A
Mark Tooze	1882	Toronto	1911	N/A
Chuck Tyner	1879	Orillia	1910	1967
Lawson Whitehead	1876	Dronfield, U.K.	1909	1934
Fred Young	1886	Kingston	1909	N/A
Rolly Young	1883	Toronto	1910	1961

INDEX

Page numbers in *italics* refer to illustrations.